FUNCTIONAL
LANGUAGES

CONSTRUCTIVE FOUNDATIONS FOR FUNCTIONAL LANGUAGES

Raymond Turner

Department of Computer Science
University of Essex

McGRAW-HILL BOOK COMPANY

London · New York · St Louis · San Francisco · Auckland
Bogotá · Caracas · Hamburg · Lisbon · Madrid · Mexico
Milan · Montreal · New Delhi · Panama · Paris · San Juan
São Paulo · Singapore · Sydney · Tokyo · Toronto

Published by
McGRAW-HILL Book Company (UK) Limited
SHOPPENHANGERS ROAD · MAIDENHEAD · BERKSHIRE · ENGLAND
TEL: 0628-23432; FAX: 0628-770224

British Library Cataloguing in Publication Data
Turner, Raymond
  Constructive foundations for functional languages.
  1. Programming languages
  I. Title
  005.13

  ISBN 0-07-707411-4

Library of Congress Cataloging-in-Publication Data
Turner, Raymond
  Constructive foundations for functional languages/Raymond Turner.
    p.   cm.
  Includes bibliographical references and index.
  ISBN 0-07-707411-4
  1. Functional programming languages.   I. Title.
QA76.73.F86T87   1991   90-25942
005.13—dc20   CIP

12345 CUP 94321

Typeset by Mid-County Press, London
and printed and bound in Great Britain at the University Press, Cambridge

To Tony

CONTENTS

PREFACE

This book is primarily an introduction to the axiomatic foundations of functional programming languages. It attempts to elucidate the nature of such languages by viewing them as axiomatic theories of functions and types. This perspective highlights the fact that they are closely related to the *constructive theories of functions and types* developed by logicians concerned with the foundations of constructive mathematics. The second goal of the book is to investigate these connections. The outcome not only provides a new slant on the nature of functional languages but also leads to a different style of functional programming.

Much effort has been made to render the book self-contained. However, it is mainly aimed at graduate students in computing science and advanced undergraduates who have taken a first course in predicate logic and have had some exposure to functional programming and the lambda calculus.

This book would never have been completed without the encouragement, endless discussion and detailed comments of my colleagues. Sam Steel, Mike Sanderson and Rans Ghosh-Roy read various drafts and located many errors and obscurities. Many other members of the Essex department have suffered my obsession with the book over the last two years. Jeff Reynolds, Nadim Obeid, Dave Lyons, Chris Lewington, Iain MacCallum and Sue Babiker deserve special mention for their patience and advice. All my students have contributed in one way or another—either through discussion or detailed comments. In particular, the development of Chapter 4 leans upon the work of Ali Hamie. My secretaries Ann Cook and Marisa Bostock also helped in the preparation of the manuscript. My greatest debts are to Martin Henson and Roxana Berretta. Roxana proofread draft after draft and never lost her patience when I replaced one error by another. Her insights and comments have been indispensable. My debts to Martin Henson will be obvious to any reader of the book. Not only have I incorporated much of his and our joint research in the book but I have called upon his advice on so many occasions that it is difficult to do justice to his contribution in this short acknowledgement.

This book was conceived in 1987 while I was a research fellow on an SDF grant at the University of Massachusetts. I would like to thank Barbara Partee for supplying such a wonderful research environment where I was able to pursue my ideas unhindered by teaching and administrative duties.

Raymond Turner
University of Essex

1

FUNCTIONAL LANGUAGES AND CONSTRUCTIVE THEORIES OF FUNCTIONS AND TYPES

This book has two interconnected themes: functional programming languages and foundational systems for constructive mathematics. At one level it is meant to be an introduction to the axiomatic foundations of functional languages but at another it is an exploration of the connections between these topics.

In its guise as an introduction to the foundations of functional languages the book can be seen as an attempt to set up a formal framework for their axiomatic description. The view adopted is that a functional language is an implicit axiomatic theory of functions and types and it is this theory that supports the formal argumentation about programs and their types. We shall study the lazy lambda calculus, various theories of types, including inductive and polymorphic types, and many other notions that are present in current functional languages. However, our approach will be somewhat more formal than usual. We shall be most concerned with the development of an axiomatic system that is rich enough to encompass all the aspects in one coherent theory. In designing such a theory we shall employ a principle of parsimony: we largely see our task as descriptive and generally any concept included in the theory must be justified in terms of current practice. If not, good reasons have to be offered for its potential usefulness.

Such formal theories have much in common with the constructive theories of functions and types developed by logicians to capture the practice of constructive mathematics. The second theme of the book centres upon the close connection between our axiomatic accounts of functional languages and these constructive theories of functions and types. The constructive paradigm has certain built-in advantages for program development which we shall explore in the last sections of the book on *constructive functional programming*.

1.1 THE NATURE OF FUNCTIONAL PROGRAMMING

It is hard to start a book and even harder to finish it. The difficulty with the present one is knowing where to start since there are so many preliminary issues that need to be addressed. Nevertheless, one has to start somewhere and a discussion of the distinction between imperative and functional languages seems like a good place.

1.1.1 Imperative and Functional Languages

It is spurious to suggest that *functional* programs denote functions whereas *imperative* programs do not. At least it is under the standard semantic paradigm known as *denotational semantics*. To illustrate this, consider the simple assignment statement:

$$x := 4$$

This can be construed as a function from states to states where a state consists of some attachment of numbers to variables, e.g. single-valued pairs of variables and numbers. The statement can then be semantically unpacked as that function which alters the state by replacing the second component of the pair, containing x as its first component, by 4. This is roughly the semantics the assignment statement would be given in a denotational semantics of the language. Under this account all programs can be considered as functions. More generally, the semantics of imperative programs is furnished in terms of their impact upon the state of some underlying abstract machine: programs are viewed as state-to-state functions. Indeed, the design of imperative languages has been heavily influenced by the model of computation introduced by the von Newmann machine. Within this tradition much of the computation is initiated by the assignment of values to named locations within the machine. Nevertheless, under this semantic theory imperative programs denote functions. So this attempt to force a wedge between the two styles of language fails.

A second try appeals to the notion of *referential transparency*. Roughly, a language is referentially transparent if the *meaning* of a complex program is a function of the *meaning* of its grammatical constituents. In other words, if p is a complex program made up from component programs q and r via a construct of the language, then the meaning of p is completely determined by the meaning of the construct together with the meanings of q and r. This is a semantic notion in that its very statement appeals to the *meaning* or *denotation* of programs. Unfortunately, this idea will not work either. Indeed, denotational semantics was set up with referential transparency as its major goal. An imperative language can be given a referentially transparent semantics where the meanings of programs are state-to-state functions (or more complex functions involving *continuations* if the language admits *jumps*).

To see what is meant by the term *functional programming* we have to search a little deeper. The classical mathematician's notion of function is that given in standard set theory: functions are single-valued sets of pairs. However, as we have seen, under this definition all programs can be construed as functions provided the domain and range of the function have sufficient structure. So the term functional programming does not derive from this notion of function. Rather it stems from the computing science distinction between *procedures* and *functions* and this distinction is best understood in terms of the above semantic view: procedures alter the state of the underlying machine whereas *pure* functions do not. It is this implicit semantic appeal to the notion of *state* that marks the difference between functional and imperative programs. Functional programs do not semantically require the notion of state whereas imperative programs do.

1.1.2 Why Functional Programming?

One can now be a little more explicit about the distinction and at the same time bring out the main attraction of the functional programming style. The move towards functional programming stems from the laudable desire to ensure that programs are correct. Consider the following program:

$$f0 = 1$$
$$f(n + 1) = (n + 1) * fn$$

Classically, functions come equipped with a domain and a range. In this case f defines a function from natural numbers to natural numbers. In the semantic paradigm sketched above the function denoted by this program is clear from its definition (factorial). There is no need to appeal to a *global* notion of state to express the denoted function; in functional languages the meaning of an expression is not dependent upon its global context. Programs can therefore be manipulated and argued about in a state-independent way and this makes life much more pleasant. Indeed, the style of argument is much closer to *ordinary* mathematical argumentation.

In contrast, consider the following program:

$$k := 0; f := 1;$$

while $k < n$ do begin $k := k + 1; f := k * f$ end

Denotational semantics would need to assign a state-to-state function to this program since it implicitly appeals to some *global* notion of state in order to account for the changing values of the variables. Programs cannot transparently denote simple functions acting on the data types of the language. Their semantics must go beyond these simple data types and appeal to the notion of state. As a consequence, the order of statements is important. For example, in the program above, if one changed the order of the assignment statements in the *while-loop* a completely different program would emerge. It is in this sense, and this sense alone, that imperative programs are not *referentially transparent*. However, this has important implications.

Reasoning about, and consequently constructing, imperative programs is a more hazardous enterprise than its functional counterpart. Of course, correctness is a relative notion and programs can only be taken to be correct relative to some specification. In the imperative paradigm the specification of a program is viewed as the relation between the *state of affairs* prior to its execution and the *state of affairs* at termination. These *state descriptions* contain information about variable bindings and shadow the states of the formal semantics. Roughly, a program is tagged with a sequence of assertions; adjacent pairs of assertions in the sequence govern the 'input–output' behaviour of the various parts of the program. Associated with each programming construct is a *proof rule* which reflects the relationship between the states of the program variables before and after the execution of the construct. A program is taken to be correct when the sequence of assertions constitutes a proof—according to these rules of proof. This is a much more difficult task than the corresponding functional enterprise and the difficulty stems from the necessity to appeal to the notion of state. Although many ingenious logical systems have resulted from attempts to formalize our intuitive reasoning about changes of state, the corresponding logics are quite difficult to work with. None of them come close to the simplicity of the logic required for reasoning about functional programs.

1.2 AXIOMATIC FOUNDATIONS FOR FUNCTIONAL LANGUAGES

Having outlined the major difference between functional and imperative languages we now examine the nature of the former a little more closely. Cut down to its essentials, a functional language has two main components:

1. A language of expressions or functions
2. A language of types

The first informs us what functions there are while the second dictates the possible types that functions or expressions can possess. This is a rather crude picture but it is a good starting point from which to reflect upon the nature of functional languages.

1.2.1 A Theory of Functions or Operations

Most functional languages have their intellectual roots in the lambda calculus. It is a rather austere language of functions (or operations) whose constructs enable only (implicit) function definition and function application. However, despite its syntactic simplicity, the lambda calculus has much to teach us about the design and implementation of functional languages. This is confirmed by its abiding influence on language designers and implementors alike.

In particular, the lambda calculus is more than just a *language* of functions—it is also a *theory of functions* or *operations*. The calculus comes equipped with an axiomatic theory of function equality, function definition and function application. It is this theory that sustains reasoning about the nature and equality of functions. Such an axiomatic theory is not a luxury but a necessity. One cannot establish that programs are correct or that two programs are equal without some such theory. Of course, this observation is as old as computing science itself and the development of axiomatic semantics reaches back to the very beginnings of the subject. We are therefore not making any original claims but only asserting the familiar and uncontroversial.

However, it is worth pointing out that the calculus is not primarily a theory of functions in the, by now classical, sense of axiomatic set theory. Within the latter paradigm functions are analysed as sets of ordered pairs (or tuples) and come equipped with a *domain* and *range*. Moreover, equality between such functions is given extensionally: two functions are equal if they produce equal results (with respect to their range) for equal arguments (in their domain). On the other hand, the calculus is better described as a theory of *operations* or *operational functions*, where operations simply transform data and have no predetermined domain and range. For example, the identity operation sends any object to itself no matter what the type of the object. Similarly, the operation of forming pairs seems not to be confined to any particular domain and range. It is not that one cannot assign types to operations but rather that they can possess many different types. Chapter 3 contains a reasonably self-contained account of the calculus. There we shall not only say a little more about this distinction between operations and functions but present a fairly detailed and gentle introduction to the calculus as a theory of operations or operational functions.

Actually, in order to reason about programs one requires more than a theory of functional equality, which is basically what the axioms of the calculus provide. We also need to reason about program termination. This is a tricky topic since it is not just a matter of adopting some evaluation strategy such as *applicative-order* reduction or *lazy evaluation*. We are most often required to establish that a particular program terminates, and to achieve this we require a theory of program termination not just a description of the adopted evaluation strategy. This argues for an axiomatic theory of program termination in addition to the theory of equality delivered by the axioms of the pure calculus. Obviously, before any such axiomatization is possible we need to decide upon the evaluation strategy—should we adopt a *strict* or *lazy* regime? Such a design decision is built into most functional languages. For example, ML is *strict* whereas Miranda™ is *lazy*. Consequently, Chapter 4 discusses the various options before launching into an axiomatization of the *lazy lambda calculus*.

Moreover, in practice, the austere simplicity of the calculus is a handicap to program development. Practical functional languages contain many other facilities or constructs (e.g. conditionals, pattern-directed recursion equations, guarded expressions, lists, natural numbers, basic arithmetic) which enable the direct formulation of more elegant and efficient programs. However, we cannot just nonchalantly add new constructs. We are under an obligation to provide an axiomatic account of any such additional features. Indeed, one of the most important morals to be drawn from the calculus is that a complete description of a functional language has to go beyond an elaboration of its syntax. It must include an axiomatic account of the *higher-level* constructs of the language. While it is true that such a theory would be no more expressive than the calculus (in principle any function that can be defined in a functional language can be implemented in the calculus), the programmer needs access to a *higher-level* description of the theory since reasoning about functions is hampered by having to trace the function definition through its calculus implementation to a point where the axioms of the calculus can take over. This perspective demands that a functional language should be presented as a *higher-level* theory of functions with axioms that directly pertain to the *higher-level* constructs of the language. Even from the implementation perspective this higher-level presentation is important since many features of current languages are not actually represented in the calculus but are supported by direct hardward implementations. We shall take up this topic in Chapter 5, where we present an axiomatic account of various features found in current functional languages.

1.2.2 A Theory of Types

The second component of a functional language concerns the notion of type. At one level types are employed in functional languages to classify objects as natural numbers or Booleans or even as more complex types. A theory of types imposes a structure upon the universe of objects available to the programmer which would otherwise remain in a pre-theoretical anarchic soup. They provide the programmer with a conceptual scheme within which program development must proceed and thus demand a level of mental hygiene that forces the programmer to go some way to ensuring the correctness of programs. In this role, which we shall dub *computational*, their main task is to prevent silliness, i.e. trying to subtract six from true. Although we might be able to do this in some languages it is conceptually indefensible.

This role is often supported by a compile-time type checker which seeks to capture errors that infringe upon the type regime. While such a type checker contains an *implicit* theory of types, by itself this is not enough. The programmer requires more direct access to this implicit conceptual scheme; the theory of types must be stated in a precise and explicit manner. Otherwise programming would be a very hit and miss affair. Write a program and see if it type-checks; if wrong, try again and so on. Indeed, such an explicit theory is necessary in order to specify the type checker. More generally, a program specification is a mathematical assertion to the effect that a program satisfies certain conditions. Types that appear in such specifications have a more mathematical flavour to them. We need to be able to argue that programs meet their specifications and for this purpose it is not sufficient to implement a compile-time type checker. Obviously, the language of types is not sufficient to enable the programmer to reason about the type of a program, to prove that a program meets its specification or indeed even to construct a halfway coherent one. This more mathematical activity requires some reasonably explicit account of the content of the type constructors. This demands that the membership conditions for types are made explicit in the form of axioms or rules and this amounts to the demand for an *axiomatic* theory of types.

To begin with (Chapter 6) we study a very rudimentary theory of types in which the only type constructors are function spaces, cartesian products and disjoint unions. Such constructors are present in one form or another in most functional languages, but our presentation is more rigorous than most in that we provide an axiomatic theory of type membership. The following four chapters take up additional type constructors which arise not only from within computing science but also from the second theme of the book, namely, constructive set theory.

This demand for an explicit axiomatic theory of functions and types is not in conflict with the denotational view of a functional language. The latter would provide a theory of functions and types but in a less direct fashion. For example, the theory of functions would be implicitly defined as all those functions named (via the semantic function) by the expressions of the formal language. On the other hand, the axiomatic approach is more explicit since the theory of functions and types is directly axiomatized. There is a sense in which the axioms of the lambda calculus *constitute* the calculus and the denotational semantics is then best seen as a metamathematical tool for the investigation of its formal properties. However, whether conceptual priority is to be given to the axiomatic formulation or its semantic theory is not that important. The main point at issue is whether the former needs to be made explicit, and this seems beyond argument. The level at which formal argumentation about programs and their types takes place is given by the axiomatic theory—or at the very least some informal approximation to it.

In conclusion, a mathematical description of a functional language has to go beyond a purely syntactic one. If we adopt the axiomatic perspective we end up with two interconnected axiomatic theories:

1. A theory of operational functions
2. A theory of types

We shall refer to such as a *programming theory*. This book is largely concerned with an elaboration of this perspective. In the course of the book we shall develop an axiomatic approach to functional languages. In doing so we shall very much have the Miranda™ style of language in mind. Different language features and notions of type would evolve if, for example, ML were adopted. However, it should be stressed that the theory we develop is not exactly that of Miranda™. We have tried to develop an abstract framework for the axiomatic approach to functional languages and as such we have not slavishly followed any existing language. Of course, certain design decisions have to be taken and by and large we have adopted the Miranda™ option but, as the reader will perceive, the approach is reasonably generic. Our major goal is the development of a *programming* theory which is *descriptively adequate* for the Miranda™ *style* of functional programming. As such, it must not only reflect the language features and notions of type but also enable a formalization of informal argumentation about such programs. However, our goal is not entirely descriptive. In some instances we have parted company with, or at least extended, tradition. This brings us nicely to the second theme of the book.

1.3 LOGICAL FOUNDATIONS OF CONSTRUCTIVE MATHEMATICS

There is a second, apparently distinct, intellectual endeavour that will inform the development of our *programming theory*. The last twenty years have seen the invention of axiomatic theories of functions and types that bear a remarkable resemblance to the axiomatic theories that underpin modern functional languages. These theories have arisen from work in the foundations of constructive mathematics. To some extent their role will be secondary since we take our major objective to be a descriptive one, i.e. the axiomatic description of current functional languages or rather the construction of a framework where this becomes a viable possibility. Constructive formal systems will guide the development of the theory in a slightly different way.

Firstly, such theories provide a formal paradigm for the actual formulation of our programming theories. This is particularly so in the case of the constructive theories of functions and types developed by Saul Feferman. Secondly, these theories offer new and useful notions of type and provide some ideas for the future development of functional languages. This will be the central theme of Chapter 7 and to some extent Chapter 9. Finally, the constructive paradigm heralds a new style of functional programming where constructive proofs of program specifications are little more than disguised functional programs. As a consequence, our two apparently distinct major endeavours, namely program construction and proofs of correctness, are just two sides of the same coin.

1.3.1 Constructive Mathematics

Before we discuss any of these theories, even in outline, we must say a little about the nature of constructive mathematics itself. The term *constructive mathematics* is generally employed to cover any mathematical activity where the existence of a mathematical object has to be explicitly demonstrated by *constructing* it. This is to be seen in contrast to the *classical* enterprise where the existence of an object can be deduced without *producing* the actual object. Classically, arguments can be *indirect*. By way of example consider the following problem: locate irrational numbers a and b such that a^b is rational. The classical solution proceeds as follows. Let a be the square root of 2. Then either a^a is rational or it is not. If it is, then we are done. If not, then $(a^a)^a$, being 2, is rational. In either case we have a solution: we have shown that there are irrationals a and b such that a^b is rational. However, the argument is *indirect* since we have not located the actual irrational numbers. As a consequence, this argument would not convince a constructive mathematician who would demand that the actual irrationals be produced. This has important implications for the logic of the underlying system and, as we shall see in Chapter 2, forces the adoption of a subsystem of classical logic called *constructive* or *intuitionistic logic*. In particular, certain logical principles such as *argument by contradiction* and the *law of excluded middle* are not upheld. For instance, the reader may have noticed that the above argument made implicit appeal to the *law of excluded middle*—'either a^a is rational or it is not'.

Indeed, it is this strong interpretation of existence claims that makes constructive mathematics interesting for computing scientists since a constructive proof that an object exists must produce the object. In particular, a constructive proof of a function specification must produce the function. In other words, given a constructive proof of a specification, we can automatically abstract a function that meets the specification. This aspect will occupy the last third of the book, which is devoted to *constructive functional programming*.

This strong notion of existence is one of the central features of constructive mathematics. However, there are various schools of *constructivism* and they depart from classical mathematics in some subtly different ways. Indeed, perhaps the best way to further explain the nature of constructive mathematics is through a brief exposition of its main brands. For our purposes these can be classified as follows:

1. Bishop's constructive mathematics
2. Intuitionism
3. Recursive mathematics

We shall say a brief word about each of these in order to set the scene for the discussion of constructive formal systems.

(a) Bishop's style constructivism (BISH) The first form is historically the latest of the three and is due to Errett Bishop (1967) (*Foundations of Constructive Analysis*), and Bishop and Bridges (1985). In the work of this school there is little philosophical defence of constructivism and the emphasis is on the *practice* of mathematics. The key idea in understanding this form of constructivism is Bishop's phrase 'mathematical statements should have numerical content'. One consequence of this is that existential assertions must, in principle at least, be capable of being made explicit: one can only show that an object exists by giving a *finite routine* for finding it. It is not assumed, however, that such *routines* are to be identified with the *general recursive functions*. The insistence that all routines be given by recursive functions is known as Church's thesis (CT). Informally, CT can be expressed as follows:

> For every putative formalism for the notion of *finite routine* there exists an algorithm (itself a recursive function) for correctly translating the formalism into that of the general recursive functions.

Evidence for CT is empirical: every attempt to formalize the notion of finite routine has resulted in a class of computable functions equal to the general recursive ones. The proofs proceed by showing that every function computable in the proposed formalism is general recursive. To achieve this an algorithm is constructed for translating between the systems. Typical examples are the equivalences between the general recursive functions, Turing machines, post-production systems and the lambda calculus. However, to assert CT constructively one requires more than these piecemeal equivalences. One would have to establish that for every putative formalism such an algorithm exists, and this would itself have to be given as a general recursive function. Given the constructive notion of existence, this could only be achieved by producing a recursive function that uniformly mapped any putative formalism to that of the recursive functions and no such recursive function has been produced. Indeed, this would be a striking result since the construction of the algorithms in the individual cases often requires great ingenuity. It is not that BISH claims that CT is false, but, given its explicit notion of existence, it can only be asserted if such a recursive function is produced.

Bishop's constructivism ought to be attractive to computing scientists since he thought of the language of mathematics as 'a high-level programming language' in which proofs should be written. Algorithms then naturally accompany existence proofs. It is this form of constructive mathematics that has largely been responsible for many of the recent developments in constructive formal systems. Despite the fact that Bishop offers little philosophical defence for his brand of constructivism, it is the most philosophically neutral of the three paradigms in that it is consistent with classical mathematics (CLASS); the other two are not.

(b) Intuitionism (INT) This is the oldest systematic philosophy of constructive mathematics and emanates from the writings of Brouwer. It shares with BISH the insistence that the notion of algorithm or finite routine should be taken as *sui generis* and certainly not to be identified with the general recursive functions. Moreover, both schools demand that proofs should be direct and constructive in the sense alluded to above.

However, intuitionism goes further than BISH. The concept most closely tied to Brouwer's name is that of the *choice sequence*. This concept was fundamental to his attempt to *constructivize* the continuum. Reflection on the nature of choice sequences led to his proof that every real-valued function on the interval $[0, 1]$ is point-wise continuous. This is, of course, classically false; classically there are non-continuous functions. Although we shall not employ this aspect of intuitionism it has been recently advocated in connection with a constructive analysis of *lazy data types* (Martin-Löf, 1990).

For our purposes the differences between INT and BISH are not very important and the most pertinent aspect of intuitionism concerns the underlying logic of intuitionistic mathematics which we shall explore in Chapter 2. This was developed by Heyting (1958) and it forms one of the cornerstones of the present book.

(c) Recursive constructivism (REC) This form of constructivism emanates from Markov and was further developed by Shanin and their students in the 1950–1967 period. It has very different philosophical roots from INT and stems from the work in *recursive function theory* whose foundations were laid in the early thirties. In this school the objects of mathematics are words in various alphabets. There are no abstract mathematical concepts and in particular no abstract notion of rule or finite routine: all number theoretic functions are given by general recursive functions. This is obviously inconsistent with classical mathematics. Therefore, on the one hand, Markov is a more strict constructivist than Bishop and Brouwer in that CT is upheld. In other respects he is more liberal. This is illustrated by his justification of what is now known as *Markov's principle*:

> If it is impossible that an algorithm does not terminate then we may assume that it does.

Thus, to show that an algorithm terminates we do not have to produce a direct proof; it is sufficient to show that the assumption that it does not terminate leads to a contradiction. This is rejected by both the other schools. We shall say more about this issue in Chapter 4 when we discuss the whole question of program termination in some detail.

This is not meant to be a detailed description of these three schools. At this point we we are only attempting to provide the reader with some general perspectives on the nature of constructive mathematics. We have included this brief discussion in order to provide a little background for our discussion of formal systems.

1.3.2 Constructive Theories of Functions and Types

Having said a little about the nature of constructive mathematics we shall now say a little about some of the actual formal systems that have been developed in response to this mathematical activity. Since the publication of Bishop's book there has been a flurry of activity in the logical community concerned with the formalization of constructive mathematics, the goal of this activity being to capture the *informal* mathematical activity of constructive mathematics within a formal system. In particular, this has led to the development of new axiomatic theories of functions and types, the most notable, at least from the present perspective, being the theories of Saul Feferman and Per Martin-Löf.

(a) Feferman's formal systems Feferman's theories are an attempt to formalize the content of Bishop in a way that reflects actual mathematical practice. The formalization is meant to be *descriptively adequate* in the strong intensional sense that the formal theory directly captures the style of argumentation and the basic ontology of the mathematics. It goes beyond a purely extensional characterization of the theorems of the system. The core of Feferman's formal systems consists of two interconnected axiomatic theories:

1. A theory of functions or operations
2. A theory of types

The first is an axiomatic theory of functions which is intended to be an abstract theory of rules or operations. Feferman (1979, 1990) has formulated various versions using both the theory of combinators and the lambda calculus itself. The theory of types is intended to reflect the notion of set or type as it is employed in BISH. More precisely, informal mathematics employs various means of constructing new types or sets from old ones (e.g. cartesian products, function spaces) and the aim of such a theory is to develop a formal theory of types that is rich enough to capture these informal concepts in a formally precise fashion. Moreover, it ought not to go too far beyond actual practice. The aim is to reflect practice as closely as possible and keep the theories as *weak* as possible, consistent with descriptive adequacy. This is more important within constructivism than its classical counterpart since constructivism places certain strictures on the very notion of type or set. For example, the concept of the *power set*, which is available in classical set theories, is not normally admitted in constructive foundational systems.

We have hopefully predisposed the reader to see, superficially at least, that these theories have a similar structure to the axiomatic formulation of a functional language. There are, of course, some differences. Feferman's theories were designed to reflect the practice of constructive mathematics, not the mathematics of functional programming. Nevertheless, there is a great measure of agreement. Most of the types admitted in Feferman's theories have their counterparts in functional languages. Indeed, where there is a difference it turns out to be instructive for programming language design. Feferman's type theories, in one respect, go beyond the type theories of most functional languages in that they offer a richer way of characterizing objects. In other respects, the early versions of the theories did not go far enough. They do not, for example, support any explicit form of polymorphism. This has since been remedied by Feferman (1990). Most of the chapters on types are concerned with a discussion of the various type constructors which arise not only within functional languages but also within constructive formal systems. The hope is that the interplay between the two will benefit both disciplines. What is clear is that the similarities are sufficiently strong to employ Feferman's style of formalization as the basis for the development of an axiomatic framework for the formalization of functional languages.

(b) The theories of Martin-Löf Strictly speaking, the theories of Martin-Löf were not motivated by the desire to capture mathematical practice but rather stem from more philosophical considerations. For Martin-Löf, *types* arise by reflection on the constructive meaning of the logical connectives and quantifiers. For each connective and quantifier there corresponds a type constructor which enables the construction of the type of the *witnesses* for a compound assertion (constructed by the connective) from the types of *witnesses* for the component assertions. In other words, the types arise in response to the attempt to provide a semantics for the logical connectives rather than as a direct attempt to formalize the practice of constructive mathematics.

Martin-Löf's theories have occupied centre-stage in the middle ground between computing science and constructive mathematics and there is already an extensive literature on the subject. By comparison, very little attention has been given to *Feferman-style* theories. Hayashi and Nakano (1988) and Henson and Turner (1988) are exceptions. We believe this to be unfortunate since the latter seem to offer a more direct way of formalizing not only the practice of constructive mathematics but also that of functional programming. Part of the purpose of this book is to argue for this claim.

(c) Intuitionistic Zermelo–Fraenkel set theory (IZF) There are other theories that attempt to formalize the content of Bishop and one worthy of mention takes as its point of departure *classical Zermelo–Fraenkel* set theory (ZF). This is a pure theory of sets constituted by set constructors which facilitate the construction of new sets from old ones, the most characteristic being the operation of forming power sets. IZF is a constructive reformulation where minimal changes are made in order to avoid certain embarrassing logical consequences. In their classical form several of the axioms (e.g. foundation) imply the law of excluded middle and so render the underlying logic classical. IZF is constructed by reformulating these troublesome axioms.

This theory is not obviously useful for our purposes. For example, the notion of function is the classical one in that functions are sets of ordered pairs. As such they come equipped with predetermined domains and ranges. This does not directly meet our need for a polymorphic notion of operation. Beeson (1989) has recently partly addressed this problem by supplementing IZF with a theory of operations. However, the sets made available in IZF go far beyond anything we are likely to meet in programming practice now or in the future. Our goal is the development of a descriptively adequate theory that only goes beyond existing practice where matters can be justified by pragmatic considerations. At first glance, IZF does not meet this criterion.

We hope that this rather inadequate introduction to constructive mathematics and its foundations is not too inadequate. Most of the points which have only been touched upon will be taken up in the chapters that follow. The book by Beeson (1985) is the best and most comprehensive introduction to constructive set theory on the market, but it is not for the faint-hearted.

1.4 ABOUT THE BOOK

This book is an attempt to develop a theory of functions and types which reflects the current paradigms in functional language design and directly supports the style of argumentation employed in program development and analysis. This argues for a style of theory similar if not identical to that of Feferman. More generally, we shall be guided by the constructive paradigm, but we shall not be a slave to it. Where we believe that computing science parts company with constructivism (although it is not entirely clear that it ever does), we shall by and large take sides with the former. This is how it should be. Our goal is not evangelical but descriptive. However, we believe that constructive formal systems have much to offer the future designer of functional languages and we shall explore certain extensions to current systems that arise from within the constructive paradigm.

Apart from an introductory chapter on intuitionistic logic, which sets the basic scene, the book has three main components:

1. A theory of functions (Chapters 3 to 5)
2. A theory of types (Chapters 6 to 10)
3. Constructive functional programming (Chapters 11 to 14)

In Chapters 3 to 5 we develop the lambda calculus and its extensions and a theory of termination. In the chapters on types we shall consider most of the type constructors present in functional languages and a few others that come from constructive type theories. In the final four chapters we cash in on the constructive nature of the programming theory.

2

THE INTUITIONISTIC PREDICATE
CALCULUS

A *programming theory* is to consist of a *theory of functions* and a *theory of types*. A theory of functions has to inform us about which functions there are and equip us with an account of their properties. A theory of types must do likewise for types. Such theories have to be formally expressed in some language, and this is the major conceptual and technical role of the predicate calculus. In particular, it enables the formulation of the axioms of functional equality and type membership. This role of the calculus will emerge as we proceed through the book. However, in this chapter we shall motivate the calculus from a somewhat different perspective.

In addition to its conceptual role as the language of our programming theory, the calculus will be the central vehicle of program specification. Every program performs some task but, unfortunately, it may not be the intended one—it may not even be coherent. In order to determine whether or not a program performs correctly it is necessary to have a precise and independent characterization of the intended goal. This has led to the development of languages and theories of program specification. Many of these theories have the predicate calculus as their nucleus. It provides a means of presenting an abstract description of the task to be programmed without commitment to a detailed presentation of how it is to be achieved. Furthermore, the underlying logic of the calculus provides a way of reasoning about programs and data. In particular, it enables the programmer to establish whether the program meets the stipulated specification. Indeed, the particular version of the calculus we adopt goes further. We shall develop the *intuitionistic predicate calculus* which actually facilitates the construction of programs from the proofs of their specifications.

2.1 THE LANGUAGE OF THE PREDICATE CALCULUS

Our version of the predicate calculus is geared for the task of reasoning about functions and their types. The intended domain of discourse includes both terms and types, and typical assertions will express membership in types, equality between terms and, eventually, program termination. This leads to the following syntactic categories:

1. Well-formed formulae (wff)
2. Terms
3. Types

This chapter is largely concerned with the sublanguage of wff which forms the core language of the logic. The language of terms is primarily a language of functions. In this chapter it will only be crudely described but in the next three chapters it will be fully developed to form the basis of a functional programming language. The final category is that of types. Again we shall reserve a full development of the language and theory of types for later. Here we shall present only a fairly rudimentary syntax.

2.1.1 Well-formed Formulae (wff)

The language of wff is made up of assertions of two kinds: atomic assertions and complex assertions which are formed using the propositional connectives and quantifiers. It is given by the following syntax:

$$\phi ::= \alpha \,|\, (\phi \wedge \psi) \,|\, (\phi \vee \psi) \,|\, (\phi \rightarrow \psi) \,|\, (\forall x \phi) \,|\, (\exists x \phi)$$

Wff are either atomic (α) or are formed from existing ones by use of the connectives and the quantifiers. The propositional connectives $\wedge$, $\vee$, $\rightarrow$ stand for conjunction, disjunction and implication respectively; the quantifiers $\forall$, $\exists$ denote universal and existential quantification. Negation, which is not included as a primitive, will be discussed shortly. We shall employ ϕ, ψ (and in general lower-case Greek letters) to denote wff and u, v, x, y, z, f, g for variables. We may omit parentheses from wff when they are not necessary to indicate the structure. Where we adopt rules of precedence we shall assume an *association to the right rule* for implication [i.e. we shall write $\phi \rightarrow \psi \rightarrow \eta$ for $\phi \rightarrow (\psi \rightarrow \eta)$]. More often, for the sake of clarity, we shall use pairs of square brackets [...], braces {...} and spaces rather than parentheses to indicate structure.

In order to unpack the language further we need to discuss the syntax of atomic wff and for this we need to keep in mind our intended application. The calculus is to be employed as a means of specifying and reasoning about programs and types. The atomic assertions must reflect this intended application. Initially, atomic assertions will be of three kinds. The first states that two terms are equal, the second that a term has a certain type and the final one is the assertion of absurdity:

$$\alpha ::= (t = s)|(t \in T)|\Omega$$

The first category concerns term equality: $t = s$ asserts that the terms t and s are equal where we employ t, s, r to denote arbitrary terms. Although the exact nature of equality will occupy much of the next chapter, the intention behind such an assertion should be intuitively clear. The second kind of atomic wff asserts that a term has a particular type. For example, the atomic wff $t \in$ Bool asserts that t is a Boolean. The wff Ω is the assertion of absurdity and will play a central role in our formulation of negation. We shall add further atomic assertions in Chapter 4 to cope with program termination.

2.1.2 Terms

The language of *terms* is the language of functions and, more generally, data items. We shall not provide the full syntax of terms until we introduce the lambda calculus in the next chapter. For the moment we only assume that variables and constants are terms:

$$t ::= x|c|\cdots$$

where c, d, e will be used to denote arbitrary constants.

2.1.3 Types

Types are employed to characterize objects as natural numbers. Booleans, characters or as more complex types. The following syntax is not hard and fast; it is only introduced at this point to enable the reader to grasp the overall structure of the language:

$$T ::= \text{Bool}|\text{Char}|\text{N}|\text{List}[\text{N}]|(T \oplus S)|(T \otimes S)|(T \Rightarrow S)$$

Upper-case letters T, S, R, etc., will be employed to denote arbitrary types. Bool, Char, N, List[N] can be considered as basic types where Bool is the type of Boolean values, Char that of characters, N that of the natural numbers and List[N] the type of lists of numbers. The three type constructors are $\oplus$ (*disjoint union*), $\otimes$ (*cartesian product*) and $\Rightarrow$ (*function space*). These type constructors are present in one form or another in most current functional languages. $T \otimes S$ is the type of ordered pairs of objects, the first being of type T and the second of type S. Intuitively, $T \oplus S$ is the type of those objects that are explicitly marked as either of type T or of type S, and $T \Rightarrow S$ is the type of objects that are functions from objects of type T to those of type S. The exact meaning of all these types will be explored in later chapters.

2.1.4 Defined Constructs

We shall also have occasion to employ other logical connectives and quantifiers which are introduced by definition. For example, negation is introduced as follows:

$$\sim\phi =_{\text{def}} \phi \to \Omega$$

The negation of a wff ϕ is thus understood as the statement that ϕ implies a contradiction or absurdity. Negation can be taken as primitive but we shall unpack it in the above way. Formally, it makes no difference.

A second definitional extension to the language involves the biconditional. This is defined in terms of implication and conjunction:

$$\phi \leftrightarrow \psi =_{\text{def}} (\phi \to \psi) \wedge (\psi \to \phi)$$

Finally, the introduction of types provides a means of expressing *bounded quantification*. For any type T we define the *bounded quantifiers* as follows:

$$(\forall x \in T)\phi =_{\text{def}} \forall x(x \in T \to \phi)$$

$$(\exists x \in T)\phi =_{\text{def}} \exists x(x \in T \wedge \phi)$$

This allows universal and existential quantification to be restricted to elements of a particular type, whether it be natural numbers, characters, Booleans or some complex type.

2.1.5 Free and Bound Variables

Before we can give the inference rules of the calculus we need some preliminary notions, namely the *scope of a quantifier*, *free* and *bound* variables and *substitution*. We shall deal with these one by one.

Definition 2.1 Every intermediate wff used in building up a wff ϕ is a *subformula* of ϕ. Let ϕ be any wff with subformula $(Qx\psi)$, where Q ($Q = \forall$ or $\exists$) is a quantifier. The *scope* of this occurrence of Q is the subformula ψ.

For example, the scope of the first existential quantifier in the wff $[\exists x(x = y)] \vee [\exists x(x \in T)]$ is the wff $x = y$; the scope of the second is the wff $x \in T$.

Definition 2.2 An *occurrence* of a variable x in a wff ϕ is said to be *bound* if that occurrence is in a quantifier Qx or is in the scope of a quantifier with the same variable; otherwise the occurrence is *free*. If a variable has a free occurrence in a wff it is said to be a *free variable* of that wff. When we wish to indicate that x and y are free in ϕ we shall write $\phi[x, y]$, etc.

For example, x occurs bound in $\forall x(x = y)$ whereas y occurs free. A variable can occur both free and bound in the same wff, e.g. x in $(\exists x(x = y)) \vee (x \in T)$. The scope of the existential quantifier is the sub-formula $(x = y)$ and does not extend to the second atomic assertion.

Definition 2.3 The *substitution* of a term t for a variable x in a wff ϕ shall consist in replacing, simultaneously, each free occurrence of x in ϕ by t. We shall employ the notation $\phi[t/x]$ (or just $\phi[t]$ where there is no danger of confusion) for the result of substituting t for every free occurrence of x in ϕ. We shall say that a term t is *free for* x in $\phi[x]$ if and only if the substitution of t for x in $\phi[x]$ does not introduce t into $\phi[x]$ at any place where a (free) variable y of t becomes a bound occurrence of y in $\phi[t/x]$.

For example, if $\phi[x, y]$ is the wff $(\exists x(x = y)) \wedge (x \in T)$, then $\phi[t, y]$ is the wff $(\exists x(x = y)) \vee (t \in T)$. Notice that x is not free for y in $\forall x\phi[x, y]$. When a term t is free for x in $\phi[x]$ then t may be substituted for every free occurrence of x in ϕ without introducing any unwanted quantifier bindings. This account of substitution is the standard one in the literature on the predicate calculus. However, for the lambda calculus we shall adopt a rather different approach in which the actual act of substitution renames bound variables to avoid such accidental bindings. The fact that the two languages have adopted such different conventions is partly a historical accident. We shall say more about this when we discuss the lambda calculus notion of substitution.

This completes the exposition of the preliminary tedious technical devices and we now turn to the contents of the calculus.

2.2 INTUITIONISTIC LOGIC

In order to employ the calculus we must spell out a *logic* for the connectives. This is achieved by providing rules of proof which govern the use of the calculus as a vehicle of reasoning. With each connective we associate two rules of proof. The first (introduction rule) provides the means of introducing a complex wff, involving a particular connective, as the conclusion of a *derivation*. The second (elimination rule) does the opposite: it provides the means of eliminating the connective from the conclusion. Our plan is to visit each of the logical connectives and for each provide and motivate the two rules of proof. In doing so we shall inductively build up the formal notion of a *derivation*.

2.2.1 Conjunction

The introduction and elimination rules for conjunction are the simplest rules to grasp and take the following form. We shall employ the decorations to the left of the inference rules (e.g. $\wedge$ i) to name the rules.

<table>
<tr><td>Conjunction
introduction</td><td>Conjunction
elimination</td></tr>
</table>

$$(\wedge i) \quad \frac{\overset{\pi}{\phi} \quad \overset{\pi'}{\psi}}{\phi \wedge \psi} \qquad\qquad (\wedge e) \quad \frac{\overset{\pi}{\phi \wedge \psi}}{\phi} \quad \frac{\overset{\pi}{\phi \wedge \psi}}{\psi}$$

According to the first rule, if we have derivations π and π' with *conclusions* ϕ and ψ respectively, then we can conclude $\phi \wedge \psi$. In other words, given derivations for the premises, the introduction rule generates a new derivation with conclusion $\phi \wedge \psi$. The elimination rules operate in the other direction: given a derivation of $\phi \wedge \psi$ we can conclude ϕ (or ψ). These rules are in keeping with our intuitive understanding of conjunction and indeed appear to exhaust that understanding. The above rules can be understood both as providing the operational meaning of conjunction and as two clauses in the inductive definition of the class of valid derivations. In this regard we must indicate how such an inductive definition gets off the ground: what are atomic derivations? We shall assume that every wff constitutes an atomic derivation. This may seem a little strange but matters will be clarified shortly.

2.2.2 Implication

Again there are essentially two rules. To grasp the introduction rule suppose that we have established ψ by repeatedly appealing to the assumption ϕ. In effect, we have then shown how to construct a derivation of ψ from a hypothetical one for ϕ. On the other hand, the elimination rule enables us to conclude ψ from two derivations: one for $\phi \to \psi$ and one for ϕ.

<table>
<tr><td>Implication
introduction</td><td>Implication
elimination</td></tr>
</table>

$$(\to i) \quad \frac{\overset{[\phi]}{\underset{\psi}{\pi}}}{\phi \to \psi} \qquad\qquad (\to e) \quad \frac{\overset{\pi}{\phi} \quad \overset{\pi'}{\phi \to \psi}}{\psi}$$

The introduction rule introduces the idea of *temporary* assumptions in derivations. The assumption ϕ acts as a temporary or hypothetical assumption from which we can construct a derivation of ψ. From such a derivation we are entitled to conclude $\phi \to \psi$ while throwing away or *discharging* (if we wish) the temporary assumption ϕ. The notation [ ] in the ($\to$i) rule is to indicate that ϕ is discharged. It is important to stress that this discharging of assumptions is optional. The content of the rule is perhaps better expressed as follows: given a derivation of ψ we can derive $\phi \to \psi$ and at the same time discharge some or all occurrences, if any, of ϕ. In particular,

$$\frac{\psi}{\phi \to \psi}$$

is a legitimate instance of ($\to$i) since ψ is a derivation (an instance of the base case of the inductive definition of derivations). In this case no appeal is made to any hypothesis. However, in general, the more assumptions that are discharged the stronger the result. These rules add two more clauses to our inductive definition of the notion of derivation. At this point, a derivation is either atomic or is obtained from already constructed derivations by application of the rules for conjunction and implication. This is all rather abstract but a few examples should clarify matters.

Example 2.1 For our first example we construct a derivation of the following: $\phi \to (\psi \to \phi)$. In this derivation we only employ the introduction rule. Observe also that the initial step of the derivation involves making the temporary assumption ϕ and constitutes an atomic derivation. This assumption is discharged by the implies introduction rule at the last step:

$$\cfrac{\cfrac{[\phi]}{\psi \to \phi} \to \text{i}}{\phi \to (\psi \to \phi)} \to \text{i} \qquad \text{discharge } \phi$$

This is an example of a *closed* derivation since at the completion of the derivation there are no undischarged or *open* assumptions. In general, if we can construct a closed derivation for a wff then we shall call the wff a *theorem*.

Example 2.2 The next example is more elaborate and involves both the introduction and elimination rules for implication. We establish:

$(\phi \to \psi \to \theta) \to ((\phi \to \psi) \to (\phi \to \theta))$.

$$\cfrac{\cfrac{\cfrac{\cfrac{[\phi \to \psi \to \theta] \quad [\phi]}{\psi \to \theta} \to \text{e} \quad \cfrac{[\phi \to \psi] \quad [\phi]}{\psi} \to \text{e}}{\theta} \to \text{e}}{\phi \to \theta} \to \text{i}}{\cfrac{(\phi \to \psi) \to (\phi \to \theta)}{(\phi \to \psi \to \theta) \to ((\phi \to \psi) \to (\phi \to \theta))} \to \text{i}} \to \text{i}}$$

$\qquad \qquad \qquad \text{discharge } \phi$

$\qquad \qquad \qquad \text{discharge } \phi \to \psi$

$\qquad \qquad \qquad \text{discharge } \phi \to \psi \to \theta$

In this derivation we initially make three assumptions: $\phi \rightarrow \psi \rightarrow \theta$, ϕ and $\phi \rightarrow \psi$. These are discharged during the implies introduction steps. At the end of the derivation all the assumptions have been discharged. Notice that the assumption ϕ is used twice in the two initial applications of the implies elimination rule. This is legitimate since at this point it has not been discharged: it is still available as an *open* assumption. The structure of this derivation is fairly typical of derivations in the system; they have an *analytic* phase where assumptions are made and dismembered using elimination rules and a *synthetic* phase where things are put back together using introduction rules.

2.2.3 Disjunction

We enrich the notion of derivation by the addition of the following rules of proof which govern disjunction:

Disjunction   Disjunction
introduction   elimination

$$[\phi] \quad [\psi]$$

$$\pi \qquad \pi \qquad\qquad \pi \qquad \pi' \qquad \pi''$$

$$(\vee i) \quad \frac{\phi}{\phi \vee \psi} \quad \frac{\psi}{\phi \vee \psi} \qquad (\vee e) \quad \frac{\phi \vee \psi \quad \eta \quad \eta}{\eta}$$

The introduction rule(s) simply asserts that if we have a derivation of ϕ or a derivation of ψ then we have one for $\phi \vee \psi$. This seems clear enough and is in perfect harmony with our intuitive understanding of disjunction. However, the elimination rule is more complicated and deserves further comment. The content of $(\vee e)$ can be explained as follows. Suppose that from the assumption ϕ we can construct a derivation of η and similarly from the assumption ψ. Then we can conclude η from $\phi \vee \psi$ and discharge these temporary assumptions (if we wish). In other words, if we are able to conclude η from either ϕ or ψ then we can conclude it from $\phi \vee \psi$. As with the introduction rule for implication, assumptions may be discharged when passing to the conclusion.

The elimination rule is one of a pair of rules which is distinguished from the others by its appeal to a new wff (η) that is not a component of the major wff under consideration. We shall meet this again with the elimination rule for existential quantification. This is but one indication of the distinguished nature of these connectives. We shall meet another later.

Example 2.3 We prove: $(\phi \rightarrow \eta) \rightarrow [(\psi \rightarrow \eta) \rightarrow \{(\phi \vee \psi) \rightarrow \eta\}]$. This derivation involves both the implication and the elimination rules for disjunction:

$$
\cfrac{[\phi \vee \psi] \qquad \cfrac{\cfrac{[\phi]}{\eta} \to e \qquad \cfrac{[\psi]}{\eta} \to e}{\eta}}{\cfrac{\cfrac{\cfrac{\eta}{(\phi \vee \psi) \to \eta} \to i}{(\psi \to \eta) \to \{(\phi \vee \psi) \to \eta\}} \to i}{(\phi \to \eta) \to [(\psi \to \eta) \to \{(\phi \vee \psi) \to \eta\}]} \to i}
$$

with top assumptions $[\phi \to \eta] \quad [\psi \to \eta]$

$\vee$ e discharge assumptions ϕ and ψ

discharge the assumption $\phi \vee \psi$

discharge the assumption $\psi \to \eta$

discharge the assumption $\phi \to \eta$

At the end of the derivation there are no undischarged assumptions.

2.2.4 Negation and Absurdity

Our next set of rules concern negation and the atomic assertion of absurdity. These are linked since, if you recall, negation was defined in terms of absurdity and implication:

$$\sim \phi =_{\mathrm{def}} \phi \to \Omega$$

Since negation is introduced by definition we have no need to introduce separate rules for it; the rules for implication provide us with two *derived* rules of negation:

$$
(\sim i) \quad \cfrac{\begin{array}{c}[\phi]\\ \pi \\ \Omega\end{array}}{\sim \phi} \qquad\qquad (\sim e) \quad \cfrac{\begin{array}{cc}\pi & \pi' \\ \phi & \sim \phi\end{array}}{\Omega}
$$

These are *derived* rules in the sense that they are not extensions to the system but rather special cases of already existing rules. The derived elimination rule enables us to draw the conclusion Ω from derivations of a wff and its negation. The introduction rule looks very much like another rule for negation (*classical negation*) which we shall study a little later. We mention this fact to put the reader on guard. They must not be confused.

By themselves these rules are not of much use. In addition, we require some rule that governs the absurd statement itself. The next rule addresses this omission and insists that from a contradiction or absurdity we can conclude anything:

$$
\text{absurd} \quad \cfrac{\begin{array}{c}\pi \\ \Omega\end{array}}{\phi}
$$

If we reach the conclusion Ω then something has gone wrong and so we can conclude what we like. There is a system of logic (*minimal* logic) that does not insist upon this rule but we shall not pause to investigate it. *Intuitionistic* logic, which is the logic we are building up, is the extension of *minimal* logic obtained by the addition of the above rule.

To illustrate these rules we establish the so-called *disjunctive syllogism*.

Example 2.4 We prove $((\phi \vee \psi) \wedge \sim\phi) \to \psi$:

$$
\cfrac{
\cfrac{[(\phi \vee \psi) \wedge \sim\phi]}{\phi \vee \psi}\ \wedge\,e
\qquad
\cfrac{\cfrac{\cfrac{[(\phi \vee \psi) \wedge \sim\phi]}{\sim\phi}\ \wedge\,e \qquad [\phi]}{\Omega}\ \sim e}{\psi}\ \text{absurd}
\qquad
\cfrac{[\psi]}{\cfrac{\psi \to \psi}{\psi}\ \to e}\ \to i
}{
\cfrac{\psi}{((\phi \vee \psi) \wedge \sim\psi) \to \psi}\ \to i
}\ \vee e
$$

discharge ϕ and ψ

discharge $(\phi \vee \psi) \wedge \sim\phi$

This brings us nicely to the notion of *dependence*. Let π be a derivation with conclusion ψ and with ϕ as an *open* (undischarged) assumption. Then the conclusion ψ is said to *depend* upon ϕ. For example, consider the following derivation:

$$
\cfrac{
[\phi \vee \psi] \qquad
\cfrac{\phi \to \eta \quad [\phi]}{\eta}\ \to e
\qquad
\cfrac{\psi \to \eta \quad [\psi]}{\eta}\ \to e
}{
\cfrac{\eta}{(\phi \vee \psi) \to \eta}\ \to i
}\ \vee e
$$

discharge assumptions ϕ and ψ

discharge the assumption $\phi \vee \psi$

The conclusion *depends* upon the assumptions $\phi \to \eta$ and $\psi \to \eta$ since at the conclusion they have not been discharged.

2.2.5 Universal Quantification

We continue our theme of explaining the use of the propositional connectives and quantifiers by describing their rules of derivation. We now concentrate on the conceptually more difficult rules, namely those that govern the quantifiers. For the universal quantifier we obtain the following enrichment of our notion of derivation:

Universal introduction	Universal elimination
$(\forall i) \quad \cfrac{\pi}{\cfrac{\phi}{\forall x \phi}}$	$(\forall e) \quad \cfrac{\pi}{\cfrac{\forall x \phi}{\phi[t/x]}}$

The elimination rule is straightforward in that it enables the inference from the universal statement to a particular instance of it. In this rule t must be free for x in ϕ. This is to avoid any accidental bindings of variables caused by the substitution. In the introduction rule the derivation of ϕ has to be such that the variable x does not occur free in any undischarged wff on which ϕ depends, i.e. in an open assumption on which $\phi[x]$ depends; the derivation is then intuitively independent of the variable x and so we can conclude that the wff holds for any object. The reason for this restriction is easy to illustrate:

$$\frac{\dfrac{[x \in S]}{\forall x(x \in S)} \; \forall i}{x \in S \to \forall x(x \in S)} \to i \qquad x \in S \text{ discharged}$$

The side conditions on universal introduction are not met since $x \in S$ is undischarged at the point where the universal introduction rule is applied. Indeed, we have an obviously false conclusion. This is a rather negative point with which to illustrate the universal quantifier rules, but it is essential that the reader understands the need for this restriction. We can now be more positive; the following is a correct application.

Example 2.5 We establish that

$$(\forall x(x \in T \to x \in S) \wedge \forall x(x \in R \to x \in S) \wedge \forall x(x \in T \vee x \in R)) \to \forall x(x \in S).$$

Informally, if every object of type T is of type S and every object of type R is of type S and every object is of type T or of type R, then every object is of type S:

$$
\frac{
\begin{array}{c}
\dfrac{
\dfrac{
\dfrac{
\dfrac{[\forall x(x \in T \to x \in S) \wedge \forall x(x \in R \to x \in S) \wedge \forall x(x \in T \vee x \in R)]}{\forall x(x \in T \vee x \in R)} \wedge e
}{\forall x(x \in T \vee x \in R)} \; \forall e \quad
\dfrac{\dfrac{[\ldots]}{\forall x(x \in T \to x \in S)} \wedge e}{[x \in T] \quad x \in T \to x \in S} \; \forall e \quad
\dfrac{\dfrac{[\ldots]}{\forall x(x \in R \to x \in S)} \wedge e}{[x \in R] \quad x \in R \to x \in S} \; \forall e
}{x \in T \vee x \in R \quad \dfrac{x \in S}{} \to e \quad \dfrac{x \in S}{} \to e}
}{x \in S} \; ve
}{\dfrac{x \in S}{\forall x(x \in S)} \; \forall i}
}{[\forall x(x \in T \to x \in S) \wedge \forall x(x \in R \to x \in S) \wedge \forall x(x \in T \vee x \in R)] \to \forall x(x \in S)} \to i
$$

In the initial steps the assumption $\forall x(x \in T \to x \in S) \wedge \forall x(x \in R \to x \in S) \wedge \forall x(x \in T \vee x \in R)$ is used three times. The side conditions on the rule are met since, in the instance of universal introduction in the derivation, the variable x does not occur free in any undischarged assumptions on which $x \in S$ depends.

2.2.6 Existential Quantification

These rules again involve the discharging of temporary assumptions. The first is easy to grasp; the second less so:

Existential   Existential
introduction   elimination

$[\phi]$

π π π'

$$(\exists \text{i}) \quad \frac{\phi[t/x]}{\exists x \phi} \qquad\qquad (\exists \text{e}) \quad \frac{\exists x \phi \qquad \eta}{\eta}$$

In ($\exists$i), t must be free for x in ϕ—to ensure no unwanted bindings. Notice that the elimination rule introduces a new wff which is not a component of the main one. We alluded to this in our discussion of disjunction. In ($\exists$e), we may discharge ϕ in passing to the conclusion and x must not occur free in:

1. η
2. Any assumption other than ϕ on which the upper occurrence of η depends

This is to ensure that the derivation of η is *independent* of the particular variable x. We shall illustrate the need for these restrictions shortly. The content of the introduction rule should be clear enough but the elimination rule deserves some comment: if we can deduce η from any instance of ϕ (the restrictions guarantee that the derivation is independent of x), then we can deduce it from the assertion that some x exists which satisfies ϕ.

Example 2.6 To illustrate the rules we prove that $(\forall x(x \in R \to x \in S) \land \exists x(x \in R)) \to \exists x(x \in S)$:

$$
\cfrac{
  \cfrac{
    \cfrac{
      \cfrac{[\forall x(x \in R \to x \in S) \land \exists x(x \in R)]}{\forall x(x \in R \to x \in S)} \land e
    }{
      \cfrac{[x \in R] \quad \cfrac{\forall x(x \in R \to x \in S)}{x \in R \to x \in S} \forall e}{\cfrac{x \in S}{\exists x(x \in S)} \exists i} \to e
    }
  }{\exists x(x \in S)} \exists e \quad \text{discharge } x \in R
}{
  \cfrac{\exists x(x \in S)}{\forall x(x \in R \to x \in S) \land \exists x(x \in R) \to \exists x(x \in S)} \to i
}
$$

discharge
$\forall x(x \in R \to x \in S) \land \exists x(x \in R)$

and at the right, separately: $\exists x(x \in R)$

Notice that at the point where the existential elimination rule is invoked the assumption $\forall x(x \in R \to x \in S) \land \exists x(x \in R)$ has not been discharged. Moreover, $\exists x(x \in S)$ depends upon this assumption. However, x does not occur free in $\forall x(x \in R \to x \in S)$, $\exists x(x \in R)$ or $\exists x(x \in S)$. Hence, the side conditions on the existential elimination rule are satisfied. To illustrate the actual restrictions on the rules we consider the two cases.

1. The case where x occurs free in η. Consider the following derivation:

$$
\cfrac{\exists x(x \in T) \quad \cfrac{\cfrac{\cfrac{[x \in T]}{x \in T \to x \in T} \to i}{x \in T} \to e}{x \in T} }{\cfrac{x \in T}{\forall x(x \in T)} \forall i} \exists e \quad (\text{violation, } x \text{ occurs free in } x \in T)
$$

This is clearly invalid since in effect it enables the conclusion that every object is of the type T from the assumption that some object is of type T.

2. The case where x occurs free in an assumption other than ϕ on which the upper occurrence of η depends. Consider the following derivation:

$$
\cfrac{\exists x(x \in S) \quad \cfrac{\exists x(x \in T) \quad \cfrac{\cfrac{\cfrac{[x \in T] \quad [x \in S]}{x \in T \wedge x \in S} \wedge i}{\exists x(x \in T \wedge x \in S)} \exists i}{\exists x(x \in T \wedge x \in S)} \exists e}{\exists x(x \in T \wedge x \in S)} \exists e}{\exists x(x \in T \wedge x \in S)} \quad \text{violation}
$$

Once again the conclusion is not sound since it enables the derivation of the existence of an object which is of both type T and S from the assumptions that there is an object of type S and one (possibly different) of type T.

This completes the proof rules for the connectives and quantifiers and the inductive definition of the notion of a derivation. More explicitly, a derivation is either atomic (a wff) or is obtained from existing derivations by application of the rule of absurdity, the rules for conjunction, disjunction, implication, universal and existential quantification. These rules of proof constitute *intuitionistic predicate logic* (IPC). The notation $\text{IPC} \vdash \phi$ (or just $\vdash \phi$ where the rules of IPC are understood) will be employed to indicate that there is a derivation with conclusion ϕ with no undischarged assumptions, i.e. it is a *theorem* of IPC. More generally, we shall write $\Gamma \vdash \phi$ if there is a derivation with conclusion ϕ whose only undischarged hypotheses are members of the set of wff Γ. We shall not always write out derivations in such formal detail and even when we do we shall often not employ the *tree* format.

2.3 THE PREDICATE CALCULUS AS A LANGUAGE OF PROGRAM SPECIFICATION

Much contemporary work in computing science is aimed at the development of languages and theories of program specification. A large subset of these languages (e.g. Z, VDM) have the predicate calculus at their core. Our version of the calculus, with its infrastructure of types and terms, has been designed with this application in mind. In this section we shall informally indicate how the present version fulfils this role. This will be an important theme in later sections of the book and the following is meant only to provide a taster for what is to come.

2.3.1 Program Specifications

Traditionally, the specification of functions is achieved through the statement of two conditions: the so-called *pre*- and *post*-conditions on the function. The latter constitutes a statement of the required relationship between the input and output of the function under the government of the pre-condition placed upon the input. Within the jurisdiction of IPC such specifications take the following form, where ϕ is the pre-condition and ψ the post-condition:

$$\forall x (\phi[x] \rightarrow \exists y \psi[x, y])$$

For example, the following is a specification of a simple sorting function on lists of natural numbers. The wff '$O[y]$' and '$P[x, y]$' indicate, respectively, that a list is sorted and that two lists are permutations of each other. We shall not at this point fuss about how these are expressed in the calculus.

$$\forall x [x \in \text{List}[N] \rightarrow \exists y (y \in \text{List}[N] \land O[y] \land P[x, y])]$$

Such a specification demands that, for every object that satisfies the pre-condition, there is an object, which together with the original, satisfies the post-condition. The *form* of this specification may not be quite as expected since the required function (i.e. the function that does the sorting) is left implicit. All we are told is that for every list there exists an ordered permutation of it. However, under one interpretation of the connectives the truth of the specification guarantees the existence of the required function. To see this we must present this interpretation and in doing so clarify the conditions under which a program can be said to *meet* such a specification.

2.3.2 Program Correctness

In what follows we informally describe a relation between programs and wff which can be intuitively understood in any of the following ways:

1. p is a program that verifies ϕ.

2. p is a solution to the problem described by ϕ.
3. p is a program that meets the specification ϕ.

Under the guidance of these intuitions we deal with each of the connectives in turn and for each we indicate the necessary and sufficient conditions for a program to *meet* the specification given by any sentence dominated by the connective. A slightly different way of looking at matters puts the emphasis on the programs rather than the specifications: what does a program have to look like to be a *correct* program for the specification ϕ?

(a) Conjunction Suppose we are asked to write a program to solve a problem that is specified as the conjunction of two subproblems. Presumably, a program that solves the problem must consist of a pair of programs, one being a program that is a solution to the first subproblem and the other a solution to the second. This leads to the following constraint on our relation.

> R1. A program that verifies $\phi \wedge \psi$ is given by presenting a program that verifies ϕ and one that verifies ψ.

One might be tempted by a somewhat different intuition: to solve $\phi \wedge \psi$ one program has to be located that suffices for both. This is certainly a possible interpretation but it hardly serves to break the problem into its components. R1 reflects the *divide and conquer* style of problem solving whereas the alternative seems like a recipe for a headache.

(b) Disjunction Writing a program to solve a problem that is expressed as the disjunction of two problems involves writing a program for one or the other. In addition, the programmer must indicate which of the two problems has been solved. That this further information is necessary should be clear but to emphasize the point consider the following circumstances. In an examination you are given the choice between two problems. You solve the first, pack up your pens and Pepsi, and leave the examination room feeling intellectually fulfilled. Unfortunately, you receive zero marks since the examiner (not being too bright) could not work out which of the two problems was attempted.

> R2. A program that verifies $\phi \vee \psi$ is given by presenting either a program that verifies ϕ or one that verifies ψ, together with a stipulation of which of the two has been verified.

(c) Implication Intuitively, to solve a problem expressed as an implication we must indicate how a solution to the antecedent can be turned into a solution for the consequent.

> R3. A program that verifies $\phi \rightarrow \psi$ is a program that transforms any program that verifies ϕ into a program that verifies ψ.

In terms of specifications, a program meets the specification $\phi \rightarrow \psi$ if it maps any program for the specification ϕ to one for ψ. In other words, it must constitute a *uniform procedure* which maps any solution for the antecedent to a corresponding solution for the consequent.

(d) Universal quantification The clause for universal quantification is similar to that of implication. A program that verifies or solves $\forall x \phi$ is to be a function that given any element (of the domain of discourse) returns a program that solves the corresponding instance of ϕ.

R4. A program that verifies $\forall x \phi$ is a program that maps each object d in the range of x into a program that verifies $\phi[d]$.

Under reading 3, a program meets a specification, expressed as a universally quantified assertion, if it *uniformly* meets the specification given by every instance. One can think of the function as a scheme for solving every instance of ϕ.

(e) Existential quantification This is more delicate. To solve the problem $\exists x \phi$ we must at least locate an element that satisfies ϕ. By itself, however, this is not enough. If you are asked to write a program that solves an existential problem you must not only locate an object but you are under the further obligation to establish that it satisfies the condition stipulated. Thus, in addition, one must provide evidence that the located element does indeed satisfy ϕ.

R5. A program that verifies $\exists x \phi$ is given by providing an object d in the range of x, together with a program that verifies $\phi[d]$.

Such a program thus consists of two parts: a witness to the truth of some instance of ϕ and a program that meets the specification determined by the instance in question.

(f) Negation This is a special case of implication: to solve $\sim \phi$ we must transform a program for ϕ into one for Ω. Of course, the latter has no solution; you cannot verify something that is absurd.

R6. A program that verifies $\sim \phi$ is a program that transforms any putative program that verifies ϕ into a program that verifies Ω where Ω has no verification.

In conclusion, notice that R1 to R6 only impose constraints on the relation; they do not define a specific one. To achieve this we would need to make further provision for atomic assertions; however, do not be taken aback by the absence of such provision. The meanings of atomic assertions are fixed by the universe of discourse, but at present are only concerned with the logical connectives and these are independent of any such universe.

This explanation, although very informal, in that it relies on some interpretation of the notion of *algorithm* or *program*, is nevertheless sufficiently clear for our present purposes. In particular, R1 to R6 justify our *style* of program specification. Consider the following abstract form of such a specification:

$$\forall x(\phi[x] \rightarrow \exists y \psi[x, y])$$

Suppose that p is a program that meets the specification. Then according to R4 and R3, p will be a function that, given any element x, together with a program that verifies the pre-condition, returns a program q that verifies the assertion $\exists y \psi[x, y]$. By R5, q will consist of two parts: an object y and a program that verifies that x and y satisfy the post-condition. In particular, such a program, given an object x that satisfies the pre-condition, eventually returns a y such that x and y satisfy the post-condition. Thus, in some sense, such programs determine the required function. All this will be made more precise later. For the moment, the reader is only required to grasp the outline of the general idea.

2.3.3 Constructive Semantics and IPC

Looked at from a slightly different point of view R1 to R6 provide a semantics for the predicate calculus since they address the question: 'What constitutes a verification of ϕ?' Indeed, the above is a variation on the *constructive* semantics for the predicate calculus due to Arend Heyting (1934). He not only provided the first formalization of intuitionistic logic but also the first semantic interpretation of the calculus which closely followed the practice of the intuitionistic mathematicians. We have to be a little guarded in this claim since our clauses do not quite reflect his but rather those of Kleene (1945), and to some extent we part company with the *official* semantics. Despite this disparity with intuitionism the clauses seem very natural from a computing science perspective.

Moreover, all the rules of IPC are sound under this semantic interpretation in the following sense. Suppose we have an inference rule of the following form:

$$\frac{\phi_1 \cdots \phi_n}{\phi}$$

Then soundness amounts to the demand that, given programs for the premises, we can locate a program for the conclusion. We cannot yet formally verify the *soundness of IPC*; this will have to wait until we have a more precise account of the semantics. In fact, the proof of soundness will form the basis of *constructive program development*. In this connection, we should remark that this semantics sanctions more than the strict intuitionist would accept since it validates a form of *Church's thesis*. We shall say more about this later when we formalize R1 to R6.

For the moment we are more concerned with what this semantic interpretation rules out. In particular, it does not sanction the *law of excluded middle* (LEM) (a rule with no premises):

$$\text{LEM} \quad \frac{}{\phi \vee \sim \phi}$$

Even with this level of formality it is easy to see this. According to R1 to R6, accepting LEM means that we have an algorithm for obtaining, for any wff ϕ, a program that verifies ϕ or a program that verifies $\sim \phi$ (i.e. a method of obtaining a contradiction from the assumption that a program exists that verifies ϕ). Suppose that $\phi[x]$ is the assertion that program x terminates (such assertions will be added to our language in Chapter 4 where we study partiality and termination). In this case we have an algorithm that informs us whether an arbitrary program terminates or not. However, there is no such program: one cannot have a program for testing termination. In other words, the validity of LEM, under the interpretation given by R1 to R6, amounts to the *halting problem*. This has important implications since if we employ the LEM in our logic of specification then we have to give up the constructive semantics and this undermines the present interpretation of wff as program specifications.

2.4 CLASSICAL AND INTUITIONISTIC LOGIC

The logic IPC may not be familiar to most readers. Indeed, those readers with some acquaintance with the predicate calculus will almost certainly have been exposed to its classical extension. The *classical predicate calculus* (CPC) is the extension of IPC obtained by the addition of any one of the following three rules of proof:

1. Classical negation (NEG)
2. Law of excluded middle (LEM)
3. Law of double negation (DN)

$$\text{NEG} \quad \begin{array}{c} [\sim \phi] \\ | \\ \Omega \\ \hline \phi \end{array}$$

$$\text{LEM} \quad \frac{}{\sim \phi \vee \phi}$$

$$\text{DN} \quad \frac{\sim \sim \phi}{\phi}$$

Any of the three, added to IPC, enables the derivation of the others. To illustrate matters we show that NEG implies LEM and leave the other derivations for the reader:

$$\cfrac{\cfrac{\cfrac{[\phi]}{\phi \vee \sim\phi} \vee i \quad [\sim(\phi \vee \sim\phi)]}{\cfrac{\Omega}{\sim\phi} \sim i} \sim e}{\cfrac{[\sim(\phi \vee \sim\phi)] \quad \cfrac{}{\phi \vee \sim\phi} \vee i}{\cfrac{\Omega}{\phi \vee \sim\phi} \text{NEG}} \sim e} \quad \begin{aligned} &\text{discharge } \phi \\[2em] &\text{discharge } \sim(\phi \vee \sim\phi) \end{aligned}$$

Formally, these rules constitute the difference between IPC and CPC. However, the difference between the two logics is best seen as a reflection of their underlying semantic theories. We have already seen why LEM is rejected by the constructive semantics. We now indicate why it is upheld by the classical semantics of the predicate calculus.

2.4.1 Classical Semantics

Classically, the language of the predicate calculus is given semantic life by spelling out the conditions under which a sentence is true or false. This is achieved in a recursive fashion by stipulating for each connective and quantifier the necessary and sufficient conditions for the wff to be true:

T1. $\phi \wedge \psi$ is true iff ϕ is true and ψ is true.
T2. $\phi \vee \psi$ is true iff ϕ is true or ψ is true.
T3. $\phi \rightarrow \psi$ is true iff ϕ is true implies ψ is true.
T4. $\forall x\phi$ is true iff for each d in the range of x, $\phi[d]$ is true.
T5. $\exists x\phi$ is true iff for some d in the range of x, $\phi[d]$ is true.
T6. $\sim\phi$ is true iff ϕ is not true (i.e. false); Ω is false.

These semantic clauses embody the classical understanding of the connectives and quantifiers. In particular, the clause T6 insists that the negation of wff is true just in case the wff is not true (i.e. false)—assuming a classical interpretation of the connectives of the metalanguage. Under such a regime, under the assumption that every atomic wff is either true of false, the law of excluded middle is sound. In fact, all the rules of CPC are *sound* under this semantics in the sense that if the premises of a rule are true then so is the conclusion.

The dissimilarity between these two semantic theories goes right to the heart of the difference between intuitionistic and classical reasoning. The law of excluded middle (or its equivalents) constitutes the formal proof theoretic distinction but the semantic theories offer an explanation for the discrepancy.

2.4.2 IPC and CPC

To complete this section, and indeed this chapter, we continue to explore the differences between these two logics, but we now examine some of the more obvious formal implications. For example, the following are derivable in CPC but not in IPC:

$$\sim\phi \vee \sim\sim\phi \tag{a}$$

$$(\phi \rightarrow \psi) \vee (\psi \rightarrow \phi) \tag{b}$$

$$\sim(\sim\phi \wedge \sim\psi) \rightarrow (\phi \vee \psi) \tag{c}$$

$$\sim(\sim\phi \vee \sim\psi) \rightarrow (\phi \wedge \psi) \tag{d}$$

The reader is urged to examine informally why these are not upheld by the clauses of R1 to R6. Perhaps the most striking differences arise in connection with the derived logics of the quantifiers. In CPC all the following are provable:

$$\forall x\phi \leftrightarrow \sim\exists x \sim \phi \tag{e}$$

$$\exists x \sim \phi \leftrightarrow \sim\forall x\phi \tag{f}$$

$$\exists x\phi \leftrightarrow \sim\forall x \sim \phi \tag{g}$$

$$\forall x \sim \phi \leftrightarrow \sim\exists x\phi \tag{h}$$

In contrast, only the following are theorems of IPC:

$$\forall x\phi \rightarrow \sim\exists x \sim \phi \tag{i}$$

$$\exists x \sim \phi \rightarrow \sim\forall x\phi \tag{j}$$

$$\exists x\phi \rightarrow \sim\forall x \sim \phi \tag{k}$$

$$\forall x \sim \phi \leftrightarrow \sim\exists x\phi \tag{l}$$

The failure of the others reflects the intuitionistic insistence that the assertion of existence is a strong one. For example, the failure of $(\sim\forall x \sim \phi) \rightarrow (\exists x\phi)$ is a consequence of the intuitionistic demand that existence proofs have to be *direct*. It is not sufficient, in order to establish that some object satisfies ϕ, to establish that the assumption that every object does not satisfy ϕ leads to a contradiction. Intuitionistically, one has to locate an object. This is reflected in the semantic clause of R5: in order to verify an existential assertion we need to locate an actual object. Indeed, the following is consistent in intuitionistic logic:

$$(\sim\forall x\phi) \wedge (\sim\exists x \sim \phi)$$

In other words, we cannot rule out the possibility that we may be able to simultaneously show that we can never prove that every object has a certain property and that we can never find a specific object that lacks it.

One could go on forever highlighting the differences between the two, but we assign further excavations to the reader. Many other differences will emerge as we enrich the theory. Indeed, we are not seeking to convince the reader of the inferential poverty of IPC—quite the contrary. Our aim has been to provide some preliminary evidence that IPC is a suitable logic for reasoning about programs and their specifications and that classical logic not only exceeds the requirements of this endeavour but is actually detrimental to it.

EXERCISES

2.1 Prove the following in intuitionistic logic. Write out all the details of the proofs.

(a) $\phi \to \sim \sim \phi$

(b) $\sim \phi \leftrightarrow \sim \sim \sim \phi$

(c) $\sim(\phi \vee \psi) \leftrightarrow (\sim \phi \wedge \sim \psi)$

(d) $\forall x \phi \to \sim \exists x \sim \phi$

(e) $\exists x \sim \phi \to \sim \forall x \phi$

(f) $\exists x \phi \to \sim \forall x \sim \phi$

(g) $\forall x \sim \phi \leftrightarrow \sim \exists x \phi$

(h) $(\phi \to \psi) \to (\sim \psi \to \sim \phi)$

(i) $\sim \sim (\phi \to \psi) \to (\phi \to \sim \sim \psi)$

(j) $\sim \sim (\phi \wedge \psi) \leftrightarrow (\sim \sim \phi) \wedge (\sim \sim \psi)$

(k) $(\phi \to \forall x \psi) \leftrightarrow \forall x(\phi \to \psi)$, x not free in ϕ

(l) $(\exists x \phi \to \psi) \leftrightarrow \forall x(\phi \to \psi)$, x not free in ψ

2.2 Complete the proof of the equivalence of the classical negation rule, the rule of excluded middle and the rule of double negation.

2.3 Informally verify that all the rules of IPC are sound under the interpretation given by R1 to R6; i.e. for each rule, given programs for the premises, construct programs for the conclusion. You will have to assume, informally, that certain constructs are available in your programming language. As you construct the proof make a list of these constructs.

2.4 Prove the following in classical logic:

(a) $\sim \phi \vee \sim \sim \phi$

(b) $(\phi \to \psi) \vee (\psi \to \phi)$

(c) $\sim(\sim \phi \wedge \sim \psi) \to \phi \vee \psi$

(d) $\sim(\sim \phi \vee \sim \psi) \to \phi \wedge \psi$

(e) $\forall x \phi \leftrightarrow \sim \exists x \sim \phi$

(f) $\exists x \sim \phi \leftrightarrow \sim \forall x \phi$

(g) $\exists x \phi \leftrightarrow \sim \forall x \sim \phi$

(h) $\forall x \sim \phi \leftrightarrow \sim \exists x \phi$

2.5 In CPC, define disjunction and existential quantification in terms of the other connectives. Derive the introduction and elimination rules for these defined constructs from the others.

2.6 Write a specification for a program that inserts a number into an ordered list of numbers and returns an ordered list.

REFERENCES AND FURTHER READING

Tennant (1978) presents predicate logic in terms of natural deduction rules and discusses the differences between the classical and intuitionistic versions.

Troelstra and Van Dalen (1988) also gives a detailed exposition along the same lines as that taken here. Dummett (1977) gives an elementary exposition of intuitionistic logic together with a discussion of the philosophical background. Hamilton (1989) provides a reasonably simple introduction to classical predicate logic which includes a treatment of its semantics. Manna and Waldinger (1984) give a very gentle introduction to the classical calculus with computing science applications. Jones (1986) provides an introduction to the calculus as a specification language but the emphasis is on the development of imperative programs.

3

THE LAMBDA CALCULUS

From one perspective the lambda calculus is a functional programming language. Indeed, it forms the conceptual backbone of most contemporary functional languages. It is a simple language whose explicit facilities allow only the definition of functions and their application to arguments, and yet behind this grammatical simplicity hides a language rich in expressive power. Ever since Landin (1966) the calculus has been employed as a basis for the design and implementation of functional languages. Languages such as ML, Miranda™, HOPE and HASKELL have all been inspired by the simple ideas that underlie the calculus.

From a different perspective the lambda calculus is a *theory of functions* or, more accurately, a *theory of operations*. The syntax of the calculus informs us how functions are to be constructed and the axioms of the calculus provide us with an axiomatic theory of functional equality, function definition and function application. It is in this sense that the calculus constitutes a *theory of functions*.

In contrast, the reader familiar with elementary set theory will have assimilated the idea that functions are special kinds of sets. This yields a different notion of function to that delivered by the axioms of the calculus. According to the traditional notion, sets are primary and functions are derived notions: sets of ordered pairs. As a consequence, functions come equipped with two sets: their *domain* and *range*. For example, the identity function on the natural numbers is the set $\{(x, y): x \in N \land y \in N \land x = y\}$.

Modern computing science appeals to a different notion of function—one that has more operational content. In this tradition, functions are essentially operations that transform data and it somewhat distorts computational intuitions to think of such operations as sets of ordered pairs selected from a predetermined domain and range. Instead, they are defined by simply describing their action and there is no intuitive necessity to define the domain and range of the intended action. Indeed, operations may be applied to themselves. The lambda calculus notion of function more accurately reflects this operational one and so it is fitting that we base our theory of functions upon the lambda calculus. The calculus treats functions as primary and as such they are not analysed in terms of sets or any other more putative notion. In the present theory, functions and sets/types are both taken as *first class citizens* and neither is analysed in terms of the other. This should not be taken to imply that operations cannot be assigned a domain and range but rather that they may be assigned many such. Operations are genuinely *polymorphic*. For example, the identity operation is the identity no matter what the domain. This is not just a theoretical observation but has practical consequences since the same operation can be employed in many contexts without the need for separate declarations.

The aim of this chapter and the following two is to introduce the calculus and to study its role in the foundations of functional programming. In the first section we introduce the syntax of the lambda calculus and in the second we shall provide its axiomatization. In this guise the calculus constitutes a *theory of functions/operations*. In the third and fourth sections we turn to the role of the calculus as a programming language and study the *evaluation* of lambda terms. Although this chapter is self-contained we shall refer the reader to the literature for many of the formal details, especially the proofs of the more technical results.

3.1 THE SYNTAX OF THE LAMBDA CALCULUS

As we have indicated, the language is very simple. Apart from variables and constants there are only two ways of forming new terms from old ones. Intuitively, these correspond to the definition of a function and its application to an argument. We shall follow the pattern of the previous chapter by first introducing the language and various other syntactic aspects pertaining to substitution, freedom and bondage.

3.1.1 The Language

Formally, the language is given by the following syntax:

$$t ::= x \,|\, c \,|\, (ts) \,|\, (\lambda x \,.\, t)$$

Terms are variables, constants, applications or abstractions. *Pure lambda terms* are those containing no constants. We shall continue to employ lower-case letters u, v, w, x, y, z, f, g for variables, c, d, e for constants and

t, s, r for terms. We shall not apply hard and fast rules to these conventions but the context will always determine matters. The first two clauses are inherited from the syntax given in the previous chapter. The third clause involves the application of one term to a second. This has particular force when the first term is an abstraction and the whole clause is then intuitively an instance of functional application. Functions are formed by *abstraction* on a term with respect to a variable and as such they are not explicitly named. One can think of the variable as the formal parameter of the function. In a certain sense abstraction is the reverse of application: roughly, the former corresponds to (implicit) function definition or declaration and the latter to function call. In an application (ts) we shall often refer to t as the *operator* and s as the *operand*.

In summary, terms of the lambda calculus are made up from variables (and optionally additional constants), applications and abstractions. The following are some examples:

$$(\lambda x.x) \qquad (a)$$

$$(\lambda x.(\lambda y.(xy))) \qquad (b)$$

$$((\lambda x.x)(\lambda x.x)) \qquad (c)$$

$$(\lambda x.(\lambda y.x)) \qquad (d)$$

$$(\lambda x.(\lambda y.(\lambda z.((xz)(yz))))) \qquad (e)$$

$$c(\lambda x.(\lambda y.x)) \qquad (f)$$

Example (a), $(\lambda x.x)$, called I, is an example of a term formed by abstraction on a variable and names the identity function. Example (b) is more elaborate, involving two abstractions, and is legitimate since functions are terms and so can be abstracted upon. This example is important since it illustrates how functions of more than one argument are defined in the lambda calculus: essentially, functions select their arguments one by one. Function application is represented by juxtaposing one term with another. This is illustrated by example (c) which involves two abstractions and an application. Examples (d) and (e) are *famous* lambda terms and are given the names K and S respectively.

There are various syntactic conventions that simplify the expression of terms and we shall employ the following rewrite conventions:

$$((ts)r) \text{ as } tsr \qquad (a)$$

$$(\lambda x.(ts)) \text{ as } \lambda x.ts \qquad (b)$$

$$(\lambda x.(\lambda y.(\lambda u.(\lambda z.t)))) \text{ as } \lambda xyuz.t \qquad (c)$$

These will greatly enhance readability without introducing ambiguity. Convention (a) encodes an *association to the left rule*, (b) also permits the removal of parentheses and (c) sanctions the removal of several stacked occurrences of the lambda.

This completes the basic description of the language. It may seem rather trivial, especially to those readers familiar with a conventional programming language. However, the reader should not be led into a false sense of simplicity; the calculus is syntactically simple but semantically not. The full conceptual impact will not be felt until the axioms are in place. To facilitate their presentation we need some *housekeeping* notions.

3.1.2 Substitution

The theory of the calculus is essentially concerned with an axiomatization of the equality relation between lambda terms where the notion of equality is supported by the idea of *substituting* a term for a variable. Under the intended interpretation of the language, abstractions are functions where this notion is to be interpreted *operationally*. With this understanding one would expect $(\lambda x.x)y$ to be equal to y and $(\lambda x.(\lambda y.x))cd$ to be equal to c. The theory of the calculus is a theory of equality for lambda terms which sanctions these intuitive equivalences. The formal definition of substitution is rather delicate and before we can present it we require some preliminary notions that formally capture the idea of one term *occurring* in a second. In what follows we shall employ ' $\approx$ ' for the syntactic identity of terms.

Definition 3.1 A term s *occurs* in t iff
(a) $s \approx t$
(b) $t \approx (t't'')$ and s occurs in t' or s occurs in t''
(c) $t \approx \lambda y.t'$ and $s \approx y$ or s occurs in t'
For a particular occurrence of $\lambda y.s$ in a term t, the occurrence s is called the *scope* of the λ on the left of s.

Like quantification, lambda abstraction is a binding operation and there are similar notions of *freedom* and *bondage* for variables.

Definition 3.2 A variable x, which occurs in a term t, *occurs free* in t iff
(a) $x \approx t$
(b) $t \approx (ss')$ and x occurs free in s or s'
(c) $t \approx \lambda y.s$ and $x \not\approx y$ and x occurs free in s
A variable x, which occurs in a term t, *occurs bound* in t iff
(a) $t \approx \lambda y.s$ and either $x \approx y$ or x occurs bound in s
(b) $t \approx (ss')$ and x occurs bound in s or s'
If x has any free occurrence in t then it is a *free variable* of t. A *closed* term is one without any free variables; we employ Λ° to denote the collection of closed terms.

Actually we have included these explicit definitions for completeness; we can express things more succinctly: an occurrence of a variable x in a term t occurs bound iff it is a part of t with the form $\lambda x . s$. For example, x is free in x but not in $\lambda x . (xy)$ or $\lambda y . ((\lambda x . x)(yy))$. Notice that a variable can be free and bound in the same expression as in $(\lambda x . x)(xx)$. Since terms occur in wff, variables in wff can now be bound by quantification and abstraction.

In the predicate calculus, substitution was defined in a very cavalier way and the subsequent problem of variable clashes was engineered away by placing impositions on the quantifier rules. In the case of the lambda calculus the traditional route avoids the problem by renaming offending bound variables in the very act of substitution.

Definition 3.3 Let t and s be terms and x a variable. We define $t[s/x]$, the result of *substituting* s for every free occurrence of x in t, by recursion on t as follows:

(a) If $t \approx x$ then $t[s/x] \approx s$

    If $t \approx t'$ (a variable or constant $\not\approx x$) then $t[s/x] \approx t$

(b) If $t \approx (t't'')$ then $t[s/x] \approx (t'[s/x]t''[s/x])$

(c) If $t \approx \lambda y . t'$ then there are two cases:

   (i) If $x \approx y$ then $t[s/x] \approx t$

  (ii) If $x \not\approx y$ then there are two subcases:

     (1) If y is not free in s or x is not free in t' then $t[s/x] \approx \lambda y . t'[s/x]$

     (2) If y is free in s and x is free in t' then $t[s/x] \approx \lambda z . t'[z/y][s/x]$, where z is not free in s and not free in t'

A mapping σ, from variables to closed terms, will be called a *closed substitution* and the term obtained from t, by substituting σx for each free variable x of t, will be written as $t\sigma$.

Notice that clause (c) (ii) splits into two cases. To justify its presence consider the following instance of substitution:

$$(\lambda y . x)[w/x]$$

Intuitively, this ought to be the constant function with value w. However, without the split between subcases (1) and (2) it will denote the identity function when $w \approx y$—hence the complication. This is a similar phenomenon to that encountered in the predicate calculus. There we avoided the problem by introducing the notion *free for*. The difference between these two approaches to substitution is a result of the tradition in the two disciplines. However, the substitution of a term for a variable in a wff must now appeal to this notion of term substitution since atomic wff contain terms.

3.2 THE LAMBDA CALCULUS AS A THEORY OF OPERATIONAL FUNCTIONS

In the last chapter we introduced the underlying logic of the programming theory; in this we begin the development of the theory itself. It is made up from three main groups of *axioms*:

1. Axioms of the lambda calculus and its extensions
2. Axioms of termination
3. Axioms of types

In general, an *axiom* is any wff that acts like a fixed open assumption. A theorem of the theory is then any wff for which there exists a derivation in IPC where the only undischarged assumptions are selected from the axioms. In this chapter we study the axioms of the *pure calculus* and deal with the extensions in Chapter 5. Termination will occupy all of Chapter 4 and the theory of types will run through Chapters 6 to 10.

The axioms of the pure lambda calculus are intended to capture the notion of equality between lambda terms. There are two fundamental equality axioms: the first reflects the intuitive idea of function application and the second determines the role of bound variables. In addition, there are axioms that govern equality in context. However, to begin with we introduce some axioms that bear upon the general nature of equality.

3.2.1 Basic Axioms of Equality

Intuitively, any notion of equality should be reflexive, symmetric and transitive, i.e. an equivalence relation:

e1. $\forall x(x = x)$
e2. $\forall x \forall y((x = y) \rightarrow (y = x))$
e3. $\forall x \forall y \forall z((x = y) \wedge (y = z) \rightarrow (x = z))$

Actually, such axioms are normally stated without the universal quantifiers and all free variables are implicitly universally quantified, a move justified by the universal introduction rule. They can also be stated as rules:

$$\text{e1} \quad \frac{}{x = x} \qquad \text{e2} \quad \frac{x = y}{y = x} \qquad \text{e3} \quad \frac{x = y \quad y = z}{x = z}$$

It does not matter which route we adopt but we shall, in the first instance, present all the programming theory axiomatically although we shall often also indicate the rule-based formulation. These axioms are normally taken to be part of the axioms of the predicate calculus (with equality).

3.2.2 The α and β Axioms

This brings us to the characteristic axioms of the calculus. Consider the two terms $(\lambda x.t)s$ and $t[s/x]$. The first represents the application of the operation $(\lambda x.t)$ to the argument s. Intuitively, the second term is a *simplification* of the first, in that it represents the result of carrying out the application represented by the first. Our notion of equality should reflect this intuition and indeed this is the content of the first axiom:

$$\beta. \ (\lambda x.t)y = t[y/x]$$

The right-hand side of the equality is the result of applying the operation, represented by the abstraction, to its argument. This amounts to the substitution of the argument for the variable of abstraction. Strictly speaking we ought to refer to the above as an *axiom scheme*. It does not take the form of a simple axiom since it is stated for arbitrary terms; it is a scheme with infinitely many instances which are generated as t ranges over the terms of the language. Many of the axioms will take this form. Observe that according to the convention the variable y, being free, is implicitly universally quantified.

The α axiom sanctions bound variable changes. According to it terms that are bound variable variants of each other represent the same operation:

$$\alpha. \ \lambda x.t = \lambda y.t[y/x] \quad \text{provided that } y \text{ is not free in } t$$

This is in keeping with the interpretation of the calculus as a theory of operations since the two expressions $\lambda x.t$ and $\lambda y.t[y/x]$ are operationally indistinguishable: applied to any term, under substitution, they yield the very same term as a result. The insistence that y is not free in t is to avoid accidental bindings in t. For example, without this restriction we would be able to conclude that $\lambda x.y = \lambda y.y$—a rather unfortunate consequence.

3.2.3 Contextual Axioms

The last group of axioms govern the behaviour of equality under application and abstraction. The first two insist that equality is preserved by application:

$$\mu. \ x = y \rightarrow ux = uy$$
$$\nu. \ u = v \rightarrow ux = vx$$

According to axiom μ, if the two arguments are equal then the operation yields the same results whereas axiom ν demands that equal operations yield equal results when applied to the very same argument. They are clearly in accord with the interpretation of the calculus as a language of operations. It would be a strange theory of operational equality that rejected them.

The normal formulation of the lambda calculus is *logic free*, i.e. without reference to the quantifiers and connectives of the predicate calculus. In this guise the above axioms are stated as rules:

$$\frac{s = s'}{ts = ts'}$$

$$\frac{s = s'}{st = s't}$$

We leave the reader to establish the equivalence of the two representations. The last contextual axiom is a little more delicate:

$$\xi. \ \forall x(t = s) \rightarrow (\lambda y . t = \lambda y . s) \qquad \text{where } x \approx y$$

It guarantees that two lambda abstractions are equal provided that the two terms are equal for all instantiations of the variable of abstraction. Intuitively, this is sound under the interpretation of abstractions as operational functions: if two terms are equal for all instantiations of a variable, then the functions formed by abstraction on the variable will be operationally indistinguishable since no matter what term is substituted for the variable the results will be the same. Notice that the variable of quantification and the variable of abstraction are both bound but the side condition on the axiom demands that they must be the very same variable. The need for this restriction ought to be obvious but can perhaps be seen in a more perspicuous way in terms of the corresponding proof rule:

$$\frac{t = s}{\lambda x . t = \lambda x . s}$$

In the rule, x must not be free in any assumption on which $t = s$ depends. The restriction guarantees that the variable x is implicitly universally quantified in the premise and so the conclusion intuitively follows. This accounts for the form of the axiom where the variable of abstraction is universally quantified with a narrow scope that does not extend to the whole implication.

This nearly completes the axioms of the pure calculus. There is one other option which we consider shortly. We shall refer to the theory consisting of the axioms e1 to e3, β, α, ξ, μ, ν as LC and write LC $\vdash \phi$ if there exists an IPC derivation of ϕ where the only open assumptions are instances of the axioms of LC.

3.2.4 Equality and Substitution

If two terms are equal can they be substituted in any context without change of *meaning*? This question is taken as the acid test for a notion of equality to be correct. There are two separate instances of the question which naturally arise within the current theory and correspond to the two different notions of context generated by terms and wff.

To address the first we need to be a little more precise about the notion of *context* generated by terms. A context, $C[\ ]$, is any lambda expression that contains $[\ ]$ as a new constant. Intuitively, $[\ ]$ represents a *hole* in the lambda expression. More formally, contexts are defined inductively as follows:

x is a context

$[\ ]$ is a context

if $C_1[\ ]$ and $C_2[\ ]$ are contexts then so are

$(C_1[\ ]C_2[\ ])$ and $\lambda x . C_1[\ ]$

We shall write $C[s]$ for the result of textually placing s in the holes of $C[\ ]$. This is *not* formal substitution and as a consequence the free variables of s may become bound in $C[s]$.

Theorem 3.1 For any context $C[\ ]$, $\mathrm{LC} \vdash (s = t) \rightarrow (C[s] = C[t])$.

PROOF By induction on the structure of the context. Assume that $t = s$. If C is a hole or a variable then the result is automatic. If $C[\ ]$ is of the form $\lambda x . C_1[\ ]$ then, by induction, $C_1[t] = C_1[s]$. By universal introduction we have: $\forall x(C_1[t] = C_1[s])$; the result now follows directly from axiom ξ. If C has the form $(C_1[\ ]C_2[\ ])$ then employ induction, e3, μ and ν.

In regard to the second question the following principle captures the obvious substitutivity requirement for wff:

e4. $x = y \rightarrow (\phi[x] \rightarrow \phi[y])$

First observe that axiom e4 implies axioms μ and ν. We illustrate with axiom μ. Let $\phi[x]$ be $ts = tx$. Then by axiom e4, $s = r \rightarrow (\phi[s] \rightarrow \phi[r])$. Since $\phi[s]$ holds the result follows. More to the point, axiom e4 is actually derivable from LC—at least where the only atomic wff are equality and absurdity. With this proviso we have the following.

Theorem 3.2 $\mathrm{LC} \vdash (x = y) \rightarrow (\phi[x] \rightarrow \phi[y])$.

PROOF We establish each instance by induction on the wff. The tricky case is the base step; the rest follows directly from the induction assumptions and the details are left for the reader. For the base step we must prove $(x = y) \rightarrow (\phi[x] \rightarrow \phi[y])$ where $\phi[x]$ is the atomic formula $t[x] = s[x]$. From Theorem 3.1, setting the context to $t[\ ]$, we obtain $t[x] = t[y]$ and, similarly, $s[x] = s[y]$. By assumption, $t[x] = s[x]$ and so, by the axioms e1 to e3, $t[y] = s[y]$.

Actually, principle e4 is generally dispensable provided that all the atomic instances are stated as axioms. If we consider the full language of the theory with type membership as an atomic formula then principle e4 is derivable provided that the atomic instance $(x \in T \wedge x = y) \rightarrow y \in T$ is included as a new axiom. We shall return to this when we deal with the axioms for types.

3.2.5 Extensionality

The theory LC is a theory of *operational functions*: it provides us with a syntax or language of functions together with axioms that inform us when two expressions or terms are equal. Classically, if two functions are equal on all arguments then they are equal as functions. This is the so-called principle of extensionality:

ext. $\forall x(tx = sx) \rightarrow (t = s)$ x is not free in t nor s

The theory extended with this axiom we denote as LC + ext. The axiom ξ is often referred to as *weak* extensionality. The only difference between the two theories is summarized as follows:

η. $\lambda x . tx = t$ x not free in t

Theorem 3.3 LC + ext is equivalent to LC + η.

PROOF Assume ext. We have $(\lambda x . tx)z = tz$ where x is not free in t. Hence, by ext, $\lambda x . tx = t$. Conversely, assume η. Then assume that $\forall x(tx = sx)$ where x is not free in t nor s. By ξ, we have $\lambda x . tx = \lambda x . sx$. By η, we can conclude that $t = s$.

In other words, extensionality enables us to conclude that $\lambda x . tx = t$ and that is all there is to it. We shall not, however, adopt ext as part of the basic theory. Instead, in the next chapter we shall see that this full version is not available in the context of a *lazy* programming language.

This completes the basic theory of the calculus. In the rest of this chapter we shall be concerned with the computational role of the calculus as a prototypical functional programming language. The reader who requires a more detailed account of the basic material of the calculus should consult Hindley and Seldin (1986) and the more advanced Barendregt (1984).

3.3 THE LAMBDA CALCULUS AS A PROGRAMMING LANGUAGE

The axioms of the lambda calculus provide a precise notion of equality for lambda terms. Implicitly, they also provide a notion of evaluation which facilitates the simplification of terms. From a computational perspective this is essential since we need to treat the language as a *calculus*, i.e. we need to calculate with it.

3.3.1 Reduction and Normal Forms

We first discuss the notions of simplification and reduction, in general, and then study some specific evaluation strategies. The central idea is to treat the axioms of the calculus as *rewrite rules* where each central axiom underwrites a rewrite rule.

We concentrate first on the axiom of β equality. This sanctions the replacement of terms of the form $(\lambda x . t)s$ by $t[s/x]$.

Definition 3.4 A term of the form $(\lambda x . t)s$ is called a β *redex* and $t[s/x]$ its *contractum*. If a term t' contains an occurrence of such a redex and we replace it by its corresponding contractum we say we have β-*contracted* the term.

Notice that a redex (reducible expression) can be replaced anywhere in a term but the axioms of the lambda calculus justify this reduction step since by Theorem 3.1 the axioms guarantee that, for any context $C[\ ]$, if $t = s$ then $C[t] = C[s]$. Moreover, this notion of β contraction has an important idea associated with it.

Definition 3.5 A term that contains no β redexes is in β-*normal form* (NF).

A term in normal form cannot be further contracted. It is as simple as possible. In the following examples, (a), (b), (d) and (e) are in normal form but (c) is not:

$$(\lambda x . x) \qquad\qquad (a)$$

$$(\lambda x . (\lambda y . (xy))) \qquad\qquad (b)$$

$$((\lambda x . x)(\lambda x . x)) \qquad\qquad (c)$$

$$(\lambda x . (\lambda y . x)) \qquad\qquad (d)$$

$$(\lambda x . (\lambda y . (\lambda z . ((xz)(yz))))) \qquad\qquad (e)$$

However, there is a further operation that can be performed which involves treating the axiom of α equality as a rewrite rule.

Definition 3.6 A replacement of a term $\lambda x . t$ by $\lambda y . t[y/x]$ (y not free in t) is called an α *reduction*. If t can be obtained from s by a finite number of α reductions we say that t is *congruent* to s.

The notion of congruence is stronger than equality since terms can be equal without being congruent but not vice versa. Together, these operations form the basis of the simplification or reduction process.

Definition 3.7 We shall say that t *reduces* to s (and write $t \geq s$) if s can be obtained from t by a finite sequence (possibly empty) of β reductions or α reductions. We shall say that t is *equivalent* to s (and write $s \equiv t$) if s can be obtained from t by a finite sequence (possibly empty) of β reductions (or reversed β reductions) or α reductions. A term that can be reduced to a term in normal form is said to be *normalizable* or to *have a normal form*.

The following examples illustrate the idea. Observe that the last does not terminate in a normal form.

$$(\lambda x \, . \, x)(\lambda x \, . \, x) \geq (\lambda x \, . \, x) \qquad\qquad (a)$$

$$(\lambda x \, . \, (\lambda y \, . \, (xy)))(\lambda z \, . \, z) \geq (\lambda y \, . \, ((\lambda z \, . \, z)y)) \geq \lambda y \, . \, y \qquad\qquad (b)$$

$$(\lambda xyz \, . \, xz(yz))uvw \geq (\lambda yz \, . \, uz(yz))vw \geq (\lambda z \, . \, uz(vz))w \geq uw(vw) \quad (c)$$

$$((\lambda x \, . \, xx)(\lambda x \, . \, xx)) \geq ((\lambda x \, . \, xx)(\lambda x \, . \, xx)) \geq ((\lambda x \, . \, xx)(\lambda x \, . \, xx)) \cdots \quad (d)$$

The last term, $((\lambda x \, . \, xx)(\lambda x \, . \, xx))$, which we shall write as $\perp$, is usually taken to be the *canonical* term without a normal form and will play a fairly substantial role in our discussion of termination in the next chapter.

3.3.2 The Church–Rosser Theorem

With the basic idea of reduction in position we can say a little about its general nature. One important property of the lambda calculus is contained in a theorem due to Church and Rosser. To grasp its content suppose that we can reduce a lambda term t to normal form by two different routes:

$$t(= t_0) \geq t_1 \geq \cdots \geq t_n = t'$$

$$t(= t_0) \geq s_1 \geq \cdots \geq s_n = t''$$

One would like to be assured that the result is independent of the actual reduction sequences. For example, consider the term $(\lambda x \, . \, x)((\lambda y \, . \, y)(\lambda y \, . \, (yy)))$. This has two possibilities for reduction. One can reduce $(\lambda y \, . \, y)(\lambda y \, . \, (yy))$ first or reduce the redex farthest to the left. This generates the following sequences:

$$(\lambda x \, . \, x)((\lambda y \, . \, y)(\lambda y \, . \, (yy))) \geq (\lambda x \, . \, x)(\lambda y \, . \, (yy)) \geq (\lambda y \, . \, (yy)) \qquad (a)$$

$$(\lambda x \, . \, x)((\lambda y \, . \, y)(\lambda y \, . \, (yy))) \geq (\lambda y \, . \, y)(\lambda y \, . \, (yy)) \geq (\lambda y \, . \, (yy)) \qquad (b)$$

In this example the order is not germane to the result. The Church–Rosser theorem informs us that this is always so.

Theorem (Church–Rosser) 3.4 If $t \geq s$ and $t \geq s'$ then there exists a term s'' such that $s \geq s''$ and $s' \geq s''$.

We shall not pause to prove this result. It is quite combinatorial and we refer the reader to Hindley and Seldin (1986) for details. However, the theorem has the following obvious consequence.

Corollary 3.1 If s has two normal forms then they are congruent.

This follows directly from the theorem: if s reduces to two normal forms t and t' then there exists a term t'' such that t and t' both reduce to t''. Since t and t' are in normal form, these reductions can only be the result of renaming bound variables and so they are congruent.

Thus, the order of evaluation does not affect the result in the sense that if we obtain a normal form, by whatever reduction steps, it will be unique up to renaming of bound variables.

3.4 REDUCTION STRATEGIES

The Church–Rosser theorem does not guarantee that every reduction strategy will locate a normal form, even if the term possesses one; it only guarantees that if a normal form is located it will be essentially unique. As one might imagine, there are many possible evaluation strategies and these have important consequences for program implementation. Here we review some of the major techniques and the ideas associated with them. For this section we shall restrict our attention to the pure lambda terms.

3.4.1 Normal and Applicative Order Reduction

A *reduction strategy* is essentially an algorithm for the evaluation of lambda terms. Two common techniques rely on the notion of *leftmost redex* where the *leftmost redex* of a lambda term is the β redex which is syntactically to the left of all other β redexes. More precisely, the leftmost redex of (st) is indentified by the beginning of the operator s. For example, the leftmost redex of $(\lambda x.(\lambda y.y)z)w$ is that with operator $(\lambda x.(\lambda y.y)z)$ and the leftmost redex of the term $(\lambda x.y)(\lambda x.xx)(\lambda z.zz)$ is the leftmost redex of $(\lambda x.y)(\lambda x.xx)$ which has $(\lambda x.y)$ as operator and $(\lambda x.xx)$ as operand. With this notion to hand we can introduce two common reduction strategies.

Definition 3.8 A reduction sequence is *normal order reduction* if at every stage the leftmost redex is reduced. A reduction sequence is *applicative order* if at every stage the leftmost redex, free of internal redexes, is reduced.

There are important differences between these two. On the one hand, applicative order can be more efficient since it demands that internal redexes are reduced first and this may avoid reducing the same redex twice. For example, consider the following evaluations:

Applicative order:

$$(\lambda x . xyxx)((\lambda z . z)w) \qquad \beta \text{ reduction}$$

$$(\lambda x . xyxx)w \qquad \beta \text{ reduction}$$

$$wyww$$

Normal order:

$$(\lambda x . xyxx)((\lambda z . z)w) \qquad \beta \text{ reduction}$$

$$((\lambda z . z)w)y((\lambda z . z)w)((\lambda z . z)w) \qquad \beta \text{ reduction}$$

$$wy((\lambda z . z)w)((\lambda z . z)w) \qquad \beta \text{ reduction}$$

$$wyw((\lambda z . z)w) \qquad \beta \text{ reduction}$$

$$wyww$$

On the face of it, applicative order looks preferable, but despite this apparent gain in efficiency there are occasions when the operand may not need to be evaluated. This has particular force when the evaluation of the argument does not terminate. Normal order reduction reflects the intuition that arguments to functions may be discarded: we apply the operator before evaluating the operand. Consider the term $(\lambda x . y)((\lambda x . xx)(\lambda x . xx))$. The leftmost redex free of internal redexes is the term with $(\lambda x . xx)$ as the operator and $(\lambda x . xx)$ as the operand. Applicative order takes this term to $(\lambda x . y)((\lambda x . xx)(\lambda x . xx))$ and thus does not terminate. With normal order the situation is different. In this case the leftmost redex has $(\lambda x . y)$ as the operator and $(\lambda x . xx)(\lambda x . xx)$ as the operand. Normal order reduction immediately terminates with the normal form y. This is not a contrived example. Indeed, the impact of normal order evaluation will become clearer when we consider the implementation of recursion in the lambda calculus.

Actually, there is a general property of normal order evaluation that is illustrated by our example. The following (the *second Church–Rosser theorem*) informs us that if a term has a normal form then normal order reduction will locate it. The proof can be found in Barendregt (1984). In contrast, applicative order is not guaranteed to terminate even when the term being evaluated has a normal form.

Theorem 3.5 If $s \geq t$ and t is in normal form then the normal order reduction sequence starting with s terminates with t.

Apart from these two strategies there are many others which have various advantages and disadvantages both theoretically and practically. We next review the two that have occupied centre-stage in computing science.

3.4.2 Head Reduction and Head Normal Form

A further notion of reduction changes the point at which reductions terminate. This idea has arisen from theoretical considerations which pertain to the appropriate analysis of *termination* in the lambda calculus. According to one paradigm a term is taken to be *meaningful* or terminating if it can be reduced to *head normal form*.

> **Definition 3.9** A term s is in head normal form (HNF) if it has the form $\lambda x_1 \cdots x_n \cdot y t_1 \cdots t_m$ for some y, $x_1, \ldots, x_n$ and $t_1, \ldots, t_m$ for some $n \geq 0$ and $m \geq 0$. A term s *has a head normal form* if it can be reduced to a term in HNF.

The following examples illustrate the idea: (a) is an example of a term that is both an NF and an HNF; (b) is in HNF but not in NF—it does, however, have an NF, namely $\lambda z . zy$; (c) has an HNF, namely $\lambda x . x((\lambda x . xx)(\lambda x . xx))$, but no NF:

$$\lambda z . zxy \qquad (a)$$

$$\lambda z . z((\lambda x . x)y) \qquad (b)$$

$$(\lambda zx . xz)((\lambda x . xx)(\lambda x . xx)) \qquad (c)$$

It is not hard to see that every normal form is an HNF but as we have just seen there are terms with no normal form that do possess an HNF. The notion of having an HNF is therefore less stringent: the terms with normal forms form a proper subclass of those with HNF. Associated with the notion HNF is a reduction strategy called *head reduction*.

> **Definition 3.10** $(\lambda x . t)t_1$ is the *head redex* of the term
> $$\lambda x_1 \cdots \lambda x_n . (\lambda x . t)t_1 \cdots t_m$$
> where $n \geq 0$ and $m \geq 1$. A reduction sequence is a *head reduction sequence* if at every stage the head redex is reduced.

A term has no head redex iff it is an HNF. Note that the head redex of a term is also the leftmost redex but the converse is false [e.g. $\lambda x . x((\lambda y . y)z)$]. We can bring out the relation between head and normal order reduction as follows. For the former we reduce the head redexes (which are also the leftmost) until an HNF is obtained. Further reduction to NF then involves leftmost redexes which are not head redexes (inner redexes):

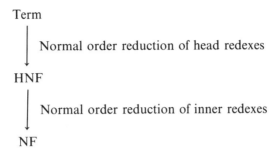

Head reduction thus reflects the normal order evaluation strategy but stops at HNFs. Naturally, this stopping place has to be justified. Why should the notion of HNF be given such a status? Intuitively, this should be assigned to NFs. We have already alluded to the reason which centres upon the appropriate analysis of termination in the calculus. As we will see in the next chapter, the notion of NF will not support a formal theory of termination. HNF has been devised with exactly this criterion in mind. For example, in the *standard* models of the lambda calculus all terms with no HNF are equal to $\perp$.

The important information about HNF and head reduction, at least from our perspective, is summarized in the following theorem. The proof can be found in Chapter 11 of Barendregt (1984).

Theorem 3.6

(*a*) $\lambda x . t$ has an HNF iff t has an HNF

(*b*) If st has an HNF then s has an HNF

(*c*) s has an HNF iff the head reduction sequence of s terminates in an HNF

This result provides some insight into the structure of HNFs and how they behave under abstraction and application. Part (*c*) parallels that for normal reduction and normal form: if s has an HNF then head reduction will locate it. However, notice that a term may have several HNFs; for example the term $\lambda x . Ix(II)$ has HNFs $\lambda x . x(II)$ and $\lambda x . xI$. This is unlike the NF analysis. However, we can employ the previous result to make a *canonical* choice. The *principal* HNF of a term with HNFs is the last term of the terminating head reduction sequence. For example, the term $(\lambda x . xx)Iy(Iz)$ has the principal HNF $y(Iz)$.

Despite being a step forward (especially from the perspective of a *theory of termination*), head reduction has one obvious practical drawback which concerns the so-called *name clash problem*. Consider the following lambda expression:

$$\lambda x.((\lambda y.\lambda x.yx)x)$$

This is not in HNF. Moreover, further reduction involves the contraction of the redex $(\lambda y.\lambda x.yx)x$. This demands an implicit α conversion to rename the bound variable x. This is a potentially expensive operation which any implementation should seek to minimize. For this reason head reduction is seldom used in practice.

3.4.3 Lazy Reduction and Weak Head Normal Forms

In fact, most implementations do not evaluate inside the body of lambda abstractions: most implementations are *lazy*. To introduce this notion first observe that every pure lambda term has one of the following forms:

$$\lambda x.t \qquad\qquad (a)$$

$$xt_1\cdots t_n, \qquad n \geq 0 \qquad\qquad (b)$$

$$(\lambda x.t)t_1\cdots t_n, \qquad n \geq 1 \qquad\qquad (c)$$

Just a little reflection on the syntax of the language should convince the reader of this. In a lazy regime, (a) and (b) are deemed to be fully evaluated. In particular, lambda abstractions are considered so. This leads to the following idea.

Definition 3.11 A lambda term is in *weak head normal form* (WHNF) iff it is of the form (a) or (b).

Notice that any term in HNF is in WHNF but not vice versa, since every lambda abstraction is in WHNF. Parallel to the notion of HNF there is an associated reduction procedure.

Definition 3.12 The term $(\lambda x.t)t_1$ is called the *lazy redex* of the term $(\lambda x.t)t_1\cdots t_n$ $(n \geq 1)$. The *lazy reduction path* is the unique reduction path where the lazy redex is always reduced. A term *has a WHNF* if its lazy reduction sequence terminates in WHNF.

Normal order, head reduction and lazy reduction all employ leftmost reduction. At each stage all contract the leftmost redex but the lazy reduction sequence may be shorter than the head reduction sequence which in turn may be shorter than the full normal order one. Every lazy redex is a head redex which is in turn the leftmost. The converse inclusions fail. In particular, the normal order and head reduction may continue to evaluate redexes after lazy reduction has ceased. In short we have the following picture:

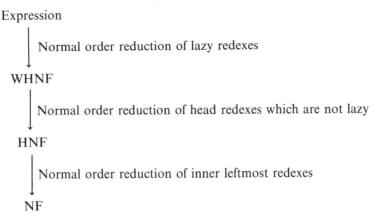

Expression

| Normal order reduction of lazy redexes

WHNF

| Normal order reduction of head redexes which are not lazy

HNF

| Normal order reduction of inner leftmost redexes

NF

One advantage of reducing an expression to WHNF rather than to HNF or NF is that it avoids the need to perform β reductions in the presence of free variables. The only way we can encounter free variables is by *passing through* λ since all references to the variable it introduces will be free only to the right of the '.'. By terminating the evaluation at the λ we avoid entering the function body and thus do not encounter any free variables. For example, $\lambda x . ((\lambda y . \lambda x . yx)x)$ is in WHNF and so there is no need for further evaluation.

Our final result parallels that for HNFs (Theorem 3.6). The proof is simple so we provide the details. The first part of the theorem is exactly the demand that lambda terms are to be considered fully evaluated and the second part insists that if an application reduces to WHNF then the operator does.

Theorem 3.7
(*a*) $\lambda x . t$ has a WHNF
(*b*) If *st* has a WHNF then *s* has a WHNF

PROOF Part (*a*) is obvious. Part (*b*) is also clear from the nature of lazy reduction. Suppose that the lazy reduction sequence for *st* terminates. Then since the lazy redex is always the leftmost redex the lazy reduction sequence for *s* must also terminate.

This completes our introduction to the main techniques for evaluating lambda terms. It would take us way beyond the scope of this book to enter into the proofs of all the results or provide further discussion of the more practical implications of the various strategies. The interested reader should consult Peyton-Jones (1986) for more implementation information and Barendregt (1984) and Ong (1988) for the proofs. The main reason for the present discussion concerns our need to develop a theory of *partiality* or *termination*.

EXERCISES

3.1 Complete the proof of Theorem 3.2.

3.2 Prove that if the axiom $\lambda xy . x = \lambda xy . y$ is added to the theory LC then all terms would be provably equal.

3.3 Reduce the following as far as possible:
  (a) $(\lambda x . x(xy))(\lambda z . zx)$
  (b) $(\lambda x . xy)(\lambda z . zx)(\lambda z . zx)$
  (c) $(\lambda x . xy)((\lambda z . zx)(\lambda z . zx))$
  (d) $(\lambda x . (\lambda y . yx)z)((\lambda z . zx)(\lambda z . zx))$
  (e) $(\lambda x . xxy)(\lambda x . xxy)(\lambda x . (\lambda y . yx)z)$
  (f) $\lambda x . y((\lambda x . xxy)(\lambda x . xxy))$
  (g) $(\lambda x . xxy)((\lambda x . xxy)(\lambda x . (\lambda y . yx)z))$
  (h) $(\lambda y . yyy)((\lambda xy . x)(\lambda x . x)(SS))$
  (i) $(\lambda yz . zy)((\lambda x . xxx)(\lambda x . xxx))(\lambda z . (\lambda x . x))$
  (j) $SSSSSSS$
  (k) $(SSSS)(SSSS)$

3.4 Evaluate (a) to (k) of Exercise 3.3 using applicative order and normal order reduction.

3.5 Which of the following terms has an HNF and which has a WHNF?
  (a) $\lambda x . ((\lambda x . xxy)(\lambda x . xxy))$
  (b) $\lambda x . y((\lambda x . xxy)(\lambda x . xxy))$
  (c) $\lambda x . Ix(II)$
  (d) $\lambda x . ((\lambda x . xx)(\lambda x . xx))$
  (e) $(\lambda x . xxy)(\lambda x . xxy)$
  (f) $(\lambda x . (\lambda y . yx)z)(\lambda x . (\lambda y . yx)z)$

3.6 Find lambda terms p, l, r such that

$$l(pxy) = x$$

$$r(pxy) = y$$

In other words, show that the lambda calculus supports *pairing*.

3.7 Find a closed lambda term Y such that $Yx = x(Yx)$. Such a Y is a *fixpoint operator* and will be used to implement recursion in Chapter 5. What impact does the order of evaluation have on a term of the form Yx?

REFERENCES AND FURTHER READING

The original source for the lambda calculus is Church (1941). The early pages provide much insight into the original motivation behind the development of the calculus. For an elementary introduction the reader should consult Hindley and Seldin (1986). The original encyclopaedia is the two-volume Curry and Feys (1958). Barendregt (1984) is the more up-to-date encyclopaedic text. Peyton-Jones (1986) is a good source for the implementation aspects of the calculus. Most books on functional languages (e.g. Field and Harrison, 1988; Henson, 1987; Reade, 1989 contain accounts motivated by computing science considerations. The recent thesis of Ong (1988) is the best source for more theoretical information about WHNFs.

4

PARTIALITY AND TERMINATION

In any programming language it is possible to write programs that do not terminate and the lambda calculus is no exception. In fact, we have already seen examples of lambda terms that fail to terminate under any reduction strategy. One aspect of a *programming theory* must be a theory of termination. Such a theory is essential in order to reason about the termination and divergence of programs. However, the axioms of the calculus give us no information about termination and divergence. Indeed, the language of the theory does not even permit the articulation of such notions—thus far all reference to such ideas has been banished to the metalanguage. This chapter is entirely concerned with the development of such a theory.

The major conceptual question concerns the nature of termination. When is a program to be considered *fully evaluated*? We shall address this question by reference to the various notions of reduction and normal form. *Meaningful* or *terminating* terms are those that can be reduced (via some reduction strategy) to *fully evaluated* ones. From our discussion in the previous chapter we know there are various options available and these will generate different theories of termination. There is, of course, an obvious choice: terminating terms are those with a normal form. However, there are technical problems with this proposal which we shall come to shortly. Indeed, our first task will be to clear the ground for the development of such a theory by investigating these options and laying out the criteria for choosing between them.

4.1 THREE PROPOSALS FOR MEANINGFUL LAMBDA TERMS

There are three obvious candidates for the notion of *meaningful* or *terminating* lambda term. They result from the three different notions of normal form discussed in the previous chapter.

1. t is *meaningful* iff t has a normal form
2. t is *meaningful* iff t has a head normal form
3. t is *meaningful* iff t has a weak head normal form

Initially, we reflect upon these proposals and investigate their advantages and drawbacks. We shall eventually adopt proposal 3 but it will be instructive to rehearse the arguments in its favour.

4.1.1 Meaningfulness = Has a Normal Form

The notion of normal form arises quite naturally from the very notion of reduction itself. The basic move in the reduction process is to replace a redex by its substitution instance. It therefore seems right to single out those terms that are normalizable as special or in some sense *meaningful*; the others are to be dubbed uninteresting or *meaningless*. Indeed, it is tempting to take things a stage further and strengthen the axioms of the calculus by adding a rule that identifies all terms which do not admit of a normal form. Intuitively, such a move seems justified since we do not want our theory to articulate any differences between non-terminating programs: they are all equally silly and as such we have no good reason to distinguish between them. We can put matters on a more formal footing by adopting the following stricture:

($*$) If s and t have no normal forms then $s = t$

Unfortunately, this rule leads to the collapse of the calculus since under its government all terms become identified—not just those without a normal form.

Theorem 4.1 The principle ($*$) forces us to identify all terms.

PROOF Let $s = (\lambda x . x(\lambda xy . x)(rr))$ and $s' = (\lambda x . x(\lambda xyz . xz(yz))(rr))$ where r is the terms $(\lambda x . xx)$. Neither s nor s' have normal forms so by ($*$) we may identify them. Consequently, we have $s(\lambda xy . x) = s'(\lambda xy . x)$, by the axioms of equality. Moreover, $s(\lambda xy \cdot x) = \lambda xy \cdot x$ and $s'(\lambda xy \cdot x) = \lambda xyz \cdot xz(yz)$. Hence, $\lambda xy \cdot x = \lambda xyz \cdot xz(yz)$. Now consider the following:

$$\lambda x \cdot x = (\lambda x \cdot x)(\lambda x \cdot x) = (\lambda xy \cdot x)(\lambda x \cdot x)((\lambda xy \cdot x)t)(\lambda x \cdot x)$$

$$= (\lambda xyz \cdot xz(yz))(\lambda x \cdot x)((\lambda xy \cdot x)t)(\lambda x \cdot x)$$

$$= (\lambda x \cdot x)(\lambda x \cdot x)(((\lambda xy \cdot x)t)(\lambda x \cdot x))$$

$$= (\lambda x \cdot x)t = t$$

Hence, $\lambda x \cdot x = t$, for any term t. By transitivity, all terms are equal.

The upshot of this is that the notion of normal form cannot furnish us with the appropriate tool for an analysis of partiality within the calculus—at least not if we embrace (∗). In one sense this is unfortunate since it is a very natural notion. In another, it is fortunate since it has been the inspiration for the development of elegant and useful alternative theories.

4.1.2 Meaningfulness = Has an HNF

One such alternative is based upon the notion of head normal form. On this account the *meaningless* terms are delineated by the criterion of not having a head normal form. This proposal was made by Wadsworth (1971) via the extensionally equivalent notion of *unsolvability*. Barendregt (1984) offers a detailed analysis of the proposal. It has a great deal going for it. Firstly, it is consistent to identify all terms without an HNF.

(∗∗) If s and t have no head normal forms then $s = t$

Theorem 4.2 The principle (∗∗) can be consistently added to the theory of the lambda calculus, i.e. not all terms are forced equal.

There are several proofs of this result available in Barendregt (1984) but they will all take us beyond the scope of the present book. One such proof establishes that all terms with no HNF can be identified with a canonical term with no HNF. Secondly, the concept of HNF has a semantic correlate, namely *solvability*. The major result due to Wadsworth (1971) states that a term has no HNF iff it is unsolvable. The latter is a semantic notion, i.e. solvability is best characterized in terms of the set theoretic models of the calculus. Finally, it can be employed as the basis for the development of elementary computability theory. More explicitly, the notion of a *lambda computable function* on the natural numbers can be based upon this notion where the concept of a partial function is unpacked in terms of the HNF model of termination.

As a consequence of these and other related considerations, Barendregt adopts the principle that the unsolvable terms should be taken as the *meaningless* or non-terminating terms. This theory should not be put aside lightly. The theory is mathematically elegant and has a rich semantic foundation. The underlying domain theoretic models are a source of great enjoyment for the mathematically inclined computing scientists.

4.1.3 Meaningfulness = Has a WHNF

However, there are other criteria that argue for a different notion of termination or meaningfulness. Most current functional languages are *lazy* in that their interpreters do not evaluate lambda abstractions; they evaluate to weak head normal form. In a recent thesis, Ong (1988) has developed a parallel analysis to that of the HNF model. He demonstrates that this notion also has a semantic counterpart, namely *strong unsolvability*. Indeed, all the mathematical elegance of the HNF analysis is matched by the WHNF regime. In particular, we have the consistency of model.

(∗∗∗) If s and t have no weak head normal forms then $s = t$

Theorem 4.3 It is consistent to add (∗∗∗) to the theory of the lambda calculus.

This of course follows from Theorem 4.2, since if it is consistent to identify all terms with no HNF it is consistent to identify those with no WHNF—the latter class is smaller. In addition to these conceptual benefits, which match the HNF model of computation, the WHNF model has the laudable property of reflecting current computational practice.

We have seen three proposals for the definition of *meaningful* lambda terms. The first proposal leads to inconsistency. If all terms without a normal form are identified, then the theory becomes inconsistent in the sense that all terms are provably equal. The second theory, while consistent and elegant, fails to reflect actual programming practice. The third is consistent, elegant and lazy. It should therefore come as no surprise that we chose the lazy model of computation as the basis for the theory of partiality/termination. It is worth saying that any notion of evaluation implicitly determines a theory of partiality and our choice constitutes a design decision.

4.2 THE LAZY LAMBDA CALCULUS

Our objective is to develop a theory of *partiality* or *termination* based upon the *lazy model of computation*. Initially, we extend the language of wff to include two new atomic assertions:

$$\alpha ::= (t = s)|(t \in T)|\Omega|(t\downarrow)|(t\uparrow)$$

The atomic wff $t\!\downarrow$ asserts that t *terminates* or is *meaningful* while $t\!\uparrow$ asserts that t *diverges* or is *meaningless*. The interpretation given to these wff is to be gleaned from the lazy model of computation. In particular, $t\!\downarrow$ is to be interpreted as 't has a WHNF'. In this section we shall use this interpretation, in an informal way, to guide our search for appropriate axioms. Later we shall formally prove that the resulting axioms are sound under this interpretation.

We first unpack this interpretation in a more explicit way. Let t be a term and let $t(\,= t_0), t_1, t_2, \ldots$ be the lazy reduction sequence of t. Then our two new atomic assertions are informally interpreted as follows:

$t\!\downarrow$ There exists an n such that t_n is in WHNF
$t\!\uparrow$ For every n, t_n is not in WHNF

Strictly speaking, this is the interpretation given to closed terms; it is extended to arbitrary terms by appeal to the notion of a closed substitution where, if you recall, a *closed substitution* is a mapping σ from variables to closed terms. We extend the interpretation by insisting that $t\!\downarrow$ iff for all closed substitutions σ, $(t\sigma)\!\downarrow$, and similarly for the other predicate $t\!\uparrow$.

4.2.1 The Axioms of Termination

The first and most transparent axiom concerns lambda abstraction. Every lambda abstraction is, by definition, in WHNF. Hence, the following:

L1. $(\lambda x . t)\!\downarrow$

L1 simply asserts that every lambda abstraction is defined or meaningful. It captures the idea that one does not evaluate the body of *stand-alone* lambda terms.

The next axiom is also almost immediate and forms part of the essence of the lazy model: if an application terminates, then the operator does:

L2. $(ts)\!\downarrow \rightarrow t\!\downarrow$

More precisely, this is justified by the following fact: if an application reduces to a WHNF, under lazy evaluation, then the operator does. In fact, this is just a restatement of Theorem 3.7(b). Notice that L2 does not demand that the operand terminates if the application does. This would not be in keeping with laziness and indeed reflects a *strict* model of computation. Such theories have been proposed (cf. Feferman, 1979, 1990; Beeson, 1985).

Our third axiom demands that termination is preserved under equality:

L3. $((t\!\downarrow) \wedge (s = t)) \rightarrow s\!\downarrow$

This is in keeping with any sensible model of computation and seems forced upon us by the very nature of equality: it is an instance of the principle (e4) that demands the substitutivity of equals for equals. Indeed, with this axiom in place principle e4 extends to this new language.

The next axiom stems from the desire to identify all undefined terms as equally meaningless:

L4. $((s{\downarrow} \lor t{\downarrow}) \to s = t) \to s = t$

According to L4, if two terms are equal, on the assumption that either terminates, then they are indeed equal. It encodes the intuition that equality is determined in relation only to termination: non-terminating terms are forced to be equal by default (we shall see this shortly). However, since we may not be able to determine whether a term terminates or not, L4 goes beyond this and offers a positive criteria for equality. We shall say more about this axiom in a moment but first we need to say a little about the predicate of non-termination.

The following amounts to the definition of divergence as the negation of convergence:

L5. $t{\uparrow} \leftrightarrow \sim(t{\downarrow})$

Is this intuitionistically sound? Under the construction placed upon our two predicates it amounts to the following:

$$\forall n[\sim(t_n \text{ WHNF})] \leftrightarrow \sim\exists n(t_n \text{ WHNF})$$

This is intuitionistically legitimate since we can decide whether or not a term is in WHNF, i.e. $\forall n[(t_n \text{ WHNF}) \lor \sim(t_n \text{ WHNF})]$.

With L5 in place we can offer some further insight into L4. First observe that L4 implies that all non-terminating terms should be identified. More formally, consider the following alternative to L4:

L4'. $(s{\uparrow} \land t{\uparrow}) \to s = t$

This is a direct formulation of the requirement that all non-terminating terms be identified. Moreover, L4 implies L4' since, if s and t both diverge, then the antecedent of the conditional L4 is immediately satisfied. Indeed, the two axioms are equivalent under the following assumption which claims that every term is meaningful or meaningless or, more evocatively, every program either terminates or diverges:

HP. $t{\downarrow} \lor t{\uparrow}$

Under the government of HP either $(s{\downarrow} \lor t{\downarrow})$ or $(s{\uparrow} \land t{\uparrow})$. In either case, given L4' and the antecedent of L4, we obtain $s = t$. Hence L4' implies L4. Classically, this is unproblematic. However, intuitionistically, HP is far from true and indeed formed the counterexample to the *law of excluded middle* in Chapter 2. Classically, it does not matter which of the two principles L4 and

L4′ we endorse, but L4 is more in keeping with a general maxim of constructive mathematics that insists that axioms should be *positive* assertions. We might also add a final axiom which demands that something is meaningless. Axiom L1 informs us that every lambda abstraction is meaningful but so far we have no guarantee that there is anything that is meaningless.

$$\bot =_{\text{def}} (\lambda x.(xx))(\lambda x.(xx))$$

$\bot$ will act as our so-called *canonically* meaningless element. The axiom for it simply demands that it diverges.

L6. $\bot\uparrow$

We know that $(\lambda x.(xx))(\lambda x.(xx))$ has no WHNF (indeed no normal form of any kind). Moreover, the choice of canonical element does not matter, given L4, since they are all to be identified.

This completes the basic axioms of the *lazy* theory of partiality. The theory LP is to be made of the theory LC plus L1 to L6. In the last section of this chapter we shall provide a more formal interpretation of the axioms in terms of the lazy model. However, the above informal remarks should provide sufficient intuitive motivation. We now explore the theory a little and draw out some of its obvious consequences.

Theorem 4.4 The following are consequences of LP:

$$s\uparrow \to (st)\uparrow \qquad\qquad (a)$$

$$(t\uparrow \wedge (s = t)) \to s\uparrow \qquad\qquad (b)$$

$$\sim(t\uparrow \wedge t\downarrow) \qquad\qquad (c)$$

$$t\uparrow \leftrightarrow (t = \bot) \qquad\qquad (d)$$

$$\sim(\lambda x.\bot = \bot) \qquad\qquad (e)$$

$$\bot t = \bot \qquad\qquad (f)$$

PROOF Part (a) follows from L5 and L2 and (b) from L5 and L3. Part (c) is a direct consequence of L5. For (d), from left to right, use L6 and L4 and L5; from right to left use L6 and (b). For (e) assume that $\lambda x.\bot = \bot$. By L6 and (b), we have $(\lambda x.\bot)\uparrow$. This contradicts L1—hence (e). For (f), we have by L6, $\bot\uparrow$ and so, by (a), $(\bot t)\uparrow$. Hence by L4′ (which follows from L4) and L5, $\bot t = \bot$, as required.

LP is a simple and elegant theory and appears to be in accord with both the lazy model of computation and the basic tenets of intuitionism. There is, however, one further axiom we need to consider.

4.2.2 Conditional Extensionality

The principle of extensionality, or equivalently the axiom η, is not valid in this lazy environment. In fact, it is inconsistent to assume it.

$\eta.\ \lambda x.tx = t$ where x is not free in t

The simple counterexample is the instance $\lambda x.\bot x = \bot$. From the latter, L1, L3, L6 and L5 lead to a contradiction: hence we have $\lambda x.\bot x \neq \bot$. However, a weaker version of extensionality is available, namely the following:

$\eta\downarrow.\ t\downarrow \rightarrow (\lambda x.tx = t)$ where x is not free in t

We shall find little employment for this axiom and we include this brief discussion only for reference and to point out that full extensionality is not available.

This completes the development of the lazy theory of termination. A version of it can be found in the thesis of Ong (1988) where the theory L1 to L5 $+\ \eta\downarrow$ is called the theory of the *lazy lambda calculus*.

4.3 ALTERNATIVE FORMULATIONS

There are various alternative ways of formulating the theory which flow from the selection of different sets of primitives. One is based on *strong equality* and the other on *divergence*. We briefly investigate these in order to put a little mathematical flesh on the theory.

4.3.1 Strong Equality

Two terms can be equal even when both are divergent. Indeed, L4 forces them to be so. However, one intuition demands that equality should imply termination. This desire is motivated by the feeling that we can only legitimately assert that two terms are equal when they are both terminating. This does not harmonize with the intuitions that underlie the axioms of the lambda calculus since they support a theory of equality for all terms— terminating or otherwise. However, matters are somewhat more subtle than this remark suggests. In fact, it is easy enough to formulate a notion of *strong* equality within the present theory. We denote this new notion by '$\simeq$':

L7. $s \simeq t =_{\text{def}} (s\downarrow \wedge t\downarrow \wedge s = t)$

Moreover, we can even reverse the order and take this new (*strong*) notion of equality as primitive. In this case it is governed by the following axioms:

S1. $x\downarrow \leftrightarrow (x \simeq x)$
S2. $x \simeq y \rightarrow y \simeq x$
S3. $(x \simeq y \wedge y \simeq z) \rightarrow x \simeq z$

In this theory the original concept of *weak equality* can be introduced by definition:

S4. $x = y =_{\text{def}} ((x\downarrow \vee y\downarrow) \rightarrow x \simeq y)$

Furthermore, within this setup, S1 can be taken as the definition of termination. Let SLP be the theory $\{\beta, \alpha, \xi, \mu, \nu\} + \{L1, L2, L5, L6\} + \{S1, S2, S3\}$ with S4 acting as the definition of weak equality. In other words, SLP is obtained from LP by replacing e1, e2, e3, L3, L4 by S1 to S3. The exact connection between the two theories is summarized below.

Theorem 4.5 SLP and LP are intuitionistically equivalent where, in SLP, S4 acts as the definition of weak equality and, in LP, L7 acts as the definition of strong equality.

PROOF We have only to worry about the interderivability of e1, e2, e3, L3, L4 and S1 to S3 and establish that the respective definitions follow as theorems. First assume LP with L7 acting as the definition of strong equality. S1 follows from L7 and e1; S2 follows from e2 and L7; S3 follows from e3 and L7. Moreover, the equivalence $x = y \leftrightarrow (x\downarrow \vee y\downarrow \rightarrow x \simeq y)$ holds: from left to right we employ L3 and from right to left we employ L4. For the converse, e1 follows from S1 and S4; e2 from S2 and S4; while e3 requires a little work. First observe that S1 to S3 yields: $(x \simeq y) \rightarrow (x \simeq x \wedge y \simeq y)$. We then employ this result together with S1, S3 and S4. L3 is a consequence of S4, $(x \simeq y) \rightarrow (x \simeq x \wedge y \simeq y)$ and S1; L4 is a direct consequence of S4. Finally, we establish that $s \simeq t \leftrightarrow (s\downarrow \wedge t\downarrow \wedge s = t)$. From let to right we employ L1 and L4 and for the other direction we employ S4.

We can summarize this result by saying that the two theories LP and SLP have a common *definitional extension*. Consequently, it does not matter which route we take since both lead to the same class of theorems.

4.3.2 A Classical (?) Version of The Theory

In presenting the basic theory the termination predicate has been selected as primitive where L5 acts as the definition of non-termination. However, we might proceed in a rather different way by selecting the canonically undefined element as the main primitive. In this regard consider the following theory:

CL1. $\lambda x . \perp \neq \perp$
CL2. $\perp t = \perp$
CL3. $t\uparrow \leftrightarrow (t = \perp)$
CL4. $t\downarrow \leftrightarrow \sim(t\uparrow)$

CLP is the theory obtained from LP by replacing L1 to L6 by CL1 to CL4. In CLP, CL3 and CL4 can be taken as definitions of the undefined and defined predicates in terms of the canonically undefined element. We refer to CLP as the classical (?) version precisely because CL4 is intuitionistically controversial. Unpacked in terms of our intended interpretation it takes the following form:

$$\exists n(t_n \text{ WHNF}) \leftrightarrow \sim \forall n[\sim(t_n \text{ WHNF})]$$

Despite the fact that $\forall n[(t_n \text{ WHNF}) \vee \sim(t_n \text{ WHNF})]$, the implication from right to left is intuitionistically questionable. It is in fact an instance of a principle known as *Markov's principle* which generally takes the following form:

MP. $\forall x(\phi[x] \vee \sim\phi[x]) \wedge (\sim\forall x \sim \phi[x] \rightarrow \exists x\phi[x])$

Notice that $\sim\forall x \sim \phi$ is intuitionistically equivalent to $\sim \sim \exists x\phi[x]$. Hence, MP can be paraphrased as: when there is an algorithm to decide ϕ, and by indirect means we can establish that we cannot avoid locating an x such that $\phi[x]$, then the algorithm supplies an x such that $\phi[x]$. This may sound quite acceptable under a certain constructive reading. Indeed, MP is accepted in *recursive* constructivism. However, it is intuitionistically moot. Moreover, in the present formal setting the two theories are only classically equivalent.

Theorem 4.6 CLP is classically equivalent to LP.

PROOF A previous theorem (4.4) informs us that CL1 to CL3 follow (intuitionistically) from LP and, moreover, CL4 is classically equivalent to L5. The converse requires a little more work. For L1, assume that $\lambda x.t = \bot$. Then $\forall x[(\lambda x.t)x = (\bot x)]$. Hence, by CL2 and β, $\forall x(t[x] = \bot)$. By ξ we can conclude that $\lambda x.t = \lambda x.\bot$. However, by CL1, $(\lambda x.\bot) \neq \bot$. Hence, $(\lambda x.t) \neq \bot$. This contradicts the assumption. Hence, $(\lambda x.t) \neq \bot$. The result now follows by CL3 and CL4. For L2, first observe that (a) of Theorem (4.4) follows from CL3 and CL2. L2 follows from Theorem 4.4(a) and CL4. For L3, first observe that Theorem 4.4(b) is a consequence of CL3; L3 follows from Theorem 4.4(b) and CL4. L4 follows classically from CL3 and CL4. L5 is (classically) equivalent to CL4. L6 follows from CL3.

Despite this result, this version of the theory is intuitionistically controversial and since our overall aim is to keep the theory as constructive as possible we shall stick with the original.

4.4 THE QUANTIFIERS OF FREE LOGIC

Not only does partiality introduce a new notion of equality but also a new form of quantification, where quantification is restricted to terminating objects. These new quantifiers are introduced by definition as follows:

$$\exists°x\phi[x] =_{\text{def}} \exists x(x{\downarrow} \wedge \phi[x])$$

$$\forall°x\phi[x] =_{\text{def}} \forall x(x{\downarrow} \rightarrow \phi[x])$$

There are obvious derived rules which are precisely the rules of the *free* logic of Scott (1970).

Quantifier rules of free logic

Introduction			Elimination

$$\begin{array}{cc} \pi & \pi' \\ \phi[t/x] & t{\downarrow} \\ \hline \exists°x\phi \end{array} \quad \begin{array}{l} \text{Existential} \\ \text{quantification} \end{array} \quad \begin{array}{c} \\ \\ \exists°x\phi \end{array} \quad \begin{array}{c} [x{\downarrow} \wedge \phi[x]] \\ \pi' \\ \eta \\ \hline \eta \end{array}$$

$$\begin{array}{c} [x{\downarrow}] \\ \pi' \\ \phi \\ \hline \forall°x\phi \end{array} \quad \begin{array}{l} \text{Universal} \\ \text{quantification} \end{array} \quad \begin{array}{cc} \pi & \pi' \\ \forall°x\phi & t{\downarrow} \\ \hline \phi[t/x] \end{array}$$

In the existential introduction rule we cannot conclude $\exists°x\phi$ from $\phi[t/x]$ unless we already know that t is meaningful. From a certain perspective this makes perfect sense since we would not want to conclude that a computation returned an object, which possessed a certain property, unless the computation terminated. In the case of the existential elimination rule we need to add the additional assumption that the free variable x is meaningful since the new existential quantifier only ranges over terminating objects. With the universal elimination rule we ensure that the universal quantifier only sanctions the attribution of the property to terminating objects and with its introduction rule we have only to consider terminating objects in the derivation of the wff. The side conditions on the rules are the same as with the original quantification rules. We leave the following as an exercise.

Theorem 4.7 The above rules are derivable in LP.

There will be occasions where we shall wish to restrict quantification, and these *total* quantifiers will then prove useful. Indeed, Scott (1979) takes these rules, together with the following rule of substitution, as constitutive of *the logic of partial elements*:

$$\text{SUBT} \quad \begin{array}{c} \pi \\ \phi[x] \\ \hline \phi[t/x] \end{array}$$

In this rule, t must be free for x in $\phi[x]$ and ϕ must not depend on assumptions containing x free. If quantification is restricted to terminating objects, this additional rule is necessary since otherwise we cannot get the full force of universal quantification.

We might be tempted to take these quantifiers as primitive with the following acting as definitions of the original quantifiers of IPC:

$$\exists x \phi [x] =_{\text{def}} (\exists^{\circ} x \phi [x]) \vee \phi [\perp]$$

$$\forall x \phi [x] =_{\text{def}} (\forall^{\circ} x \phi [x]) \wedge \phi [\perp]$$

Unfortunately, the original quantifier rules can only be derived with the aid of HP. However, it is possible, and for certain applications quite convenient, to develop the whole theory in free logic, but we shall not adopt this route. Instead, we shall employ these strong quantifiers only when it proves necessary and convenient. We are not identifying *termination* with *existence*. This is in keeping with the basic philosophy which supports the lambda calculus. Indeed, the intended models of the theory are the domain theoretic models of the lazy lambda calculus (Abramsky, 1987) and we intend the quantifiers to range over the whole domain of the model. We shall discuss the semantics of the theory in the last chapter.

4.5 THE BISIMULATION INTERPRETATION OF LP

The aim of this section is to spell out the interpretation of the lazy lambda calculus alluded to in Sec. 4.2. This model is due to Abramsky (1987) and centres upon his notion of *applicative bisimulation*. To provide an interpretation of the theory LP we must fix the interpretation of the two atomic assertions $t\downarrow$ and $t = s$. We set the scene in the next two sections and provide the actual interpretation in the third. For the rest of this chapter we restrict attention to pure lambda terms. The reader who is prepared to take the axioms of LP on trust can safely skip this section on a first reading. The rest of the book does not depend upon a knowledge of this material.

4.5.1 Convergence

Plotkin (1985) and Abramsky (1987) give an alternative characterization of lazy reduction which will prove more convenient than a direct appeal to the notion of a lazy reduction sequence. We introduce a binary relation $t \Downarrow s$, which is to be read as *t converges to principal weak head normal form s*. The relation is specified inductively, over the closed lambda terms, by two rules:

$$(\text{abs-}\Downarrow) \quad \frac{}{\lambda x . t \Downarrow \lambda x . t}$$

$$(\text{app-}\Downarrow) \quad \frac{s \Downarrow \lambda x . t \qquad t[r/x] \Downarrow w}{(sr) \Downarrow w}$$

The assertion, $s \Downarrow$ (s *lazily converges*) is then defined as follows:

$$s \Downarrow \quad \text{iff} \quad \text{there is a term } w \text{ in WHNF such that } s \Downarrow w.$$

For closed terms, $s \downarrow$ is to be interpreted as $s \Downarrow$ and, more generally, for arbitrary terms $s \downarrow$ will be interpreted as $(s\sigma) \Downarrow$, for all closed substitutions σ.

We must first prove that such an interpretation is in harmony with the lazy model, i.e. that lazy reduction and lazy convergence coincide over closed terms. This will be achieved by a simple induction on the length of the reduction sequence. To facilitate the proof we impose a finer structure on the relation of lazy convergence by explicitly indicating the number of steps required for convergence. The relation s *converges to t in n steps*, written as $\langle s \Downarrow t, n \rangle$, is also introduced inductively:

$$(\text{abs}'\text{-}\Downarrow) \quad \frac{}{\langle \lambda x.t \Downarrow \lambda x.t, 0 \rangle}$$

$$(\text{app}'\text{-}\Downarrow) \quad \frac{\langle s \Downarrow \lambda x.t, n \rangle \quad \langle t[r/x] \Downarrow w, m \rangle}{\langle (sr) \Downarrow w, n + m + 1 \rangle}$$

It should be clear that $s \Downarrow t$ iff there exists an n such that $\langle s \Downarrow t, n \rangle$. This provides us with the structure to prove that lazy reduction and lazy convergence coincide.

Theorem 4.8 For a closed lambda term s, the lazy reduction sequence for s terminates in WHNF w iff $s \Downarrow w$.

PROOF Observe that if s lazily reduces to w then, for all sequences of closed terms r, sr lazily reduces to wr. First assume that $\langle s \Downarrow w, n \rangle$. We show that the lazy reduction sequence terminates in n steps by induction on n. For $n = 0$ the result is immediate. Let $\langle sr \Downarrow w, n + 1 \rangle$. By definition, we have $\langle s \Downarrow \lambda x.t, m \rangle$ and $\langle t[r/x] \Downarrow w, k \rangle$ for some $m, k \leq n$, $m + k = n$. By induction, s lazily reduces to $\lambda x.t$ in m steps and $t[r/x]$ lazily reduces to w in k steps. Hence, by the initial observation of the proof, sr lazily reduces to $(\lambda x.t)r$, which lazily reduces to $t[r/x]$—the whole process taking $m + k + 1$ steps. For the converse, the zero case is again trivial. Assume that sr lazily reduces to w in $n + 1$ steps. Consider the lazy reduction sequence for sr:

$$sr \geq p_0 \geq p_1 \geq \cdots \geq p_{n+1} = w$$

Hence, for some m, k ($0 \leq m, k < n, n = m + k$), s lazily reduces to $\lambda x.t$ in m steps and $t[r/x]$ lazily reduces to w in k steps. By induction, we have $\langle s \Downarrow \lambda x.t, m \rangle$ and $\langle t[r/x] \Downarrow w, k \rangle$. The definition of $\Downarrow$ yields the result.

This provides a more manageable account of the interpretation of the first predicate and paves the way to the more substantial notion associated with the second.

4.5.2 Applicative Bisimulation

The equality relation will be interpreted in terms of Abramsky's notion of *applicative bisimulation*. This notion derives its impetus from the computational perspective that applicative behaviour is the wedge that individuates programs. The latter is determined by performing *experiments* on the program aimed at unpacking its computational content. More precisely, we attempt to glean the computational outcome that is *observable* when the program is applied to all possible inputs. Suppose that t is some closed term. The simplest experiment we can perform on t is to evaluate it and check to see whether it converges to a lambda abstraction $\lambda x.s$. If it does so, we continue by applying the abstraction to a new term and repeat the experiment. At each stage we are only able to observe convergence. More specifically, we are interested in comparing two terms with respect to their applicative behaviour. Two (closed) terms are compared by performing such experiments on them in tandem where each experiment consists in applying each of the terms to a closed term and observing their applicative behaviour; the outcomes are then subject to a further family of experiments, in a recursive fashion. This is the essence of the bisimulation interpretation of equality.

Given these intuitions we see that the applicative bisimulation ordering, written as $\leq^B$, is to satisfy the following requirement. For the moment it is restricted to closed terms.

$s \leq^B t$ iff if $s \Downarrow \lambda x.r$ then there exists a term q such that $t \Downarrow \lambda x.q$
and for all closed terms p, $r[p/x] \leq^B q[p/x]$

This is of course not a definition since as it stands it is circular. Rather it is intended as a stipulation of a requirement we intuitively wish to place upon the ordering. To define the actual relation of equality we first define a sequence of *approximations*.

Definition 4.1 Define a sequence of relations $\{\leq_k\}$ on closed lambda terms, inductively, as follows:

$s \leq_0 t$

$s \leq_{k+1} t$ iff if $s \Downarrow \lambda x.r$ then there exists a term q such that
$t \Downarrow \lambda x.q$ and for all closed terms p, $r[p/x] \leq_k q[p/x]$

This sequence reflects the intuitive idea of performing experiments at various depths. At depth $k + 1$ we check to see whether s reduces to a lambda abstraction. If it does then we require t to reduce to a second lambda abstraction and we continue the experiment at depth k, this time comparing their applications on all closed arguments. The depth 0 test is always true. We can then define the relation $s \leq^B t$ (to be read as s *is less than t in the bisimulation ordering* or s *is a bisimulation less than t*) by insisting that s is less than t for all experiments, i.e.

$$s \leq^B t \text{ iff for all } k, s \leq_k t$$

The relation so defined clearly satisfies the original stipulation and is in fact the largest relation that does. Suppose that $\leq$ is any other such relation. Then claim that, for all closed terms s, t, if $s \leq t$ then for all k, $s \leq_k t$. This is achieved by induction on k. For $k = 0$ the result is immediate. If the result holds for some k, then suppose that $s \leq t$. By stipulation we have the following: if $s \Downarrow \lambda x . r$ then there exists a term q such that $t \Downarrow \lambda x . q$, and for all closed terms p, $r[p/x] \leq q[p/x]$. By induction, $r[p/x] \leq q[p/x]$ implies that $r[p/x] \leq_k q[p/x]$ and so, by definition, $s \leq_{k+1} t$, as required.

From now on we shall write $s \leq^B t$ as $s \leq t$. The relation is extended to arbitrary terms s, t in the (by now) standard way:

$$s \leq t \text{ iff for all closed substitutions } \sigma, s\sigma \leq t\sigma$$

Finally, we define $s \equiv t$ (s *is bisimulation equal to t*):

$$s \equiv t \text{ iff } s \leq t \text{ and } t \leq s$$

This definition formally captures the idea of performing a suite of experiments on the terms and that for two terms s, t, $s \equiv t$ exactly when they have identical observable applicative behaviour.

So much for the basic notion. However, it will prove convenient to work with a reformulation that is more in keeping with lambda calculus tradition.

Definition 4.2 For closed terms s and t we define $s \leq^c t$ iff for all closed contexts $C[\ ]$, $C[s] \Downarrow$ implies $C[t] \Downarrow$. This relation is extended to arbitrary terms as: $s \leq^c t$ iff for all closed substitutions σ, $s\sigma \leq^c t\sigma$.

The following result can be found in Chapter 6 of Abramsky's thesis. The proof employs *domain logic* and as the author points out it does not seem possible to give a more direct proof. We refer the interested reader to the original source for the details.

Theorem (Abramsky) 4.9 $s \leq^c t$ iff $s \leq t$.

We can now summarize all the information about bisimulation which will prove necessary for the proposed interpretation.

Theorem 4.10 For all terms s, t, r we have:

(a) $t \leq t$

(b) $s \leq r$ and $r \leq t$ implies $s \leq t$

(c) $s \leq t$ implies $s[r/x] \leq t[r/x]$

(d) $s \leq t$ implies $r[s/x] \leq r[t/x]$

(e) $\lambda x . t \equiv \lambda y . t[y/x]$, y not free in t

(f) $s \leq t$ implies $\lambda x . s \leq \lambda x . t$

(g) $s \leq t$ implies $sr \leq tr$ and $rs \leq rt$

(h) $(\lambda x . t)s \equiv t[s/x]$

(i) $t \Downarrow$ implies $\lambda x . tx \equiv t$, x not free in t

(j) $\perp \leq t$ and $t \leq YK$ for all terms t, where $K = \lambda xy . x$

PROOF Parts (a) to (c) are straightforward; they follow directly from the definitions. For (d) we employ Theorem 4.9. We have to prove: $s \leq^c t$ implies $r[s/x] \leq^c r[t/x]$. First rename all bound variables in r and replace x by a context $[\ ]$ to obtain a context $r[\ ]$ such that $r[s/x] = r[s]$ and $r[t/x] = r[t]$. Now let $C[\ ]$ be some closed context and σ be some closed substitution instance. Let $C_1[\ ]$ be $C[r[\ ]]\sigma$. Since $s \leq^c t$, if $C_1[s\sigma] \Downarrow$ then $C_1[t\sigma] \Downarrow$. Notice that $(r[s/x])\sigma = (r[\ ])\sigma[s\sigma]$. Hence, $C[(r[s/x])\sigma] \Downarrow$ implies that $C[(r[t/x])\sigma] \Downarrow$, as required. Parts (e) and (f) are easy and (g) follows from (d): use the contexts $[\ ]r$ and $r[\ ]$. Part (h) is left to the reader. For (i), suppose that $t \Downarrow$ and let σ be some closed substitution. Then for any closed term r, $(t\sigma)r \Downarrow q$ iff $((t\sigma)x)[r/x] \Downarrow q$ (x not free in t) iff $((\lambda x . tx)\sigma)r \Downarrow q$. For (j), $\sim(\perp \Downarrow)$ and hence $\perp \leq t$, for all closed terms t. For the second part, note that $YK \Downarrow \lambda y . s$, where $s = (\lambda x . K(xx))(\lambda x . K(xx))$ and furthermore for all r, $s[r/y] \Downarrow \lambda y . s$. It follows that for all $r_1, \ldots, r_n$, for $n \geq 0$, $YKr_1 \cdots r_n \Downarrow$. Hence $t \leq YK$, for all closed t.

The first eight provide a justification for the axioms of LC. Part (i) informs us about conditional extensionality. Notice that the axiom of extensionality is not valid in general since it is false that $\lambda x . \perp \leq_1 \perp$. This follows since $(\lambda x . \perp) \Downarrow$. According to part (i) only the conditional form is available. Part (j) informs us that $\perp$ is a least and YK a greatest element in the ordering.

This completes our discussion of the notion of bisimulation. We are now in a position to provide the promised semantics for the theory LP.

4.5.3 Soundness of the Lazy Lambda Calculus

We shall construct a formal model of LP from the closed terms of the lambda calculus. More exactly, we establish that each of the axioms of the theory LP is sound under the bisimulation interpretation. For closed terms we interpret the atomic statements of the theory as follows:

$t \downarrow$ is to be interpreted as $t \Downarrow$

$t = s$ is to be interpreted as $t \equiv s$

The atomic assertions concerning type membership play no role in the interpretation so we can safely ignore them. More precisely, we recursively define a mapping $[\phi]_\sigma$, relative to closed substitutions σ, which interprets each wff as a statement about convergence and bisimulation:

b1. $[t \downarrow]\sigma$ is true   iff $(t\sigma) \Downarrow$
b2. $[t = s]\sigma$ is true   iff $(t\sigma) \Downarrow$ iff $(s\sigma) \Downarrow$
b3. $[\phi \wedge \psi]\sigma$ is true   iff $[\phi]\sigma$ is true and $[\psi]\sigma$ is true
b4. $[\phi \vee \psi]\sigma$ is true   iff $[\phi]\sigma$ is true or $[\psi]\sigma$ is true
b5. $[\phi \rightarrow \psi]\sigma$ is true   iff $[\phi]\sigma$ is true implies $[\psi]\sigma$ is true
b6. $[\exists x\phi]\sigma$ is true   iff   for some closed term t, $[\phi]_{\sigma[x/t]}$ is true
b7. $[\forall x\phi]\sigma$ is true   iff   for all closed terms t, $[\phi]_{\sigma[x/t]}$ is true
b8. $[\Omega]\sigma$ is false

In the above, $\sigma[x/t]$ is that substitution identical to σ except that x is mapped to t. This interpretation essentially assigns truth values to each wff, relative to a closed substitution. We shall say that wff is *true under this interpretation* iff it is true relative to all closed substitutions. The reader should not necessarily take this as a classical semantics. It may look like one but it all depends upon the interpretation of the logical connectives on the right-hand side. They can be understood either classically or intuitionistically.

Theorem 4.11 All the axioms of LP $+ (\eta\downarrow)$ are true under this interpretation.

PROOF Axiom L1 is obvious. For L2 we appeal directly to Theorem 3.7. For L3, assume that for all closed substitutions σ, $(t\sigma) \Downarrow$ and $t\sigma \equiv s\sigma$. Then, by definition, $(s\sigma) \Downarrow$. For L4, we have, by assumption, $(t\sigma) \Downarrow$ or $(s\sigma) \Downarrow$ implies that $(t\sigma) \Downarrow$ iff $(s\sigma) \Downarrow$. Consequently, $(t\sigma) \Downarrow$ iff $(s\sigma) \Downarrow$. The axioms of the lambda calculus follow directly from Theorem 4.10. L6 is immediate. The axiom $\eta\downarrow$ also follows directly from Theorem 4.10(i).

In this section we have merely touched the surface of a topic on which there is much more of importance to say, but our objective was only to provide the lazy interpretation of the theory and this has been achieved. The reader who wishes to pursue the topic further should consult Abramsky (1987) and Ong (1988).

EXERCISES

4.1 Consider the following lambda terms:

$$T =_{def} \lambda xy.x$$

$$F =_{def} \lambda xy.y$$

$$A =_{def} \lambda xy.xyF$$

$$O =_{def} \lambda xy.xTy$$

$$N =_{def} \lambda x.xFt$$

According to LP, which of the following lambda terms terminate?

(a) $AT\bot$
(b) $A\bot T$
(c) $AF\bot$
(d) $A\bot F$
(e) $N\bot$
(f) $OT\bot$
(g) $O\bot T$
(h) $OF\bot$
(i) $O\bot F$

Prove all your conclusions from the axioms of LP. The above provides a representation of the Boolean connectives in the lambda calculus.

4.2 Find a lambda term C which satisfies the following, where T and F are given as in Exercise 4.1:

C1. $CTxy = x$
C2. $CFxy = y$
C3. $C^{\bot}xy = \bot$

This provides a representation of the conditional expression.

4.3 Prove the following in LP:

(a) $\{s \simeq t \wedge (sr)\!\downarrow\} \rightarrow (sr \simeq tr)$
(b) $\{s \simeq t \wedge (rs)\!\downarrow\} \rightarrow (rs \simeq rt)$
(c) $\forall x(s \simeq t) \rightarrow (\lambda x.s \simeq \lambda x.t)$

4.4 Consider the following relativized quantifiers:

$$\exists^{\circ}x\phi[x] =_{def} \exists x(x\!\downarrow \wedge \phi[x])$$

$$\forall^{\circ}x\phi[x] =_{def} \forall x(x\!\downarrow \rightarrow \phi[x])$$

Prove that these quantifiers obey the rules of *free logic*. Conversely, from the rules of *free logic* and the following definitions derive the quantifier rules of IPC. You have to assume HP.

$$\exists x\phi[x] =_{def} (\exists^{\circ}x\phi[x]) \vee \phi[\bot]$$

$$\forall x\phi[x] =_{def} (\forall^{\circ}x\phi[x]) \wedge \phi[\bot]$$

4.5 Prove that $s \equiv t$ iff for all sequences of closed terms r, $sr \Downarrow$ iff $tr \Downarrow$.

4.6 Axiomatize the HNF model of computation along the same lines as the analysis of Sec. 4.2 for WHNF. This requires a fair amount of thought.

4.7 (For students familar with Miranda™) Does the theory LP reflect the 'intended' interpretation of Miranda™ (cf. Thomson, 1989)?

REFERENCES AND FURTHER READING

Abramsky (1987) and Ong (1988) are the central references for the lazy lambda calculus. The head normal form model of computation is covered in Barendregt (1984). Troelstra and Van Dalen (1988) contain a full discussion of weak and strong equality as well as further discussion of *free* logic and its alternative *partial logic*.

5

TOWARDS A FUNCTIONAL LANGUAGE

The language of the lambda calculus is a very austere one. Its only explicit constructs are function definition and function application. In this chapter we introduce a more realistic programming language. The language will more directly support many features found in current functional languages such as guarded expressions, recursion equations and certain built-in constants and data items. This goal will be achieved by gradually adding features to the lambda calculus.

There are various ways of *extending* the calculus. Roughly, these can be grouped under three headings:

1. Definitions
2. Axiomatic specifications of new constants
3. New syntactic classes

Route 1 involves the introduction of language features by definition. In these extensions new language features are introduced directly as lambda terms. Such definitions amount to an implementation of the new construct within the pure calculus. Properties of the new construct can then be derived as theorems. Certain constructs will be introduced in this way and as such they are to be regarded as *syntactic sugar*.

The second more abstract route proceeds in the opposite direction: a new constant is regarded as *built-in* and not defined in any way. In these extensions a new constant is introduced by stipulating its logical content axiomatically rather than by *compiling* it into the pure calculus. The conditional forms a simple example; it is axiomatically specified in terms of its behaviour on the truth values. Within this paradigm one is not committed to any particular implementation even if one is provided. Indeed, in a few cases we will not actually provide an implementation but instead justify the extension by indicating that the Church–Rosser theorem remains intact. This general procedure will be justified in Sec. 5.2 where the general conditions for the addition of axiomatically introduced constants will be outlined.

From one perspective it makes little difference which of these two routes is adopted since the amount of trivial verification required is pretty much identical in both approaches. If the construct is introduced axiomatically we must establish that consistency is preserved; if the construct is added as *sugar* we need to spell out its important properties since these will play a crucial role in program correctness. However, in general, the second abstract approach has a distinct conceptual advantage: the new constructs are characterized via the specification and not in terms of any particular implementation. The axiomatic approach thus reflects the important differ-ence between a program specification and its implementation. Indeed, this distinction forms the basis of the notion of a *high-level* language. Moreover, it leaves open the possibility for more efficient (e.g. hardware) implemen-tations. Nevertheless, not everything can be built in. Exactly what is determines the language and theory of functions.

Finally, we add a new class of items to the language, namely *pattern abstractions*. This is slightly different to the other extensions since the language is enriched by a new recursive class. To implement this class we would need to provide a compiler from the extended language into the lambda calculus. Although we indicate how this might be achieved we actually treat the extension axiomatically in that we supply axioms for pattern abstraction.

5.1 BOOLEANS AND CONDITIONALS

We begin our study with the rather simple notions associated with Boolean values and the Boolean connectives. We shall be very pedantic in this initial section in order to highlight the main ideas.

5.1.1 Boolean Constants and Boolean Operations

These are familiar to all programmers whether they are of the functional variety or not. The normal facilities for Booleans consist of two truth values t (true) and f (false) together with a collection of Boolean connectives. The standard ones are conjunction (and), disjunction (or) and negation (not). The following specification unpacks their behaviour on these standard truth values. For convenience we employ infix notation.

B1. t and t = t
B2. t and f = f
B3. f and t = f
B4. f and f = f
B5. t or t = t
B6. t or f = t
B7. f or t = t
B8. f or f = f
B9. not t = f
B10. not f = t

We might also wish to state their behaviour on the canonically undefined value. Within the lazy regime these connectives are governed by the following conditions:

B11. t and $\bot$ = $\bot$
B12. $\bot$ and t = $\bot$
B13. f and $\bot$ = f
B14. $\bot$ and f = $\bot$
B15. t or $\bot$ = t
B16. $\bot$ or t = $\bot$
B17. f or $\bot$ = $\bot$
B18. $\bot$ or f = $\bot$
B19. not $\bot$ = $\bot$
B20. t$\downarrow$ $\wedge$ f$\downarrow$ $\wedge$ t $\neq$ f
B21. $\bot$ and $\bot$ = $\bot$
B22. $\bot$ or $\bot$ = $\bot$

The Boolean functions agree with the classical connectives on the ordinary truth values, i.e. t and f. However, where $\bot$ is involved they reflect the lazy model of computation. For example, consider B13 and B14; they are asymmetrical. If the undefined value is passed as the first argument, the result is undefined whereas, if f is passed first, a truth value is returned. We summarize this by saying that conjunction is *strict* in its first argument but not in its second.

Now we have a choice to make. We could regard these as built-in constants governed axiomatically by B1 to B22 or we could implement them in the pure calculus. In general, the choice is influenced by the usefulness of the construct and the efficiency of any such implementation. In this particular case not too much hangs on the decision and it is easy enough to provide a direct implementation.

Theorem 5.1 The lambda terms (a) to (e) below satisfy B1 to B22:

$\lambda xy.x$	t	(a)
$\lambda xy.y$	f	(b)
$\lambda xy.xy\text{f}$	and	(c)
$\lambda xy.xty$	or	(d)
$\lambda x.x\text{ft}$	not	(e)

PROOF We prove B1 and B20 and leave the rest for the reader. For B1, $(\lambda xy.xy\text{f})(\lambda xy.x)(\lambda xy.x) = (\lambda xy.x)(\lambda xy.x)\text{f} = \text{t}$. For B20, the first part follows from L1. To prove that $\text{t} \neq \text{f}$ assume $\text{t} = \text{f}$. Applying both to $\perp$ and then to $\lambda x.x$ we obtain: $\perp = \lambda x.x$ which contradicts L1 and L6.

Normally, however, languages come equipped with a *conditional* operator and this is marshalled to implement the logical connectives. We follow this tradition and assume that the truth values are built-in constants whereas the Boolean connectives are implemented in terms of the conditional.

5.1.2 The Conditional Operator

This is a three place operator constrained by the following considerations: if the first argument of the conditional is true then the second is returned; if the first argument is false the third is returned; if the first argument is undefined then so is the whole conditional.

C1. cond $\text{t}xy = x$
C2. cond $\text{f}xy = y$
C3. cond $\perp xy = \perp$

The conditions C1 to C3 reflect the lazy model. For example, cond $\text{t}xy$ returns the value x even when y is not defined. In the future we shall write cond xyz more naturally as $x \longrightarrow y, z$. An implementation that meets this specification is simple enough to concoct.

Theorem 5.2 The following lambda terms satisfy the axioms C1 to C3:

$\lambda zxy.zxy$	conditional
$\lambda xy.x$	true
$\lambda xy.y$	false

PROOF The result follows by the β-equality axiom of the calculus: $(\lambda zxy.zxy)tuv = tuv = u$ and $(\lambda zxy.zxy)fuv = fuv = v$. For C3, notice that cond $\perp xy = \perp$, by Theorem 4.4.

Notice that this implementation of the conditional only works for the implementation of the Boolean values given previously. Actually, this is rather beside the point; this implementation is provided only for completeness. As we have already indicated, in keeping with pragmatic tradition we shall adopt the second route to our treatment of the conditional and assume that the truth values and the conditional are new built-in constants given axiomatically by C1 to C3 and B20. The logical connectives of Theorem 5.1 can then be implemented in terms of the conditional (see the exercises).

5.2 NEW CONSTANTS

A large fraction of what follows involves the addition of new axiomatically introduced constants. We are therefore under more than a little obligation to point out the foundational implications of such additions. There are various aspects to this issue but perhaps the most urgent concerns the problem of consistency: are the resulting axiomatic theories consistent? At one level this is addressed by providing an implementation. The new theory is then a *definitional extension* of the old. While this is sufficient in theory, in practice it constrains matters too much. We are forced to view the new construct in exactly the way dictated by the representation and we consequently block the possibility for a more efficient implementation. A more abstract route seeks to ensure that the Church–Rosser theorem remains in place. There are several general results that guarantee this. We shall briefly review the main two. The reader who is prepared to take such matters on trust can safely omit the rest of this section.

5.2.1 Delta Reduction

One first result is due to Mitschke (1976) and admits *delta reduction* as a special case. Let c be some constant and R and S be n-place relations on the lambda terms (including c as a constant). Suppose that c is given by the following reduction rules:

$$ct_1 \cdots t_n > r \quad \text{if } R(t_1, \ldots, t_n)$$

$$ct_1 \cdots t_n > r' \quad \text{if } S(t_1, \ldots, t_n)$$

Let $>'$ be the new relation of reduction (i.e. with the above reduction rules added). Suppose that R and S are disjoint and are closed under reduction and substitution, i.e.

1. R and S are *closed under reduction* iff if $t_i >' s_i$ $(1 \leq i \leq n)$, then $R(t_1, \ldots, t_n)$ implies $R(s_1, \ldots, s_n)$ and $S(t_1, \ldots, t_n)$ implies $S(s_1, \ldots, s_n)$.

2. R and S are *closed under substitution* iff if s_i is a substitution instance of $t_i (1 \leq i \leq n)$ (i.e. s_i is obtained from t_i by substituting terms for variables), then $R(t_1, \ldots, t_n)$ implies $R(s_1, \ldots, s_n)$ and $S(t_1, \ldots, t_n)$ implies $S(s_1, \ldots, s_n)$.

Under these conditions the new notion of reduction, $>'$, satisfies the Church–Rosser theorem. The result extends to any number of relations and supports the addition of new axiomatically introduced constants where the following axiomatic formulation, viewed as rewrite rules, generates the new notions of reduction:

$$ct_1 \cdots t_n = r \text{ if } R(t_1, \ldots, t_n)$$

$$ct_1 \cdots t_n = r' \text{ if } S(t_1, \ldots, t_n)$$

As an example, consider the conditional:

$$\text{cond } str = t \text{ if } s = \text{t}$$

$$\text{cond } str = r \text{ if } s = \text{f}$$

$$\text{cond } str = \bot \text{ if } s = \bot$$

This clearly conforms to the above stipulations: the relations on the right are disjoint and closed under substitution and reduction. The reader who wishes to pursue the details further should consult Barendregt (1984, Chapter 15).

5.2.2 *R* Reduction

The best exposition of this can be found in Chapter 2 of Stenlund (1972). We assume that some constants have no reduction rules associated with them. Call these S constants. R constants will be associated with the following notion of R reduction. An R *redex* for an R constant c is of the form:

$$(*) \quad ct_0 \cdots t_{n-1}(dt_n)$$

for some S constant d. The arity n ($n \geq 1$) is uniquely determined by c itself. For each S constant d, for which each term of the form $(*)$ is an R redex, there is a uniquely determined term $t_{c,d}[x_0, \ldots, x_n]$ such that:

1. $t_{c,d}[x_0, \ldots, x_n]$ is not of the form $cx_0 \cdots x_{n-1}(dx_n)$
2. All the free variables in $t_{c,d}[x_0, \ldots, x_n]$ are in the sequence $x_0, \ldots, x_n$

The *contractum* of the R redex $(*)$ is the following term:

$$t_{c,d}[t_0, \ldots, t_n]$$

Under these conditions the extended notion of reduction is *Church–Rosser*. The result admits of some simple generalizations where in particular the S constants can select more than one argument. The pairing and projections of the next section form an example where the projections are R constants and, pairing itself, which has no contraction rules, an S constant.

It would take us too far from our present concerns to give a complete account of all of this work. This section is only included to provide the reader with a little insight into what is at stake when such constants are added axiomatically.

5.3 PAIRING AND CASE STATEMENTS

We next consider two constructs that are closely associated with the data-type constructors of cartesian product and disjoint union. The exact connection will not be made explicit until the next chapter but roughly the first construction enables us to construct elements of the Cartesian product type from elements of the component types while the second does the same for disjoint union.

5.3.1 Pairing and Tuples

Most functional languages permit the representation of ordered pairs of objects and more generally of ordered tuples. The concept of an ordered pair is captured via three operations p, 1 and r, where p forms the actual ordered pair and 1 and r select the left and right components respectively. These operations are introduced by the following axiomatic demands.

P1. $l(pxy) = x$
P2. $r(pxy) = y$

These two axioms capture the basic notion of an ordered pair but in a lazy regime the pairing operation is taken to be lazy in both its arguments whereas the projection operations are taken to be strict.

P3. $(pxy)\downarrow$
P4. $(1\bot)\uparrow \wedge (r\bot)\uparrow$

In future we shall often write pxy as (x, y). Observe that $(\bot, x)$, $(y, \bot)$ and $(\bot, \bot)$ are all distinct provided that x and y are not $\bot$. The following provides an implementation but, given the ubiquitous nature of these operations, it makes sense only to constrain them axiomatically.

Theorem 5.3 The following lambda terms satisfy P1 to P4:

$$\lambda xyz \, . \, zxy \qquad \text{pairing}$$

$$\lambda u \, . \, u(\lambda xy \, . \, x) \qquad \text{left selector}$$

$$\lambda u \, . \, u(\lambda xy \, . \, y) \qquad \text{right selector}$$

PROOF Observe that $1(x, y) = (\lambda z.zxy)(\lambda xy.x) = (\lambda xy.x)xy = x$. The argument for P2 is similar. Axiom P3 follows from L1 and P4 from $\bot t = \bot$.

In general, we cannot insist that $z = (1z, rz)$, i.e. everything is a pair. In fact, no such *surjective pairing* exists in the lambda calculus (see Barendregt, 1984, Chapter 15). However, it will prove convenient to single out those objects that are pairs. The following predicate does the trick:

$$\text{pair}(z) =_{\text{def}} z = (1z, rz)$$

Furthermore, the pairing and projection operations can be extended to form tuples of arbitrary length. These notions are determined by the following axioms which generalize P1 to P4:

P5. $\pi_{ni}(\text{tuple}_n x_1 \cdots x_n) = x_i, 1 \le i \le n$
P6. $(\text{tuple}_n x_1 \cdots x_n) \downarrow$
P7. $(\pi_{ni} \bot) \uparrow$

Thus tuple_n forms an ordered n-tuple (the pairing operator is the special case, tuple_2) and π_{ni} selects its ith component. The non-strictness of tuple parallels that for pairing. In line with the convention adopted for pairing we shall most often write $\text{tuple}_n x_1 x_2 \cdots x_n$ as $(x_1, x_2, \ldots, x_n)$. Again, we shall consider these constructs as new built-in constants governed by axioms P5 to P7. However, the following provides an implementation.

Theorem 5.4 The following lambda terms satisfy P5 to P7:

$$\lambda x_1 \cdots x_n z.zx_1 \cdots x_n \qquad \text{tuple}$$

$$\lambda u.u(\lambda x_1 \cdots x_n.x_i) \qquad \text{selection}$$

PROOF Exercise.

In the standard way of representing functions of more than one argument in the calculus a function selects its arguments one by one. However, there is an alternative perspective which can be gleaned from the pairing constructor. To investigate this we introduce two functions, Curry and Uncurry.

P8. Curry $=_{\text{def}} \lambda fxy.f(x, y)$
P9. Uncurry $=_{\text{def}} \lambda fz.f(1z)(rz)$

The function Curry takes a function that expects one argument and returns a function that expects two by coding the two arguments as a pair. The function Uncurry does the reverse: it takes a function that expects two arguments and returns one that expects one by employing the selection operations.

Theorem 5.5

(a) $\text{Curry}(\text{Uncurry } f) = \lambda xy . fxy$

(b) $\text{Uncurry}(\text{Curry } g) = \lambda z . g(\text{lz}, \text{rz})$

(c) $\text{Curry}(\text{Uncurry } f)xy = fxy$

(d) $\text{pair}(z) \rightarrow \text{Uncurry}(\text{Curry } g)z = gz$

PROOF For (a) we have: $\text{Curry}(\text{Uncurry } f) = \lambda xy . (\text{Uncurry } f)(x, y) = \lambda xy . ((\lambda z . f(\text{lz})(\text{rz}))(x, y)) = \lambda xy . fxy$. The derivation for (b) is similar. Parts (c) and (d) follow directly.

Notice that (a) does not establish that $\text{Curry}(\text{Uncurry } f) = f$, but only that it equals $\lambda xy . fxy$. However, according to (c) the two functions are extensionally equal in that for all x and y, $(\lambda xy . fxy)xy = fxy$. In the case of (d) we have even less: the two functions $\text{Uncurry}(\text{Curry } g)$ and g are extensionally equal only when their arguments are pairs.

These operations facilitate the introduction of another idea, namely pair abstraction.

P10. $\lambda(x, y) . t =_{\text{def}} \text{Uncurry}(\lambda x . \lambda y . t)$

This idea will prove quite useful and indeed forms the basis of *pattern abstraction*. In this regard it will prove necessary to generalize matters.

P11. $\text{Uncurry}_n =_{\text{def}} \lambda fz . f(\pi_{n1} z) \cdots (\pi_{nn} z)$

P12. $\text{Curry}_n =_{\text{def}} \lambda f x_1 \cdots x_n . f(x_1, \ldots, x_n)$

P13. $\lambda(x_1, \ldots, x_n) . t =_{\text{def}} \text{Uncurry}_n(\lambda x_1 \cdots \lambda x_n . t)$

These ideas also supply a convenient tool for the representation of simultaneous recursion which we shall come to in a moment. We leave the reader to formulate the obvious generalization of Theorem 5.5.

5.3.2 Case Statements

The pairing construction is related to the cartesian product construction on types in that elements of a cartesian product of two types are ordered pairs of objects made up from elements of the component types. We now consider a construction that is similarly related to the type constructor of disjoint union where the disjoint union of two types is the type of those elements which are *tagged* versions of elements of the component types; elements of the union are tagged according to their origin. For example, we might form the disjoint union of Booleans and natural numbers where the elements of the union are *tagged* numbers or *tagged* Booleans. We shall study this construction in some detail in the next chapter. Here we are concerned only with the constructors and destructors that go with it.

Case analysis is supported by two/three operators: the actual case statement itself together with a means of tagging the elements. The injections

(in_L, in_R) act as the tags and the case statement provides the means of selecting an operation depending on the nature of the element (its tag). The axioms for these constructs reflect these informal remarks.

CS1. case $(in_L x)fg = fx$

CS2. case $(in_R x)fg = gx$

We shall write case zfg more conventionally as case z of $[f, g]$.

CS1 and CS2 encode the notion that a case statement selects f or g to apply to the element according to its origin. In addition, we might also insist on a *destructor* which recovers the injected element from the injection.

CS3. $proj(in_L x) = x \wedge proj(in_R x) = x$

CS3 demands that an injection followed by a projection returns the original element. To complete the picture, we spell out the strictness criteria for these constructs: we insist that the case statement, like the conditional, is strict in its first argument, whereas the projection is taken to be strict and the injections lazy.

CS4. case $\perp$ of $[f, g] = \perp$

CS5. $(proj \perp)\uparrow \wedge (in_L x)\downarrow \wedge (in_R x)\downarrow$

It follows that $(in_R x) \neq (in_L x)$—use CS1 and CS3 with two non-equal functions. One implementation is given in Theorem 5.6. The proof is left in order to bore the reader.

Theorem 5.6 The following lambda terms satisfy CS1 to CS5:

$$\lambda x.(t, x) \qquad \text{left injection}$$

$$\lambda x.(f, x) \qquad \text{right injection}$$

$$\lambda x.\lambda f.\lambda g.lx \longrightarrow f(rx), g(rx) \qquad \text{case statement}$$

$$\lambda x.rx \qquad \text{projection}$$

Although we shall not employ this implementation it does provide the reader with a more concrete analysis of injections and case statements. In particular, the tags are Booleans and the injections pairs whose origin is identified by the nature of the Boolean value.

Finally, this construction can also be generalized. In the following the in_{ni} are the generalized injection operations, $proj_n$ the projections and $case_n$ the n-place case statement:

CS6. $case_n(in_i x)$ of $[f_1, \ldots, f_n] = f_i x$

CS7. $proj(in_i x) = x$

CS8. $case_n \perp$ of $[f_1, \ldots, f_n] = \perp$

CS9. $(proj \perp)\uparrow \wedge (in_i x)\downarrow$

This time we leave the whole implementation as an exercise. Nothing depends upon the details since these constructs are also to be taken as new constants defined by CS6 to CS9 which subsume CS1 to CS5. Alternatively, we could take simple pairing and case analysis as basic and implement the generalizations in terms of them.

5.4 LISTS AND NATURAL NUMBERS

Lists and natural numbers are omnipresent data items in functional programming, and in the course of the book we shall study these notions from several perspectives. In particular, we shall later introduce the actual data types of lists and numbers. However, for the moment, we are only concerned with the basic operations necessary to construct and manipulate objects of these types.

5.4.1 Lists

Traditionally, lists are built using two operations: one that denotes the empty list ([ ]) and one (cons) that builds a new list from an element and an old list. In addition, we require operations hd and tl which select the head and tail of a list respectively. At the outset we shall write cons xy as $x:y$. The basic axioms for these constants require little further explanation.

LT1. hd $x:y = x$
LT2. hd [ ] = $\perp$
LT3. tl $x:y = y$
LT4. tl [ ] = $\perp$

The standard notation demands that we write $x:[\ ]$ as $[x]$ and, more generally, $[x, y, z]$ for $x:(y:(z:[\ ]))$, etc.

In addition to these basic constructors we might also require a test function which detects the presence of an empty list.

LT5. empty [ ] = t
LT6. empty $x:y = f$
LT7. empty $\perp = \perp$

Finally, we insist that [ ] is defined, cons is lazy, hd and tl are strict and [ ] is never equal to $(x:y)$.

LT8. $[\ ]\!\downarrow \wedge (x:y)\!\downarrow \wedge (hd\perp)\!\uparrow \wedge (tl\perp)\!\uparrow \wedge ([\ ] \neq (x:y))$

The implementation is slightly tricky since we have several interconnected operations to consider.

Theorem 5.7 The lambda terms that follow satisfy LT1 to LT8:

$\lambda xyz . zxy$	cons
$\lambda x . \text{t}$	the empty list
$\lambda x . x(\lambda u . \lambda v . \text{f})$	empty test function
$\lambda z . (\text{empty } z) \longrightarrow \bot, z(\lambda xy . x)$	head
$\lambda z . (\text{empty } z) \longrightarrow \bot, z(\lambda xy . y)$	tail

PROOF LT5 and LT6 are straightforward to verify. LT1 to LT4 follow from LT5 and LT6. LT7 and LT8 are immediate from the axioms of the theory LP and the strictness of the conditional in its first argument. In particular, if $\lambda x . \text{t} = \lambda z . zxy$ then, by L2, applying both sides to $\bot$, we obtain: $\text{t} = \bot$. By B20, this is impossible.

Of course, it would be rather silly to employ this or indeed any other lambda calculus representation. Lists are such a fundamental notion in functional programming that they demand *first class* status. Moreover, it is more efficient to opt for a direct hardware implementation. We cannot provide that here. All we can do is to leave matters open: the constructs are only constrained by LT1 to LT8.

5.4.2 The Natural Numbers

The natural numbers are generated by two constructors: zero and successor which gain substance through the following axioms.

N1. $(\text{succ } x) = (\text{succ } y) \quad \rightarrow \quad x = y$
N2. $x = y \quad \rightarrow \quad (\text{succ } x) = (\text{succ } y)$
N3. $(\text{succ } x) \neq 0$

N1 to N3 form part of the theory known as *first-order arithmetic*. The principle of induction is missing but we shall return to this when we discuss the data type of the natural numbers. The first condition informs us that two numbers with the same successor are equal while the second insists that equal numbers have the same successor. In fact, the latter follows from the axioms of the calculus. The third demands that zero is not the successor of any number.

If we are feeling pedantic we might also demand that all the natural numbers are defined and, in addition, throw in a couple of other functions:

one that tests for zero and one that selects the predecessor of non-zero numbers.

N4. $0\!\downarrow \wedge \forall x((\text{succ } x)\!\downarrow)$
N5. zero $0 = t$
N6. zero (succ x) $= f$
N7. zero $\perp = \perp$
N8. pred (succ x) $= x$
N9. pred $0 = \perp$
N10. pred $\perp = \perp$

We write 1 for (succ 0), 2 for (succ 1), etc., and, often, (succ x) as x'. There are various ways of representing the natural numbers in the lambda calculus, all of which have their peculiar and useful properties. For illustrative purposes we provide a fairly standard one.

Theorem 5.8 The following lambda terms satisfy N1 to N10:

$\lambda x . x$	zero object
$\lambda x . (f, x)$	successor
$\lambda u . ut$	zero test function
$\lambda x . (\text{zero } x) \longrightarrow \perp, (x(\lambda uv . v))$	predecessor

PROOF The definedness conditions N4 are straightforward, given the conditions imposed on pairing. For N1 to N3, the only non-trivial one is N3. Assume that succ $x = 0$; succ x applied to t yields f, 0 applied to t yields t. By B20, $f \neq t$. Hence we have a contradiction. We leave the rest to the reader.

Once again this implementation is provided only for illustrative purposes. Like those for lists, the natural number constructors and destructors are to be regarded as new constants given by N1 to N10.

There is much more to say about natural numbers and lists. In particular, the actual type of natural numbers is yet to be studied. We have a name for it but little else. The same goes for lists. This will be rectified when we study inductive types.

5.5 FIXPOINTS AND RECURSION

The claim that the lambda calculus is a functional *programming language* admits many different interpretations. At one level it refers to the ability of the calculus to act as a vehicle for the implementation of functional languages. In other words, any functional (in principle, any) programming language can be compiled into the calculus. One important aspect of this *computational completeness* of the calculus is its ability to support recursion.

5.5.1 The Form of Recursive Function Definitions

In one traditional format, recursive functions are introduced by conditional expressions of the following form:

$$\text{add } xy \quad = \quad (\text{zero } y) \longrightarrow x, \text{ succ} (\text{add } x\,(\text{pred } y))$$

$$\text{mult } xy \quad = \quad (\text{zero } y) \longrightarrow 0, \text{ add} (\text{mult } x\,(\text{pred } y))x$$

$$\text{fac } x \quad = \quad (\text{zero } x) \longrightarrow 1, \text{ mult } x\,(\text{fac}\,(\text{pred } x))$$

$$\text{append } xy \quad = \quad (\text{empty } x) \longrightarrow y, (\text{hd } x){:}(\text{append}\,(\text{tl } x)y)$$

$$\text{EQ}_N xy \quad = \quad lx \longrightarrow ly, (ly \longrightarrow lx, \text{EQ}_N\,(\text{pred } x)(\text{pred } y))$$

The first defines addition, the second multiplication, the third factorial, the fourth appends two lists together and the last tests for numerical equality. More generally, we are concerned with recursive functions of the following form (where t is any term in which the variables f and $x_1, \ldots, x_n$ may be free):

$$f x_1 \cdots x_n = t[\,f, x_1, \ldots, x_n]$$

The first thing to observe about such definitions is their *equational form*. The functions so defined are not expressed as lambda terms but rather express conditions that lambda terms must satisfy. Logically, they are function specifications. This is the central observation which underlies the representation of such functions in the calculus. We shall establish that such equations can be *solved* within the theory of the lambda calculus, i.e. there are lambda terms that satisfy such equations.

5.5.2 Fixpoints

To see how such functions might be represented consider the third example above:

$$\text{fac } x = (\text{zero } x) \longrightarrow 1, \text{ mult } x\,(\text{fac}\,(\text{pred } x))$$

A sufficient condition for fac to satisfy this equation is given by the following equation:

$$\text{fac} = \lambda x.\,[(\text{zero } x) \longrightarrow 1, \text{ mult } x\,(\text{fac}\,(\text{pred } x))]$$

It is easy to see that lambda equality yields the first equation. Indeed, we can carry out one further transformation:

$$\text{fac} = F(\text{fac})$$

where $F = \lambda f.\,\lambda x.\,[(\text{zero } x) \longrightarrow 1, \text{ mult } x(f(\text{pred } x))]$.

Any solution to the above will be a solution to the original. In other words, a solution is obtained by taking fac to be a *fixpoint* of the lambda term *F*. The notion of a *fixpoint* may be new to some readers but there is nothing mysterious about it. A *fixpoint* of a function is any element that is mapped to itself by the function. For example, 1 is a fixpoint of $\lambda x . x$.

This way of looking at matters holds the key to the calculus representation of recursive functions. Suppose we can locate some lambda term *Y* which satisfies the following *fixpoint* property:

FP. $YF = F(YF)$

How does this enable us to define recursive functions? To illustrate, consider again the factorial function. The above discussion suggests that we define fac as *YF*. We then have the following:

$$\text{fac } x = (YF)x = (\text{zero } x) \longrightarrow 1, \text{ mult } x \, (\text{fac } (\text{pred } x))$$

This is exactly as demanded by the original equation. More generally, if the function is given by the following equation:

$$f x_1 \cdots x_n = t\lfloor f, x_1, \ldots, x_n \rfloor$$

then we set $f = YF$ where $F = \lambda f . \lambda x_1 \cdots x_n . t[f, x_1, \ldots, x_n]$.

It is an important feature of the lambda calculus that a term which satisfies FP is definable. Without recursive facilities the lambda calculus could not provide the foundations for functional programming since it would not be *computationally complete*. This leaves us to check that such a *Y* exists.

Theorem 5.9 The lambda term $Y = \lambda f . (tt)$ where $t = \lambda x . f(xx)$ satisfies FP.

PROOF $(YF) = (t[F/f]t[F/f]) = F(t[F/f]t[F/f]) = F(YF)$.

One further observation about fixpoint constants is important. Notice that the particular *Y* chosen as the source of the implementation is a lambda abstraction and so we have $Y\downarrow$. This follows from L1. We cannot conclude that *YF* is defined nor, in general, that *YFx* will be. This will depend upon the nature of *F* and *x*. Of course, in particular cases or even in certain general recursive forms, we can establish termination. In this connection consider again the factorial function:

$$\text{fac } x = (YF)x = (\text{zero } x) \longrightarrow 1, \text{ mult } x \, (\text{fac } (\text{pred } x))$$

If *x* is zero then fac *x* is defined, so the base case is clear. Otherwise, on the assumption that (fac (pred *x*)) is defined and mult is defined for all natural numbers, then (fac *x*) will be. We must establish the totality of functions individually or according to their general form. We cannot impose any general definedness conditions on *YFx*. Even to formalize this argument we require induction on the natural numbers.

5.5.3 Simultaneous Recursions

In general, we may wish to define several functions by a simultaneous recursion. Fortunately, the whole development can be easily extended to simultaneous recursive definitions using the machinery of tuples and tuple abstraction:

$$f_1 x_1 \cdots x_n = t_1$$
$$\cdots\cdots\cdots$$
$$f_m x_1 \cdots x_n = t_m$$

These equations can be implemented as follows. We leave the reader to check that this gives the correct function.

$$(f_1, \ldots, f_m) = Y[\lambda(f_1, \ldots, f_m).(\lambda x_1 \cdots x_n . t_1, \ldots, \lambda x_1 \cdots x_n . t_m)]$$

This completes our preliminary discussion of recursive functions. However, writing recursive functions in terms of conditional expressions generally leads to rather opaque programs. We shall shortly provide a remedy for this lunacy in terms of *guarded expressions* and *recursion equations*.

5.6 LET EXPRESSIONS

Thus far we have not introduced any facilities that enable simple declarations. Obviously, this is inconvenient in practice since we often wish to refer to objects directly. To address this issue we introduce two equivalent forms of definition:

$$\text{let } x = t \text{ in } s$$

$$s \text{ where } x = t$$

In these expressions x is a variable and s, t terms. These encode the idea that s is to be evaluated in the context where x is bound to t. Their exact meaning is unpacked by the following definitions.

DEF1. let $x = t$ in s $\quad =_{\text{def}} \quad (\lambda x . s)t$
DEF2. s where $x = t$ $\quad =_{\text{def}} \quad (\lambda x . s)t$

These are just pieces of *syntactic sugar* and do not involve the addition of new constants. They can be used in the same way as any other expression and, in particular, can be nested:

$$\text{let } y = 3 \text{ in (let } x = 4 \text{ in (add } yx))$$

Moreover, we can add a little more *sugar* to make things even more palatable.

DEF3. $\quad$ (let $fx = t$ in s) $\quad =_{\text{def}} \quad$ (let $f = \lambda x . t$ in s)
DEF4. (letrec $fx = t$ in s) $\quad =_{\text{def}} \quad$ (let $f = Y(\lambda fx . t)$ in s)

We leave the reader to generalize the definitions to allow for functions of more than one argument. To bring out the implications of this last definition we establish a simple result which highlights how the recursion is unwound in DEF4.

Theorem 5.10 (letrec $fx = t$ in s) = (let fx = (letrec $fx = t$ in t) in s).

PROOF

$\quad$ letrec $fx = t$ in s

$\quad = $ let $f = Y(\lambda fx . t)$ in s $\qquad\qquad$ DEF4

$\quad = $ let $f = (\lambda fx . t)(Y(\lambda fx . t))$ in s $\qquad$ by FP

$\quad = $ let $f = \lambda x . t[Y(\lambda fx . t)/f]$ in s

$\quad = $ let fx = (let $f = Y(\lambda fx . t)$ in t) in s $\qquad$ DEF3 and DEF1

$\quad = $ let fx = (letrec $fx = t$ in t) in t) in s $\qquad$ DEF4

All this goes some way to alleviating the original inconvenience since we can now explicitly declare a variable as the name of a function. We shall take matters a stage further in the last section where we extend these definitions to cater for functions defined via *patterns*.

5.7 GUARDS AND CONDITIONAL EQUATIONS

In this section we introduce an idea that facilitates a more natural expression of certain forms of function definition. The facilities currently available are rather cumbersome, especially where a function is defined via several cases. At present, in general, we must appeal to the conditional expression; while this is simple enough when there are only two cases, it becomes rather messy when the function involves multiple splits.

5.7.1 Simple Guarded Expressions

The following expression returns the first term when the second evaluates to true; otherwise a *failure message* is returned.

$\quad$ G1. t when $s =_{\text{def}} s \longrightarrow t$, fail

This simple construct is useful in function definitions of the following form:

$$\text{let } fx = (t \text{ when } s) \text{ in } r$$

The function f has the value t when s is true; otherwise a failure message is returned. Here, fail is a new constant that indicates that a failure has occurred; this will be returned when s returns the value f. We need to ensure that failures are *infectious* (i.e. if a failure is returned and applied to a further argument the whole term fails). We shall come to the reason for this shortly.

G2. fail x = fail

Notice that, according to G2, we could directly implement the fail constant using the fixpoint constructor.

5.7.2 Fatbar and Conditional Function Definitions

Guarded expressions are most useful when they occur in the form of a conditional equation such as the following definition of gcd (*greatest common divisor*):

$$\text{gcd } xy = \text{gcd } (x - y)y \qquad \text{when } x > y$$
$$= \text{gcd } x(y - x) \qquad \text{when } x < y$$
$$= x \qquad \text{when } x = y$$

In the above $<$ is the standard ordering on the natural numbers or more precisely a Boolean-valued function for the relation. The function gcd is defined by cases. Intuitively, the function gcd returns a value according to the guard/Boolean expression that governs it.

More generally, we wish to admit function definitions of the following form:

$$\text{let } fx = t_1 \text{ when } s_1$$
$$\dots\dots\dots\dots$$
$$t_n \text{ when } s_n$$

in s

Intuitively, the idea behind such definitions is simple enough: the guards are tested in sequence until one is true. The result corresponding to this guard is then returned. If no guard is true a failure occurs. To provide an exact account of these informal remarks we axiomatically introduce a further constant ▌ (fatbar).

G3. $x \, ▌ \, y = y$ for x = fail

$x \, ▌ \, y = x$ for $x \neq$ fail and $x \neq \perp$

$x \, ▌ \, y = \perp$ for $x = \perp$

This will return x provided it is not a failure; otherwise y will be returned. Observe that fatbar is an associative operation with identity, namely the constant fail.

Actually, $\blacksquare$ can be defined by employing the following idea. We shall assume that, for every built-in constant c, there is a further built-in constant Eq_c that acts as a partial equality test for c, i.e. it satisfies the following.

EQ. $Eq_c\ s = t$ if $c = s$

     $Eq_c\ s = f$ if $c \neq s$ and $s \neq \perp$

     $Eq_c\ s = \perp$ if $s = \perp$

Fatbar can then be implemented as $\lambda xy.\ Eq_{fail}\ x \longrightarrow y, x$.

Whether we adopt this implementation or not, with the aid of fatbar we can unpack these more elaborate definitions.

G4. let $fx = t_1$ when s_1

        $\dots\dots\dots\dots$

           t_n when s_n

in $s =_{def}$
let $fx = (t_1$ when $s_1) \blacksquare \cdots \blacksquare (t_n$ when $s_n)$
in s

This is in agreement with the operational account: if the first guard fails we move on to the second and so on. For example, in the case of gcd we obtain the following representation:

let gcd $xy =$
$(gcd(x - y)y$ when $x > y)\blacksquare(gcd\ x(y - x)$ when $x < y)\blacksquare(x$ when $x = y)$
in s

Conditional equations provide the facility for the construction of elegant and perspicuous programs. In particular, they remove the need for cumbersome nested conditionals. These are laudable properties which are also possessed by our last addition to the calculus.

5.8 RECURSION EQUATIONS

Current functional languages allow functions to be defined via a set of *recursion equations*. This style of function definition not only leads to a more elegant and transparent form of programming but often facilitates the proofs of correctness and termination. In this paradigm functions are defined according to their behaviour on certain selected *patterns*. The following are some simple examples:

$$\text{cond } \mathrm{t} xy \quad = x$$

$$\text{cond } \mathrm{f} xy \quad = y$$

$$\text{pred } 0 \quad\quad = \bot$$

$$\text{pred}(\text{succ } y) = y$$

$$\text{append } [\ ] x \quad\quad = x$$

$$\text{append }(\text{cons } ay)x = \text{cons } a(\text{append } yx)$$

$$\text{reverse } [\ ] \quad\quad = [\ ]$$

$$\text{reverse }(\text{cons } ay) \quad = \text{append }(\text{reverse } y)[a]$$

$$\text{add } x0 \quad\quad\quad = x$$

$$\text{add } x\,(\text{succ } y) \quad\quad = \text{succ }(\text{add } xy)$$

In the first the conditional is defined according to its behaviour on the *patterns* t and f. The second and last employ the natural number *patterns* 0 and (succ y). The third and fourth employ the list *patterns* [ ] and (cons ay). To understand these equations we need to appeal to the notion of a *pattern match*. Consider the first. This is given via two equations. To apply the function to an argument we try and *match* the argument with one of the *patterns*. If we obtain a match then the corresponding right-hand side determines the result. In the case of append the two patterns are the constant [ ] and the pattern (cons ay). Notice that they are exhaustive and disjoint. The idea here is pretty much as before except there is the possibility of a recursive call. We attempt to *match* the argument with [ ]. If it *matches* then the second argument is returned. If this attempted *match* fails then we move on and attempt a *match* with the cons form of the argument. If this *matches* then we instigate a recursive call of append. If both fail then, presumably, a failure message should be returned.

These examples well illustrate the idea of a function defined by pattern-directed recursion equations, but the above explanation of the intended semantics is rather informal. What exactly is meant by the term 'match'? This is a rather tricky issue and will occupy us for most of this section. The first thing we need to be clear about is the notion of *pattern* itself.

5.8.1 Patterns

In general, patterns are built up from the constants, variables and *constructors* of the language. The actual patterns we shall study are summarized by the following syntax:

$$p ::= x \mid c \mid (k p_1 \ldots p_n)$$

Patterns are variables, constants or a constructor (k) together with an appropriate number of patterns—the arity of the constructor. We shall insist that all constructors and constants are distinct (i.e. for any two k and k', $k \neq k'$) and that all the variables in a pattern are distinct. *Constructors* form a distinguished class of constants and, following Peyton-Jones (1986), are divided into two classes: *product* constructors $[\text{tuple}_n (n > 1)]$ and *sum* constructors which, for example, include those for lists ($[\ ]$, cons) and natural numbers (0, succ). We shall employ S, S', etc., to denote sum constructors. We can consider the constants as sum constructors of arity zero. Intuitively, patterns are partially specified values built up from the variables, constants and data constructors.

There are some general axiomatic requirements specific to patterns which require elaboration.

pat$\downarrow$ $(c x_1 \cdots x_n)\downarrow$

pateq $(c x_1 \cdots x_n) = (d u_1 \cdots u_m)$
$$\leftrightarrow \quad (n = m \wedge c = d \wedge x_1 = u_1 \wedge \cdots \wedge x_n = u_n)$$

The first demands that the constructors are lazy. Here we assume that c is a constructor of arity n. The second insists that patterns are *structured* objects whose equality is completely determined by the constructor and its components: two patterns are equal iff they have the same *structure* and equal components.

5.8.2 Pattern Abstraction

The notion of a pattern is simple enough but this is only part of the story; we also need to formalize the concept of a *pattern match*. One route, and the one we adopt, employs the idea of a *pattern abstraction*. To see how this arises consider again the definition of pred. Using fatbar and pattern abstraction we can reformulate the requirement as follows:

$$\text{pred } y = [(\lambda 0 . \perp) y] \blacksquare [(\lambda(\text{succ } x) . x) y]$$

It is similar to the original but the expressions on the right involve abstraction with respect to the patterns 0 and (succ x). If we apply pred to an argument then it must match one of the pattern abstractions; otherwise a failure will occur. According to this representation matching will now take place with respect to the pattern abstracted. However, to facilitate this representation we must add pattern abstractions to the language:

$$t ::= x \mid c \mid (ts) \mid (\lambda p . t)$$

This extension is unlike the addition of new constants since it involves the addition of a new class of expressions. Notice that since patterns include variables, pattern abstraction subsumes simple variable abstraction.

Ordinary lambda abstraction is governed by the axioms of the lambda calculus. In extending abstraction to patterns we are under an obligation to extend this theory, i.e. provide *axioms of pattern abstraction*. Indeed, it is these axioms that constitute the formal notion of *match*. Variable abstraction forms part of the basic theory so we are left with constant patterns, products and sums.

(a) Constant abstraction These axioms reflect the idea that the abstraction only bites when the argument equals the constant of abstraction.

PA1. $(\lambda c.t)d = t$ if $d = c$
$(\lambda c.t)d = \text{fail}$ if $d \neq c \wedge d \neq \perp$
$(\lambda c.t)\perp = \perp$

Actually, this form of pattern abstraction can be easily implemented using the built-in equality test for constants: $\lambda c.t$ can be implemented as the lambda term $\lambda x.\text{Eq}_c\, x \longrightarrow t$, fail (where x is not free in t).

By way of example, consider the following function definition which is a representation of the negation function using fatbar and constant patterns:

$$\text{Neg } x = [(\lambda t.f)x]\blacksquare[(\lambda f.t)x]$$

Operationally, we try to match against the first constant abstraction; if the match fails we move to the second.

(b) Product patterns Following Peyton-Jones (1986), we employ a *lazy pattern matching* regime for product patterns. We first provide the axioms and then indicate why they reflect lazy pattern matching.

PA2. $\lambda(\text{tuple}_n p_1 \cdots p_n).t = \text{Uncurry}_n(\lambda p_1 \cdots \lambda p_n.t)$

According to PA2, we postpone the evaluation of the argument—hence the tuple patterns are lazily evaluated. For example, consider the following function:

$$\text{zeropair} = \lambda(\text{tuple}_2\, xy).0$$

If we apply this to $\perp$ we obtain the following:

$$\text{zeropair } \perp = (\lambda x.\lambda y.0)(l\perp)(r\perp)$$
$$= (\lambda y.0)(r\perp)$$
$$= 0$$

This is the option adopted by Miranda™. Peyton-Jones (1986) provides a detailed defence of this approach to product matching. In contrast, we could insist that product patterns be *strict*, i.e.

$$(\lambda(\text{tuple}_n p_1 \cdots p_n).t)\perp = \perp$$

In this case zeropair $\perp = \perp$. There is, however, no obvious sense in which either approach is correct. The important point is that there is a choice to be made and the axioms must reflect this choice.

(c) Sum patterns Finally, we turn to sum constructor patterns. The axioms insist that the argument to a sum abstraction must be dominated by the same constructor; otherwise a failure will occur. The last clause insists on strictness.

PA3. $(\lambda(Sp_1 \cdots p_n).t)(St_1 \cdots t_n) = (\lambda p_1 \cdots \lambda p_n.t)t_1 \cdots t_n$

$\quad\quad (\lambda(Sp_1 \cdots p_n).t)(S't_1 \cdots t_m) = \text{fail for } S \neq S'$

$\quad\quad (\lambda(Sp_1 \cdots p_n).t)\perp \quad\quad\quad = \perp$

PA1 to PA3 provide us with a precise account of pattern abstraction. Moreover, the above axioms, employed as rewrite rules, provide a way of recursively compiling away all reference to pattern abstraction. To see this one only needs to observe that in the product and sum cases the complexity of the pattern abstraction is reduced.

Before we leave the theory of pattern abstraction there is a small technical matter that needs to be addressed. We must establish that pattern abstraction is *sound* in the sense of the *principle of abstraction*.

Theorem 5.11 For all patterns p and all terms t, $(\lambda p.t)p = t$.

PROOF We prove, by induction on patterns, that for all terms t, $(\lambda p.t)p = t$. The cases where p is a variable or constant are clear. Assume that p is a tuple pattern. We need to prove that for all terms t, $(\lambda(p_1,\ldots,p_n).t)(p_1,\ldots,p_n) = t$. By PA2, we have to prove

$$(\lambda p_1 \cdots \lambda p_n.t)p_1 \cdots p_n = t.$$

By induction applied n times we obtain the result. The analysis for sums is similar.

5.8.3 Recursion Equations

With this machinery in place we can return to our original task of providing a more formal account of recursion equations. In general, we shall employ recursion equations of the following form:

$$fp_{1,1} \cdots p_{1,m} = t_1$$
$$\cdots\cdots\cdots\cdots\cdots$$
$$fp_{n,1} \cdots p_{n,m} = t_n$$

We shall not employ equations with overlapping patterns. Intuitively, such equations are to be understood as follows. Given an argument sequence

$s_1 \cdots s_m$, we try to match it against one of the pattern sequences in the function definition. If successful the corresponding right-hand side determines the result; otherwise a failure occurs. Given our theory of pattern abstraction this can now be made precise. We need to see the above as an equation in need of a solution. Matters are a little more involved than with ordinary recursive definitions since we must employ both the fixpoint operator and the pattern abstractions. However, with these tools at our disposal it is easy enough to *solve* such equations:

$$f = Y[\lambda f x_1 \cdots x_m \cdot \{((\lambda p_{1,1} \cdots \lambda p_{1,m}.t_1)x_1 \cdots x_m)\blacksquare \cdots \blacksquare((\lambda p_{n,1} \cdots \lambda p_{n,m}.t_n)x_1 \cdots x_m)\}]$$

There is a restriction on this representation, namely that the variables x_i must be fresh, i.e. not free in any t_j.

As a simple example consider the following definition of append:

$$\text{append} \quad [\ ]y \qquad = y$$

$$\text{append} \quad (\text{cons } ax)y = \text{cons } a(\text{append } xy)$$

This is unpacked as the fixpoint equation:

$$\text{append } uv = ((\lambda[\ ] . \lambda y . y)uv)\blacksquare((\lambda(\text{cons } ax). \lambda y . (\text{cons } a \,(\text{append } xy)))uv)$$

In most of the examples we consider we shall implicitly appeal to this representation, but the matching will be so obvious that many of the formal details will be suppressed.

5.8.4 Let Expressions and Patterns

Finally we extend *let expressions* to allow for patterns. The following exactly mirror the definitions for the case of variable abstraction. Moreover, they can be employed as rewrite rules to remove all reference to patterns.

> DEFP1. let $p = t$ in r $\quad =_{\text{def}} (\lambda p . r)t$
> DEFP2. letrec $fp = t$ in $r =_{\text{def}}$ let $f = Y[\lambda f . \lambda p . t]$ in r
> DEFP3. r where $p = t$ $\quad =_{\text{def}} (\lambda p . r)t$

More importantly, since function definitions always occur in context, we must indicate how the combination pans out.

> DEFP4. let $f p_{1,1} \cdots p_{1,m} = t_1$
> $\qquad \dots\dots\dots\dots\dots\dots$
> $\qquad f p_{n,1} \cdots p_{n,m} = t_n$
> in s
>
> $\qquad =_{\text{def}}$
> letrec $f x_1 \cdots x_m =$
> $((\lambda p_{1,1} \cdots \lambda p_{1,m}.t_1)x_1 \cdots x_m)\blacksquare \cdots \blacksquare((\lambda p_{n,1} \cdots \lambda p_{n,m}.t_n)x_1 \cdots x_m)$
> in s

With the append example we have the following reduction:

$$\text{let append} \quad [\ ]y \quad = y$$
$$\text{append} \quad (\text{cons } ax)y = \text{cons } a\,(\text{append } xy)$$
$$\text{in append} \quad (\text{cons } al)l'$$

By DEFP4 this unpacks to the following:

letrec append $uv =$
$$((\lambda[\ ].\lambda y.y)uv)\blacksquare((\lambda(\text{cons } ax).\lambda y.(\text{cons } a\,(\text{append } xy)))uv)$$
in append $(\text{cons } al)l'$

This further unpacks as follows:

$(\lambda(\text{cons } ax).\lambda y.(\text{cons } a\,(\text{append } xy))))(\text{cons } al)l'$	DEF3, DEF4, PA1 and G3
$(\lambda a.\lambda x.\lambda y.(\text{cons } a\,(\text{append } xy)))al'$	PA3
cons a (append ll')	by PA1

This is as expected. The exercises contain other examples for the reader to study. There are implementation delicacies that relate to *conformality checking*, but we refer the reader to Peyton-Jones (1986) for more details.

5.9 AXIOMATIC FORMULATIONS OF FUNCTIONAL LANGUAGES

We have now extended the lambda calculus in several ways and in fact have at our disposal most of the facilities of the functional language Miranda™. Throughout the development we have added many new constants and syntactic classes to the calculus and, in parallel, provided axioms that define the logical content of such features. As such we have provided an extended programming language and, via the axioms, an *extended* axiomatic theory of functions or operations. From one perspective the new theory is no more expressive than the calculus itself—it is a *conservative extension* of the calculus. However, practically, the theory is essential since otherwise we are forced, in reasoning about such constructs, to trace their implementation history through to the pure calculus. To grasp the content we only need access to their axiomatic definitions. The axioms provide a *high-level* view of the theory which operates at the level at which we need to reason about the language features. In particular, the programmer only needs knowledge of the equality and termination axioms for the construct. The reader can take the axioms of the various language features as providing an axiomatic formulation of the programming language. For future reference we let PL* be the theory LP of Chapter 4 extended with the axioms for the constructs of the present chapter.

EXERCISES

5.1 Complete the proof of Theorem 5.1. Implement the Boolean connectives in terms of the conditional and prove that your implementation satisfies B1 to B22.

5.2 Complete the proof of Theorem 5.4. Implement tuples by the following recursion:

$$\text{tuple}_1\, t \qquad = t$$

$$\text{tuple}_{n+1}\, t_1 \cdots t_{n+1} = (t_1, (\text{tuple}_n t_2 \cdots t_{n+1}))$$

Define the corresponding projections and prove the implementation correct.

5.3 Formulate and prove the generalization of Theorem 5.5 for generalized Currying.

5.4 Implement generalized case statements in the pure calculus and prove your implementation correct. Given simple case statements and projections implement the generalized forms in terms of them.

5.5 Consider the following implementation of zero and succ:

$$0 = \lambda fx\,.\,x$$

$$\text{succ} = \lambda xyz\,.\,y(xyz)$$

Prove that this implementation satisfies N1 to N3. Implement the other natural number operations. Define addition and multiplication directly without appeal to the fixpoint finder.

5.6 Let $F = \lambda y\,.\,\lambda f\,.\,f(yf)$. Prove that for any term t, $(YF)t = t((YF)t)$, i.e. YF is itself a *fixpoint finder*. Is $YF = Y$? What can you conclude from your answer?

5.7 Prove that fatbar is associative with fail as its identity.

5.8 Employ the axioms for pattern abstraction to simplify the following:
  (*a*) let addpair $= \lambda(\text{pair } xy)\,.\,(\text{add } xy)$ in addpair (pair 3 4)
  (*b*) let reverse [ ] $=$ [ ]
      reverse (cons ax) $=$ append (reverse x) [a]
    in reverse (cons a (cons b [ ]))
  (*c*) let reflect (leaf n) $=$ leaf n
      reflect (branch ts) $=$ branch (reflect s) (reflect t)
    in reflect (branch (branch (leaf n) (leaf m)) (leaf n))

REFERENCES AND FURTHER READING

The main source for this chapter is Peyton-Jones (1986), and in particular Chapters 3 to 6. For an introduction to Miranda™ and indeed functional programming the reader should consult Bird and Wadler (1988) and the slightly more advanced Henson (1987). Reade (1989) is also worthy of study but is based upon a strict language.

6

A SIMPLE THEORY OF TYPES

In modern programming languages not only are there basic types such as natural numbers, characters, Booleans, etc., but also ways of building new types from old ones. These involve type constructors such as disjoint union, Cartesian product and the type of functions from one type to another. In addition, there are inductive or recursive types and various notions of polymorphism. In the next few chapters we shall study all these type constructors and certain others that are not usually found in programming languages. However, before we proceed with the development of any form of type theory we need to be clear about the role that types play in computing science. In order to organize our thoughts on this matter we isolate two possible roles for the notion of type.

(a) **The programming role of types** At one level types are an organizational tool for the development of reliable software. In this guise they are employed as a conceptual scheme for the systematization of data and the construction of algorithms. A theory of types imposes a net upon the universe of objects which enables the programmer to locate trivial conceptual errors such as attempting to subtract a number from a Boolean value. This first role is best classified as *computational*. Objects are classified in order to provide structure to the programmer's universe and algorithm development has to proceed in harmony with this structure. Indeed, many systems have built-in compile-time *type checkers* which aid the programmer in the detection of such errors. This role of types has much in common with *dimensional* analysis in physics where one has to ensure that both sides of an equation have the same physical dimension. This is the traditional and familiar role of types in computing science. Most of the type constructors we shall study arise from this computational role of types and in designing our theory we shall be largely guided by the implicit-type theories of current languages.

(b) The mathematical role of types However, in a *programming theory* types also play a more mathematical role. In this guise types function in much the same way as sets in mathematics and here objects are classified for mathematical purposes. Classifying an object as a natural number or a function from natural numbers to natural numbers often has a mathematical motivation. We may, for example, wish to prove that all natural numbers have a specified property. The classification enables the objects to be grouped together as an entity which can then be mathematically investigated. This is the familiar role of sets in mathematics and it is not one that we can dispense with: a *programming theory* must provide not only a means of assigning types to programs but also a means of formulating and proving properties about them. In this capacity the types form part of the mathematical apparatus necessary for the specification of programs. For example, the following is a traditional specification of a sorting algorithm where O and P indicate that a list is ordered and two lists are permutations of each other:

$$\forall x [x \in \text{List}[N] \to (fx \in \text{List}[N] \land O[fx] \land P[x, fx])].$$

Whatever means we employ to locate such a function we must still prove that it meets such a specification and this is essentially a mathematical activity.

In summary, even though the computational role of types is the fundamental one in computing science this role must be supported by a mathematical account of the types. This may seem so obvious that it is hardly worth pointing out. However, most programming languages are normally not presented in this manner. In this chapter we attempt to provide a framework for such presentations.

6.1 AN OUTLINE OF THE SIMPLE THEORY

Before we launch into the details of the various type constructors we need to clear the way a little. There are several preliminary notions and concepts that need to be discussed including the actual syntax of the simple theory.

6.1.1 The Syntax of Types

In Chapter 2 we introduced a simple language of types which included certain basic types and we alluded to the possibility of forming new types via type constructors. In this chapter we shall be concerned with the following language of types:

$$T ::= B \mid (T \oplus S) \mid (T \otimes S) \mid (T => S) \mid (T \Rightarrow S) \mid (T \Rrightarrow S)$$

Where we omit parentheses in type expressions we shall adopt the convention that disjoint union and Cartesian product take precedence over the function space constructors and that function space constructors associate to the right, i.e. $T => S => R$ for $T => (S => R)$. We shall also freely use layout, [ ] and { } to indicate structure. According to this ontology, types are either basic (B) or constructed by means of type constructors from already existing types. We shall outline the structure of the basic types shortly. The first two constructors form disjoint unions ($\oplus$) and cartesian products ($\otimes$). The last three introduce various notions of function space: the first is the space of *general* functions, the second that of *total* functions and the last that of *partial* functions. This richness of function spaces stems from the ability of the theory to articulate a notion of termination.

6.1.2 Invariance

The derived principle e4 allows the substitutivity of equals for equals. This principle is generally derivable from its atomic instances. Thus far the instances for equality and termination are in place. The following implicitly extends the principle to the full language.

INV. $[x \in T \wedge x = y] \rightarrow y \in T$

It is a simple principle of *invariance*: if an object has a certain type then all objects equal to it have the type. It is difficult to imagine a type theory which did not uphold INV.

With these preliminaries in place we begin the development of the actual theory of types. To initiate the discussion we introduce certain *basic* types.

6.1.3 Enumerated Types

There is always a degree of ambivalence about which types should be taken as basic. Booleans and the natural numbers are prime candidates. However, the natural number type forms an example of an *inductive type* and we shall delay our study of it until we consider the general class of such types. In the first instance, the basic types are generated by a *scheme* of enumeration.

In general, types will be defined via an axiom which states the necessary and sufficient conditions for being a member of the type. In the case of enumerated types this amounts to little more than an enumeration of their elements. Let $c_1, \ldots, c_n$ be any constants. The *enumerated type* $\{c_1, \ldots, c_n\}$ is the type given by the following axiom.

ENUM. $x \in \{c_1, \ldots, c_n\} \leftrightarrow (x = c_1 \vee \cdots \vee x = c_n)$

Notice that this is an axiom scheme since it introduces a new type for each finite collection of constants. For example, Bool is a type whose only elements are the constants t (true) and f (false). Consequently, the (derived) axiom for Bool simply asserts that a member of Bool is either t or f.

Bool. $x \in \text{Bool} \leftrightarrow (x = t \lor x = f)$

With this axiom in place it is intuitively clear that the Boolean connectives and functions should have the following types:

$$\text{and} \in \text{Bool} \Rightarrow \text{Bool} \Rightarrow \text{Bool}$$
$$\text{or} \in \text{Bool} \Rightarrow \text{Bool} \Rightarrow \text{Bool}$$
$$\text{not} \in \text{Bool} \Rightarrow \text{Bool}$$
$$\text{cond} \in \text{Bool} \Rightarrow T \Rightarrow T \Rightarrow T$$

Once the axioms for the general function space are in place we shall be able to verify these facts formally. A second example is the type of symbolic atoms. Here certain constants are singled out to stand as symbolic atoms.

Sym. $x \in \text{Sym} \leftrightarrow (x = \text{"Engine"} \lor \cdots \lor x = \text{"Polly"})$

The choice of symbols is arbitrary and the above is introduced only for illustrative purposes. We could go on and on adding such examples but there seems little point since the general idea of an enumerated type should be familiar to most readers. What might be less so is the axiomatic presentation. The axiom for enumerated types simply asserts the necessary and sufficient conditions for membership and the axiom says no more and no less than one would expect: to be a member of the type it is necessary and sufficient to be one of the specified constants. In general, all the type axioms will be presented in this way. For each constructor the axiom (scheme) states the necessary and sufficient conditions for membership.

6.1.4 Some Useful Basic Types

A second group of basic types, although not strictly necessary at this stage, will prove convenient when we introduce the type constructors. Their membership conditions are given by the following axioms:

$$z \in \text{PAIR} \quad \leftrightarrow \quad z = (lz, rz)$$

$$z \in \text{TUPLE}_n \quad \leftrightarrow \quad z = (\pi_{n1}z, \ldots, \pi_{nn}z)$$

$$z \in \text{INJ} \quad \leftrightarrow \quad (z = \text{in}_L(\text{proj } z) \lor z = \text{in}_R(\text{proj } z))$$

$$z \in \text{INL} \quad \leftrightarrow \quad z = \text{in}_L(\text{proj } z)$$

$$z \in \text{INR} \quad \leftrightarrow \quad z = \text{in}_R(\text{proj } z)$$

The first is the type of pairs, the second the type of n-tuples and the third the type of injections; the fourth and last are the types of left and right injections respectively. These types can be viewed as special cases of both *inductive* and *comprehension* types, but for the present we shall take them as basic.

6.2 THE GENERAL FUNCTION SPACE

We have alluded to the function space construction on several occasions but actually things are more involved than we have admitted. There are many different options available to us and thus far we have been somewhat ambiguous about which is being employed. The major source of ambiguity stems from considerations that pertain to termination. However, the first, and probably the most obvious, notion places no demands upon termination.

6.2.1 The Axiom of General Function Spaces

For types S and T, $S => T$ is *the general type of functions from S to T.* For a function to be a member of this type it has only to map every element of the *domain* to a member of the *codomain.*

GFS. $f \in (S => T) \leftrightarrow \forall x (x \in S \rightarrow fx \in T)$

We can immediately put this notion to work. The following provides types for some of the basic operations of the previous chapter.

Theorem 6.1
(a) and $\in$ Bool => Bool => Bool
(b) or $\in$ Bool => Bool => Bool
(c) not $\in$ Bool => Bool
(d) For any type S, cond $\in$ Bool => S => S => S

PROOF We shall not strain the reader's patience too much. We shall only prove (c) by way of illustration. The others are left as exercises. We have to show that $\forall x (x \in$ Bool $\rightarrow$ (not $x) \in$ Bool). An inspection of the axioms for negation yield the result: if x is t then (not x) is f and if x is f then (not x) is t. In either case the result is in Bool.

When are two functions equal? The theory of lambda equality addresses this question in general but the full principle of extensionality is not available in the lazy theory. However, it will prove useful to have a notion of extensional equivalence relativized to types. Essentially, two functions are *extensionally equal on T* if they give equal results for all elements of T.

Definition 6.1 Define $f \equiv_T g =_{\text{def}} \forall x \in T(fx = gx)$. Where no danger of ambiguity arises we shall write $f \equiv g$ for $f \equiv_T g$.

This notion will prove to be convenient later. For the moment it plays a minor role in the formulation of the following properties of the general function space which provide some insight into its elementary closure properties.

Theorem 6.2 Let T, S, R and U be any types. Then:

(a) $I \in T \Rightarrow T$

(b) If $f \in T \Rightarrow S$ and $g \in S \Rightarrow R$ then $g \circ f \in T \Rightarrow R$, where $g \circ f = \lambda x . g(fx)$.

(c) If $f \in T \Rightarrow S$, $g \in S \Rightarrow R$ and $h \in R \Rightarrow U$ then $(h \circ g) \circ f = h \circ (g \circ f)$.

(d) If $f \in T \Rightarrow S$ then $f \circ I \equiv_T f$ and $I \circ f \equiv_T f$.

PROOF All are routine and are left for the reader.

Part (a) informs us that the identity is in every function space, (b) that the spaces are closed under functional composition, (c) that composition is associative and (d) that I is an identity (modulo extensional equivalence) with respect to functional composition.

6.2.2 Abstraction and Application: the Type System TA[λ]

There is a tight connection between the general function space and the basic operations of the lambda calculus. In computing science, type systems are generally introduced in a *logic-free* way. This is achieved through rules of proof which provide type introduction and elimination rules for the various programming constructs. The most basic operations of the theory are those of the lambda calculus itself and their rules employ function spaces.

	Introduction		Elimination

$$(\Rightarrow\text{i}) \quad \dfrac{\begin{array}{c} [x \in S] \\ | \\ t \in T \end{array}}{\lambda x . t \in S \Rightarrow T} \qquad\qquad (\Rightarrow\text{e}) \quad \dfrac{f \in S \Rightarrow T \qquad x \in S}{fx \in T}$$

In the introduction rule x must not occur free in any undischarged assumption, other than $x \in S$, on which $t \in T$ depends. These rules should be self-explanatory but we shall illustrate their employment shortly. First we establish their soundness.

Theorem 6.3 The abstraction and application rules are derivable from GFS.

PROOF The second rule is clear from the axiom from left to right. For the first, notice that $(\lambda x . t)x = t$ and then employ the axiom from right to left to conclude, from the assumptions of the rule and universal introduction, that $\lambda x . t \in S \Rightarrow T$.

These rules are the standard *type checking* rules for abstraction and application. They provide a means of locating types for complex expressions (of the pure calculus) in terms of the types of their subexpressions; they enable the assignment of a type to an expression in a way that reflects the syntactic structure of the expression. These remarks are probably best illustrated by way of a couple of examples.

Example 6.1 $\lambda xyz . x(yz) \in (S \Rightarrow R) \Rightarrow (T \Rightarrow S) \Rightarrow T \Rightarrow R$

$$
\cfrac{
[x \in S \Rightarrow R] \quad
\cfrac{
\cfrac{[y \in T \Rightarrow S] \quad [z \in T]}{yz \in S} \Rightarrow e
}{
\cfrac{
\cfrac{
\cfrac{x(yz) \in R}{\lambda z . x(yz) \in T \Rightarrow R} \Rightarrow i
}{\lambda yz . x(yz) \in (T \Rightarrow S) \Rightarrow T \Rightarrow R} \Rightarrow i
}{\lambda xyz . x(yz) \in (S \Rightarrow R) \Rightarrow (T \Rightarrow S) \Rightarrow T \Rightarrow R} \Rightarrow i
} \Rightarrow e
}
$$

The next is a slightly more complex example with a very similar structure.

Example 6.2 $\lambda xyz . xz(yz) \in (S \Rightarrow T \Rightarrow R) \Rightarrow (S \Rightarrow T) \Rightarrow S \Rightarrow R$

$$
\cfrac{
\cfrac{[x \in S \Rightarrow T \Rightarrow R] \quad [z \in S]}{xz \in T \Rightarrow R} \Rightarrow e \quad \cfrac{[y \in S \Rightarrow T] \quad [z \in S]}{yz \in T} \Rightarrow e
}{
\cfrac{
\cfrac{
\cfrac{xz(yz) \in R}{\lambda z . xz(yz) \in S \Rightarrow R} \Rightarrow i
}{\lambda yz . xz(yz) \in (S \Rightarrow T) \Rightarrow S \Rightarrow R} \Rightarrow i
}{\lambda xyz . xz(yz) \in (S \Rightarrow T \Rightarrow R) \Rightarrow (S \Rightarrow T) \Rightarrow S \Rightarrow R} \Rightarrow i
}
$$

The type system generated by these rules (together with a rule-based version of the lambda calculus and INV) is known as TA$[\lambda]$ (see Hindley and Seldin 1986, Chapter 15). In the classical lambda calculus, under extensionality, the rules are equivalent to the axiomatic formation. Unfortunately, full extensionality is not available in the lazy lambda calculus. Since we shall take GFS as our main notion of function space we shall not pursue TA$[\lambda]$ further, but refer the reader to Hindley and Seldin for more details.

6.3 CARTESIAN PRODUCT

We alluded to this type constructor in the previous chapter when we discussed pairing. It enables the formation of types whose elements are pairs of objects selected from the component types. Although it is one of the most simple and common of all the type constructors, in the present setting it raises a few subtle issues.

6.3.1 The Axiom for Cartesian Products

The axiom for this constructor straightforwardly captures the above intuition.

CP. $z \in S \otimes T \leftrightarrow (z \in \text{PAIR} \wedge \text{l}z \in S \wedge \text{r}z \in T)$

Informally, an element of the Cartesian product of S and T is a pair whose left component is a member of S and whose right component is a member of T. For example, the pair (f, 'Fred') is of type $\text{Bool} \otimes \text{Sym}$. We can of course iterate the construction: (t, (f, 'Fred')) has type $\text{Bool} \otimes (\text{Bool} \otimes \text{Sym})$. Notice that the elements of this type are not three-tuples but pairs. However, the construction can be generalized to yield objects that are n-tuples, $(n > 0)$:

$$z \in S_1 \otimes S_2 \otimes \cdots \otimes S_n \leftrightarrow ((z \in \text{TUPLE}_n) \wedge (\pi_{n1}z) \in S_1 \wedge \cdots \wedge (\pi_{nn}z) \in S_n)$$

For example, we could form the three-place product $\text{Bool} \otimes \text{Bool} \otimes \text{Sym}$ whose members take the form (b, b', c), where b and b' are Booleans and c is a symbolic atom. Notice that this is different to $\text{Bool} \otimes (\text{Bool} \otimes \text{Sym})$ since the latter has elements that are pairs whose second elements are pairs. This is a consequence of the fact that tuples are not defined in terms of pairs. The spaces are of course *isomorphic* (see the exercises). We shall write S^n for $S \otimes \cdots \otimes S$—the n-place Cartesian product of S.

With CP in place we can provide types for some more interesting functions. Recall the following definitions:

$$\text{Curry} \quad =_{\text{def}} \lambda f x y . f(x, y)$$

$$\text{Uncurry} =_{\text{def}} \lambda f z . f(\text{l}z)(\text{r}z)$$

Theorem 6.4

$$\text{Curry} \in (S \otimes T \Rightarrow U) \Rightarrow (S \Rightarrow T \Rightarrow U) \qquad (a)$$

$$\text{Uncurry} \in (S \Rightarrow T \Rightarrow U) \Rightarrow (S \otimes T \Rightarrow U) \qquad (b)$$

PROOF   For (a), let $f \in (S \otimes T \Rightarrow U)$. We need to show $(\text{Curry } f) \in S \Rightarrow (T \Rightarrow U)$. Let $x \in S$. We then need to show that $(\text{Curry } fx) \in (T \Rightarrow U)$, i.e. for all y in T, $(\text{Curry } fxy) \in U$. However, this follows since the latter equals $f(x, y)$. Part (b) is similar.

Although this type constructor is really simple, there are some subtle issues that need to be discussed. In particular, there is an alternative axiomatization which implicitly forces members to be pairs.

CP'. $z \in S \otimes T \leftrightarrow \exists x \exists y (x \in S \wedge y \in T \wedge z = (x, y))$

Indeed, this might appear to be the obvious definition. Fortunately, these two axiomatic specifications of the idea are equivalent: the addition of either to the existing theory (i.e. that accumulated thus far including PL∗) yields the other.

Theorem 6.5 $CP \leftrightarrow CP'$.

PROOF Assume $z = (lz, rz) \land lz \in S \land rz \in T$. Then, immediately, we have $\exists x \exists y (x \in S \land y \in T \land z = (x, y))$. Conversely, assume

$$\exists x \exists y (x \in S \land y \in T \land z = (x, y)).$$

By the axioms of pairing, $z \in \text{PAIR} \land lz \in S \land rz \in T$.

Hence, either leads to the same *extensional* characterization of the notion of Cartesian product. However, the former has certain *intensional* properties which are not possessed by the latter. In particular, the first characterization makes no explicit existential assumptions and this will be important for later developments. At this point, these remarks may be somewhat opaque, but the reader should take note that types that are definable without reference to existential quantification or disjunction possess some important properties which play a crucial role in program development.

The second issue of some delicacy concerns the *totality* of the Cartesian product constructor. Since the pairing construct is lazy, every element of the Cartesian product is defined, i.e. $l\bot = \bot$ and $r\bot = \bot$ but $(\bot, \bot) \neq \bot$ and so $\bot$ is not a pair and thus cannot be an element of the Cartesian product of any two types, even if the component types contain it. With lazy pairing all the elements of the Cartesian product of any two types are total or terminating. Of course, we might drop the demand that elements of the Cartesian product be pairs, i.e. adopt the following axiom.

CP''. $z \in S \otimes T \quad \leftrightarrow \quad (lz \in S \land rz \in T)$

This provides us with a somewhat different notion of product. Not all elements are pairs and, in particular, $\bot \in S \land \bot \in T \leftrightarrow \bot \in S \otimes T$. The original is best thought of as the *lazy product*. In contrast, CP'' exactly captures the notion of product given by the introduction and elimination rules for pairing.

6.3.2 Pairing and Projections

As we have already indicated on several occasions, there is an intimate relationship between the notion of Cartesian product and the pairing and projection operations. The axiom does not make this connection explicit. It is best brought out in terms of the following proof rules:

Introduction   Elimination

$$\frac{x \in S \quad y \in T}{(x, y) \in S \otimes T} \otimes i \qquad \frac{z \in S \otimes T}{\text{l}z \in S} \otimes e \qquad \frac{z \in S \otimes T}{\text{r}z \in T} \otimes e$$

The first rule informs us that a pair of objects has type $S \otimes T$ when the first member has type S and the second has type T. The other two rules determine the types of the projections. Together with the rules for application and abstraction they extend our ability to type expressions in a *syntax-directed* way, where expressions can contain the pairing and projection operations as well as those of the pure calculus.

Example 6.3 Uncurry $\in (S \Rightarrow T \Rightarrow U) \Rightarrow (S \otimes T \Rightarrow U)$.

$$\cfrac{[f \in S \Rightarrow T \Rightarrow U] \quad \cfrac{\cfrac{[x \in S \otimes T]}{\text{l}x \in S} \otimes e \quad \cfrac{[x \in S \otimes T]}{\text{r}x \in T} \otimes e}{\cfrac{\cfrac{f(\text{l}x) \in T \Rightarrow U}{f(\text{l}x)(\text{r}x) \in U} \Rightarrow e}{\cfrac{\lambda x. f(\text{l}x)(\text{r}x) \in S \otimes T \Rightarrow U}{\text{Uncurry} \in (S \Rightarrow T \Rightarrow U) \Rightarrow (S \otimes T \Rightarrow U)} \Rightarrow i} \Rightarrow i}}{} \Rightarrow e}$$

Again these rules are not quite equivalent to the axiomatic formulation but in this case matters are easily rectified by the addition of a rule which insists that elements of the product are pairs:

$$\frac{z \in S \otimes T}{z \in \text{PAIR}}$$

Theorem 6.6 The above rules are equivalent to CP.

PROOF The first (introduction) rule follows from the axiom from right to left. The second (elimination) rule follows from the opposite direction. The final rule follows from the axiom from left to right. Conversely, to obtain the axiom from right to left we proceed as follows. By assumption, $z \in \text{PAIR} \wedge \text{l}z \in S \wedge \text{r}z \in T$. Hence, $z = (\text{l}z, \text{r}z)$ and $(\text{l}z, \text{r}z) \in S \otimes T$; the left-hand side now follows. Conversely, if $z \in S \otimes T$, then by the additional rule $z \in \text{PAIR}$ and by the elimination rules $\text{l}z \in S \wedge \text{r}z \in T$.

Thus the two formulations are equivalent and we could employ either in practice. However, the introduction and elimination rules do not, by themselves, guarantee that an element of the Cartesian product is a pair. Of course, if we adopt CP″ as the basic axiom for products then we have complete agreement with the introduction and elimination rules.

6.3.3 Cartesian Products and General Function Spaces

Suppose that R is the type of employees, T is the type that indicates their status and S their current salary and we wish to define a function that returns, for each employee, a pair that consists of status and salary. More generally, usuppose that we are given functions $f \in R => T$ and $g \in R => S$. Is there a *natural* way of defining a function from R to $T \otimes S$? The answer is given by the following result which not only displays the form of such a function but also insists that it is unique (up to extensionality).

Theorem 6.7 Let $f \in R => T$ and $g \in R => S$. Define

$$[f, g] = \lambda x . (fx, gx).$$

Then $[f, g] \in (R => T \otimes S)$, $\text{l} \circ [f, g] \equiv f$ and $\text{r} \circ [f, g] \equiv g$. Moreover, for any $h \in (R => T \otimes S)$ such that $\text{l} \circ h \equiv f$ and $\text{r} \circ h \equiv g$ we have $[f, g] \equiv h$.

PROOF Clearly, $[f, g] \in (R => T \otimes S)$ and $\text{l} \circ [f, g] = \lambda x . (\text{l}(fx, gx)) = \lambda x . fx \equiv f$. Let $h \in (R => T \otimes S)$ and $\text{l} \circ h \equiv f$ and $\text{r} \circ h \equiv g$. Let $x \in R$; then we have $[f, g]x = (fx, gx)$. By hypothesis, the latter equals $(\text{l}(hx), \text{r}(hx))$. Since $hx \in T \otimes S$, hx is a pair. It follows that $hx = (\text{l}(hx), \text{r}(hx))$.

Notice that the proof requires the elements of the product to be pairs. This result would not go through with the less demanding notion of product. A picture might help to clarify matters. The theorem states that $[f, g]$ is the unique (up to extensional equivalence on R) function that makes the following commute:

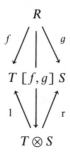

There is one further link between these two constructors that is worth a mention. The following provides an extensional characterization of the Curry function.

Theorem 6.8 Let $g \in R \Rightarrow U$ and $h \in S \Rightarrow V$. Define

$$g \otimes h \in ((R \otimes S) \Rightarrow (U \otimes V))$$

by $g \otimes h = [g \circ \mathsf{l}, \ h \circ \mathsf{r}]$. Let $f \in R \otimes S \Rightarrow U$; then $f \equiv \mathrm{App}_\circ((\mathrm{Curry}\ f) \otimes I)$ where $\mathrm{App} = \lambda(f, x) . fx$. Moreover, for $g \in R \Rightarrow S \Rightarrow U$ such that $f \equiv \mathrm{App}_\circ(g \otimes I)$ we have $\forall x \in R(gx \equiv (\mathrm{Curry}\ f)x)$.

PROOF First notice that $\mathrm{App}(((\mathrm{Curry}\ f) \otimes I)(x, y)) = \mathrm{App}(\lambda z . f(x, z), y)$ $= f(x, y)$. Also, if $f(x, y) = (\mathrm{App}_\circ(g \otimes I))(x, y)$ then $f(x, y) = gxy$. Hence $gx \equiv (\mathrm{Curry}\ f)x$.

In other words, given $f \in R \otimes S \Rightarrow U$, Curry is the unique function (up to extensionality) that makes the diagram commute:

These simple results should give the reader some insight into the use of the theory in a more mathematical guise as a theory of types. In particular, they establish that our notions of function space and Cartesian product behave in a standard way.

6.4 DISJOINT UNION

The next type constructor also forms part of the core of any type theory for functional programming. To introduce the idea we consider the following problem. Suppose that we wish to form a type from the following two types, which, in some sense, *contain* the elements of both:

| Pres | the type of present employees |
| Past | the type of past employees |

The new type is to consist of all employees both past and present. One obvious solution, but one that will not quite work, is to form the union: an object is in the new type if it is in either of the component types. To see the problem with this proposal, assume that we require a function that returns the current salary of present employees but indicates an error for past employees. By lumping together the two types in a union we have no obvious way of defining such a function, since given an element of the union we cannot determine its origin. More generally, we are frequently required to consider programs that operate on the *union* of two types with the proviso that we can discern the origin of the elements. This leads us to the notion of *disjoint* or *discriminated* union.

6.4.1 The Axiom of Disjoint Union

The axiom for this constructor reflects the intuition that the origin of the elements must be recoverable. Intuitively, an object z is in the disjoint union of S and T (written $S \oplus T$) if z is either a left injection from S or a right injection from T.

DU. $z \in S \oplus T \;\leftrightarrow$

$[z \in \text{INJ} \wedge (z \in \text{INL} \rightarrow (\text{proj } z) \in S) \wedge (z \in \text{INR} \rightarrow (\text{proj } z) \in T)]$

This may seem a little complicated but it simply demands that the elements are injections built from elements of the component types.

This construction can also be generalized to form the disjoint union of any finite number of types in a straightforward way. We leave the reader to carry the investigation further. As with the Cartesian product, the disjoint union of any two types is *total* in the sense that all its members are defined or terminating. This follows simply because injections are always defined.

Parallel to the Cartesian product there is an alternative formulation involving existential quantification. Here we guarantee that members are injections by explicit appeal to the existence of an object from one of the component types.

DU'. $z \in S \oplus T \;\leftrightarrow\; [\exists x \in S(z = (\text{in}_L x)) \vee \exists y \in T(z = (\text{in}_R y))]$

We leave the reader to check that these two formulations result in extensionally equivalent types (i.e. prove the analogue of Theorem 6.5). However, as with Cartesian products, the original is to be preferred since it makes no explicit existential demands.

6.4.2 Case Statements and Injections

The natural programming constructs that accompany this type are the injection functions and the case statement. There are derived rules that govern these constructs: one for the case statement and two for the injection functions.

Introduction   Elimination

$$\frac{u \in S}{(\text{in}_L u) \in S \oplus T}(\oplus i) \qquad \frac{u \in T}{(\text{in}_R u) \in S \oplus T}(\oplus i) \qquad \frac{z \in S \oplus T \quad \overset{[x \in S]}{\underset{t \in U}{\mid}} \quad \overset{[y \in T]}{\underset{s \in U}{\mid}}}{(\text{case } z \text{ of } [\lambda x . t, \lambda y . s]) \in U}(\oplus e)$$

Theorem 6.9 The above rules are derivable in LC from DU.

PROOF The soundness of the introduction rules follows from the axiom from right to left and the axioms of injection. For the elimination rule assume that $z \in S \oplus T$. Then either $z = \text{in}_L(\text{proj } z)$ and $(\text{proj } z) \in S$ or $z = \text{in}_R(\text{proj } z)$ and $(\text{proj } z) \in T$. If the former, by assumption $t[\text{proj } z/x] \in U$. Moreover, $(\lambda x . t)(\text{proj } z) = t[\text{proj } z/x]$. Hence, case z of $[\lambda x . t, \lambda y . s] = (\lambda x . t)(\text{proj } z) \in U$. A similar analysis applies to the other alternative.

Once again, these rules do not completely characterize our notion of disjoint union since in particular they do not guarantee that elements of the disjoint union are injections.

6.4.3 Disjoint Unions and Function Spaces

To complete the story we return to the original motivation for the introduction of disjoint unions and put matters on a more precise footing. Let $f \in T => U$ and $g \in S => U$. Suppose that we wish to define a function that operates on the disjoint union of S and T and which, in an obvious way, *extends* these functions. The case statement provides the means:

$$f \oplus g =_{\text{def}} \lambda x . (\text{case } x \text{ of } [f, g])$$

We must, of course, check that everything pans out correctly. The following not only indicates that this function works but also that it is (up to extensionality) the only one.

Theorem 6.10 Let $f \in T => U$ and $g \in S => U$. Then

$$f \oplus g \in (T \oplus S => U)$$

and $(f \oplus g) \circ \text{in}_L \equiv f$ and $(f \oplus g) \circ \text{in}_R \equiv g$. Moreover, for any $h \in (T \oplus S => U)$ such that $h \circ \text{in}_L \equiv f$ and $h \circ \text{in}_R \equiv g$, we have $h \equiv (f \oplus g)$.

PROOF Clearly, $f \oplus g \in (T \oplus S => U)$ and $(f \oplus g) \circ \text{in}_L \equiv f$, etc. Let $h \in (T \oplus S => U)$ satisfy $h \circ \text{in}_L \equiv f$ and $h \circ \text{in}_R \equiv g$. Then suppose $z \in T \oplus S$. If $z = \text{in}_L(\text{proj } z)$, $hz = h(\text{in}_L(\text{proj } z)) = f(\text{proj } z) = (f \oplus g)z$. If $z = \text{in}_R(\text{proj } z)$, $hz = h(\text{in}_R(\text{proj } z)) = g(\text{proj } z) = (f \oplus g)z$.

Again a diagram will help to clarify matters: $f \oplus g$ is the unique function (up to extensionality) that makes the following commute:

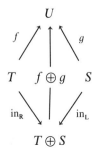

This can be seen as a general justification of the employment of disjoint union as opposed to the more obvious set theoretic variety. It is the dual result to Theorem 6.7 for Cartesian products.

6.5 TOTAL AND PARTIAL FUNCTION SPACES

The general function space provides a rather crude classification of functions. More specifically, it does not articulate the difference between partial and total functions. For this we need two further notions.

6.5.1 Total Function Spaces

For any types S and T, $S \Rightarrow T$ is the type of total functions from S to T. The axiom that governs this notion is a slight variation on that of the general function space in that it further insists on the totality of the functions.

FS. $f \in (S \Rightarrow T) \quad \leftrightarrow \quad \forall x(x \in S \rightarrow ((fx)\downarrow \wedge fx \in T))$

In other words, f is in the function space $S \Rightarrow T$ iff for every element x of S, fx terminates and is a member of T. The following provides some simple examples.

Theorem 6.11
(a) and $\in$ Bool $\Rightarrow$ Bool $\Rightarrow$ Bool
(b) or $\in$ Bool $\Rightarrow$ Bool $\Rightarrow$ Bool
(c) not $\in$ Bool $\Rightarrow$ Bool
(d) $p \in S \Rightarrow T \Rightarrow (S \otimes T)$
(e) $in_L \in T \Rightarrow (T \oplus S)$
(f) $in_R \in S \Rightarrow (T \oplus S)$
(g) Curry $\in (S \otimes T \Rightarrow U) \Rightarrow (S \Rightarrow T \Rightarrow U)$
(h) Uncurry $\in (S \Rightarrow T \Rightarrow U) \Rightarrow (S \otimes T \Rightarrow U)$

PROOF Here we illustrate with a few examples. For (c), we have to show that $\forall x(x \in$ Bool $\rightarrow ((not\ x)\downarrow \wedge (not\ x) \in$ Bool$))$. An inspection of the Boolean axioms should be sufficient to convince the reader of the truth of the claim. For (d) we have to prove that $\forall x(x \in S \rightarrow ((px)\downarrow \wedge (px) \in T \Rightarrow (S \otimes T)))$. Axioms P3 and L2 yield $(px)\downarrow$. This leaves us to prove: $(px) \in T \Rightarrow (S \otimes T)$, i.e. $\forall y(y \in T \rightarrow (pxy)\downarrow \wedge (pxy) \in S \otimes T)$. By P3, $(pxy)\downarrow$. Obviously, $pxy \in S \otimes T$, by the axiom of Cartesian products. For (g), let $f \in (S \otimes T) \Rightarrow U$. By L1, $(\lambda xy . f(x, y))\downarrow$. Moreover, for $x \in S$, $(\lambda y . f(x, y))\downarrow$ and for $y \in T$, $f(x, y)\downarrow$ and $f(x, y) \in U$.

Notice that provided that S is non-empty (i.e. $\exists x(x \in S)$) then every element of $S \Rightarrow T$ will be defined. With this proviso, $\bot$ therefore cannot be a member of the total function space—by definition. It can, of course, be a member of the general function space and will be just in case $\bot$ is a member of the target type.

The derived rules for abstraction and application are similar to those of the general function space. The side conditions are the same but there are additional conditions for termination.

$$\text{Introduction} \qquad \text{Elimination}$$

$$\frac{\begin{array}{c}[x \in S]\\ |\\ t \in T \wedge t\downarrow\end{array}}{\lambda x . t \in S \Rightarrow T} \qquad \frac{f \in S \Rightarrow T \qquad x \in S}{fx\downarrow \wedge fx \in T}$$

The abstraction rule can be paraphrased as follows: if under the assumption that $x \in S$ we can prove that $t \in T$ and $t\downarrow$, then we can conclude that $\lambda x . t \in S \Rightarrow T$. The application rule is self-explanatory. These rules can be derived from FS. We leave the proof to the reader since it is similar to that for the general space.

Theorem 6.12 The abstraction and application rules are derivable from FS.

Although we strive to ensure that all functions will be total we cannot in general restrict our programming language so that only total functions are admitted, at least not without severely constraining the expressive power of the language. This leads to the demand for a notion of function space that corresponds to partial functions.

6.5.2 Partial Function Spaces

Let S and T be types; then $S \Rightarrow T$ is *the type of partial functions from S to T.* Here we do not demand that the function be defined on all elements of the domain in question but only that where it is defined it will be a member of the codomain.

PFS. $f \in (S \Rightarrow T) \quad \leftrightarrow \quad \forall x(x \in S \wedge (fx)\downarrow \quad \rightarrow \quad fx \in T)$

For example, $\text{pred} \in N \Rightarrow N$, but it is not a member of $N \Rightarrow N$ nor of $N \Rightarrow N$. This has to be proven (by numerical induction) but it should be clear since $(\text{pred}\, x)$ is only undefined when applied to zero. For the list functions we have $\text{hd} \in \text{List}[N] \Rightarrow \text{Bool}$ and $\text{tl} \in \text{List}[N] \Rightarrow \text{Bool}$, where $\text{List}[N]$ is the type of lists on N. Even though we have not yet formally introduced these types these claims should be intuitively obvious.

Whereas the undefined element is not a member of any total function space it is, by definition, a member of every partial space. To see this notice that $\forall x((\perp x)\uparrow)$. Consequently, $\perp$ is, by default, a member of every partial function space.

There are also derived rules that can be lifted off the partial function space construction.

<table>
<tr><td>Introduction</td><td>Elimination</td></tr>
</table>

$$[x \in S \wedge t\downarrow]$$
$$|$$
$$\frac{t \in T}{\lambda x.t \in (S \Longrightarrow T)} \qquad \frac{f \in S \Longrightarrow T \quad x \in S \quad fx\downarrow}{fx \in T}$$

The following is also left to the reader.

Theorem 6.13 The abstraction and application rules are derivable from PFS.

Most of the time we shall operate with these notions of function space, however, there are other options that arise from the total quantifiers and strictness criteria. These are introduced by the following axiomatic requirements.

FS°. $f \in (S \Rightarrow {}^{\circ}T) \quad \leftrightarrow \quad \forall^{\circ}x(x \in S \quad \rightarrow \quad fx\downarrow \wedge fx \in T)$

PFS°. $f \in (S \Longrightarrow {}^{\circ}T) \quad \leftrightarrow \quad \forall^{\circ}x(x \in S \wedge fx\downarrow \quad \rightarrow \quad fx \in T)$

SFS. $f \in (S \Rightarrow {}^{s}T) \quad \leftrightarrow \quad f \in (S \Rightarrow {}^{\circ}T) \wedge (f \perp)\uparrow$

SPFS. $f \in (S \Longrightarrow {}^{s}T) \quad \leftrightarrow \quad f \in (S \Longrightarrow {}^{\circ}T) \wedge (f \perp)\uparrow$

The first two restrict attention to the defined objects. For example, a function is of the first type if it is defined when applied to all defined objects in the domain. The next two function spaces further insist that the functions in the respective total and partial spaces are strict. There are still more options available but we shall examine them if and when the need arises. What should be clear is that matters are getting a little out of hand. We seem to have many different options available and each seems to require the introduction of a new type constructor. This is a little inelegant and constitutes one reason for the introduction of *comprehension* types in the next chapter.

Finally, observe that the partial space is the least demanding of the three: it is the easiest to get into. Next comes the general space and finally the total one. However, to express all this formally we require the notion of a *subtype*.

6.6 SUBTYPES

Now that a simple theory of types is in place we can address certain questions about the general nature of types. These pertain to the more mathematical role of types as an axiomatic theory of sets or types. In this section we concentrate on the following: when is one type a subtype of a second? Presumably this is so when every element of one is an element of the other.

Definition 6.2 $S \subseteq T =_{\text{def}} \forall x (x \in S \to x \in T)$.

The enumeration construction provides a simple means of constructing a subtype of a given type. Trivially, Bool is a subtype of any enumeration type of which the truth values are members. More interestingly, how does this notion of subtype interact with the other type constructors? We have the following simple consequences. Notice in particular how the conditions on the function spaces in (c) to (e) are reversed in the first conjunct of the premise. The function spaces are *monotone* in the codomain but *antimonotone* in the domain.

Theorem 6.14

$$T \subseteq S \wedge T' \subseteq S' \quad \to \quad T \otimes T' \subseteq S \otimes S' \qquad (a)$$

$$T \subseteq S \wedge T' \subseteq S' \quad \to \quad T \oplus T' \subseteq S \oplus S' \qquad (b)$$

$$T' \subseteq T \wedge S \subseteq S' \quad \to \quad (T \Rightarrow S) \subseteq (T' \Rightarrow S') \qquad (c)$$

$$T' \subseteq T \wedge S \subseteq S' \quad \to \quad (T =\!\gg S) \subseteq (T' =\!\gg S') \qquad (d)$$

$$T' \subseteq T \wedge S \subseteq S' \quad \to \quad (T =\!> S) \subseteq (T' =\!> S') \qquad (e)$$

$$T \Rightarrow S \quad \subseteq \quad T =\!> S \quad \subseteq \quad T =\!\gg S \qquad (f)$$

PROOF All of these are entirely routine and can be safely left as exercises.

Part (f) displays the inclusions that hold between the three main notions of function space: the general space lives between the total and partial spaces. We leave as an exercise the exploration of the other notions of function space.

At present we have no non-trivial means of constructing subtypes. We can enumerate some of the elements, at least in certain cases, but we have no general means of *picking* out some collection of elements. For example, we might want to select the subtype of natural numbers consisting of the primes. This cannot be done by enumeration. We shall address this issue in the next chapter where we study the axiom scheme of *separation*.

Given the notion of subtype we can also introduce a notion of *extensional equivalence* between two types. In fact we have already implicitly appealed to this notion on several occasions.

Definition 6.3 $T \equiv S =_{\text{def}} (T \subseteq S \wedge S \subseteq T)$.

There are some obvious properties of this notion. In particular, it is an equivalence relation on types.

Theorem 6.15

$$T \equiv T \tag{a}$$

$$(T \equiv S) \to (S \equiv T) \tag{b}$$

$$(T \equiv T' \wedge T' \equiv S) \to T \equiv S \tag{c}$$

Furthermore, we have an immediate corollary to Theorem 6.14.

Theorem 6.16

$$(T \equiv S \wedge T' \equiv S') \to (T \otimes T' \equiv S \otimes S') \tag{a}$$

$$(T \equiv S \wedge T' \equiv S') \to (T \oplus T' \equiv S \oplus S') \tag{b}$$

$$(T' \equiv T \wedge S \equiv S') \to ((T \Rightarrow S) \equiv (T' \Rightarrow S')) \tag{c}$$

$$(T' \equiv T \wedge S \equiv S') \to ((T \Rrightarrow S) \equiv (T' \Rrightarrow S')) \tag{d}$$

$$(T' \equiv T \wedge S \equiv S') \to ((T \Rightarrow S) \equiv (T' \Rightarrow S')) \tag{e}$$

We shall have more to say about this notion and its connection with *type equality* in the next chapter. For the present we shall adopt it as our working notion of type equivalence.

6.7 DECIDABILITY

We finally address one further issue. It concerns the following problem. Suppose we have a predicate (given by a well-formed formula) and some type T. Under what circumstances can we replace this predicate by a Boolean-valued function on the type T? In other words, when can we implement the predicate in the programming language? We shall not provide a complete answer to this question but only put a little flesh on the notion. First we must be more precise about what is at stake.

6.7.1 Strongly Decidable wff

Intuitively, a relation is *strongly decidable relative to types* $T_1, \ldots, T_n$, just in case there is a function that decides the matter. More exactly we have the following.

Definition 6.4 A wff $\phi[x_1, \ldots, x_n]$ is *strongly decidable relative to types* $T_1, \ldots, T_n$ just in case:

$$\exists f \in (T_1 \Rightarrow \cdots \Rightarrow T_n \Rightarrow \text{Bool}) \forall x_1 \in T_1 \cdots \forall x_n \in T_n (f x_1 \cdots x_n = \mathsf{t} \leftrightarrow \phi[x_1, \ldots, x_n])$$

We shall call f a *witness* function for ϕ relative to $T_1, \ldots, T_n$. If all the types are T we shall say that the wff is *strongly decidable relative to T*.

There are some immediate implications that provide some closure conditions for the notion.

Theorem 6.17 If $\phi[x]$ and $\psi[x]$ are both strongly decidable relative to T, then so are $\sim\phi[x]$, $(\phi \wedge \psi)[x]$, $(\phi \rightarrow \psi)[x]$ and $(\phi \vee \psi)[x]$.

PROOF We illustrate with conjunction. Let f and g be the witness functions for ϕ and ψ respectively. The witness function for the conjunction is given as $\lambda x.(fx \text{ and } gx)$. Let x be in T. Then $(fx \text{ and } gx) = t$ iff $(fx = t) \wedge (gx = t)$ iff $\phi[x] \wedge \psi[x]$.

These results are all very obvious but they at least give us some insight into the notion. In summary, they inform us that strong decidability is preserved by the propositional connectives. No such result is forthcoming for the quantifiers. However, this is all a bit abstract. To convince the reader that this notion is of interest we need to look at some of its specific instances.

6.7.2 Equality

For which types is equality decidable? This is obviously of some importance since we would like to know when the equality relation on a type can be implemented.

Definition 6.5 A type T has *strongly decidable equality* iff the wff $x = y$ is strongly decidable relative to T.

For example, Bool has strongly decidable equality where the witness function is given as follows:

$$
\begin{aligned}
fxy &= t & &\text{when } (x \text{ and } y) \\
&= t & &\text{when } ((\text{not } x) \text{ and } (\text{not } y)) \\
&= f & &\text{when } ((\text{not } x) \text{ and } y) \\
&= f & &\text{when } (x \text{ and } (\text{not } y))
\end{aligned}
$$

Indeed, any enumeration type has strongly decidable equality: we employ the built-in equality tests for constants. Moreover, we have closure under disjoint union and Cartesian product.

Theorem 6.18 If T and S have strongly decidable equality then so do $T \otimes S$ and $T \oplus S$.

PROOF We illustrate with Cartesian product and leave the other case as an exercise. Let x and y be members of $T \otimes S$. First observe that the equality predicate for $T \otimes S$ takes the following form: $(\mathrm{l}x = \mathrm{l}y) \wedge (\mathrm{r}x = \mathrm{r}y)$. Since the first conjunct is strongly decidable relative to T, there is a witness function f and similarly one, g, for S. Put $hxy = (f(\mathrm{l}x)(\mathrm{l}y)$ and $g(\mathrm{r}x)(\mathrm{r}y))$. This is the witness function for the product.

The natural number type also has strongly decidable equality where the witness function is given by the following recursion equation:

$$f\,0\,y \qquad\quad = \mathrm{zero}\ y$$

$$f\,x\,0 \qquad\quad = \mathrm{zero}\ x$$

$$f(\mathrm{succ}\ x)(\mathrm{succ}\ y) = f\,x\,y$$

At the moment we cannot prove that this function does the trick since we require a more formal account of the type. However, as we shall see, lists, trees and indeed all *structural* inductive types have decidable equality.

In contrast, the universal type which we introduce in the next chapter does not have strongly decidable equality since this would mean that we could test for the equality of any two terms. In particular, we could test for equality with the canonical non-terminating element and this amounts to a test for termination, which we know to be impossible: equality in the lambda calculus is undecidable.

6.7.3 Membership

A second instance of the general idea concerns the following question. Given that S is a subtype of T, when can we determine whether an element of T is a member of S? This is really the membership problem relativized to a given type. In particular, if T is the universal type it amounts to the *membership problem* for S: when can we decide whether an element is a member of S? More formally, we have the following specialization of strong decidability.

Definition 6.6 Let T and S be types with $T \subseteq S$. Then T is *strongly decidable relative to* S iff $\exists f \in S \Rightarrow \mathrm{Bool}[\forall x \in S(f x = \mathrm{t} \leftrightarrow x \in T)]$.

For example, the types of left and right injections are strongly decidable relative to the type of injections since we can employ the built-in equality tests for the injection constants. In addition, we have the following closure conditions for this notion.

Theorem 6.19 If T and T' are strongly decidable relative to S and S' respectively, then $T \otimes T'$ and $T \oplus T'$ are strongly decidable relative to $S \otimes S'$ and $S \oplus S'$ respectively.

PROOF For Cartesian product let f_T be the witness function for T in S and $f_{T'}$ be that for T' in S'. Define

$$fx = f_T(\mathrm{l}x) \text{ and } f_{T'}(\mathrm{r}x)$$

Since f_T and $f_{T'}$ are total functions from S to Bool and S' to Bool respectively, f is a total function from $S \otimes S'$ to Bool. Moreover, $fx = \mathrm{t}$ exactly when $f_T(\mathrm{l}x) = \mathrm{t}$ and $f_{T'}(\mathrm{r}x) = \mathrm{t}$, i.e. iff $(\mathrm{l}x \in T \wedge \mathrm{r}x \in T')$ iff $x \in T \otimes T'$. For disjoint union we proceed in a similar manner. Let f_T be the witness function for T in S and $f_{T'}$ be that for T' in S'. Define

$$fx = \text{case } x \text{ of } [\lambda y . f_T y, \lambda z . f_{T'} z]$$

Since f_T and $f_{T'}$ are total functions from S to Bool and S' to Bool respectively, it follows that f is a total function from $S \oplus S'$ to Bool. Furthermore, $fx = \mathrm{t}$, just in case x is a left injection and $f_T(\text{proj } x) = \mathrm{t}$ or x is a right injection and $f_{T'}(\text{proj } x) = \mathrm{t}$, i.e. just in case x is a member of $T \oplus T'$.

There is no similar result for forthcoming for the function space constructors. We might try and appeal to the derived type checking rules. For the general function space these rules can be employed to assign types to pure lambda terms. We have seen examples of their application to this end. Indeed, it is known that for $\text{TA}[\lambda]$ it is decidable whether a term is typeable—the rules provide the guts of the algorithm (see Hindley, 1969). However, as we remarked before, these rules do not completely determine our notion of *general function space*. They only do so under extensionality and *extensional* equality for functions is not decidable. To see this let $\phi[x]$ be strongly decidable relative to T, with witness function w. Assume further that $\forall x \in T(\phi[x])$ is not strongly decidable. Notice that $\forall x \in T(wx = \mathrm{t})$ iff $\forall x \in T(\phi[x])$, which we have assumed to be not strongly decidable. Hence, we cannot decide whether the two functions w and $\lambda x . \mathrm{t}$ are extensionally equal on T.

We have only skimmed the surface of these ideas. There is a great deal left unsaid but we have done enough for the applications that follow. However, there is one further issue we must clarify.

6.7.4 Decidability

There is a prima facie different notion of decidability that arises from the very nature of intuitionistic logic. In intuitionistic logic the law of excluded middle, $\phi \vee \sim \phi$, fails: not every instance is provable. However, certain instances of it will hold. Statements that satisfy the law of excluded middle are called *decidable*. More generally, a predicate or relation will be dubbed decidable if its universal closure is. The following is the relativized version. The original is recoverable as the special case induced by the universal type (see next chapter).

Definition 6.7 A wff $\phi[x_1, \ldots, x_n]$, where $x_1, \ldots, x_n$ are all the free variables of ϕ, is *decidable relative to types* $T_1, \ldots, T_n$ just in case:

$$\forall x_1 \in T_1 \cdots \forall x_n \in T_n(\phi[x_1, \ldots, x_n] \vee \sim\phi[x_1, \ldots, x_n])$$

When all the types are T we shall say that the wff is *decidable relative to T*.

What is the exact relationship between these two notions of decidability? One direction is easy; the other is less so.

Theorem 6.20 If $\phi[x]$ is strongly decidable relative to T, then it is decidable relative to T.

PROOF We know that $\forall x \in T(fx = \mathrm{t} \leftrightarrow \phi[x])$. Consequently, since f is total, $\forall x \in T(\phi[x] \vee \sim\phi[x])$.

In classical logic, these two notions part company since the notion of decidability is vacuous: every predicate is decidable but not all are strongly so. However, in intuitionistic logic, at least for the types of the present chapter, the converse of Theorem 6.20 is also true, but it will be some time before we are able to establish this fact. However, we can already outline the argument. If $\phi[x]$ is decidable then, according to our verification interpretation of intuitionistic logic (see Chapter 2), there will be a program that verifies the fact (uniformly for each x in T), and this is essentially the requirement for strong decidability. The actual proof employs the idea of *realizability*, which is a precise formulation of our algorithmic interpretation of the connectives.

6.8 THE THEORY STT

Before we press on further with the development of the type theory it might be prudent to collect our thoughts a little and summarize the progress made. In Chapters 3 to 5 we introduced the lambda calculus, a theory of partiality and a more pragmatic theory of operations/functions. We referred to this theory as PL*. This forms the first component of a programming theory, namely a theory of operations or functions. In this chapter we made a further move in the development of such a theory by introducing a rather rudimentary theory of types. Although the theory is not yet complete, its final shape is roughly in place. For this reason we take stock of what we have. We shall refer to the present theory as STT (simple theory of types).

1. Syntax

$$t ::= x \mid c \mid (ts) \mid (\lambda x . t)$$

(plus the syntax of Chapter 5)

$$T ::= B \mid (T \otimes S) \mid (T \oplus S) \mid (T => S) \mid (T \Rightarrow S) \mid (T \Rrightarrow S)$$

$$\phi ::= \alpha \mid (\phi \wedge \psi) \mid (\phi \vee \psi) \mid (\phi \rightarrow \psi) \mid (\forall x \phi) \mid (\exists x \phi)$$

$$\alpha ::= (t = s) \mid (t \in T) \mid \Omega \mid (t \downarrow)$$

2. Axioms
   (a) The axioms of the lambda calculus and partiality including the axioms for constants (i.e. PL*)
   (b) The axioms for basic types and INV
   (c) $z \in S \otimes T \leftrightarrow (z \in \text{PAIR} \wedge \text{lz} \in S \wedge \text{rz} \in T)$
   (d) $z \in S \oplus T \leftrightarrow (z \in \text{INJ} \wedge (z \in \text{INL} \rightarrow (\text{proj } z) \in S) \wedge (z \in \text{INR} \rightarrow (\text{proj } z) \in T))$
   (e) $f \in (S => T) \leftrightarrow \forall x (x \in S \rightarrow fx \in T)$
   (f) $f \in (S \Rightarrow T) \leftrightarrow \forall x (x \in S \quad \rightarrow \quad (fx \downarrow) \wedge fx \in T)$
   (g) $f \in (S \Rrightarrow T) \leftrightarrow \forall x (x \in S \wedge (fx \downarrow) \quad \rightarrow \quad fx \in T)$

This theory will serve as the base theory for the development of further notions of type. It is a very simple theory with no notion of inductive ₅or polymorphic type. These concepts will occupy us in later chapters. First we turn to some further type constructors which arise not so much from functional languages but rather from within *constructive set theory*.

EXERCISES

6.1 State derived proof rules for generalized Cartesian products and derive them from the axiom. Generalize the type constructor of disjoint union to arbitrary finite numbers of types. State the axiom and derived proof rules.

6.2 Define a notion of *isomorphism* between types. Prove that $S \otimes (T \otimes R)$ is isomorphic to $S \otimes T \otimes R$.

6.3 Prove the following in STT:
   (a) $\lambda xy . x \in S => T => S$ for all types S, T
   (b) $\lambda xyz . xzy \in (S => T => R) => (T => S => R)$, for all types S, T, R

In the above, under what circumstances, if any, can the general spaces be replaced by total ones? Use the derived introduction and elimination rules for pairing, projection, abstraction and application to type the Curry function.

6.4 State and prove all the inclusion relations that exist between all the following function spaces:

$$FS°. \quad f \in (S \Rightarrow °T) \quad \leftrightarrow \quad \forall°x(x \in S \quad \rightarrow \quad fx{\downarrow} \land fx \in T)$$

$$PFS°. \quad f \in (S \Rightarrow\!\!\!\!\Rightarrow °T) \quad \leftrightarrow \quad \forall°x(x \in S \land fx{\downarrow} \quad \rightarrow \quad fx \in T)$$

$$SFS. \quad f \in (S \Rightarrow {}^sT) \quad \leftrightarrow \quad f \in (S \Rightarrow °T) \land (f{\perp}){\uparrow}$$

$$SPFS. \quad f \in (S \Rightarrow\!\!\!\!\Rightarrow {}^sT) \quad \leftrightarrow \quad f \in (S \Rightarrow\!\!\!\!\Rightarrow °T) \land (f{\perp}){\uparrow}$$

$$GFS. \quad f \in (S \Rightarrow T) \quad \leftrightarrow \quad \forall x(x \in S \quad \rightarrow \quad fx \in T)$$

$$FS. \quad f \in (S \Rightarrow T) \quad \leftrightarrow \quad \forall x(x \in S \quad \rightarrow \quad fx{\downarrow} \land fx \in T)$$

$$PFS. \quad f \in (S \Rightarrow\!\!\!\!\Rightarrow T) \quad \leftrightarrow \quad \forall x(x \in S \land fx{\downarrow} \quad \rightarrow \quad fx \in T)$$

6.5 State and prove similar results to Theorems 6.7, 6.8 and 6.10 for the total function space. What problems are there in extending matters to partial function spaces?

6.6 Prove that if $\phi[x]$ and $\psi[x]$ are both decidable relative to T, then so are $\sim\phi[x]$, $(\phi \land \psi)[x]$, $(\phi \rightarrow \psi)[x]$ and $(\phi \lor \psi)[x]$.

6.7 A type T is said to have *decidable equality* iff $\forall x \in T \forall y \in T((x = y) \lor \sim(x = y))$. Prove that if T and S have decidable equality then so do $T \otimes S$ and $T \oplus S$.

6.8 Let T and S be types with $T \subseteq S$. Then T is said to be *decidable relative to S* iff the predicate $x \in T$ is decidable relative to S. Let $T \subseteq S$ and $T' \subseteq S'$. Prove that if T and T' are decidable relative to S and S' respectively, then $T \otimes T'$ and $T \oplus T'$ are decidable relative to $S \otimes S'$ and $S \oplus S'$ respectively.

REFERENCES AND FURTHER READING

For the programming role of types see Reade (1989, Chapter 11). Indeed, any of the elementary books on functional languages contain a discussion of the simple type constructors—with different degrees of formality. For an elementary account of lambda calculus type schemes see Barendregt (1990) and Hindley and Seldin (1986).

7

CONSTRUCTIVE TYPE THEORIES

All of the type constructions considered so far are familiar and occur in one form or another in most current functional languages. Together with some basic inductive types they constitute a rather elegant type theory. However, it is not very expressive. One measure of the expressive power of such a theory concerns its ability to discriminate between objects; the more expressive the more *fine grained* the mesh it places upon the universe of objects. The present theory only classifies objects in a rather rude way. For example, even if the natural numbers were in place we could not form any interesting subtypes. We could not, for example, form the type of all odd numbers. The type constructors we now study go some way towards alleviating this problem.

Indeed, the constructors of this chapter are closely tied to the view that a programming theory is constituted by a *theory of functions* and a *constructive theory of types*. However, before we launch into a discussion of these types we need to say a little about the general nature of such theories. There are two general criteria that are usually employed as a guide to the development of a *constructive type theory*:

(*a*) *Types are non-extensional*
(*b*) *Types are predicative*

The first concerns the identity criteria for types and the second dictates the nature of the type constructors that are admitted into the theory.

(a) Extensionality In any theory of sets/types the question of equality has to be addressed: when are two sets/types taken to be identical? This question is important because, in general, identity is taken to imply indiscernibility, i.e. if two objects of any kind are equal then they share all properties. In standard set theory sets are identified *extensionally*. In other words, the following is imposed:

EXT. $T = S \leftrightarrow T \equiv S$

Should we adopt this axiom? There is an obvious answer: we cannot. The point is that our formal language does not even permit the expression of equality between types as a notion distinct from extensional equivalence. Of course, this could be easily rectified but it would be rather pointless to do so. Type terms only ever occur in extensional positions in wff: i.e. to the right of $\in$. As a consequence it is easy to prove, by a simple induction on wff, that extensionally equivalent types already share the same properties, i.e.

$$T \equiv S \rightarrow (\phi[T] \rightarrow \phi[S])$$

where $\phi[T]$ indicates that T occurs in an atomic subformula of ϕ. We therefore have no need to take a stance on the extensionality question since expressions never occur in positions that would force the issue. If types were permitted to occur as arguments to functions or on the left of $\in$, then matters would be different. We would then need to distinguish between a type given in extension and its *intensional correlate*. For our purposes $\equiv$ can be taken as the working definition of type equivalence. The theory is extensional but in a rather neutral sense: type expressions never occur in positions that demand an intensional notion.

(b) Predicativity A type is taken to be *predicative* if it is introduced in a way that does not make reference to the type itself. In particular, it must not, in its definition, refer to the whole collection of types—including itself. It is quite hard to be precise about this notion except by employing the idea of type quantification which we shall come to later. Indeed, it is not obviously clear that constructive mathematics entirely banishes such *impredicative* types. We shall adopt a cautious attitude and attempt to keep the theory predicative but we shall not be a slave to this constructive stricture. In fact, we will not be forced to take a stand on this issue until we study *polymorphism* in Chapter 10.

7.1 SUBTYPES AND SEPARATION

The first new type constructor we study is motivated by the desire to form subtypes of a given type. Enumeration types provide one means of doing this but they are very restricted. For example, if the natural number type N were in place, we could classify a function as a member of the total function space $N \Rightarrow N$, but we could not classify it further. It might always return an even number but the present theory does not permit the articulations of such a fact. We cannot, in any non-trivial way, form subtypes of given types.

7.1.1 The Axiom Scheme of Separation

Standard set theory and certain constructive set theories sanction the formation of sets by *separation* on some given set. We now introduce a similar construction into the present theory.

$$T ::= B | (T \oplus S) | (T \otimes S) | (T => S) | (T \Rightarrow S) | (T =\!\gg S) | \{x \in T : \phi\}$$

Notice that since type expressions refer to wff they can now contain variables. Variables other than x which occur free in T or ϕ are considered as *free variables of* $\{x \in T : \phi[x]\}$ and x itself is considered *bound*. Thus separation introduces a new binding operation which operates exactly as the quantifiers. We shall employ the notation $T[x, y, z]$, etc., to indicate that x, y, z are free variables in the type expression T. We shall also write $T[t/y]$ for the result of substituting t for each free occurrence of y in $T[y]$. Since we are introducing a new binding operation into the language, which can affect the binding of variables in wff, we must insist that our notion of *free for* is extended to include this new binding operation: t is *free for* x in $\phi[x]$ iff the substitution of t for x in $\phi[x]$ does not introduce t into $\phi[x]$ at any place where a (free) variable y of t becomes a bound occurrence (by a quantifier or a separation type) of y in $\phi[t/x]$. In particular, this affects the elimination rule for the universal quantifier since we must ensure, in its application, that the term substituted is *free for* the variable of substitution—in this extended sense. The necessity to extend this notion never arose with lambda binding since the definition of substitution automatically catered for illegal replacements.

With these technical preliminaries in place we can get to the main issue, namely the axiom that governs this constructor. Intuitively, the elements of $\{x \in T : \phi\}$ are those elements of T that satisfy the wff ϕ. This leads to the following *axiom of separation*.

SP. $z \in \{x \in T : \phi\} \leftrightarrow (z \in T \wedge \phi[z/x])$

Observe that this is actually an axiom scheme since although it expresses one idea it covers an infinite number of cases generated by the types and wff. The following are some immediate consequences of the axiom.

Theorem 7.1

$$\{x \in T : \phi\} \subseteq T \qquad (a)$$

$$(S \subseteq T \wedge (\phi \rightarrow \psi)) \rightarrow \{x \in S : \phi\} \subseteq \{x \in T : \psi\} \qquad (b)$$

$$(S \equiv T \wedge (\phi \leftrightarrow \psi)) \rightarrow \{x \in S : \phi\} \equiv \{x \in T : \psi\} \qquad (c)$$

The major role of separation concerns the formation of subtypes. We now spend a little time exploring this idea. We cannot say too much since our stock of interesting types is still rather limited. Indeed, for illustrative purposes we employ the natural number type even though it is still to be formally introduced.

7.1.2 Subtypes

Separation facilitates the introduction of potentially more *informative types*. It provides greater discriminating power than the constructors of STT alone, i.e. it facilitates a more *fine-grained* classification of objects. This is illustrated by the following types:

$$\{x \in N : \exists y \in N(x = 2 * y)\} \qquad (a)$$

$$\{x \in N : \exists y \in N(x = (2 * y)')\} \qquad (b)$$

$$\{x \in N : \exists y \in N(x = y * y)\} \qquad (c)$$

$$\{x \in N : \exists y \in \{0, 1, 2, 3\}(x = y * y)\} \qquad (d)$$

$$\{x \in N : x > 0\} \qquad (e)$$

We have employed the type of natural numbers to introduce various subtypes by separation. The first is the type of even numbers, the second the type of odd numbers and the third that of numbers which are squares. The fourth defines a type that is extensionally equal to a finite type and the last selects the non-zero numbers.

A further illustration concerns the domain and range of a partial function.

Definition 7.1 Let $f \in S \Rightarrow T$ then define the *domain* and *range* of f respectively as $\mathrm{Dom}(f) =_{\mathrm{def}} \{x \in S : fx \downarrow\}$ and $\mathrm{Ran}(f) =_{\mathrm{def}} \{y \in T : \exists x \in S(fx \downarrow \wedge fx = y)\}$.

This is a good instance of the mathematical role of types. We have singled out two subtypes that can now be employed as entities in their own right. Without separation we could not refer to these notions within the theory and they would have to remain at an informal level.

One further and related application concerns the generalization of Theorem 6.7 to partial function spaces. Let $f \in R \Rightarrow T$ and $g \in R \Rightarrow S$. Define $[f, g] = \lambda x . (fx, gx)$ as before. However, now we have a problem. We need to prove that $[f, g] \in R \Rightarrow T \otimes S$ but we cannot. In general it is false since the product is lazy and so $[f, g]x$ will always be defined even when fx or gx are not. Consequently, we cannot conclude that $[f, g]x$ will be a member of $T \otimes S$. However, with the finer control provided by separation we can rectify matters. Even though $[f, g]$ is not a member of $R \Rightarrow T \otimes S$ it is a member of the partial function space $\{x \in R : (fx) \downarrow \wedge (gx) \downarrow\} \Rightarrow T \otimes S$.

In addition to the greater expressive power introduced by separation there are other benefits. The inclusion of separation results in a more compact presentation of certain aspects of STT. Firstly, the various notions of function space can be derived from one notion by separation:

$$S \Rightarrow T =_{\mathrm{def}} \{ f \in S \Rightarrow T : \forall x \in S(fx\downarrow) \}$$

$$S => T =_{\mathrm{def}} \{ f \in S \Longrightarrow T : \forall x \in S(fx \in T) \}$$

We leave the reader to ponder these definitions and establish that the axiom scheme of separation yields the correct axioms for each of the notions of function space. Furthermore, given the types PAIR, INJ, INL and INR we can form Cartesian products and disjoint unions as separation types:

$$S \otimes T =_{\mathrm{def}} \{ z \in \mathrm{PAIR} : \mathrm{l} z \in S \wedge \mathrm{r} z \in T \}$$

$$S \oplus T =_{\mathrm{def}} \{ z \in \mathrm{INJ} : (z \in \mathrm{INL} \to (\mathrm{proj}\, z) \in S) \wedge (z \in \mathrm{INR} \to (\mathrm{proj}\, z) \in T) \}$$

Hence, given certain basic types, STT + SP reduces to INV + SP + PFS + PL*. However, one cannot form the partial function space by separation—there is no larger type to separate from.

This type constructor has a long history in mathematical logic and set theory but so far has had little impact on computing science. The only approximation to the notion are the subtypes introduced in Martin-Löfs theory and *subrange types*, but the latter form a very special case of separation. This lack of impact is probably because the computational role of types has occupied centre-stage. Computing scientists have been concerned with the development of computationally tractable theories of types which are supported by compile-time type checkers. Consequently, they have not sought the expressive richness offered by type constructors such as separation. Within the present paradigm type checking is part of the general process of program construction and is, as we shall see, carried out in an interactive fashion. This opens the way for the employment of much richer theories of types.

7.2 DEPENDENT TYPES AND PROPOSITIONS AS TYPES

A second vein of constructors, which spring from the constructive paradigm, focus upon the notion of a *dependent type*. Such constructors form part both of Feferman's theories and those of Martin-Löf. If you recall, we mentioned these theories in our discussion of constructive formal systems in Chapter 1. In the former theories they are obtained by the addition of the *join* axiom to a basic theory based upon a simple scheme of *comprehension* whereas for Martin-Löf they occupy a more central position. In this section we study these constructors within the setting of STT + SP.

7.2.1 Dependent Types

Since type expressions can contain free variables they can be seen as denoting a *family of types paramaterized by a free variable*. This can be exploited to introduce two new type constructors that generalize the simple notions of function space and Cartesian product:

$$T ::= B|(T \oplus S)|(T \otimes S)|(T => S)|(T \Rightarrow S)|(T =\gg S)|\{x \in T:\phi\}$$
$$(\pi x \in T.S)|(\sigma x \in T.S)$$

$\pi x \in T.S$ is the type of *dependent products* and $\sigma x \in T.S$ that of *dependent sums*. In these expressions the variable x is considered bound.

Dependent products correspond to the types of functions whose range type depends not only on their domain but also on the actual argument. This idea is captured by the following axiom.

DP. $f \in (\pi x \in S.T) \leftrightarrow \forall x[x \in S \rightarrow fx \in T]$

If the type expression T contains the variable x free (x not free in S) then we obtain the notion of a *dependent product* type. The important point is that the type of fx will be $T[x]$ and so the type of fx *depends upon* x itself, not just the type of x. This generalizes the ordinary notion of general function space which is the special case where x is not free in T.

As a simple illustration of this notion consider the following representation of arrays of Booleans:

$$N[n] = \{y \in N:y < n\}$$
$$A[n] = N[n] => \text{Bool}$$

$A[n]$ is a Boolean array of size n and $\pi x \in N.A[x]$ captures the notion of a dynamic array: its elements will be functions that given a natural number n return a Boolean array of dimension n. Although a rather simple example, it clearly illustrates how the type of function application can depend on the actual argument as well as its type. A more interesting example is afforded by the function left, which, given a list of numbers l and an number n which is a member of l, returns a sublist of l whose members are all the numbers less than n. Such a function forms part of the standard definition of quicksort. What type does this function have? It is easy enough to characterize it in terms of partial function spaces but dependent products provide a more informative characterization.

$$\text{left} \in \pi x \in \{y \in \text{List}[N]:y \neq [\ ]\}.[\{z \in N:\text{Member}(z,x) = t\} \Rightarrow \text{List}[N]]$$

We are able to use the total function space constructor since the second argument to the function left is forced to be a member of the first. These examples demonstrate the increase in expressive power afforded by dependent types.

Since dependent products generalize the general function space one would expect the derived rules to generalize and they do. We leave the reader to check their derivability. In the introduction rule x must not be free in S or in any undischarged assumption.

Introduction   Elimination

$$(\pi i) \quad \frac{\begin{array}{c}[x \in S]\\ \mid\\ t \in T\end{array}}{\lambda x.t \in \pi x \in S.T} \qquad\qquad (\pi e) \quad \frac{f \in \pi x \in S.T \qquad y \in S}{fy \in T[y/x]}$$

These are the actual rules that constitute Martin-Löf's notion of dependent product. One should say that he has formulated several such systems but the changes mostly concern the nature of equality. Moreover, his framework is quite different and so one should interpret these remarks with a little caution. They are also the rules of the AUTOMATH system of de Bruijn (1970), but his system does not have a separate syntactic class of types.

Whereas the dependent product generalizes the function space construction the *dependent sum* does the same for Cartesian products. The following determines its content.

DS. $\quad z \in (\sigma x \in S.T) \leftrightarrow (z \in \text{PAIR} \wedge \text{rz} \in S \wedge \text{lz} \in (T[\text{rz}/x]))$

An object is in the dependent sum $\sigma x \in S.T$ if it is a pair whose right component is a member of S and whose left is a member of the instance of T obtained by substituting the right component for the variable x. The Cartesian product $(T \otimes S)$ is the special case where x is not free in T. There are also derived rules that characterize Martin-Löf's dependent sum.

Introduction   Elimination

$$(\sigma i) \quad \frac{x \in S \qquad u \in T[x]}{(u,x) \in \sigma x \in S.T} \qquad (\sigma e) \quad \frac{z \in \sigma x \in S.T \qquad \begin{array}{c}[x \in S, u \in T[x]]\\ \mid\\ s \in R\end{array}}{(\text{let}\,(x,u) = (\text{rz},\text{lz})\,\text{in}\,s) \in R[\text{rz}/x][\text{lz}/u]}$$

In the elimination rule x and u must not occur free in any assumptions on which $x \in S$ and $u \in T[x]$ depend. Moreover, x must not be free in S and u must not be free in $T[x]$. We leave the reader to show that these rules are derivable from DS.

These type constructors form the core of Martin-Löf's theory of types which offers an alternative constructive paradigm to the one presented here. Indeed, his theory has been taken up by computing scientists and is currently under fairly intensive investigation as a complete framework for program specification and development. The theory is *logic free* in the sense that the proof rules make no appeal to the logical connectives and quantifiers. Program specifications are formulated in terms of the actual types. To understand this remark, and indeed the relationship between these two approaches, we need to grasp the following concept.

7.2.2 Propositions as Types

The idea that there is a close connection between propositions and types has its roots in the early semantic accounts of intuitionistic logic. It was first made explicit in the work of Curry and Howard and has been given full philosophical import in the theories of Martin-Löf. The central idea is implicit in the intuitive semantics for the connectives and quantifiers given in Chapter 2. There we established a connection between wff and terms by describing a recursive relation (t *verifies* ϕ) on wff. Suppose that for each wff we *collect together* the *verifiers* into a type. This provides a correspondence between wff and types where the type corresponding to a wff is the type of its verifiers. We can actually make this more precise. *Propositions* can be construed as types under a recursive mapping which associates a type (*the type of its verifiers*) with each wff:

$$R(\phi \wedge \psi) = R(\phi) \otimes R(\psi)$$
$$R(\phi \vee \psi) = R(\phi) \oplus R(\psi)$$
$$R(\phi \rightarrow \psi) = R(\phi) => R(\psi)$$
$$R((\forall x \in T)\phi) = \pi x \in T . R(\phi[x])$$
$$R((\exists x \in T)\phi) = \sigma x \in T . R(\phi[x])$$

This mapping provides a precise correspondence between wff and types and formally captures the intuitive semantics given in Chapter 2.

Martin-Löf takes matters one stage further. For him, there is not just a correspondence between propositions and types; they are actually identical. His theory is set up in a logic-free way: grammatically, there is no separate class of wff; there are only types and terms and a relation of membership between them. This relation is intuitively unpacked in much the same way as the notion of *verification*. Program specifications are not presented (as in the present theory) as wff but rather by the types themselves. It would take us too far from our present concerns to go into the details of the theory, but there is now an abundance of literature both on the foundations and on its application to computing science (see, for example, Smith, Petersson and Nordström, 1990). There is, however, one further point that we need to address.

In the definition of the function R we surreptitiously ignored the fact that the quantifiers are bound by a type. This is in keeping with one perspective in constructive mathematics which insists that quantification must be bound by some type. In Martin-Löf's theory quantification is given in terms of the dependent types since for him propositions are types and so, in traditional terms, he only admits bound quantifiers. Feferman, on the other hand, imposes no such restriction. The debate (such as it is) will no doubt continue forever. We shall continue to employ unbound quantification. However, if we wish to carry through the above correspondence then we require the following concept.

7.3 UNIVERSAL TYPES

Many of our expressions cannot be assigned a type within the present theory. For example, the expression $\lambda x . xx$ causes real problems. If we try and type this expression within STT we seem to require a type S which is equivalent to its own general function space—or at least the latter must be a subtype of it. Can we extend the theory so that every object has a type? One rather crude way is to force the issue by adding a *universal type*.

UT. $\quad x \in \Delta \leftrightarrow x = x$

The type Δ is the *universal type* in that every object is a member.

There are some surprising consequences of the existence of such a type. One obvious observation is that every type is a subtype of the universal one—by definition. In particular, $\Delta \Rightarrow \Delta$ is a subtype of Δ. Furthermore, let $Ev = \lambda fx . fx$. Then it is clear that $Ev \in (\Delta \Rightarrow (\Delta \Rightarrow \Delta))$. Obviously, $I \in (\Delta \Rightarrow \Delta) \Rightarrow \Delta$ and, moreover, $\forall f \in \Delta \Rightarrow \Delta \forall x \in \Delta \{Ev(If)x = fx\}$.

To some readers all this may seem rather mysterious. Indeed, to some it may even appear paradoxical: surely, *Russell's paradox* bans such sets or types? Therefore, before we proceed any further we should try and dispel this mystery.

7.3.1 The Universal Type and Set Theory

Readers familiar with standard set theory will know that the existence of a universal set is not guaranteed. Indeed, in standard *Zermelo–Fraenkel* set theory (ZF) the existence of such a set is inconsistent with the theory. This is because the separation axiom of ZF is more powerful than ours. The wff allowed in ZF separation are not restricted as in the present theory. In particular, the separation axiom of ZF permits the formation of the following:

$$\{x \in y : \sim (x \in x)\}$$

If the universal set is admitted in ZF then the following set is available:

$$\text{Russell} = \{x \in \Delta : \sim (x \in x)\}$$

The axiom of separation immediately yields a contradiction: Russell $\in$ Russell $\leftrightarrow$ $\sim$ (Russell $\in$ Russell). In the present theory this derivation is blocked: the expression $x \in x$ is not part of our language since the right-hand side is not a type expression. Despite the existence of the universal type, the present theory, in other respects, is very rudimentary. Not only is separation restricted but it does not include other set constructors that are available in standard set theory, e.g. *power* sets. This is blocked for the same reason that Russell's is.

$$P(x) = \{y \in \Delta : \forall z(z \in y \to z \in x)\}$$

The present theory is mathematically quite weak and, in particular, it is *strongly sorted*: types and terms occupy separate and distinct syntactic categories. One can build a model of the present theory in ZF but not vice versa.

7.3.2 Separation and the Universal Type

According to UT there is a type that everything has. However, this type is highly uninformative since it does nothing to classify objects: if every object has this type then it tells us nothing distinctive about any particular object. Its real usefulness springs from its mathematical contribution: it adds a new layer of expressive power to separation. Indeed, with just UT and separation we can define all the other types.

$$\{c_1, \ldots, c_n\} =_{\text{def}} \{x \in \Delta : x = c_1 \vee \cdots \vee x = c_n\}$$

$$\text{PAIR} =_{\text{def}} \{z \in \Delta : z = (lz, rz)\}$$

$$\text{INJ} =_{\text{def}} \{z \in \Delta : z = \text{in}_L(\text{proj } z) \vee z = \text{in}_R(\text{proj } z)\}$$

$$\text{INL} =_{\text{def}} \{z \in \Delta : z = \text{in}_L(\text{proj } z)\}$$

$$\text{INR} =_{\text{def}} \{z \in \Delta : z = \text{in}_R(\text{proj } z)\}$$

$$S \otimes T =_{\text{def}} \{z \in \Delta : z \in \text{PAIR} \wedge lz \in S \wedge rz \in T\}$$

$$S \oplus T =_{\text{def}} \{z \in \Delta : z \in \text{INJ} \wedge (z \in \text{INL} \to (\text{proj } z) \in S)$$
$$\wedge (z \in \text{INR} \to (\text{proj } z) \in T)\}$$

$$S \Longrightarrow T =_{\text{def}} \{f \in \Delta : \forall x(x \in S \wedge (fx)\downarrow \to fx \in T)\}$$

$$\pi x \in S . T =_{\text{def}} \{f \in \Delta : \forall x(x \in S \to fx \in T)\}$$

$$\sigma x \in S . T =_{\text{def}} \{z \in \Delta : z \in \text{PAIR} \wedge rz \in S \wedge lz \in (T[rz/x])\}$$

Theorem 7.2 Under the above definitions SP + UT implies CP, DU, PFS, DP, DS and the axioms for the basic types.

This follows immediately from the definitions of the above type constructors and the axiom of separation. So SP + UT renders all the other constructors redundant. Indeed, we get more than we bargained for. Not only does the theory UT + SP subsume all the present types but it supports several other *natural* type constructors:

$$S \cup T =_{def} \{x \in \Delta : x \in S \vee x \in T\}$$
$$S \cap T =_{def} \{x \in \Delta : x \in S \wedge x \in T\}$$
$$S - T =_{def} \{x \in \Delta : x \in S \wedge \sim (x \in T)\}$$
$$V =_{def} \{x \in \Delta : x \neq x\}$$

We obtain ordinary union, intersection and type difference. The last is the empty type. These are not available in STT + SP. Moreover, we can even form unions and intersections of *families of types*:

$$\bigcup x \in S . T =_{def} \{y \in \Delta : \exists x \in S((y, x) \in \sigma x \in S . T)\}$$
$$\bigcap x \in S . T =_{def} \{y \in \Delta : \forall x \in S((y, x) \in \sigma x \in S . T)\}$$

We have thus reached a point where the whole theory of types can be generated by just two simple axioms. In terms of mathematical elegance this is to be welcomed. However, some of the types it admits are slightly problematic from the perspective of program construction. In fact, it is not clear that they are ever required for this particular purpose. For example, the disjoint union constructor can always be employed in place of the union. Indeed, there are good reasons for doing so. When we introduced disjoint union we indicated that ordinary union was of little value since we could not effectively determine the origin of an element. In this regard, notice that the union types involve disjunction and existential quantification. This is to be seen in contrast to all the other constructors. For certain purposes we would prefer a slightly more constrained version of the theory in which all the types are, in some sense, *completely presented*, i.e. involve no disjunction and existential quantification. We approach this by way of a slight reformulation of SP + UT.

7.4 COMPREHENSION

The addition of UT to separation greatly enhances its power. Indeed, we can characterize matters exactly. The axiom scheme of separation (SP) provides a means of forming the subtype of a given type delineated by some property. Comprehension, on the other hand, enables the formation of types just through a particular property. This is a more weighty idea and precisely captures the power of SP + UT.

7.4.1 The Axiom Scheme of Comprehension

The formation rule takes the form: if ϕ is a wff then $\{x:\phi\}$ is a type. This leads to the following extension to the syntax for types:

$$T ::= B \mid \Delta \mid (T \otimes S) \mid (T \oplus S) \mid (T => S) \mid (T \Rightarrow S) \mid (T =\gg S) \mid$$
$$(\pi x \in T.S) \mid (\sigma x \in T.S) \mid \{x \in T:\phi\} \mid \{x:\phi\}$$

The *free variables* of $\{x:\phi\}$ are those of ϕ (other than x) and x is *bound*. The conventions regarding substitution, which applied to separation, also apply here. For convenience, we shall often write $\{(x, y):\phi[x, y]\}$ for $\{z:z \in \text{PAIR} \wedge \phi[lz, rz]\}$.

The axiom that governs this type constructor is a simple axiom (scheme) of *comprehension*.

COMP. $z \in \{x:\phi\} \leftrightarrow \phi[z/x]$

One might question the constructive nature of this notion of type; is it not impredicative? This thought is easy to dispel. We can view the comprehension types as being constructed in a *layer-by-layer* fashion: one begins with some basic types (for example given enumeration). This allows the formation of wff whose only atomic membership wff are of the form $t \in B$, where B is some basic type. Comprehension can then be employed to form types by abstraction on these wff. Once these types are in place we can form wff which contain atomic assertions that reference these types and so on. In other words, the types permitted by comprehension only involve types that have already been constructed.

What is the exact relationship between SP + UT and COMP? Firstly, COMP supports SP and UT:

$$\{x \in S:\phi\} =_{\text{def}} \{x:x \in S \wedge \phi\}$$

$$\Delta =_{\text{def}} \{x:x = x\}$$

so that COMP is at least as powerful a theory as SP + UT. On the other hand, given SP + UT we can define every instance of comprehension:

$$\{x:\phi\} =_{\text{def}} \{x \in \Delta:\phi\}$$

In summary we have the following.

Theorem 7.3 The theory SP + UT is equivalent to the theory based upon COMP.

Hence, the two theories are *equivalent* in the sense that for any type available in one theory there is an equivalent type available in the other. All this is pretty obvious, but we have taken this rather long-winded route in order to pinpoint the exact assumptions that underlie the acceptance of full comprehension.

7.4.2 Negative Comprehension and Program Development

This is certainly an elegant theory, but elegance by itself is not enough to justify a theory. It might, for example, be elegant and wrong. Fortunately, nothing so definitive can be said about the present theory. However, it does seem to go beyond what is actually required for certain applications. More particularly, not all instances of comprehension will prove necessary for the purposes of program specification and development. This is, of course, an empirical claim, but it appears to be a fact that for such applications a restricted form of comprehension suffices. This is not to say that full comprehension will not prove useful for certain mathematical purposes but rather that for program development a more conservative version is sufficient. In this regard, consider the definitions of the types of STT + DP + DS given by comprehension:

$$S \otimes T =_{\text{def}} \{z : z \in \text{PAIR} \wedge \text{l}z \in S \wedge \text{r}z \in T\}$$

$$S \oplus T =_{\text{def}} \{z : z \in \text{INJ} \wedge (z \in \text{INL} \rightarrow (\text{proj } z) \in S) \wedge$$

$$(z \in \text{INR} \rightarrow (\text{proj } z) \in T)\}$$

$$S \Rightarrow\!\!\!> T =_{\text{def}} \{f : \forall x (x \in S \wedge (fx){\downarrow} \rightarrow fx \in T)\}$$

$$S \Rightarrow T =_{\text{def}} \{f : f \in S \Rightarrow\!\!\!> T \wedge \forall x \in S (fx \in T)\}$$

$$S \Rightarrow T =_{\text{def}} \{f : f \in S \Rightarrow T \wedge \forall x \in S (fx{\downarrow})\}$$

$$\pi x \in S . T =_{\text{def}} \{f : \forall x (x \in S \rightarrow fx \in T)\}$$

$$\sigma x \in S . T =_{\text{def}} \{z : z \in \text{PAIR} \wedge \text{r}z \in S \wedge \text{l}z \in (T[\text{r}z/z])\}$$

Each of these types is defined by a comprehension formula which, apart from atomic formulae, is constructed by conjunction, negation, implication and universal quantification. There are no disjunctions or existential quantifications. The enumeration and base types will be dealt with later. Such formulae play an important role in program specification and construction and so they deserve special attention.

Definition 7.2 A wff ϕ is *negative* or $\exists, \vee$ *free* iff ϕ does not contain $\vee$ or $\exists$. We shall refer to the class of negative formulae by nwff.

The term $\exists, \vee$ *free* is more accurate but we shall mainly employ the term *negative* to refer to these formulae. With this notion in place we can introduce a restricted form of comprehension. For want of a better name we call it *negative comprehension*.

NCOMP. $z \in \{x : \phi\} \leftrightarrow \phi[z/x]$ where ϕ nwff

Types formed by negative comprehension cover the whole of STT + DP + DS. In addition, the empty and universal type are provided for and indeed the above subsumes those instances of separation induced by negative formulae and negative types. We shall return to this scheme later when we discuss program development. In fact, we shall generally operate with the full scheme but restrict it where convenient.

EXERCISES

7.1 Prove Theorem 7.1. Prove that the definitions of the general and total function spaces given in terms of separation satisfy the axioms for these types.

7.2 Using Definition 7.1 state and prove a version of Theorem 6.7 for partial function spaces.

7.3 Prove the soundness of the derived rules for dependent products and sums.

7.4 Provide direct definitions of the union and intersection of families of types without direct resource to dependent sums.

7.5 Axiomatize notions of dependent products that generalize the total and partial function spaces. The one supplied in the text corresponds to the general function space construction. State and prove the derived proof rules.

REFERENCES AND FURTHER READING

The best source for further discussion of the axioms of separation and comprehension is Beeson (1985, Chapter 10). Beeson (1981) and Beeson (1986) are also relevant. Our presentation is different but the central idea is the same, although our notion admits dependent types whereas in Beeson (1985) and Feferman (1979) this is achieved by the addition of the *join* axiom. Feferman (1990) is closer to the present formulation. The reader should also consult Martin-Löf (1975, 1979, 1982) for more discussion of dependent types and their role in computing science. Other introductions to Martin-Löf's theory are Backhouse (1986) and Smith, Petersson and Nordström (1990). A further variation is given in Constable (1986).

8

STRUCTURAL INDUCTIVE TYPES

Although our programming language supports the definition of recursive functions we cannot, in the present theory, assign a type to them—at least not in any really informative sense. Nor can the present theory sustain formal reasoning about such functions. To classify such functions we need to *enrich* the theory with *inductive/recursive* types. There are many general forms of such types worthy of exploration. However, initially we restrict ourselves to a very special subclass and leave the more general schemes for the next chapter.

In this chapter we concentrate on the scheme that generates *structured types*. Such types are *constructor induced types*; the elements of the types are built in an inductive fashion by application of constructors. This aspect of the type is provided by an axiom of *closure* which insists that the type is closed under the application of the constructors. In addition, the type comes equipped with a principle of *structural induction* which provides the means of proving properties about the type. Functions acting on these types are naturally defined via recursion equations that stipulate their behaviour for each of the constructor induced objects of the type. The principle of induction then enables the proof of their properties.

Initially, we examine some common *standard types* which form the backbone of much functional programming. The three most ubiquitous members of the genre are the following:

1. The natural numbers
2. Lists
3. Sexpressions

The early sections of this chapter are devoted to an exploration of these three examples. This paves the way for the introduction of the general scheme in the later sections.

8.1 THE NATURAL NUMBER TYPE

We have continually alluded to the natural number type without spelling out its exact nature. The time has come to remedy this. Natural numbers form the most interesting simple example of a *structural inductive* type and we devote this initial section to their exploration.

8.1.1 Axioms of Closure and Induction

For the natural numbers the axioms of closure and induction take on the following familiar form.

NC. $0 \in N \wedge \forall y(y \in N \to y' \in N)$

NI. $[\phi[0] \wedge \forall y \in N(\phi[y] \to \phi[y'])] \to \forall x \in N(\phi[x])$

The first axiom expresses the idea that N contains 0 and is closed under the successor constructor. In other words, the type is *inductively generated* from the constant constructor 0 by application of the constructor succ. The second axiom (scheme) is the principle of numerical induction. We shall refer to the formula ϕ as the induction formula. The content of the induction scheme should be clear enough: in order to prove that all natural numbers possess a certain property it is sufficient to prove 0 has the property and, under the assumption that a natural number has the property, its successor does. As we shall see later, the induction axiom implies that the elements guaranteed to be in the type by closure are all the elements of the type.

We can immediately put these principles to use by establishing some basic facts about the natural numbers and their associated operations.

Theorem 8.1

$$\forall x \in N(x \downarrow) \qquad (a)$$

$$\text{succ} \in N \Rightarrow N \qquad (b)$$

$$\text{pred} \in N \Rightarrow\!\!\!\gg N \qquad (c)$$

$$\text{zero} \in N \Rightarrow \text{Bool} \qquad (d)$$

PROOF For part (a) we employ induction with the induction formula $\phi[x]$ set to $x \downarrow$. Both the base step and the induction step follow immediately from axiom N4 of the natural numbers which insists that $0 \downarrow$ and $(\text{succ } x) \downarrow$. For part (b) we employ induction with the induction formula set to $(\operatorname{succ} x) \in \mathbb{N}$. This is sufficient by N4. Both the base case and the induction step follow from closure. For (c) we have to prove $\forall x \in \mathbb{N}((\operatorname{pred} x) \downarrow \to (\operatorname{pred} x) \in \mathbb{N})$. Set the induction formula $\phi[x]$ to $((\operatorname{pred} x) \downarrow \to (\operatorname{pred} x) \in \mathbb{N})$. The base case, $x = 0$, follows since $(\operatorname{pred} 0)$ is undefined. Assume $x \in \mathbb{N} \wedge \phi[x]$. We know $\operatorname{pred}(\operatorname{succ} x) = x$. Since by assumption $x \in \mathbb{N}$ we have $\operatorname{pred}(\operatorname{succ} x) \in \mathbb{N}$. For (d) we use induction with the induction formula $\phi[x]$ set to $(\operatorname{zero} x) \in \operatorname{Bool}$.

This should give the reader a little insight into the use of the induction and closure axioms. However, they are all very trivial and do not illustrate numerical induction very well. The principal employment of induction is to be found in its close connection with recursive functions on the natural numbers.

8.1.2 Recursive Functions and Numerical Induction

The relationship between induction and recursively defined functions will be an important theme for the rest of the book. We here consider numerical induction and recursively defined functions on the natural numbers. We begin with the most obvious examples:

$$\operatorname{add} x0 = x$$

$$\operatorname{add} xy' = (\operatorname{add} xy)'$$

$$\operatorname{mult} x0 = 0$$

$$\operatorname{mult} xy' = \operatorname{add} (\operatorname{mult} xy)x$$

An option available is to treat addition and multiplication as built-in constants where the above are taken as axioms. Indeed, for efficiency reasons this is a sensible option. Whether or not we adopt this route is of little logical consequence since they will have the same properties under either alternative. Intuitively, these functions should have type $\mathbb{N} \Rightarrow \mathbb{N} \Rightarrow \mathbb{N}$, and we employ induction to establish these facts. For ease of expression we shall often write $(\operatorname{add} xy)$ as $x + y$ and $(\operatorname{mult} xy)$ as $x * y$.

Theorem 8.2

$$\operatorname{add} \in \mathbb{N} \Rightarrow \mathbb{N} \Rightarrow \mathbb{N} \quad \text{and} \quad \operatorname{mult} \in \mathbb{N} \Rightarrow \mathbb{N} \Rightarrow \mathbb{N}$$

PROOF We illustrate with addition. We must establish that $\forall x \in \mathbb{N}[(\operatorname{add} x) \downarrow \wedge \forall y \in \mathbb{N}((x + y) \downarrow \wedge (x + y) \in \mathbb{N})]$. By L2, $(x + y) \downarrow \to (\operatorname{add} x) \downarrow$. Moreover, by Theorem 8.1, $(x + y) \in \mathbb{N} \to (x + y) \downarrow$. Hence it is sufficient to prove that $\forall y \in \mathbb{N} \forall x \in \mathbb{N}((x + y) \in \mathbb{N})$. Use induction with the induction formula $\phi[y]$ set to $\forall x \in \mathbb{N}((x + y) \in \mathbb{N})$. The base step follows from the definition. For the induction step assume that $(x + y) \in \mathbb{N}$.

Consider the following proof:

$x + y' = (x + y)'$	(i) By definition of $+$
$(x + y)' \in N$	(ii) By closure, since $(x + y) \in N$
$(x + y') \in N$	(iii) From (i) and (ii) and INV
$\forall x \in N((x + y') \in N)$	(iv) From (iii) by universal introduction

The result now follows by NI. The argument for $*$ is similar.

As a further illustration of numerical induction we establish some elementary facts about addition and multiplication.

Theorem 8.3

$$\forall z \in N \forall x \in N \forall y \in N \{ x + (y + z) = (x + y) + z \} \qquad (a)$$

$$\forall x \in N \forall y \in N \forall z \in N \{ (x * y) * z = x * (y * z) \} \qquad (b)$$

$$\forall x \in N \forall y \in N \{ (x + y) = (y + x) \} \qquad (c)$$

$$\forall x \in N \forall y \in N \{ (x * y) = (y * x) \} \qquad (d)$$

$$\forall x \in N \forall y \in N \forall z \in N \{ x * (y + z) = (x * y) + (x * z) \} \qquad (e)$$

$$\forall x \in N \forall y \in N \forall z \in N \{ (x + y) * z = (x * z) + (y * z) \} \qquad (f)$$

PROOF For (a) we proceed by induction on z, where the induction formula $\phi[z]$ is $\forall x \in N \forall y \in N \{ x + (y + z) = (x + y) + z \}$. We first establish the base step:

$x + (y + 0) = x + y$	(i) Definition of addition
$(x + y) + 0 = x + y$	(ii) Definition of addition
$x + (y + 0) = (x + y) + 0$	(iii) From (i) and (ii)

The following derivation yields the induction step:

$[\phi[z]]$	(i) Induction hypothesis
$(x + y) + z' = ((x + y) + z)'$	(ii) Definition of addition
$((x + y) + z)' = (x + (y + z))'$	(iii) From (i) and axioms for succ
$(x + (y + z))' = x + (y + z)'$	(iv) Definition of addition
$x + (y + z)' = x + (y + z')$	(v) Definition of addition
$\phi[z']$	(vi) From (ii) to (v), transitivity of $=$ and $\forall i$

This yields part (a). We leave the others as exercises.

The induction proofs are now getting a little more involved and display the intimate connection between recursion and induction: the former is a way of defining functions while the latter enables the proof of their properties. We shall later revisit this relationship and drive it in the opposite direction. More precisely, induction will be employed as a method of constructing recursive functions.

8.1.3 Equality and Orderings on N

One cannot proceed very far with numerical programming without equality and the standard orderings on the numbers. Since we have made no built-in provision for these relations we must provide an implementation. The following proof is a little more interesting since the form of the recursion equations naturally leads to a *nested* induction.

Theorem 8.4 Natural number equality is strongly decidable.

PROOF Consider the function given by the following recursion equations:

$$EQ\,0y = \text{zero}\,y$$

$$EQ\,x0 = \text{zero}\,x$$

$$EQ\,x'y' = EQ\,xy$$

We leave the reader to check that EQ has type $N \Rightarrow N \Rightarrow Bool$. We establish by induction that EQ is the witnessing function for natural number equality. Let $\phi[n]$ be $\forall m \in N[n = m \leftrightarrow (EQ\,nm = t)]$. For the base case we require: $\forall m \in N[0 = m \leftrightarrow (EQ\,0m = t)]$. This follows by a simple induction and the definition of EQ. For the induction step the induction hypothesis is $\forall m \in N[n = m \leftrightarrow (EQ\,nm = t)]$. We must prove $\forall m \in N[n' = m \leftrightarrow (EQ\,n'm = t)]$. To achieve this we employ a further induction, this time on m. The base step demands that $n' = 0 \leftrightarrow EQ\,n'0 = t$, and this follows directly from the second equation of the definition of EQ. For the induction step we have to show that $n' = m' \leftrightarrow EQ\,n'm' = t$. By the axioms of succ and the definition of EQ, this amounts to proving that $n = m \leftrightarrow EQ\,nm = t$. This follows from the main induction hypothesis. Hence the subinduction is established and also consequently the main one.

We can now employ numerical equality in our programming language since the function EQ encodes it. In this connection, programming with the natural numbers will certainly involve the comparison of two numbers with respect to their standard orderings. Logically, these notions are normally introduced as follows.

Definition 8.1

$$x \leq y =_{\text{def}} [x \in N \land y \in N \land \exists u \in N(y = x + u)] \qquad (a)$$

$$x < y =_{\text{def}} [x \in N \land y \in N \land \exists u \in N(u \neq 0 \land y = x + u)] \qquad (b)$$

$$x =_N y =_{\text{def}} [x \in N \land y \in N \land x = y] \qquad (c)$$

One can view these as abstract specifications of the orderings and our task is to provide an implementation. Before we do so we establish a few basic facts about them.

Theorem 8.5

$$\forall x \in N \forall y \in N[x < y \leftrightarrow (x \leq y \land x \neq y)] \qquad (a)$$

$$\forall x \in N \forall y \in N[x \leq y \leftrightarrow (x < y \lor x = y)] \qquad (b)$$

$$\forall x \in N \forall y \in N[y \leq x \lor x \leq y] \qquad (c)$$

$$\forall x \in N \forall y \in N[x < y' \rightarrow ((x = y) \lor (x < y))] \qquad (d)$$

PROOF We leave (a), (b) and (d) as exercises. We prove (c). We employ induction with the induction formula set to $\phi[x] = \forall y \in N(y \leq x \lor x \leq y)$. $\phi[0]$ is clear since $0 \leq y$. For the induction step assume $\phi[x]$. There are two possibilities we must consider: $x \leq y$ or $y \leq x$. We establish in both cases that $y \leq x' \lor x' \leq y$. We consider the latter first. Assume $\exists v \in N(x = y + v)$. We have by definition of addition, $\exists v \in N(x' = y + v')$, and, consequently, $y \leq x'$. Hence, trivially, $y \leq x' \lor x' \leq y$. This deals with the latter possibility. Assume that $x \leq y$. This splits into two cases: $x = y$ or $x < y$. Assume that $x = y$. Then $x' = y'$ and so $\exists w \in N(x' = y + w)$; hence $y \leq x'$. If $x < y$ then $\exists v \in N(y = x + v \land v \neq 0)$. We leave the reader to show that $\exists w \in N(y = x' + w)$, i.e. $x' \leq y$. Thus, in either case we have $y \leq x' \lor x' \leq y$, as required.

Together, Theorems 8.4 and 8.5 establish that equality and the orderings are decidable. In fact Theorem 8.5 implicitly guarantees strong decidability, i.e. that the orderings can be implemented. We alluded to this in our discussion of decidability in Chapter 6. However, since the formal proof of this result is not yet in place we provide some of the details.

Theorem 8.6 $<$ and $\leq$ are strongly decidable relative to N.

PROOF Let leq (less than or equal) be given by the following recursion equations:

$$\text{leq } 0y = \text{t}$$

$$\text{leq } x0 = \text{zero } x$$

$$\text{leq } x' y' = \text{leq } xy$$

It is easy to establish, by induction on N, that it has type $N \Rightarrow N \Rightarrow Bool$. For the main part of the proof we employ a similar argument to that used for the equality predicate. We leave the reader to program the function lt for $<$.

These results enable us to extend the repertoire of relations that we can employ in numerical programming. For example, the results justify the following definition in the sense that the guards are satisfied in the intuitively correct circumstances. We assign the definition of ' $-$ ', the subtraction function, to the reader.

$$
\begin{aligned}
\gcd xy &= \gcd(x - y)y & &\text{when } y < x \\
&= \gcd x(y - x) & &\text{when } x < y \\
&= x & &\text{when } x =_N y
\end{aligned}
$$

More often these functions are built in to the programming language and their inclusion is then justified via the general theorems for the addition of axiomatically defined constants. It is a matter of taste and convenience as to which functions are built in but, whatever choice is made in these particular cases, some functions and relations will need to be developed and analysed in the above manner; not everything can be built in.

8.2 LISTS

The natural numbers form one common example of an inductive data type; lists form another. Indeed, lists are probably the most commonly used data type in functional programming. We shall proceed, as with the natural numbers, by setting up a new form of inductive type, but here matters are a little more complicated. Initially, we extend our syntax of types to include lists: if T is a type then $List[T]$ is a type. This is more complex than the natural number type since the above syntax permits the formation of the type of $List[T]$ for any previously defined type T.

8.2.1 The Data Type of Lists

$List[T]$, *the type of lists on* T, is given by the following closure and induction axioms.

LC. $[\ ] \in List[T] \wedge \forall u \in T \forall x (x \in List[T] \rightarrow (u:x) \in List[T])$

LI. $[\phi[[\ ]] \wedge \forall u \in T \forall x \in List[T](\phi[x] \rightarrow \phi[u:x])] \rightarrow$

$\forall x \in List[T](\phi[x])$

The closure axiom informs us that the empty list is a member of the type $List[T]$ and that, if u is a member of T and x is a member of $List[T]$, then

$u:x$ is a member of $\text{List}[T]$. Lists are formed by the constructor cons from the empty list. The induction axiom is the *principle of list induction*: to prove that some property holds of all members of $\text{List}[T]$ we must establish the base case (i.e. that it holds for the empty list) and under the assumption that a list x has the property we must prove that, for any member u of T, $u:x$ has the property.

Theorem 8.7

$$\forall x \in \text{List}[T](x\downarrow) \tag{a}$$

$$\text{cons} \in (T \Rightarrow \text{List}[T] \Rightarrow \text{List}[T]) \tag{b}$$

$$\text{hd} \in (\text{List}[T] \Rrightarrow T) \tag{c}$$

$$\text{tl} \in (\text{List}[T] \Rrightarrow \text{List}[T]) \tag{d}$$

$$\text{empty} \in (\text{List}[T] \Rightarrow \text{Bool}) \tag{e}$$

PROOF We prove (b) and leave the others as exercises in list induction. We use list induction with the induction formula $\phi[x]$ set to $\forall u \in T((u:x) \in \text{List}[T])$. This is sufficient by part (a), List closure and L2. For the base case we have to prove that $\forall u \in T\{[u] \in \text{List}[T]\}$. This follows from closure. For the induction step suppose that $x \in \text{List}[T]$, $v \in T$ and $\forall u \in T((u:x) \in \text{List}[T])$. Then $v:x$ is a member of $\text{List}[T]$. Let $u \in T$. By closure, $u:(v:x) \in \text{List}[T]$. Hence, we have the following: $\forall v \in T \forall x \in \text{List}[T][\forall u \in T\{(u:x) \in \text{List}[T]\} \rightarrow \forall u \in T\{u:(v:x) \in \text{List}[T]\}]$. List induction now yields the result.

Observe that hd and tl are partial functions since they are undefined on the empty list. However, these proofs do not provide very interesting examples of list induction. To obtain more demanding instances we must seek out recursively defined list functions.

8.2.2 Establishing the Formal Properties of List Functions

We are now in a position to begin elementary list programming. Our strategy will be to survey some of the more familiar operations on lists and establish their various formal properties. The examples have been selected mainly to illustrate the employment of the axioms in formally establishing properties of list functions and, in particular, to emphasize the relationship between list induction and simple pattern-directed list functions.

The function ($*$) appends two lists to form a third where for convenience we employ infix notation:

$$[\ ] * y = y$$

$$(u:x) * y = u:(x * y)$$

The following provides a little more substance for the list axioms.

Theorem 8.8

$$* \in \text{List}[T] \Rightarrow \text{List}[T] \Rightarrow \text{List}[T] \qquad (a)$$

$$\forall x \in \text{List}[T](x * [\ ] = x) \qquad (b)$$

$$\forall x \in \text{List}[T]\forall y \in \text{List}[T]\forall z \in \text{List}[T][(x * y) * z = x * (y * z)] \qquad (c)$$

PROOF For (a), by list closure, L2 and Theorem 8.7 it is sufficient to prove the following: $\forall x \in \text{List}[T]\forall y \in \text{List}[T](x * y \in \text{List}[T])$. To achieve this we employ list induction where the induction formula $\phi[x]$ is defined as $\forall y \in \text{List}[T](x * y \in \text{List}[T])$. For the base case we must prove $\forall y \in \text{List}[T]([\ ] * y \in \text{List}[T])$, and this is clear from the definition. The induction step amounts to the claim that for all u in T, $x * y \in \text{List}[T]$ implies $(u{:}x) * y \in \text{List}[T]$. By the definition of $*$ the consequent of this implication is just $u{:}(x * y) \in \text{List}[T]$, and this follows immediately from closure. For part (b) we again employ list induction with the induction formula defined as $\phi[x] = (x * [\ ] = x)$. The base step is clear from the definition of $*$. For the induction step assume that $y * [\ ] = y$. Then $(z{:}y) * [\ ] = z{:}(y * [\ ])$, which by induction equals $z{:}y$. For part (c) we set the induction formula $\phi[x]$ to $\forall y \in \text{List}[T]\forall z \in \text{List}[T][(x * y) * z = x * (y * z)]$. For the base step we must prove that $([\ ] * y) * z = [\ ] * (y * z)$. From the definition of append, $([\ ] * y) * z = y * z$. Indeed, $y * z = [\ ] * (y * z)$, as required. For the induction step, consider $((u{:}x) * y) * z$. By the definition of append, $((u{:}x) * y) * z = (u{:}(x * y)) * z = u{:}((x * y) * z)$. By the induction hypothesis we obtain $u{:}(x * (y * z))$. Employing the definition of $*$ we obtain $(u{:}x) * (y * z)$, as required.

The next example is interesting since in order to define the function we need to know that the equality relation on the base type is implementable. Let T have strongly decidable equality. The following purports to delete all occurrences of an element of the base type from a list:

$$\text{delete } u[\ ] = [\ ]$$

$$\text{delete } u(v{:}x) = \text{delete } ux \qquad \text{when } \text{EQ}_T uv$$

$$\text{delete } u(v{:}x) = v{:}(\text{delete } ux) \text{ when not } (\text{EQ}_T uv)$$

Theorem 8.9

$$\text{delete} \in T \Rightarrow \text{List}[T] \Rightarrow \text{List}[T]$$

PROOF Since $\text{List}[T]$ is total it is sufficient to show that $\forall u \in T\forall x \in \text{List}[T]((\text{delete } ux) \in \text{List}[T])$. Use list induction with $\phi[x]$ set to

$\forall u \in T((\text{delete } ux) \in \text{List}[T])$. The base case follows immediately from the first equation for delete. For the induction step assume $\phi[x]$. There are two cases to consider. If $u = v$ then $(\text{delete } u(v:x)) = (\text{delete } ux)$. By induction, this is a member of $\text{List}[T]$. If $u \neq v$ then $(\text{delete } u(v:x)) = v:(\text{delete } ux)$. By induction, $(\text{delete } ux) \in \text{List}[T]$ and consequently, by closure, we have $v:(\text{delete } ux) \in \text{List}[T]$.

We could avoid the decidability restriction in the definition of the function if we permit an additional argument:

$$\text{del } pu[\ ] = [\ ]$$

$$\text{del } pu(v:x) = \text{del } pux \quad \text{when } puv$$

$$\text{del } pu(v:x) = v:(\text{del } pux) \quad \text{when not } (puv)$$

This then has type $(T \Rightarrow T \Rightarrow \text{Bool}) \Rightarrow (T \Rightarrow \text{List}[T] \Rightarrow \text{List}[T])$. We leave the reader to verify this claim.

Together with append and delete the next function completes a basic repertoire of elementary list functions:

$$\text{reverse} \quad [\ ] = [\ ]$$

$$\text{reverse} \quad u:x = (\text{reverse } x) * [u]$$

Theorem 8.10

$$\text{reverse} \in \text{List}[T] \Rightarrow \text{List}[T] \qquad (a)$$

$$\forall x \in \text{List}[T] \forall y \in \text{List}[T][\text{reverse } x * y = (\text{reverse } y) * (\text{reverse } x)] \qquad (b)$$

$$\forall x \in \text{List}[T][(\text{reverse } (\text{reverse } x)) = x] \qquad (c)$$

PROOF We leave (a) as an exercise. For (b) we use induction with the formula equal to $\forall y \in \text{List}[T](\text{reverse } x*y = (\text{reverse } y)*(\text{reverse } x))$. The proof is straightforward. We concentrate on (c); it is more interesting. We employ induction where the induction formula is set to $(\text{reverse } (\text{reverse } x)) = x$. The base step requires: $(\text{reverse } (\text{reverse } [\ ])) = [\ ]$, which follows from the definition. For the induction step assume $(\text{reverse } (\text{reverse } x)) = x$. Observe that, by the definition of reverse, $(\text{reverse } (\text{reverse } u:x)) = (\text{reverse } ((\text{reverse } x)*[u]))$. By (b) the latter equals $(\text{reverse } [u])*(\text{reverse } (\text{reverse } x))$, i.e. $[u]*(\text{reverse } (\text{reverse } x))$. By induction, this equals $[u]*x$, i.e. $u:x$.

So far we have not mixed the data types but this is easy to put right. We next consider an example that employs both the data types N and Lists;

it returns the length of a list:

$$\text{len} [\ ] = 0$$
$$\text{len } u{:}x = 1 + (\text{len } x)$$

Theorem 8.11

$$\text{len} \in \text{List}[\,T\,] \Rightarrow \text{N} \qquad\qquad\qquad\qquad (a)$$

$$\forall x \in \text{List}[\,T\,]\,y \in \text{List}[\,T\,](\text{len}(x * y) = (\text{len } x) + (\text{len } y)) \qquad (b)$$

PROOF Exercise.

The next example is somewhat more interesting. The function map applies a function to each element of a list, and the function filter removes elements of a list that do not satisfy some Boolean function. These are defined by the following recursion equations:

$$\text{map } g[\ ] = [\ ]$$
$$\text{map } g(u{:}x) = gu{:}(\text{map } gx)$$
$$\text{filter } p[\ ] = [\ ]$$
$$\text{filter } p(a{:}x) = a{:}(\text{filter } px) \quad \text{when } pa$$
$$\text{filter } p(a{:}x) = \text{filter } px \qquad \text{when not}(pa)$$

The main properties of these functions, including their relationship, is summarized by the following.

Theorem 8.12

$$\text{filter} \in (T \Rightarrow \text{Bool}) \Rightarrow (\text{List}[\,T\,] \Rightarrow \text{List}[\,T\,]) \qquad (a)$$

$$\text{map} \in (T \Rightarrow T) \Rightarrow (\text{List}[\,T\,] \Rightarrow \text{List}[\,T\,]) \qquad (b)$$

$$\forall x \in \text{List}[\,T\,]\forall p \in T \Rightarrow \text{Bool}\forall g \in T \Rightarrow T \qquad (c)$$

$$[\text{filter } p(\text{map } gx) = \text{map } g(\text{filter}(p \circ g)x)]$$

PROOF We leave (a) and (b) as exercises and prove (c). We use list induction with the induction formula set to the following: $\phi[x] = \forall p \in T \Rightarrow \text{Bool}\forall g \in T \Rightarrow T[\text{filter } p(\text{map } gx) = \text{map } g(\text{filter}(p \circ g)x)]$. The base case follows from the definitions since both sides are $[\ ]$. Inductively, assume that filter $p(\text{map } gx) = \text{map } g(\text{filter}(p \circ g)x)$. We have filter $p(\text{map } g(u{:}x)) = \text{filter } p(gu{:}(\text{map } gx))$. This follows by the definition of map. To expand further we have to consider the two cases. If $p(gu) = \text{t}$ then we have filter $p(gu{:}(\text{map } gx)) = gu{:}(\text{filter } p(\text{map } gx))$. By induction this equals $gu{:}(\text{map } g(\text{filter}(p \circ g)x))$, i.e. map $g(u{:}(\text{filter}(p \circ g)x))$—by

definition of map. By definition of filter the latter is equal to
map g(filter($p \circ g$)(u:x)), as required. If, on the other hand, $p(gu)$ is
false, then filter $p(gu$:(map gx)) = filter p(map gx), which by induction
equals map g(filter($p \circ g$)x), which by definition of filter equals
map g(filter($p \circ g$)(u:x)).

Although all these examples are straightforward they illustrate well the
employment of the list axioms. In particular, the reader should take note
that all the reasoning is internal to the theory. Indeed, this is one of the main
features of a programming theory. A complete description of a programming
language ought to be an axiomatic theory which supports all the argumentation
about objects and their types. Inductive types are no exception.

8.2.3 List Equality and Membership

To complete our brief introduction to the data type of lists we examine the
implementation on some useful list relations. We begin with list equality. Its
decidability follows from that of the base type.

Theorem 8.13 If T has strongly decidable equality then so does List[T].

PROOF Let the strong decidability of T equality be witnessed by EQ_T.
Consider the function given by the following recursion equations:

$$EQ \ [\ ]y = \text{empty } y$$

$$EQ \ x[\ ] = \text{empty } x$$

$$EQ \ (u{:}x)(v{:}y) = EQ_T \ uv \text{ and } (EQ \ xy)$$

We leave the reader to check that EQ has type list[T] $\Rightarrow$ List[T] $\Rightarrow$ Bool.
We employ list induction to prove that EQ is the required witness
function. Let $\phi[x] = \forall y \in \text{List}[T](x = y \leftrightarrow EQ \ xy = t)$. If x is the empty
list then the result follows almost directly (use a sub-induction) from
the first equation; we leave the details for the reader. For the induction
step we have to prove that $\forall y \in \text{List}[T]((u{:}x) = y \leftrightarrow EQ(u{:}x)y = t)$. We
employ a subinduction on y. If y is the empty list the result follows
immediately from the second equation. If y has the form $v{:}z$, then it is
sufficient to prove $(u{:}x) = (v{:}z) \leftrightarrow EQ_T uv$ and EQ xz. The result now
follows from the main induction hypothesis and the axioms of pairing.

In other words, if we can implement the equality of the base type then
we can do the same for the inductive type. This is important since, presumably,
we would like to be able to effectively determine whether two lists are equal.
This would be blocked, for example, if we formed lists of functions from N
to N. Indeed, we may need to compute whether or not a member of the base

type is an element of a particular list. The following does the trick. Again the base type is assumed to have (strongly) decidable equality.

$$\text{member } u[\ ] = f$$

$$\text{member } u(y{:}x) = t \qquad \text{when } EQ_T\, uy$$

$$\text{member } u(y{:}x) = \text{member } ux \ \text{ when } not(EQ_T\, uy)$$

Theorem 8.14

$$\text{member} \in T \Rightarrow \text{List}[\,T\,] \Rightarrow \text{Bool}$$

PROOF By induction on the lists with induction formula $\phi[x]$ set to $\forall u \in T((\text{member } ux) \in \text{Bool})$. The base case is clear. For the induction step there are two cases. If $u = y$ then the result is immediate. Otherwise, the result follows directly from the induction hypothesis.

Using member we can define the obvious *sublist* ordering:

$$x \leq y =_{\text{def}} [\,x \in \text{List}[\,T\,] \ \wedge\ y \in \text{List}[\,T\,] \ \wedge\ \forall u \in T((\text{member } ux) = t$$

$$\rightarrow (\text{member } uy) = t)]$$

Theorem 8.15 If T has strongly decidable equality then the derived sublist ordering is strongly decidable relative to $\text{List}[\,T\,]$.

PROOF Define

$$\text{sub} \quad [\ ]y = t$$

$$\text{sub} \quad (u{:}x)y = (\text{member } uy) \text{ and } (\text{sub } xy)$$

This defines the witness function for the ordering relative to $\text{List}[\,T\,]$. We leave the reader to check the details.

This concludes our brief introduction to the data type of lists, our main aim being to demonstrate how the formal theory can be employed to establish simple properties of list functions. In particular, we have illustrated one aspect of the relationship between simple pattern-directed list functions and list induction. We shall later call upon the intuitions developed here to explore the relationship between induction and recursion from the opposite direction: inductive proofs will serve as a means of constructing programs.

8.3 SEXPRESSIONS

Before we turn to a general scheme for structural inductive types we study one more concrete example, namely sexpressions. We follow the pattern of previous sections and first study the axioms of closure and induction and then illustrate their use by reference to several examples. The discussion will be less protracted than the previous ones since few new points of principle arise.

8.3.1 The Type of Sexpressions

Sexpressions are built from two constructors, tip and branch. The former has arity one and the latter arity two. The elements of the type are constructed from the base type via tip or built from existing members by the constructor branch. More precisely, the type Se$[T]$, *the type of sexpressions on T*, is given by the following closure and induction axioms.

SC. $\forall u \in T\{(\text{tip }u) \in \text{Se}[T]\} \land \forall x \in \text{Se}[T]\forall y \in \text{Se}[T]((\text{branch }xy) \in$

$\text{Se}[T])$

SI. $[\forall u \in T\{\phi[\text{tip }u]\} \land \forall x \in \text{Se}[T]\forall y \in \text{Se}[T](\phi[x]\land\phi[y] \rightarrow$

$\phi[\text{branch }xy])] \rightarrow \forall x \in \text{Se}[T](\phi[x])$

These principles reflect the informal comments given above. The closure axiom informs us that a sexpression on the base type T is either a *tip* constructed from a member of T or a *branch* constructed from two sexpressions. The induction principle again parallels the structure of the closure axiom: to prove that every sexpression has some property we have to prove that every tip constructed from a member of T has the property and, under the assumption that sexpressions x and y both possess the property, (branch xy) has the property.

8.3.2 Sexpression Programming

We shall study only a few key notions. To begin with we introduce a couple of functions to illustrate the principle of sexpression induction. The first function, fringe, lists the elements of the base type T that occurs as the *leaves* of a sexpression while the second forms the *mirror image* of a sexpression:

$$\text{fringe}(\text{tip }u) = [u]$$

$$\text{fringe}(\text{branch }xy) = (\text{fringe }x) * (\text{fringe }y)$$

$$\text{mirror}(\text{tip }u) = \text{tip }u$$

$$\text{mirror}(\text{branch }xy) = \text{branch}(\text{mirror }y)(\text{mirror }x)$$

In the following inductive proofs the induction step involves two assumptions which correspond to the two parts of the sexpression. The proofs employ the inductive hypothesis twice. This is unlike the case of lists and natural numbers where the constructors selected at most one argument from the inductive type.

Theorem 8.16

$$\text{fringe} \in \text{Se}[\,T\,] \Rightarrow \text{List}[\,T\,] \qquad (a)$$

$$\text{mirror} \in \text{Se}[\,T\,] \Rightarrow \text{Se}[\,T\,] \qquad (b)$$

PROOF We illustrate with (a). We prove the main part by induction where $\phi[x]$ is $(\text{fringe } x) \in \text{List}[\,T\,]$. The base case is obvious. For the induction step consider $(\text{fringe } x) * (\text{fringe } y)$. By induction, $(\text{fringe } x) \in \text{List}[\,T\,] \wedge (\text{fringe } y) \in \text{List}[\,T\,]$. Hence, from the type of $*$, $(\text{fringe } x) * (\text{fringe } y) \in \text{List}[\,T\,]$.

There is also a simple relationship between these functions and the reverse function on lists.

Theorem 8.17

$$\forall x \in \text{Se}[\,T\,]\{(\text{reverse}(\text{fringe } x)) = (\text{fringe}(\text{mirror } x))\}$$

PROOF We employ sexpression induction, where the induction formula is $\phi[x] = \{\text{reverse}(\text{fringe } x) = \text{fringe}(\text{mirror } x)\}$. The base case is routine. For the induction step we proceed as follows:

$$\text{reverse }(\text{fringe}(\text{branch } xy))$$

$= \text{reverse }((\text{fringe } x) * (\text{fringe } y))$	definition fringe
$= (\text{reverse }(\text{fringe } y)) * (\text{reverse}(\text{fringe } x))$	Theorem 8.10
$= (\text{fringe}(\text{mirror } y)) * (\text{fringe}(\text{mirror } x))$	induction
$= \text{fringe}(\text{branch}(\text{mirror } y)(\text{mirror } x))$	definition fringe
$= \text{fringe}(\text{mirror}(\text{branch } xy))$	definition mirror

Hence, by induction, we are finished.

Finally, the function smember purports to decide whether an element of T is a member of a sexpression on T:

$$\text{smember } u(\text{tip } v) = \text{EQ}_T\, uv$$

$$\text{smember } u(\text{branch } xy) = (\text{smember } ux) \text{ or } (\text{smember } uy)$$

We leave the following as an exercise in sexpression induction.

Theorem 8.18

$$\text{smember} \in T \Rightarrow \text{Se}[\,T\,] \Rightarrow \text{Bool}$$

This short discussion should be sufficient to give the reader a flavour of sexpression programming and the employment of sexpression induction. Further excavations are left to the reader. Henson (1987) provides a fairly rich source of examples.

Obviously there is much more to say about all three of these types. We could, for example, pile up numerical, list and sexpression programs but this would be at best rather tiresome. We might also introduce new forms of inductive type such as general trees, but it seems clear that a general scheme is required—who knows what inductive types might be needed in practice. In most functional languages natural numbers and lists are taken as basic built-in types, but they also admit schemes of *user-defined* types. In the rest of this chapter we shall explore one such scheme which naturally subsumes our three examples.

8.4 STRUCTURAL INDUCTIVE TYPES (SITs)

Each of the simple inductive types has been assembled from constructors. In the natural number case the constructors were 0 and successor, for lists they were the empty list and concatenation and for sexpressions they were tip and branch. In this section we examine a general scheme for such types. To extract the pattern, recall that each of our examples involves an axiom of closure and an axiom of induction. Moreover, each closure axiom consists of a conjunction of clauses, each of which consists of a wff which asserts that the type is closed under the constructor. The induction axioms take a similar shape and in each case constitute a principle of *structural induction*. In formulating the general scheme we must also take into account the fact that inductive types may involve *parameters* (e.g. List$[T]$, Se$[T]$).

8.4.1 General Scheme

In general, an SIT is given relative to two families:

(*a*) **T**   a finite collection of parameter types
(*b*) **C** $= \langle c_i : 1 \leq i \leq n \rangle$ a finite collection of distinct constructors

We employ the notation SI$[\mathbf{T}, \mathbf{C}]$ for the *structural inductive type generated by* **T** *and* **C**. Each constructor has an associated *signature* which consists of its arity (≥ 0) and the types of its arguments, selected from **T** or SI$[\mathbf{T}, \mathbf{C}]$ itself. To ensure a base case we need to insist that one constructor selects no arguments from SI$[\mathbf{T}, \mathbf{C}]$.

The closure axiom for SI$[\mathbf{T}, \mathbf{C}]$ consists of the conjunction of several closure conditions, each of which provides a sufficient condition for being in the type under definition and corresponds to closure under a constructor.

For each constructor c_i in the collection **C**, we introduce a *closure clause* $\delta[c_i]$, which takes the following form. For convenience, we write T for $SI[\mathbf{T}, \mathbf{C}]$.

$$(\forall x_1 \in T_1 \cdots \forall x_k \in T_k)((c_i x_1 \cdots x_k) \in T)$$

In the above, $k(\geq 0)$ is the arity of the constructor c_i, and for $1 \leq j \leq k$, T_j is a parameter type or T itself. In essence, this clause states that the type is closed under the application of the constructor. A complete closure axiom is the conjunction of such clauses with respect to the collection **C**. It thus takes the following form.

CLO. $\delta[c_1] \wedge \cdots \wedge \delta[c_n]$

We could express the closure conditions in a piecemeal way by splitting the closure axiom into its components, and we shall often do this for typographical convenience.

The general form of the induction principle is predictable from the closure axiom. Again each constructor contributes a component. Let $\delta'[c_i]$ be the following wff:

$$(\forall x_1 \in T_1 \cdots \forall x_k \in T_k)(\phi[y_1] \wedge \cdots \wedge \phi[y_r] \quad \rightarrow \quad \phi[c_i x_1 \cdots x_k])$$

In the above, $y_1, \ldots, y_r$ are those x_j's such that $T_j = T$ (i.e. of type T). According to this induction clause the constructor c_i preserves the property ϕ. The idea is simple enough but may bear a little further explanation, especially with regard to the subset of variables of type T. Let c_4 be a constructor of arity seven:

$$c_4 x_1 x_2 \cdots x_7$$

Now consider the subset of these variables whose type is T, say x_2, x_3. Then the induction clause takes the following form:

$$(\forall x_1 \in T_1 \cdots \forall x_7 \in T_k)(\phi[x_2] \wedge \phi[x_3] \quad \rightarrow \quad \phi[c_4 x_1 \cdots x_7])$$

With these clauses in place the induction axiom can be succinctly stated.

IND. $(\delta'[c_1] \wedge \cdots \wedge \delta'[c_n]) \rightarrow \forall y \in T(\phi[y])$

IND is a principle of *structural induction*: in order to prove that each member of the inductive type T has the property, it is sufficient to prove that the constructors preserve the property.

These axioms may be a little messy to state in their full generality but the underlying idea is really rather simple: each constructor induces a closure clause and an induction clause. We trust that the reader can see that each of the elementary examples of the previous chapter conforms to this general pattern. We give one further example to illustrate the idea.

Labelled trees are a generalization of sexpressions where the binary nodes are labelled with values from a further type. We introduce an SIT, Tree$[T, S]$

$(= SI[\langle T, S \rangle, \langle leaf, tree \rangle])$ with parameters T and S, by the following closure and induction axioms.

CLO1. $\forall u \in S((leaf\, u) \in Tree[T, S])$

CLO2. $\forall u \in T \forall x \in Tree[T, S] \forall y \in Tree[T, S]((tree\, xuy) \in Tree[T, S])$

Here the constructors are leaf and tree and CLO1 and CLO2 are the corresponding closure clauses. For convenience we shall also sometimes write the induction axiom as a proof rule. In this case, it takes the following form.

IND.

$$\frac{\forall u \in S(\phi[leaf\, u]) \quad \forall u \in T \forall x \in Tree[T, S] \forall y \in Tree[T, S](\phi[x] \wedge \phi[y] \rightarrow \phi[tree\, xuy])}{\forall x \in Tree[T, S](\phi[x])}$$

Structural inductive types give rise to many of the inductive types that occur in actual programming practice. Indeed, this scheme is more powerful than it might seem. We further illustrate the general idea by reference to some of the type constructors that we have previously introduced.

8.4.2 Other Type Constructors as SITs

Many of the other type constructors succumb to an analysis in terms of structural inductive types. The basic types, disjoint union and Cartesian product types can all be characterized in terms of SITs.

(a) Enumerated types These are special cases of inductive types. For example, in the case of Booleans we can introduce a structural inductive type by the following axioms.

CLO. $t \in Bool' \wedge f \in Bool'$

IND. $\phi[t] \wedge \phi[f] \rightarrow \forall x \in Bool'(\phi[x])$

The constructors are the constants t and f. We leave it as an exercise for the reader to check that Bool and Bool' are extensionally equivalent. One inclusion follows from closure and the other from induction. Therefore the type of Booleans can be introduced as an SIT. Indeed, this form is to be preferred since no disjunctions are employed in the axiomatic specification.

(b) Cartesian products Let T and S be types. The type $CP[T, S]$ is introduced by the following closure and induction axioms.

CLO. $\forall u \in T \forall v \in S((u, v) \in CP[T, S])$

IND. $\forall u \in T \forall v \in S\{\phi[(u, v)]\} \rightarrow \forall x \in CP[T, S](\phi[x])$

In this case we employ the pairing constructor and this constructor only selects elements from the parameter types. It follows that $T \otimes S \equiv CP[T, S]$:

the inclusion $T \otimes S \subseteq CP[T, S]$ follows from closure and the other inclusion from induction. The type PAIR is a special case where S and T are the universal type.

(c) Disjoint union Let T and S be types. Treating the injections as constructors we can form the type $DU[T, S]$.

CLO. $\forall u \in T((\text{in}_L u) \in DU[T, S]) \wedge \forall u \in S((\text{in}_R u) \in DU[T, S])$

IND. $(\forall u \in T\{\phi[\text{in}_L u]\} \wedge \forall u \in S\{\phi[\text{in}_R u]\}) \rightarrow \forall x \in DU[T, S](\phi[x])$

It is easy to see that $DU[T, S] \equiv T \oplus S$. The proof is similar to the case for Cartesian products. If S and T are the universal type we obtain the type of injections.

Thus the base types, Cartesian products and disjoint unions can be defined as structural inductive types. However, this is not the case with the function spaces. It will be instructive for the reader to try.

8.4.3 Recursive Functions on SITs

Structural inductive types are constructor-induced inductive types. Consequently, recursive functions can be naturally defined in a pattern-directed way. To define a function on such a type we stipulate its behaviour for each of the constructors. For one-place functions our recursion equations have clauses of the following form:

$$f(c_i x_1 \cdots x_k) = t_i$$

Most of the examples from the previous sections take this form. For example, in the case of Booleans we have the following simple instance:

$$\text{not t} = \text{f}$$
$$\text{not f} = \text{t}$$

Indeed, it is one of the central features of modern functional languages that such pattern-directed functions are directly definable. The corresponding induction principle then yields a method for proving properties of such functions. We have seen many examples of this already but we provide one more, this time in the more general setting.

Theorem 8.19 If each parameter type in **T** has strongly decidable equality then so does $SI[\mathbf{T}, \mathbf{C}]$.

PROOF Let f_i be the witness function for the parameter type T_i. Notice first that, by pattern equality, two elements of the type are equal iff they have the same form and equal components (by equality axioms for patterns). We thus define the witness function for $SI[T, C]$ as follows:

$$f(c_i x_1 \cdots x_k)(c_j u_1 \cdots u_k) =$$

$c_i = c_j$ and $f_1 x_1 u_1$ and ... and $f_k x_k u_k$ and $f y_1 v_1$ and ... and $f y_r v_{r'}$

where the y's and v's are the x's and u's of type $SI[T, C]$. We then employ induction for the SIT to show that for any two elements of the type, x and y, $x = y$ iff $fxy = t$. Set the induction hypothesis to $\phi[x] = \forall y \in SI[T, C](fxy = t \leftrightarrow x = y)$. To establish this use a sub-induction. The argument then proceeds from the initial observation of the proof.

The exact connection between structural induction and pattern-directed list functions is a little delicate. One is often forced to be quite inventive in formulating the induction hypothesis and it is sometimes more convenient to employ a different style of inductive argumentation. For example, certain list functions, although pattern directed, cannot be *directly* analysed by a simple structural induction. Indeed, we have already seen many examples of this where we were forced to employ a nested induction. These are special cases of so-called *well-founded* induction—the topic of the next chapter.

8.5 TYPE EQUATIONS

In the functional programming literature structural types are normally presented in a different way as *solutions to type equations*. Here we examine this form of presentation and connect it with ours. We demonstrate that any structural inductive type can be presented as the *smallest solution* to a rather simple *type equation*.

In order to set things up we require a little *meta* notation. Consider a typical closure clause for a structural type T:

$$(\forall x_1 \in T_1 \cdots \forall x_k \in T_k)((c_i x_1 \cdots x_k) \in T)$$

We shall write $C_i[T]$ for the following comprehension type:

$$\{z : \exists x_1 \in T_1 \cdots \exists x_k \in T_k (z = c_i x_1 \cdots x_k)\}$$

Notice that this is parameterized on T since T can be any, none or all of the T_i. More generally, we write $C_i[S]$ where S contextually replaces T in the comprehension type expression.

With this notation in place we can offer a different presentation of structural types.

$$(*) \quad T \equiv C_1[T] \cup \cdots \cup C_n[T]$$

The type equation $(*)$ states that T is extensionally equivalent to the type given by the union on the right. Notice that this union is really a form of *discriminated union* since the parts of the union are disjoint and we can always tell from the constructors the origin of an element. What is the exact connection between this representation and that given by closure and induction? The answer is given by the following result.

Theorem 8.20 A type J satisfies $SI[T, C]$ closure and induction iff it satisfies (a) and (b):

(a) $C_1[J] \cup \cdots \cup C_n[J] \subseteq J$
(b) For every type S, $(C_1[S] \cup \cdots \cup C_n[S]) \subseteq S \quad \rightarrow \quad J \subseteq S$

Moreover, if it satisfies (a) and (b) then it satisfies the type equation $(*)$.

PROOF Assume closure and induction. Part (a) follows directly from closure. For (b) we use induction with the formula set to $x \in S$. Assume $x_1 \in T_1 \wedge \cdots \wedge x_k \in T_k$. Further assume $y_1 \in S, \ldots, y_r \in S$ where these are the x_j's of type J. It follows that $c_i x_1 \cdots x_k$ is a member of $C_i[S]$. Hence, by assumption, it is a member of S. For the converse, the axiom of closure is automatic from (a). For induction, we put S equal to $\{x \in J : \phi[x]\}$; the result now follows from (b), since by (a) and the assumption of the induction hypothesis we obtain the following: $(C_1[\{x \in J : \phi[x]\}] \cup \cdots \cup C_n[\{x \in J : \phi[x]\}]) \subseteq \{x \in J : \phi[x]\}$. Finally, to see that $(*)$ is satisfied by any type that satisfies (a) and (b) we need only show that $J \subseteq C_1[J] \cup \cdots \cup C_n[J]$. Use (b) with S equal to $C_1[J] \cup \cdots \cup C_n[J]$.

As a consequence, we have the following special cases for natural numbers, lists and sexpressions:

(a) $N \equiv \{0\} \cup SUCC[N]$
  where $SUCC[T] = \{x : \exists y \in T(x = y')\}$
(b) $List[T] \equiv NIL \cup CONS[List[T]]$
  where $NIL = \{[\ ]\}$ and
  $CONS[S] = \{z : \exists x \in T \exists y \in S(z = (x:y))\}$
(c) $Se[T] \equiv TIP \cup BRANCH[Se[T]]$
  where $TIP = \{z : \exists x \in T(z = (tip\ x))\}$ and
  $BRANCH[S] = \{z : \exists x \in S \exists y \in S(z = (branch\ xy))\}$

In general, the result informs us that the type $SI[T, C]$ is the smallest type, in the sense of the subtype ordering, that satisfies the type equation $(*)$. The important point is that the original characterization goes beyond the simple expression of the type given by the above equation since the induction scheme guarantees its minimality.

8.6 GENERALIZATIONS OF STRUCTURAL INDUCTION

There are various ways to generalize the simple scheme and still remain within the spirit of structural induction. For completeness, we briefly consider two obvious generalizations.

8.6.1 Simultaneous Inductive Types

In certain applications we might be required to set up simultaneous inductive types. For example, consider the following closure axioms:

$$\forall x \in T((\text{node } x) \in \text{Tree})$$

$$\forall x \in T \forall y \in L((\text{branch } (\text{node } x)y) \in \text{Tree})$$

$$[\ ] \in L$$

$$\forall x \in \text{Tree} \forall y \in L((\text{cons } xy) \in L)$$

These are the closure axioms for two simultaneous inductive types (Tree and L). The elements of L are lists of trees where the trees are either nodes selected from elements of the base type T or a branch consisting of a node and a list (of trees).

It is a simple if rather tedious matter to generalize the scheme to cater for such types. Suppose, more generally, that we wish to simultaneously define inductive types $S_1, \ldots, S_m$. Let **T** be a family of parameter types and **C** be a family of constructors. A closure axiom for $S_1, \ldots, S_m$ is again a conjunction of clauses. For each constructor the clause $\delta[c_i]$ takes the following form:

$$\forall x_1 \in T_1 \cdots \forall x_k \in T_k((c_i x_1 \cdots x_k) \in S_j)$$

where T_j are members of the family **T** or $S_1, \ldots, S_m$. The induction axiom is a little more complicated. Each of the components $\delta'[c_i]$ is defined as follows. Let $\phi_1, \ldots, \phi_m$ be wff corresponding to the types under definition, i.e. we wish to prove that each member of S_j has the property ϕ_j. Then we have the following induction clauses:

$$\forall x_1 \in T_1 \cdots \forall x_k \in T_k(\phi_{j[1]}[y_1] \wedge \cdots \wedge \phi_{j[r]}[y_r] \to \phi_j[c_i x_1 \cdots x_k])$$

where in the above $\phi_{j[1]}, \ldots, \phi_{j[r]}$ and ϕ_j are selected from $\phi_1, \ldots, \phi_m$ and y_i is of type $S_{j[i]}$.

Although rather cumbersome the idea is simple enough. However, we shall not bother to investigate matters further since we shall shortly see a more elegant way of dealing with such types.

8.6.2 Pattern-Induced Structural Types

Recall that the closure and induction axioms are *constructor induced*. In particular, the closure axiom insists on closure under the constructors. This admits of an obvious generalization where we allow arbitrary patterns in the closure and induction clauses. The types are now given with respect to families of the following form:

(a) **T**   a finite family of parameter types
(b) **P** = ⟨ p_1 : 1 ≤ i ≤ n ⟩ a finite family of distinct patterns

The individual clauses for closure and induction are as follows:

$$(\forall x_1 \in T_1 \cdots \forall x_k \in T_k)(p_i \in T)$$

$$(\forall x_1 \in T_1 \cdots \forall x_k \in T_k)(\phi[y_1] \wedge \cdots \wedge \phi[y_r] \ \rightarrow \ \phi[p_i])$$

where the y_i's are the x_j's of type T, the structural type under definition. This generalizes the simple scheme since the constructor-induced clauses are simple cases of the above. The original notion employed only simple patterns obtained by application of constructors to variables or constants.

The *natural* form of functions associated with this notion of type permits arbitrary patterns on the left-hand side:

$$f p_1 = t_1$$
$$\cdots\cdots\cdots$$
$$f p_n = t_n$$

These types directly mirror the pattern-directed recursion equations we introduced in Chapter 5. This scheme is more general and elegant than the original and is certainly worthy of further exploration. However, we shall assign this task to the reader since our goal is to explore more *substantial* generalizations which subsume the above—the topic of the next chapter.

EXERCISES

8.1 Provide all the details for the proofs of Theorems 8.1 to 8.6.

8.2 Consider the function:

$$\text{del } pu[\ ] = [\ ]$$

$$\text{del } pu(v{:}x) = \text{del } pux \quad \text{when } puv$$

$$\text{del } pu(v{:}x) = v{:}(\text{del } pux) \quad \text{when not } (puv)$$

Prove that it has the type $(T \Rightarrow T \Rightarrow \text{Bool}) \Rightarrow\!\!\!> (T \Rightarrow \text{List}[T] \Rightarrow \text{List}[T])$.

8.3 Prove the following:

$$\text{reverse} \in (\text{List}[T] \Rightarrow \text{List}[T]) \tag{a}$$

$$\forall x \in \text{List}[T] \forall y \in \text{List}[T]((\text{reverse } x * y) = (\text{reverse } y) * (\text{reverse } x)) \tag{b}$$

$$\text{filter} \in (T \Rightarrow \text{Bool}) \Rightarrow (\text{List}[T] \Rightarrow \text{List}[T]) \tag{c}$$

$$\text{map} \in (T \Rightarrow T) \Rightarrow (\text{List}[T] \Rightarrow \text{List}[T]) \tag{d}$$

$$\text{mirror} \in \text{Se}[T] \Rightarrow \text{Se}[T] \tag{e}$$

8.4 Write a program of type $\text{List}[N] \Rightarrow \text{List}[N]$, which given a list returns a sorted list (with respect to the $<$ ordering on N). Prove that your program has the correct type. Extend this exercise by considering different sorting algorithms.

8.5 Prove that Bool and Bool' are extensionally equivalent. Furthermore, prove that the inductive characterizations of disjoint union and Cartesian product are extensionally equivalent to the original definitions from Chapter 6.

8.6 Define the data type of queues on a base type T as a structural inductive type. Provide its characterization in terms of type equations.

8.7 Set up a simple imperative programming language with expressions and commands/statements as a pair of simultaneous inductive types. Your language should involve statements with components that are expressions and expressions with components that are statements.

REFERENCES AND FURTHER READING

For more examples of list and sexpression programming in the Miranda™ style the reader should consult Bird and Wadler (1988) and Henson (1987). Structured types are treated informally in Peyton-Jones (1986) and somewhat more formally in Chapter 5 of Reade (1989).

9

WELL-FOUNDED INDUCTIVE TYPES

One fairly common phenomenon that arises in program correctness concerns the need to *strengthen* the induction hypothesis. This arises since often the obvious hypothesis will not support the argument and it is then necessary to establish a stronger result than the one actually required. Indeed, the main creative step in such proofs concerns the formulation of the correct hypothesis.

To illustrate the point consider the following famous function:

$$\text{fib } 0 = 0$$
$$\text{fib } 1 = 1$$
$$\text{fib } (x + 2) = (\text{fib } x) + (\text{fib } x')$$

Suppose we embark on the task of proving that fib is a total function from N to N. The obvious induction hypothesis, namely $(\text{fib } x) \in N$, will not quite work since to prove $(\text{fib } (x + 2)) \in N$ we require both $(\text{fib } x)$ and $(\text{fib } x')$ to be members of N. Ordinary numerical induction seems blocked—at least with the obvious induction hypothesis. The evident ploy is to strengthen the hypothesis to guarantee that $(\text{fib } y)$ is a member of N for each y less than x, i.e.

$$\forall y \in N[y < x \rightarrow (\text{fib } y) \in N]$$

The argument can then proceed by simple numerical induction. This form of argument is so common that it is normally singled out for special attention and given the name *complete numerical induction*. In fact, it is a special case of so-called *well-founded* induction.

There are many situations in computing science where *well-founded induction* seems both appropriate and necessary. This chapter is devoted to an exploration of this form of induction and its role in computing science.

We shall first introduce the basic concept and then explore the development of a theory of types based upon it. Finally, we shall briefly examine its natural generalization to *monotone induction*.

9.1 WELL-FOUNDED INDUCTION

Classically, there are various equivalent formulations of the idea that a relation $R \subseteq T \otimes T$ is *well founded* on a type T. However, not all are intuitionistically acceptable. The most direct formulation is the one that explicitly encodes *well-founded induction*.

Definition 9.1 $R \subseteq T \otimes T$ is *well founded* on the type T (or *well-orders* T) iff the following principle holds:

Principle 1. $\forall x \in T\{\forall y[(x, y) \in R \to \phi[y]] \to \phi[x]\} \to \forall x \in T\{\phi[x]\}$

This is the principle of *well-founded induction* itself: to prove that some property holds of every member of the type it is sufficient to show that any member does if all its R predecessors do. The following are some simple examples:

(*a*) N is well ordered by $\{(x, y) \in N \otimes N : x = y'\}$.
(*b*) N is well ordered by $\{(x, y) \in N \otimes N : y < x\}$.
(*c*) List$[T]$ is well ordered by $\{(x, y) \in \text{List}[T] \otimes \text{List}[T] : \exists z \in T(x = z:y)\}$.

We shall leave the reader to establish (*a*) and (*c*) and shall shortly examine (*b*) in some detail in order to provide some motivation for this form of induction. Indeed, we now present three small case studies which illustrate how such induction naturally arises in computing science.

9.1.1 DIVIDE AND CONQUER

A well-known technique for designing efficient algorithms is known as *divide and conquer*. The general idea involves solving a problem by dividing it into subproblems which have the same form as the original. One example is given by the following algorithm for sorting a list:

```
quicksort [ ] = [ ]
quicksort n:l = (quicksort l') * [n] * (quicksort l'')
            where (l', l'') = split nl
```

The function split, given a natural number and a list, returns two lists l', l'', where l' is a list that consists of all the elements of l less than n and l'' a list that consists of all the elements of l greater than or equal to n. At this point we shall not fuss about the exact form of split; we only require that the lengths of l' and l'' are strictly less than the length of $n{:}l$. Now suppose that we wish to prove that quicksort $\in \text{List}[\text{N}] \Rightarrow \text{List}[\text{N}]$. If we try to prove the result by structural induction then the induction step seems blocked—at least with the obvious induction hypothesis, namely (quicksort $x) \in \text{List}[\text{N}]$. At the induction stage we are inductively informed that (quicksort $l) \in \text{List}[\text{N}]$ and we need to conclude that (quicksort $(n{:}l)) \in \text{List}[\text{N}]$. However, to complete the argument we seem to require that (quicksort $l') \in \text{List}[\text{N}]$ and (quicksort $l'') \in \text{List}[\text{N}]$. One way to achieve this is to argue by induction on the *list ordering*, generated by the length of the lists. More precisely, we appeal to the following ordering:

$$R = \{(x, y) \in \text{List}[\text{N}] \otimes \text{List}[\text{N}]{:}(\text{len } y) < (\text{len } x)\}$$

This defines a relation on lists induced by their lengths. The analysis of quicksort can then proceed.

Theorem 9.1

(a) R well-orders $\text{List}[\text{N}]$
(b) quicksort $\in \text{List}[\text{N}] \Rightarrow \text{List}[\text{N}]$

PROOF For (a) assume $\forall x \in \text{List}[\text{N}]\{\forall y[(x, y) \in R \to \phi[y]] \to \phi[x]\}$. Employ $\text{List}[\text{N}]$ induction with the induction formula set to $\Phi[x] = \forall z((\text{len } z) = (\text{len } x) \to \forall y[(z, y) \in R \to \phi[y]])$. The case for $[\ ]$ is immediate. Assume that $n \in \text{N}$ and $x \in \text{List}[\text{N}]$. Assume inductively $\Phi[x]$. Further assume that $(\text{len } z) = (\text{len } (n{:}x))$ and $(z, y) \in R$. Then either $(\text{len } y) < (\text{len } x)$ or $(\text{len } y) = (\text{len } x)$. In the first case the induction assumption yields that $\phi[y]$. If $(\text{len } y) = (\text{len } x)$ then, by induction again, $\forall u[(y, u) \in R \to \phi[u]]$. By the assumption $\forall x \in \text{List}[\text{N}]\{\forall y [(x, y) \in R \to \phi[y]] \to \phi[x]\}$, we have $\phi[y]$ and thus, in either case, $\phi[y]$. Hence $\Phi[n{:}x]$. By $\text{List}[\text{N}]$ induction, $\forall x \in \text{List}[\text{N}](\Phi[x])$. From the initial assumption and the definition of Φ, we have $\forall x \in \text{List}[\text{N}](\phi[x])$. Hence, R well-orders $\text{List}[\text{N}]$. For (b) we employ this fact. Set $\phi[x]$ to be (quicksort $x) \in \text{List}[\text{N}]$. Let $x \in \text{List}[\text{N}]$ and assume that $\forall y[(x, y) \in R \to (\text{quicksort } y) \in \text{List}[\text{N}]]$. Since $x \in \text{List}[\text{N}]$ and $\text{List}[\text{N}] \equiv \text{NIL} \cup \{x{:}\exists y \in \text{List}[\text{N}]\exists n \in \text{N}(x = n{:}y)\}$ there are two possibilities for x. If $x = [\ ]$, then from the definition, (quicksort $x) \in \text{List}[\text{N}]$. If $x = (n{:}l)$, then by assumption, (quicksort l') and (quicksort l'') are both members of $\text{List}[\text{N}]$. Hence, since (quicksort $n{:}l) = (\text{quicksort } l') * [n] * (\text{quicksort } l'')$, the functionality of $*$ yields (quicksort $n{:}l) \in \text{List}[\text{N}]$.

The important moral is that the obvious induction hypothesis is not strong enough. To carry out the argument the induction hypothesis has to be strengthened. In the above analysis this insight has been raised to the level of a principle, namely well-founded induction on the relation R.

9.1.2 Complete Numerical Induction

Complete numerical induction arises from the necessity to argue about functions defined by *course-of-values* recursion. In such function definitions the function may depend upon the values of the recursive calls of all its predecessors. Generally, such functions take the following form, where $g \in N \Rightarrow N$, $h \in N^{k+2} \Rightarrow N$ and $e_i \in N \Rightarrow N$ and $(\forall x \in N)(e_i x < x')$, $i = 1, \ldots, k$.

$$f(0, y) = gy$$

$$f(x', y) = h(x, y, f(e_1 x, y), \ldots, f(e_k x, y))$$

Again, it should be clear that a simple structural induction will not directly support the analysis of such functions. At the induction step we need to know that all the predecessors have the property in question. In other words, we must appeal to the $<$ ordering on the natural numbers, i.e. argue by induction on the following relation:

$$R = \{(x, y) \in N \otimes N : (y < x)\}$$

More explicitly, we require the following principle of *complete numerical induction*:

$$[\forall x \in N(\forall y[(x, y) \in R \to \gamma[y]] \to \gamma[x])] \to \forall y \in N(\gamma[y])$$

The analysis then proceeds in much the same way as the previous example.

Theorem 9.2

(*a*) R well-orders N
(*b*) $f \in N \otimes N \Rightarrow N$

PROOF For (*a*) assume that $\forall x \in N(\forall y(y < x \to \gamma[y]) \to \gamma[x])$. In order to prove the consequent we require a more general induction hypothesis. Let $\phi[x] = \forall y(y < x \to \gamma[y])$. From the original assumption, we have: $\forall x \in N(\phi[x] \to \gamma[x])$. Thus, if we can prove the induction the result follows. $\phi[0]$ holds by default. Assume $\phi[x]$; it follows that $\gamma[x]$. By Theorem 8.5(*d*), we know that $y < x' \to ((y = x) \vee (y < x))$. Consequently, we have $\forall y(y < x' \to \gamma[y])$, i.e. $\phi[x']$. By induction $\forall y \in N(\phi[y])$ and hence $\forall y \in N(\gamma[y])$. For (*b*), we employ (*a*) with the induction formula $\forall y \in N(f(x, y) \in N)$; we leave the details to the reader.

We have thus established that f has the expected type. In doing so we have introduced a new form of induction which we have shown to be derivable from simple numerical induction. Moreover, this form of induction naturally arises from functions introduced by *course-of-values* recursion.

9.1.3 Lexicographic Orderings

The *Ackermann function* is infamous in complexity theory and elementary recursion theory. It provides the standard counterexample of a function which is *general recursive* but not *primitive recursive*:

$$A(0, y) = y'$$

$$A(x', 0) = A(x, 1)$$

$$A(x', y') = A(x, A(x', y))$$

Suppose we wish to prove that it has type $N \otimes N \Rightarrow N$. The obvious ploy is to attempt a numerical induction with the induction formula set to $\forall y \in N(A(x, y) \in N)$. The base case is clear but the only way to carry through the induction step involves a second induction, this time with respect to y. Indeed, we have seen other examples where such nested inductions proved necessary. In this particular case the nested induction amounts to a well-founded induction on the so-called *lexicographic ordering*:

$$(x, y) \ll (u, v) =_{\text{def}}$$

$$x \in N \wedge y \in N \wedge u \in N \wedge v \in N \wedge \{(x < u) \vee [(x = u) \wedge (y < v)]\}$$

The argument for the functionality of A then proceeds by a well-founded induction on the following relation:

$$R = \{(x, y): x \in N \otimes N \wedge y \in N \otimes N \wedge y \ll x\}$$

Theorem 9.3

(*a*) R is well founded on $N \otimes N$
(*b*) $A \in N \otimes N \Rightarrow N$

PROOF For (*a*) set the induction hypothesis to $\forall v \in N\{\forall y[((u, v), y) \in R \rightarrow \phi[y]]\}$. We then prove the result by a further induction, this time on v. We leave the details to the reader. We shall concentrate on (*b*). Use (*a*). Set the induction formula to $Ax \in N$. Assume that $x \in N \otimes N$ and $\forall y[(x, y) \in R \rightarrow Ay \in N]$. Since $x \in N \otimes N$, $lx = 0 \vee lx \neq 0$. In the former case the result is immediate from the first equation. In the second case we again have $rx = 0 \vee rx \neq 0$. This time the first possibility is immediate from the second equation for A. Thus we are left with the case where both components of x are successors. Suppose that $x = (u', v')$. Then by the third equation, $A(u', v') = A(u, A(u', v))$. By induction, $A(u', v) \in N$—since $(u', v) \ll (u', v')$. Moreover, $(u, A(u', v)) \ll (u', v')$ and so, by induction again, $A(u', v') \in N$.

In all three examples a common pattern can be perceived. In each case the *obvious* structural induction is blocked and to complete the analysis a more general induction hypothesis is required and this amounts to the introduction of a principle of well-founded induction. This form of argument is ubiquitous in mathematics and computing science. Somehow this ubiquity ought to be reflected in the design of a programming theory. We shall address this issue presently but first we ought to justify the claim made at the beginning of this section concerning the actual notion of a *well-founded relation*.

9.1.4 A Classical Formulation of Well-Founded Induction

Our definition of a well-founded relation directly reflects the principle of well-founded induction. However, there is an alternative definition which is more traditional—at least in classical mathematics. According to it, a relation $R \subseteq T \otimes T$ is well founded on T just in case every non-empty subset has a minimal element. More precisely:

Principle 2. $S \subseteq T \wedge \sim (S \equiv \nabla) \rightarrow \exists x \in S \forall y \in S(\sim (x, y) \in R)$

Principle 2, or some slight variant, is normally taken as the actual definition of a well-founded relation; principle 1 is then derived as the principle of well-founded induction. Classically, there is nothing to choose between them.

Theorem 9.4 Principles 1 and 2 are classically equivalent

PROOF First assume principle 2. Further assume that $\forall x \in T\{\forall y[(x, y) \in R \rightarrow \phi[y]] \rightarrow \phi[x]\}$ and $\exists x \in T\{\sim \phi[x]\}$. Let $S = \{x \in T: \sim \phi[x]\}$. By assumption S is non-empty. By principle 2 it has a minimal element: an x such that $\forall y \in S(\sim (x, y) \in R)$. Suppose that $(x, y) \in R$. Classically, by the minimality of x we have $\phi[y]$—since $R \subseteq T \otimes T$. However, by assumption $\forall x \in T\{\forall y[(x, y) \in R \rightarrow \phi[y]] \rightarrow \phi[x]\}$ and so $\phi[x]$, which is a contradiction. Conversely, assume principle 1. Let $S \subseteq T$ be non-empty and assume contrary to principle 2 that $\forall x \in S \exists y \in S((x, y) \in R)$. We prove by induction that $S \cap T$ is empty. Set the induction formula to $\sim (x \in S)$. Let $x \in T$ and $\forall y[(x, y) \in R \rightarrow \sim (y \in S)]$. Assume $x \in S$. Then $\exists y \in S((x, y) \in R)$. Let $y \in S$ and $(x, y) \in R$. It follows that $\sim (y \in S)$. This is a contradiction and so $\sim (x \in S)$. Hence, by induction, $\forall x \in T(\sim (x \in S))$, i.e. $S \cap T$ is empty. However, this contradicts $S \subseteq T$— since S is non-empty. Hence, $\sim (\forall x \in S \exists y \in S((x, y) \in R))$. Therefore, classically, we have the conclusion of principle 2.

We have used classical reasoning in the proof. Indeed, the above formulations are not intuitionistically equivalent. Suppose that we adopt principle 2 as our main definition and that, according to it, $<$ well-orders N. Then we have the following:

$$(S \subseteq N \land \sim(S \equiv \nabla)) \rightarrow \exists x \in S \forall y \in S(\sim(y < x))$$

Put $S = \{x \in N : (x = 1) \lor (x = 0 \land \phi)\}$, where ϕ is arbitrary. This is non-empty and so by the principle it has a minimal element: it is either 1 or 0. If the latter, then ϕ. If the former then $\sim(0 \in S)$, but this can only be because $\sim \phi$. Hence either ϕ or $\sim \phi$, i.e. we have derived the law of excluded middle (LEM). As a consequence, we are either forced to the conclusion that $<$ does not well-order N or to accept LEM. Intuitionistically, this discredits option 2. In particular, principles 1 and 2 cannot be intuitionistically equivalent. Suppose there were. Since $<$ well-orders N according to principle 1 it does so according to principle 2. Consequently, LEM would follow.

We have seen that well-founded induction occurs naturally in the analysis of certain forms of program. Indeed, many of these examples from the previous chapter made implicit appeal to some form of well-founded induction. It is not that structural induction does not support the arguments (at some level) but rather that setting up the induction hypothesis implicitly involves the introduction of a well-founded relation. This strongly suggests that we should explore the possibility of making well-founded induction the basis for a notion of inductive type. This is in keeping with the general pragmatic line that useful and commonly applied constructs should be given first-class status.

9.2 WELL-FOUNDED TYPES (WFTs)

Such a theory is introduced in Feferman (1975, 1979) and forms part of his *constructive set theory* T_0. We now investigate the addition of such types to the present theory. In doing so, we shall pretty much follow the presentation in Feferman (1975).

9.2.1 Axioms of Closure and Induction

Let T and R be types; then we extend the syntax of types by the addition of types $\Xi[T, R]$, *the well-founded inductive type generated by R from T*. We shall refer to T as the *base type* and R as the *generating relation*. In essence, the elements of the type $\Xi[T, R]$ are the R-accessible elements of T and may be pictured as the elements of T sitting on top of a well-founded tree that branches according to R. These types are also given by closure and induction axioms but they take a very different form to those of the structural types. In fact, both axioms reflect the principle of well-founded induction. More precisely, the type $\Xi[T, R]$ is governed by the following closure and induction principles.

CLO. $\forall x \in T\{\forall y[(x, y) \in R \rightarrow y \in \Xi[T, R]] \rightarrow x \in \Xi[T, R]\}$

IND. $\forall x \in T\{\forall y[(x, y) \in R \rightarrow \phi[y]] \rightarrow \phi[x]\} \rightarrow \forall x \in \Xi[T, R]\{\phi[x]\}$

The closure axiom insists that an object is a member of the type if all its R *predecessors* are. The induction axiom follows suit: to show that all members of the type satisfy a predicate we must show an element does when all its R predecessors do. Notice that R is not necessarily well founded on the whole of T. The axioms only guarantee that R well-orders T iff the inductive type subsumes all the members of T. More precisely, we have the following theorem.

Theorem 9.5

(*a*) $\Xi[T, R] \subseteq T$

(*b*) If $S \subseteq T$ and R well-orders S, then $S \subseteq \Xi[T, R]$

(*c*) $\Xi[T, R] \equiv T$ iff R well-orders T

PROOF For (*a*) use induction with the formula set to $x \in T$. For (*b*) assume that R well-orders S. Then, by definition, we have $\forall x \in S\{\forall y[(x, y) \in R \rightarrow \phi[y]] \rightarrow \phi[x]\} \rightarrow \forall x \in S\{\phi[x]\}$. We employ induction with the induction formula set to $x \in \Xi[T, R]$. By closure, we have $\forall x \in S\{\forall y[(x, y) \in R \rightarrow y \in \Xi[T, R]] \rightarrow x \in \Xi[T, R]\}$. Hence, since R well-orders S, $\forall x \in S(x \in \Xi[T, R])$, i.e. $S \subseteq \Xi[T, R]$. For part (*c*), notice that from (*b*) if R well-orders T then we have $T \subseteq \Xi[T, R]$; part (*a*) yields the opposite inclusion. For the converse, if $\Xi[T, R] \equiv T$, then the induction principle immediately guarantees that R well-orders T.

These types may still appear a little mysterious but some simple examples should dispel the mystery. Two obvious ones are the following:

$\Xi[N, R]$ where $R = \{(x, y) \in N \otimes N : (y < x)\}$ \hfill (*a*)

$\Xi[\text{List}[N], R]$ where $R = \{(x, y) \in \text{List}[N] \otimes \text{List}[N] : (\text{len } y) < (\text{len } x)\}$

\hfill (*b*)

Example (*a*) encodes *complete numerical induction* and (*b*) induction on the length of lists. Since these are well-orderings on N and $\text{List}[N]$ respectively, we can immediately deduce that $\Xi[N, R] \equiv N$ and $\Xi[\text{List}[N], R] \equiv \text{List}[N]$.

To provide some further insight into these types we supply an extensional characterization: if the base types and the generating relations are equivalent then so are the corresponding well-founded inductive types.

Theorem 9.6

$$R \subseteq R' \quad \to \quad \Xi[T, R'] \subseteq \Xi[T, R] \qquad (a)$$

$$T \subseteq S \quad \to \quad \Xi[T, R] \subseteq \Xi[S, R] \qquad (b)$$

PROOF For (a) we employ $\Xi[T, R']$ induction. Assume the $x \in T$ and $\forall y((x, y) \in R' \to y \in \Xi[T, R])$. By assumption, $R \subseteq R'$ and so we have $\forall y((x, y) \in R \to y \in \Xi[T, R])$. By closure for $\Xi[T, R]$, we have $x \in \Xi[T, R]$. The result now follows by $\Xi[T, R']$ induction. For (b) we employ induction for $\Xi[T, R]$ with the induction formula set to $x \in \Xi[S, R]$.

9.2.2 Recursion and WFTs

As we shall see later, there is a form of recursion that *corresponds* to well-founded induction. By this we mean that proofs involving well-founded induction give rise to recursive programs of a particular style. At this point we cannot be very specific about the connection but we can at least state the general form of the recursions.

$(*).\ fx = Fx(\lambda y. fy)$

The existence of such functions is justified by the fixpoint theorem:

$$YG = G(YG)$$

where in these instances $G = \lambda f x . F x(\lambda y . f y)$. One obvious example is supplied by the following type and function:

$T = N \otimes N$

$R = \{(x, y) : x \in N \otimes N \land y \in N \otimes N \land y \ll x\}$

where $\ll$ is the lexicographic ordering

Ackermann function:

$A(x, y) = Fxy(\lambda(u, v). A(u, v))$

   where

   $F0yg\ = y'$

   $Fx'0g\ = g(x, 1)$

   $Fx'y'g = g(x, g(x', y))$

Although this represents the general form of the recursions that *correspond* to well-founded inductions, it does not tell us very much—at least it does not unless we know a little more about the nature of the function F. In particular, what type must it have for f to be a function from $\Xi[T, R]$ to $\Xi[T, R]$?

One obvious answer is $\Xi[T, R] \Rightarrow ((\Xi[T, R] \Rightarrow \Xi[T, R]) \Rightarrow \Xi[T, R])$, but we can actually squeeze a little more information from the well-founded induction axiom which also provides employment for dependent types. Given that we require f to be of type $\Xi[T, R] \Rightarrow \Xi[T, R]$ (i.e. a total function), can we characterize the type of F in a more subtle way in terms of the types $T, R, \Xi[T, R]$?

Theorem 9.7 Let $I = \Xi[T, R]$ and $F \in (\pi x \in T)B[x]$ where $P[x] = \{y:(x, y) \in R\}$ and $B[x] = (P[x] \Rightarrow I) \Rightarrow I$. Then $f \in I \Rightarrow I$, where f is given by $fx = Fx(\lambda y . fy)$.

PROOF We employ $\Xi[T, R]$ induction with the induction formula set to $fx \in I \wedge (fx)\downarrow$. Assume that $x \in T \wedge \forall y((x, y) \in R \rightarrow fy \in I)$ [i.e. $\forall y((x, y) \in R \rightarrow (\lambda y . fy)y \in I)$]. By assumption, $\forall z \in T(Fz \in B[z])$. Therefore, in particular, $Fx \in B[x]$. Hence, $\forall g(\forall y((x, y) \in R \rightarrow gy \in I) \rightarrow ((Fx)g\downarrow \wedge (Fx)g \in I))$. It follows that $(Fx(\lambda y . fy))\downarrow$ and $Fx(\lambda y . fy) \in I$, as required.

We shall not explore matters further at this stage since it is pointless to do so without the exact nature of the correspondence between proofs and programs in place. We have only broached the topic in order to induce the reader to think a little about the *correspondence* between well-founded induction and recursion.

This type constructor is more flexible than its structural cousin since the type can be tailored to fit the application at hand. Moreover, these types are not only mathematically more interesting than the structural variety but also more elegant and succinct in their presentation.

9.3 STRUCTURAL INDUCTIVE TYPES AS WELL-FOUNDED TYPES

With the main definitions in place there are several obvious questions that need to be addressed. The first concerns their relation to the structural types. WFTs are more general in that they appeal to a generating relation as opposed to a simple pattern-directed closure condition. More exactly, any structural type can be introduced as a well-founded type in the following sense.

Theorem 9.8 For each structural inductive type there is a well-founded inductive type which is extensionally equivalent to it and the induction principles are interderivable.

PROOF For ease of exposition we simplify things a little. The following technique also applies to the most general case. Consider the SIT I, with parameter K, given by the closure and induction conditions:

$$\forall u \in K\{(du) \in I\} \wedge \forall x \in I \forall y \in I\{(cxy) \in I\}$$

$$[\forall u \in K(\phi[du]) \wedge \forall x \in I \forall y \in I(\phi[x] \wedge \phi[y] \rightarrow \phi[cxy])]$$

$$\rightarrow \forall x \in I(\phi[x])$$

There are two constructors, d and c. To set up an equivalent well-founded type we define the base type and the generating relation:

$$T = \{z : \exists u \in K(z = du) \vee \exists x \exists y(z = cxy)\}$$

$$R = \{(x, y) : \exists v(x = cvy \vee x = cyv)\}$$

We first consider the extensional equivalence. Claim first that $I \subseteq \Xi[T, R]$. This is established by I induction with the induction formula set to $x \in \Xi[T, R]$. We consider the two induction conditions. Observe that no y satisfies $(du, y) \in R$. This follows since the constructors are taken to be distinct. Hence, by $\Xi[T, R]$ closure, $du \in \Xi[T, R]$. This takes care of the base case. For the second condition, assume that $x \in I$ and $y \in I$ and $x \in \Xi[T, R]$ and $y \in \Xi[T, R]$. Claim that $\forall v[(cxy, v) \in R \rightarrow v \in \Xi[T, R]]$. If $(cxy, v) \in R$ then, for some u, $cxy = cuv$ or $cxy = cvu$. Hence, either $v = y$ or $v = x$. In either case we have $v \in \Xi[T, R]$—hence, the claim. By closure for $\Xi[T, R]$, we have $cxy \in \Xi[T, R]$. The result now follows by I induction. Next claim that $\Xi[T, R] \subseteq I$. Here we employ $\Xi[T, R]$ induction with the induction formula set to $x \in I$. We have to establish that $\forall x \in T\{\forall y[(x, y) \in R \rightarrow y \in I] \rightarrow x \in I\}$. Let $x \in T$. If $x = du$, for some u in K, then by I closure, $x \in I$. Suppose that $x = cuv$ for some u and v. By definition of R, we have, immediately, $(x, u) \in R$ and $(x, v) \in R$. Assume that $\forall y[(x, y) \in R \rightarrow y \in I]$. Consequently, $u \in I$ and $v \in I$. By I closure, $x \in I$. Hence we obtain the first part. Next we establish that the induction axioms are interderivable. The proof is similar but for completeness we provide the details. First assume I induction. We derive $\Xi[T, R]$ induction. Assume that $\forall x \in T\{\forall y[(x, y) \in R \rightarrow \phi[y]] \rightarrow \phi[x]\}$. We need to show that $\forall x \in \Xi[T, R]\{\phi[x]\}$. By extensional equivalence of the two types it is sufficient to show that $\forall x \in I\{\phi[x]\}$. This is achieved by I induction. Observe that no y satisfies $(du, y) \in R$. Hence, $\phi[du]$. For the I induction step assume that $x \in I$ and $y \in I$ and $\phi[x]$ and $\phi[y]$. Claim that $\forall v[(cxy, v) \in R \rightarrow \phi[v]]$. If $(cxy, v) \in R$ then, for some u, $cxy = cuv$ or $cxy = cvu$. Hence, either $v = y$ or $v = x$. In either case, $\phi[v]$—hence, the claim. By $\forall x \in T\{\forall y[(x, y) \in R \rightarrow \phi[y]] \rightarrow \phi[x]\}$, we can conclude that $\phi[cxy]$. The result now follows by I induction. Next assume $\Xi[T, R]$ induction. Assume that $\forall u \in K\{\phi[du]\} \wedge \forall x \in I \forall y \in I\{\phi[x] \wedge \phi[y] \rightarrow \phi[cxy]\}$. We first establish that $\forall x \in T$

$\{\forall y[(x, y) \in R \rightarrow \phi[y] \wedge y \in I] \rightarrow \phi[x] \wedge x \in I\}$. Let $x \in T$. If $x = du$ for some $u \in K$, then we are done. Otherwise we must have that $x = cuv$ for some u and v. By definition of R we have that $(x, u) \in R$ and $(x, v) \in R$. Assume that $\forall y[(x, y) \in R \rightarrow \phi[y] \wedge y \in I]$. Consequently, $\phi[u] \wedge u \in I$ and $\phi[v] \wedge v \in I$. By $\forall x \in I \forall y \in I\{\phi[x] \wedge \phi[y] \rightarrow \phi[cxy]\}$ and I closure, $\phi[x] \wedge x \in I$. Hence, $\forall x \in \Xi[T, R](\phi[x] \wedge x \in I)$. In particular, $\forall x \in \Xi[T, R](\phi[x])$ and so, by extensional equivalence, $\forall x \in I(\phi[x])$.

In particular, natural numbers and lists can be represented as well-founded types. The following representations arise naturally from the theorem:

(*a*) Natural numbers:

$$T = \{x: x = 0 \vee \exists y(x = y')\}$$
$$R = \{(x, y): x = y'\}$$

(*b*) List[S]:

$$T = \{x: x = [\ ] \vee \exists z \in S \exists y(x = z:y)\}$$
$$R = \{(x, y): \exists z \in S(x = z:y)\}$$

In conclusion, we have established that the structural inductive types are embraced by the well-founded ones. However, this should not be taken as a licence to abandon the former. Even though we can obtain SITs from WFTs the above representation is not always convenient for program development. The structural inductive types occupy such a special place in computing science that they deserve independent status.

9.4 SIMULTANEOUS WELL-FOUNDED TYPES

Our scheme of well-founded induction seems only to cater for the definition of a single type. However, this is an illusion. In this section we show that the scheme is more general than it might appear and, in particular, sanctions *simultaneous* type definitions.

9.4.1 The General Form of Simultaneous Types

One common application for such types arises when we are required to prove properties by induction on the structure of a language. For example, we might be required to prove that every term in the following programming language has some property:

$$C ::= \text{dummy} \mid \text{if } E \text{ then } C \mid \text{resultis } E$$

$$E ::= \text{true} \mid \text{false} \mid \text{valof } C$$

For pedagogical reasons we have kept matters simple. There are only two syntactic categories: commands (C) and expressions (E). That this is a pretty silly language is not important; nor are the meanings of the constructs. We are only concerned with the fact that the language consists of two syntactic categories that are mutually recursive. Our goal is the formulation of a general scheme that enables these mutually recursive categories to be defined as types, and this simple example is sufficiently complex to motivate matters.

Let S and T be the base types and A and B the generating relations. Consider the following axioms of closure and induction:

$$\forall x \in T \, \forall y \in S \{ \forall u \forall v [(x, u, v) \in A \to (u \in I \land v \in J)] \land \forall u \forall v [(y, u, v) \in B$$

$$\to (u \in I \land v \in J)] \quad \to \quad (x \in I \land y \in J) \}$$

$$\forall x \in T \, \forall y \in S \{ \forall u \forall v [(x, u, v) \in A \to (\phi[u] \land \psi[v])] \land \forall u \forall v [(y, u, v) \in B$$

$$\to (\phi[u] \land \psi[v])] \quad \to \quad (\phi[x] \land \psi[y]) \}$$

$$\to \forall x \in I \forall y \in J \{ \phi[x] \land \psi[y] \}$$

The axioms simultaneously define two inductive types I and J together with a principle of induction which enables the proof of properties by simultaneous induction.

In our example, the recursion of the language naturally generates two relations:

$$A = \{(x, u, v): x = \text{'dummy'} \lor x = \text{'if } v \text{ then } u\text{'} \lor x = \text{'resultis } v\text{'}\}$$

$$B = \{(x, u, v): x = \text{'true'} \lor x = \text{'false'} \lor x = \text{'valof } u\text{'}\}$$

The required types I and J are generated as the well-founded parts of these relations. More precisely, if we set S and T to be the type of symbolic atoms, then A and B generate two types I and J that correspond to the categories C and E. On the face of it, these principles take us beyond the simple scheme elaborated in the previous section. However, appearances can be deceptive.

9.4.2 Simultaneous Types Are Well Founded

In order to prove that such types can be defined using the general scheme of well-founded induction we need to define a base type and a generating relation. These take the following form:

$$C = T \otimes S$$

$$Q = \{(x, y): y \in \text{PAIR} \land ((\text{l}x, \text{l}y, \text{r}y) \in A \lor (\text{r}x, \text{l}y, \text{r}y) \in B)\}$$

The type $\Xi[C, Q]$ defines the simultaneous types in the following sense.

Theorem 9.9

(a) $\Xi[C, Q] \equiv I \otimes J$
(b) The induction principles are interderivable.

PROOF Write $\Xi[C, Q]$ as K. We first prove $I \otimes J \subseteq K$. We employ simultaneous induction with the following induction formulae:

$$\phi[z] = z \in T \wedge \forall y((z, ly, ry) \in A \rightarrow (ly, ry) \in K)$$

$$\psi[z] = z \in S \wedge \forall y((z, ly, ry) \in B \rightarrow (ly, ry) \in K)$$

Assume $x \in T$ and $y \in S$. Further assume that $\forall u \forall v((x, u, v) \in A \rightarrow \phi[u] \wedge \psi[v])$ and $\forall u \forall v((y, u, v) \in B \rightarrow \phi[u] \wedge \psi[v])$. If $(x, lu, ru) \in A$, then $\phi[lu] \wedge \psi[ru]$. By the definitions of ϕ and ψ, $lu \in T$ and $ru \in S$ and, moreover, $\forall z((lu, lz, rz) \in A \vee (ru, lz, rz) \in B \rightarrow (lz, rz) \in K)$. Suppose that $((lu, ru), z) \in Q$. Then it follows that $(lz, rz) \in K$. Since $z \in PAIR$, $z \in K$. By K closure, $(lu, ru) \in K$. Hence, $\forall u((x, lu, ru) \in A \rightarrow (lu, ru) \in K)$, i.e. $\phi[x]$. Similarly, $\forall u((y, lu, ru) \in B \rightarrow (lu, ru) \in K)$, i.e. $\psi[y]$. By I, J induction, $\forall x \in I \forall y \in J(\phi[x] \wedge \psi[y])$. Hence, $\forall x \in I \otimes J(\phi[lx] \wedge \psi[rx])$. By K closure, $\forall x \in I \otimes J(x \in K)$. This completes the proof of the first inclusion. To prove $\Xi[T, S] \subseteq I \otimes J$ we employ K induction with the formula set to $x \in I \otimes J$. Assume, $x \in T \otimes S$ and $\forall y((x, y) \in Q \rightarrow y \in I \otimes J)$. Then, by definition of Q, $\forall u \forall v((lx, u, v) \in A \vee (rx, u, v) \in B) \rightarrow u \in I \wedge v \in J)$. By the simultaneous closure axiom, $lx \in I \wedge rx \in J$. Hence $x \in I \otimes J$. This completes the proof of extensional equivalence. For the induction principles we proceed in a similar manner. For completeness we provide the details. To prove that simultaneous induction implies K induction, assume $(*)$: $\forall x \in T \otimes S\{\forall u[(x, u) \in Q \rightarrow \Phi[u]] \rightarrow \Phi[x]\}$. We employ simultaneous induction with the induction formulae set to the following:

$$\phi[z] = z \in T \wedge \forall y((z, ly, ry) \in A \rightarrow \Phi[(ly, ry)])$$

$$\psi[z] = z \in S \wedge \forall y((z, ly, ry) \in B \rightarrow \Phi[(ly, ry)])$$

Assume $x \in T$ and $y \in S$. Assume $\forall u \forall v[(x, u, v) \in A \rightarrow \phi[u] \wedge \psi[v]]$ and $\forall u \forall v[(y, u, v) \in B \rightarrow \phi[u] \wedge \psi[v]]$. If $(x, lu, ru) \in A$, then $\phi[lu] \wedge \psi[ru]$. By definition of ϕ and ψ, $(lu, ru) \in T \otimes S$ and, furthermore, $\forall z((lu, lz, rz) \in A \vee (ru, lz, rz) \in B \rightarrow \Phi[(lz, rz)])$. By $(*)$, $\Phi[(lu, ru)]$. Hence, $\forall u((x, lu, ru) \in A \rightarrow \Phi[(lu, ru)])$, i.e. $\phi[x]$. Similarly, $\psi[y]$. By I, J induction, $\forall x \in I \forall y \in J(\phi[x] \wedge \psi[y])$. We need to conclude that $\forall x \in K(\Phi[x])$. Since $K \equiv I \otimes J$ and, by $(*)$, $\phi[lx] \wedge \psi[rx]$ implies $\Phi[x]$, it is sufficient to show $\forall x \in I \otimes J\{\phi[lx] \wedge \psi[rx]\}$, which has been achieved. The derivation of I, J induction from K induction is also similar to the closure case: use K induction with the formula set to $\Phi[x] = (\Phi[lx] \wedge \psi[rx])$.

In other words, we can obtain such simultaneous types by *projecting out* from a simple well-founded type: I is extensionally equal to $\{x:\exists z\in\Xi[C,Q]$ $(x=lz)\}$ and J is extensionally equal to $\{x:\exists z\in\Xi[C,Q](x=rz)\}$. In conclusion, the scheme of well-founded inductive types is closed under simultaneous inductive definitions.

9.5 TYPE EQUATIONS AND MONOTONE INDUCTION

Like their structural counterparts, well-founded inductive types can also be characterized in terms of type equations. More exactly, they can be portrayed as the solution to equations induced by a certain subclass of *monotone* type constructors. Indeed, this way of viewing matters leads naturally to the class of types defined generally by *monotone operators*. We shall get to this shortly, but we first concentrate on the WFTs.

9.5.1 The Type Equations for Well-founded Induction

To set things up we must first define the comprehension types which are induced by the general form of such types. For the types S, T and R let $\Psi(S)$ be the type $\{x\in T:\forall y[(x,y)\in R\to y\in S]\}$. Now consider the following conditions on a type I. Notice that (b) is an axiom scheme, induced by type expressions.

$$\Psi(I)\subseteq I \tag{a}$$

$$\Psi(S)\subseteq S \quad\to\quad I\subseteq S \tag{b}$$

Theorem 9.10 A type I satisfies schemes (a) and (b) iff it satisfies $\Xi[T,R]$ induction and closure, i.e.

$$\forall x\in T\{\forall y[(x,y)\in R\to y\in I]\to x\in I\}$$

$$\forall x\in T\{\forall y[(x,y)\in R\to\phi[y]]\to\phi[x]\}\to\forall x\in I\{\phi[x]\}$$

PROOF Scheme (a) is just a reformulation of closure. Scheme (b) follows from induction: we set the induction formula to $x\in S$. For the converse, the premise of induction yields $\Psi(\{y:\phi[y]\})\subseteq\{y:\phi[y]\}$. Scheme (b) yields the conclusion.

We can say a little more about these comprehension types and this will pave the way for the generalization. The type constructors induced by well-founded induction are *monotone* in the sense of the following scheme. The proof is trivial and follows directly from the definition of Ψ.

$$\text{MON. } S\subseteq T \quad\to\quad \Psi(S)\subseteq\Psi(T)$$

As a direct consequence of this result, and Theorem 9.10, we can conclude that $\Xi[T, R] \subseteq \Psi(\Xi[T, R])$: use scheme (a), MON, followed by scheme (b). Hence, we have $\Psi(\Xi[T, R]) \equiv \Xi[T, R]$. Consequently, well-founded types satisfy a *monotone type equation*.

9.5.2 Monotone Inductive Types

To complete this chapter on well-founded types we briefly consider a generalization of the scheme. We shall not employ it in the sequel but it does lead to a direct comparison with the *recursive types* of *domain theory* and so is worthy of a little attention.

In order to generalize the WFTs we first generalize our informal notion of a *type constructor*. For each well-formed formula $\psi[S, x]$, let $\Psi(S)$ be the type $\{x : \psi[S, x]\}$. Assume that Ψ is monotone, i.e. MON is satisfied. Under the government of MON, the scheme of *monotone inductive types* guarantees the existence of a new type K, which satisfies the following closure and induction principles:

CLO. $\Psi(K) \subseteq K$

IND. $\Psi(S) \subseteq S \rightarrow K \subseteq S$

As a consequence of these three conditions, K is the smallest type, in the sense of the subtype ordering, that satisfies the following.

EE. $\Psi(K) \equiv K$

However, not all such comprehension-induced constructors are monotone. The following is an obvious counterexample:

$$\Psi(S) = \{f : \forall x(x \in S \rightarrow fx \in S)\}$$

Indeed, this notion is not of much use unless we know which wffs induce monotone operators. Obviously all the WFTs do. However, we can go further; the following provides a sufficient condition.

Definition 9.2 The type expression S occurs *only positively* in $\phi[S, x]$ iff:

(a) ϕ is atomic
(b) ϕ is $\eta \wedge \delta, \eta \vee \delta, \exists y\eta$ or $\forall y\eta$ and S occurs only positively in η and δ
(c) ϕ is $\eta \rightarrow \delta$ and S occurs only positively in δ and not at all in η

Theorem 9.11 If S occurs only positively in $\psi[S, x]$ then the induced type constructor Ψ is monotone.

PROOF By induction on ψ. For example, if ψ is a conjunction, $\eta \wedge \delta$, then assume that $S \subseteq T$. Then we have the following inclusions: $\{x : (\eta \wedge \delta)[S, x]\} \equiv \{x : \eta[S, x]\} \cap \{x : \delta[S, x]\} \subseteq \{x : \eta[T, x]\} \cap \{x : \delta[T, x]\}$, where the last step is justified by the induction hypothesis.

For the implication case, $\{x{:}\eta \to \delta[S,x]\} \subseteq \{x{:}\eta \to \delta[T,x]\}$ is fairly automatic.

An interesting example is a type that is equivalent to the total function space from the natural numbers to the type:

$$\Psi(K) \equiv \{f{:}\forall x(x \in \mathbf{N} \quad \to \quad (fx){\downarrow} \wedge (fx) \in K)\}$$

$$\equiv \mathbf{N} \Rightarrow K$$

From the scheme of positive induction we obtain the following closure and induction principles:

CLO. $(\mathbf{N} \Rightarrow K) \subseteq K$
IND. $(\mathbf{N} \Rightarrow S) \subseteq S \quad \to \quad K \subseteq S$
EE. $K \equiv \mathbf{N} \Rightarrow K$

The second provides a way of proving properties of the elements by a scheme of induction: to show that every element of the type has a property $\phi[x]$ we need only show that $[f \in T \wedge \forall x\{x \in \mathbf{N} \quad \to \quad (fx){\downarrow} \wedge \phi[fx]\}] \to \phi[f]$.

Can we push things any further? In particular, can we drop the monotonicity constraint? One motivation for this might stem from the desire to admit type constructors like the following:

$$\Psi(S) = \{f{:}\forall x(x \in S \quad \to \quad (fx){\downarrow} \wedge (fx) \in S)\}$$

$$= S \Rightarrow S$$

Under the government of EE we obtain a type that satisfies the following type equation:

$$K \equiv K \Rightarrow K$$

K is a type that is equivalent to its own total function space. However, there is a problem at the outset. If we drop MON then EE does not follow from CLO and IND. If we wish to admit such types the obvious solution is to adopt EE itself as the axiom scheme: for any induced type constructor Ψ, there is a new type K that satisfies EE.

As a consequence we obtain something like the *recursive types* familiar from *domain theory*. However, the analogy is nowhere near exact. For one thing, *domains* are traditionally built by only employing the type constructors of disjoint union, Cartesian product, function spaces and the recursive type constructor itself. Domains are quite different in nature to the types of the present theory and it would be wrong to push the analogy too far. Indeed, this brings us to the main point of the section: in the present theory one cannot adopt EE as the basic scheme of recursive types for in the presence of comprehension the effect is disastrous.

Theorem 9.12 EE + COMP (indeed negative comprehension) is inconsistent.

PROOF With EE and COMP we can define the following type:

$$\text{Russ} \equiv \{x: \sim(x \in \text{Russ})\}$$

This leads immediately to a contradiction: $x \in \text{Russ} \leftrightarrow \sim(x \in \text{Russ})$.

In fact we obtain a version of the infamous Russell type or class. We are therefore stuck with monotone inductive types. Fortunately, in practice this is not a major restriction. Indeed, we shall only employ at most well-founded induction in all applications.

EXERCISES

9.1 Prove the following:

(a) N is well ordered by $\{(x, y) \in \text{N} \otimes \text{N}: x = y'\}$.

(b) List$[T]$ is well ordered by $\{(x, y) \in \text{List}[T] \otimes \text{List}[T]: \exists z \in T(x = z: y)\}$.

Is List$[\text{N}]$ well ordered by the sublist ordering (see Theorem 8.2)?

9.2 Prove that a relation R on a type T is *well founded* iff there is no function $f \in \text{N} \Rightarrow T$ such that $\forall i \in \text{N}((fi, f(i + 1)) \in R)$. Is this intuitionistically provable, i.e. do you need to employ classical reasoning?

9.3 Let T be a type and R a well-ordering of T. Prove that the lexicographic ordering induced by R well-orders $T \otimes T$.

9.4 Use complete numerical induction to establish the type of fibonacci:

$$\text{fib } 0 = 0$$

$$\text{fib } 1 = 1$$

$$\text{fib } (x + 2) = \text{fib } x + \text{fib}(x + 1)$$

9.5 Set up general trees as a WFT (see Theorem 8.5).

9.6 Under what circumstances can the comprehension types introduced in the proof of Theorem 9.9 by replaced by negative comprehensions? Carry out a similar analysis for the derivation of structural types from WFTs.

REFERENCES AND FURTHER READING

Feferman (1979) is the source of well-founded induction. Monotone induction is investigated at length in Moschovakis (1974). Paulson (1986) discusses well-founded induction in relation to Martin-Löf's type theory. A good project would be to investigate the development of his paper within the confines of the present setup.

10
POLYMORPHISM AND ABSTRACT DATA TYPES

We are almost at the end of our extended excursion into the various notions of type. Our two final concepts have played a dominating role in contemporary computing science. No theory of types for functional languages would be complete without some mechanism for the articulation of *polymorphism* and *data abstraction*.

Modern functional languages allow functions to be defined *polymorphically*. Functions are not restricted to specific types but may live in many different types. Indeed, we have already seen many instances of polymorphic functions: the identity function is a member of every general function space and the append function is a member of $\text{List}[T] \Rightarrow \text{List}[T] \Rightarrow \text{List}[T]$, for every type T. This form of polymorphism demands that the function is in every type of the *appropriate form*. This is essentially the Miranda™ style of polymorphism and is often referred to as *implicit* or *universal* polymorphism. One aim of this chapter is to extend the theory so that such functions can be assigned types that reflect their polymorphic nature.

We shall also enrich the theory by the addition of *abstract data types* (and more generally *existential* types). Abstract types are to be seen in opposition to structured types. In the latter the elements are composite objects built from the constructors whereas abstract types are characterized not in terms of the elements but in terms of the fundamental operations of the type.

The plan of this chapter is as follows. In the early sections we study *universal* and *existential types*. We then consider a different notion of abstract data type which is inspired by the notion of a *universal algebra*. This will lead to an alternative version of the whole theory which is *predicative*. This desire arises since, in the form we present them, these new notions of type take us beyond a strictly predicative theory. Finally, we shall study the polymorphism of the *second-order lambda calculus*. Logically, data abstraction and polymorphism are dual notions. The latter is articulated in terms of universal type quantification and the former in terms of existential type quantification. Indeed, this characterization determines our first topic.

10.1 TYPE QUANTIFICATION

Polymorphic and abstract types are unlike any of the other types considered in one major respect: the axioms for these types, unlike their predecessors, force an enrichment of the underlying logic. For example, in the case of polymorphism, we need to express the idea that a term has *all* the types of a particular form. Within the present theory we cannot articulate such a notion; we can only do so in the metatheory.

10.1.1 An Extension to the Language

Consequently, our first task must be to extend the language of the theory. There are two aspects to this: we have to increase our stock of type expressions to allow type variables (we employ X, Y, Z to denote type variables) and at the same time upgrade the language of wff by the addition of type quantification:

$$T ::= X \mid B \mid \{x : \phi'\} \mid \Xi[T, S] \mid \text{SI}[\mathbf{T}, \mathbf{C}]$$

$$\phi ::= \alpha \mid (\phi \wedge \psi) \mid (\phi \vee \psi) \mid (\phi \rightarrow \psi) \mid (\forall x \phi) \mid (\exists x \phi) \mid (\forall X \phi) \mid (\exists X \phi)$$

Notice that comprehension types are slightly modified. In the type expression $\{x : \phi'\}$, the wff ϕ' must be *first order* (i.e. it must not admit bound type variables). Thus, for example, $\{x : \exists X(x \in X)\}$ is not permitted. We shall consider the full second-order scheme later. Furthermore, for the moment, the induction axioms for WFTs and for structural types will also be restricted to first-order wff (i.e. the induction formula must be first order).

The inclusion of type variables means that both wff and type expressions may contain them. The notions of freedom and bondage apply to type variables exactly as with individual variables. Furthermore, the substitution of a type expression for a type variable parallels that for individual substitution: we shall write $\phi[S/X]$ and $T[S/X]$ for the result of replacing the type expression S for X in ϕ and for X in T respectively. This deals with the syntax and brings us to the logic of type quantification.

10.1.2 The Proof Rules for Type Quantification

The proof rules for type quantification parallel those for individual quantification. For the universal quantifier they take the following form:

Introduction   Elimination

$$\frac{\phi}{\forall X \phi} \qquad\qquad \frac{\forall X \phi}{\phi[T/X]}$$

The normal side conditions on the introduction rule apply: the proof of ϕ has to be such that the variable X does not occur free in any undischarged assumption on which ϕ depends. In the elimination rule, T must be *free for* X in ϕ, i.e. no free variable (individual or type) of T must become bound in the substitution. Notice that variables can be bound not only by individual quantification and comprehension types but now also by type quantification. In addition, as we shall see, the polymorphic and abstract types bind type variables.

The existential rules also parallel the individual case:

Introduction   Elimination

In the existential introduction rule T must be free for X in ϕ and in the elimination rule the constant X must not be free in ψ or in any assumption, other than ϕ, on which the upper occurrence of ψ depends. These rules function in exactly the same way as the simple quantifier rules and the reader should have little difficulty with them. They will be employed mainly in connection with polymorphism and its dual and we shall illustrate their use with reference to these constructors.

10.2 UNIVERSAL TYPES: POLYMORPHISM

There are two main varieties of polymorphism: *implicit* and *explicit*. The explicit variety will be briefly discussed, but we shall deal mainly with the former which naturally arises in connection with the untyped lambda calculus. We discuss the concept according to which the same function can possess many different types provided that they are of the appropriate form. This is known as *universal* or *implicit* polymorphism. This is to be distinguished from the *explicit* variety where the terms themselves contain type information. However, before we discuss the implicit genre in detail we need to say a little more about these two options and their relationship to the alternative *monomorphic* theories.

10.2.1 Monomorphic and Polymorphic Type Systems

Programming languages like Pascal are *strongly typed*. For example, there is no general identity function. Such a function has to be introduced for all types. Type systems where functions have only a single type are called *monomorphic* and in such regimes, even though the form of a function may be the same for a whole collection of types, the system demands that separate functions be declared. For example, consider the function len which returns the length of a list. In a monomorphic system a separate function would have to be declared for every base type and, furthermore, the type of the function would have to be included as part of the declaration.

$$len \in List[N] \Rightarrow N$$

$$len [\ ] = 0$$

$$len\ a{:}x = (len\ x) + 1$$

$$len' \in List[Bool] \Rightarrow N$$

$$len' [\ ] = 0$$

$$len'\ a{:}x = (len'\ x) + 1$$

This is very restrictive since the programmer is not able to take advantage of the identical *form* of the various instances; formally they are different functions. This is really a left-over from the classical view of functions where they come equipped with a predetermined domain and range.

In contrast, with explicit polymorphism there is no necessity to duplicate the definition. Roughly, the definition would take the following form:

$$len \in Polymorphic\ X.(List[X] \Rightarrow N)$$

$$len\ X[\ ] = 0$$

$$len\ X(a{:}x) = (len\ Xx) + 1$$

Here the duplication is avoided by permitting the function to take a type as an argument and return the corresponding monomorphic instance. One can think of the function definition as a monomorphic scheme. In this regime programs contain type information but it is *loose*: functions can possess a whole variety of types.

This is a halfway house between monomorphism and implicit polymorphism. The latter is even less demanding since the actual function definition need contain no explicit type information. For example, the function len takes its familiar form:

$$\text{len} [\ ] = 0$$

$$\text{len } a{:}x = (\text{len } x) + 1$$

Implicit polymorphism removes a lot of the notational clutter present in the other schemes. In some systems, a type for a function can be deduced by the compiler, where part of the compiler is a type checker which attempts to infer the types of programs from their context. This form of type checking has found its way into many modern functional languages. It should be said, however, that this approach has its limitations since the possibility for such compile-time type checking is dependent upon the richness of the theory of types. In the constructive paradigm this issue is largely circumvented. Programs will be developed in an *interactive* way where part of the development involves the construction of a proof that the program meets its specification—including its type.

10.2.2 Implicit Polymorphism

The reader should by now have grasped the essence of the idea, but it will do no harm to illustrate matters further. Consider again the append and reverse functions on lists. With type quantification in place we can express the contents of earlier results in a more formal way:

$$\forall X (\text{append} \in \text{List}[X] \Rightarrow \text{List}[X] \Rightarrow \text{List}[X])$$

$$\forall X (\text{reverse} \in \text{List}[X] \Rightarrow \text{List}[X])$$

These functions clearly illustrate the idea of *universal polymorphism*. Such functions have a whole variety of types governed by the *form* of the type expression. However, within the present theory we cannot assign a type to them; the above assertions only guarantee their membership in all the appropriate types.

To take matters further, we require a type that reflects the idea that such functions possess all the types of the correct form. To this end we add a new clause to the syntax of types:

$$T ::= X \,|\, B \,|\, \cdots \,|\, (\Pi X . T)$$

The types of the form $\Pi X . T$ are the intended types of polymorphic functions where the type variable X is bound in type $\Pi X . T$. The axiom for this new type constructor follows the intuitions already alluded to: we require the function to have all instances of the type in question.

PM. $f \in \Pi X . T \leftrightarrow \forall X (f \in T)$

$\Pi X . T$ can be viewed, informally, as the intersection, taken over all types, of all its instances. PM is almost self-explanatory and rather than dwell upon it further we illustrate its content with some examples:

(*a*) $\Pi X . (X \Rightarrow X)$. This is the type of function that is in every general function space. An obvious example is the constant function $\lambda x . x$.

(*b*) $\text{cond} \in \Pi X . (\text{Bool} \Rightarrow X \Rightarrow X \Rightarrow X)$

(*c*) $\text{append} \in \Pi X . (\text{List}[X] \Rightarrow \text{List}[X] \Rightarrow \text{List}[X])$
$\text{reverse} \in \Pi X . (\text{List}[X] \Rightarrow \text{List}[X])$
$\text{map} \in \Pi X . ((X \Rightarrow X) \Rightarrow \text{List}[X] \Rightarrow \text{List}[X])$
$\text{len} \in \Pi X . (\text{List}[X] \Rightarrow N)$

(*d*) $\text{fringe} \in \Pi X . (\text{Se}[X] \Rightarrow \text{List}[X])$
$\text{mirror} \in \Pi X . (\text{Se}[X] \Rightarrow \text{Se}[X])$

Notice that, in all these examples, the Π constructor has the widest scope. If out intended application of the concept went no further than these rudimentary examples there would be little point in the rather elaborate syntax for type expressions which, in particular, allow the operator to be nested and combined with the other constructors. However, it is not difficult to dream up examples that demand the full force of this theory.

(*e*) $1 \in \Pi X . \Pi Y . (X \otimes Y \Rightarrow X)$; $r \in \Pi X . \Pi Y . (X \otimes Y \Rightarrow Y)$;
$p \in \Pi X . \Pi Y . (X \Rightarrow Y \Rightarrow (X \otimes Y))$

(*f*) $\text{Curry} \in [\Pi X . (X \otimes X \Rightarrow X)] \Rightarrow [\Pi X . (X \Rightarrow X \Rightarrow X)]$;
$\text{Uncurry} \in [\Pi X . (X \Rightarrow X \Rightarrow X)] \Rightarrow [\Pi X . (X \otimes X \Rightarrow X)]$

(*g*) $\text{diag} = \lambda f x . f(x, x) \in [\Pi X . (X \otimes X \Rightarrow X)] \Rightarrow [\Pi X . (X \Rightarrow X)]$

In (*e*) the polymorphic constructor is nested and in (*f*) and (*g*) it occurs within the scope of the function space constructor. Indeed, example (*f*) illustrates the advantage of this enriched theory. If we only allowed the polymorphic operator to have wide scope then we could only assign the following type to Curry:

$$\Pi X . [(X \otimes X \Rightarrow X) \Rightarrow (X \Rightarrow X \Rightarrow X)]$$

In the enriched theory this is a subtype of $[\Pi X . (X \otimes X \Rightarrow X)] \Rightarrow [\Pi X . (X \Rightarrow X \Rightarrow X)]$. This illustrates the fact that the inclusion of these type constructors increases the *expressive power* of the theory, i.e. we can assign more general types to functions. Many functional languages do not support such richness and so our theory goes beyond much existing practice. However, it does so in a uniform and natural way and seems to be a move justified by the subsequent increase in expressive power.

Before we proceed any further there is an important conceptual point that needs to be aired. The inclusion of such types enhances the expressive power of the theory since type variables now range over such types. In particular, PM is *impredicative* since it involves quantification over all types including the very type under definition. As a consequence, for f to be a member of $\Pi X . T$, it would have to be a member of $T[\Pi X . T/X]$. There is a *circularity* in the definition which some may find unacceptable. While it is true that in the intuitionistic and constructive literature the full force of impredicative definitions is not used, it is not absolutely clear whether or not certain instances are acceptable. For example, it does not obviously follow from the writings of Brouwer that impredicatively defined sets or types are to be excluded. Moreover, the present approach, even if impredicative is rather straightforward in that the polymorphic types are on the same footing as the others. However, there is a way around the problem which introduces a new layer of types or *kinds*, and we shall explore this option later.

10.3 EXISTENTIAL AND ABSTRACT TYPES

In this section we introduce one notion of an *abstract data type*. However, we shall not tackle the notion head-on. Rather, we let it emerge as a special case of the more general idea of an *existential type*. This is essentially the approach elaborated in Cardelli and Wegner (1986).

10.3.1 Existential Types.

Polymorphic types are universal in the sense that a function is of type $\Pi X . T$ if it is a member of every type instance of T. A dual notion involves the existential quantifier. Intuitively, polymorphic types represent infinite intersections and existential types infinite unions. As usual, we first get the syntax straight:

$$T ::= X \,|\, \cdots \,|\, (\Pi X . T)|(\Sigma X . T)$$

In $\Sigma X . T$ the type variable X is bound. The axiom is predictable, given the above remarks about duality.

$$\text{ADT.} \quad f \in \Sigma X . T \leftrightarrow \exists X (f \in T)$$

For example, $\Sigma X . X \otimes X$ is the type of ordered pairs of objects selected from the same type. Notice that, in the presence of the universal type, this type is equivalent to the type of objects that are pairs selected from the same type, whereas the type $\Sigma X . \Sigma Y . X \otimes Y$ is the type of ordered pairs generally. The type $\Sigma X . X$ is the type of everything that has a type. The type $\Sigma X . X \otimes (X \Rightarrow N)$ is the type of any object together with an integer-valued function on that type. For example, the pair $(7, \text{succ})$ has this type. This type contains a certain amount of information since it forces a relation between the object and the function. For example, $(3, \text{append})$ does not have this type since append has type $\Pi X . [\text{List}[X] \Rightarrow \text{List}[X] \Rightarrow \text{List}[X]]$. Existential types thus have the ability to *hide* information, and this is the crucial property that enables them to capture one notion of an abstract data type.

10.3.2 Concrete and Abstract Types

As a prerequisite to formalization we must clear the way a little by indicating the difference between *concrete* and *abstract* types. *Concrete* types stress the *form* or *structure* of objects. For example, each element of a structural type is uniquely presented as an expression manufactured from the constructors. Concrete types consist of such composite structured objects. In contrast, *abstract data types* are formulated in terms of operations. The elements of an abstract type are considered *abstract* in the sense that the structure of the elements is suppressed. It is the operations themselves that determine the type in that the logical properties of the type are completely determined by the logical relations that exist between them. Such abstract specifications permit a type to be presented and used without reference to any particular implementation. The general idea is best illustrated by reference to some examples. We shall not be too ambitious and choose some rather trite ones.

(a) Lists Let T be some type. The abstract notion of a list of objects of type T is given in two parts. The first specifies the type of the operations. This is the so-called *signature* of the abstract type. Notice that the head and tail functions are forced to be partial since they may be undefined on the empty list.

Signature:

$e \in \text{List}$	generates the empty list
$h \in \text{List} \Longrightarrow T$	the head function
$t \in \text{List} \Longrightarrow \text{List}$	the tail function
$c \in T \Rightarrow \text{List} \Rightarrow \text{List}$	concatenation

In addition, these functions are governed by *laws* which unpack the relationships between them. In the case of lists these are simple and familiar.

Laws:

$$\forall x \in T \forall y \in \text{List}[h(cxy) = x \land t(cxy) = y]$$

This second part of the specification enumerates the *laws* that the functions must obey but it does not, by itself, provide any information about how the functions are to be implemented, and nor indeed does it provide any information about the actual concrete elements of the type. The only information that can be gleaned from the specification is the type or signature of the functions together with their logical relationships.

(b) Queues A second example is provided by the notion of queue. Let T be some type. Then the abstract notion of a queue of objects of type T is given as follows. Notice that we have employed the general function space; the total one would result in a different type specification.

Signature:

$s \in$ Queue

$j \in$ Queue $=> T =>$ Queue

$f \in$ Queue $=> T$

$r \in$ Queue $=>$ Queue

Laws:

$\forall x \in T[\, f(jsx) = x\,]$

$\forall q \in \text{Queue} \forall x \in T \forall y \in T[\, f(j(jqx)y) = f(jqx)\,]$

$\forall x \in T[\, r(jsx) = s\,]$

$\forall q \in \text{Queue} \forall x \in T \forall y \in T[\, r(j(jqx)y) = j(r(jqx))y\,]$

Intuitively, these operations are to be understood as follows. The element s generates an empty queue; j adds a new last member to an existing queue; f selects the front member from a non-empty queue; and r removes the front member. The equations reflect these intuitive demands. Again, they do not inform us how to compute the required functions, but only express the algebraic laws that govern them.

(c) Sets Sets form a third common example. Let T be some type with strongly decidable equality. The signature of the abstract type of sets on T is given as follows:

Signature:

empty $\in$ Set

unit $\in T =>$ Set

union $\in$ Set $=>$ Set $=>$ Set

inter $\in$ Set $=>$ Set $=>$ Set

diff $\in$ Set $=>$ Set $=>$ Set

member $\in T =>$ Set $=>$ Bool

where empty is the empty set; unit turns an element of T into a singleton set; union returns the set whose members consist of those of the component sets; inter is set intersection; and diff is set difference. The Boolean function member tests for membership. The following laws formally unpack these intuitive remarks:

Laws:

$\forall x \in T[(\text{member } x \text{ empty}) = f]$

$\forall x \in T \forall y \in T[(\text{member } x(\text{unit } y)) = \text{Eq}_T xy]$

$\forall x \in T \forall u \in \text{Set} \forall v \in \text{Set}[(\text{member } x(\text{union } uv)) = (\text{member } xu) \text{ or } (\text{member } xv)]$

$\forall x \in T \forall u \in \text{Set} \forall v \in \text{Set}[(\text{member } x(\text{inter } uv)) = (\text{member } xu) \text{ and } (\text{member } xv)]$

$\forall x \in T \forall u \in \text{Set} \forall v \in \text{Set}[(\text{member } x(\text{diff } uv)) = (\text{member } xu)$
and not$(\text{member } xv)]$

 Each of the three examples follows a similar pattern. Each consists of a signature and a set of laws. According to our informal reflections, the abstract type is determined by the operations themselves and not by the specific structure of the elements. More explicitly, an *abstract data type* is not a single tuple of operations but rather a whole collection or family of such tuples, and a particular tuple of operations will be a member of the abstract type if there exists a type (the implementing type) with respect to which the operations satisfy the signature and the laws. In this sense each such tuple of operations constitutes a specific instance of the abstract type.

10.3.3 Abstract Types as Existential Types

Actually, abstract types really arise through the combination of existential and comprehension types. For example, the abstract data type of queues on the type T is given as follows:

$$\Sigma X . \{(s, j, f, r) : s \in X \ \wedge$$

$$j \in X \Rightarrow T \Rightarrow X \ \wedge$$

$$f \in X \Rightarrow T \ \wedge$$

$$r \in X \Rightarrow X \ \wedge$$

$$\forall x \in T[f(jsx) = x] \ \wedge$$

$$\forall q \in X \forall x \in T \forall y \in T[f(j(jqx)y) = f(jqx)] \ \wedge$$

$$\forall x \in T[r(jsx) = s] \ \wedge$$

$$\forall q \in X \forall x \in T \forall y \in T[r(j(jqx)y) = j(r(jqx))y]\}$$

The abstract type is represented as an existential (negative) comprehension type. The axioms for these constructors, applied to this example, yield the intuitive membership conditions for the abstract type of queues. The elements are four tuples (s, j, f, r), for which there exists a type X (the implementation) with respect to which the following hold:

$$s \in X \land$$

$$j \in X \Rightarrow (T \Rightarrow X) \land$$

$$f \in X \Rightarrow T \land$$

$$r \in X \Rightarrow X \land$$

$$\forall x \in T[f(jsx) = x] \land$$

$$\forall q \in X \forall x \in T \forall y \in T[f(j(jqx)y) = f(jqx)] \land$$

$$\forall x \in T[r(jsx) = s] \land$$

$$\forall q \in X \forall x \in T \forall y \in T[r(j(jqx)y) = j(r(jqx))y]$$

For lists, the abstract data type is characterized by the following existential comprehension type:

$$\Sigma X . \{(e, h, t, c) : e \in X \land$$

$$h \in X \Rightarrow\!\!\gg T \land$$

$$t \in X \Rightarrow\!\!\gg X \land$$

$$c \in T \Rightarrow X \Rightarrow X \land$$

$$\forall x \in T \forall y \in X[h(cxy) = x \land t(cxy) = y]\}$$

To reinforce the general idea one more example should suffice. In the case of arrays we have the following:

$$\Sigma X . \{(m, s, l, u) : m \in \text{List}[T] \Rightarrow X \land$$

$$s \in X \Rightarrow N \land$$

$$l \in X \Rightarrow N \Rightarrow T \land$$

$$u \in X \Rightarrow N \Rightarrow T \Rightarrow X \land$$

$$\forall x \in \text{List}[T][s(mx) = len\ x] \land$$

$$\forall x \in X \forall n \in N \forall y \in T[s(uxny) = sx] \land$$

$$\forall x \in \text{List}[T] \forall n \in N[l(mx)n = x!n] \land$$

$$\forall x \in X \forall n \in N \forall m \in N \forall y \in T[(n = m) \to (l(uxny)m = y) \land$$

$$(n \neq m) \to (l(uxny)m = lxm)]\}$$

The elements of the abstract type are four-tuples (m, s, l, u) where, intuitively, the function m forms an array from a list, s returns the size of the array, l is a lookup function, which given an array and a number returns an element at the numbered destination, and u updates the array with a new element at the provided destination. The ! function of type $\text{List}[T] \Rightarrow N \Rightarrow \text{List}[T]$ returns the element of the list at the specified place.

10.3.4 Implementation of Abstract Types

In order to implement an abstract data type, the programmer has to provide the operations and a representation of its values and establish that the operations satisfy the signature and laws. For example, for the abstract type of lists on T, a particular instance or implementation is the four-tuple $([\ ], \text{hd}, \text{tl}, \text{cons})$. To establish that this tuple is in the abstract type of lists on T we have to locate a type with respect to which the signature and laws are obeyed. This is easy; we choose the concrete structural inductive type $\text{List}[T]$.

A more interesting example is afforded by the abstract type of sets on some type T. This type can be implemented via the type $\text{List}[T]$. In particular, the operations of union and member can be implemented as follows:

$$\text{union } ss' = s * s'$$

$$\text{member } x[\ ] = \text{f}$$

$$\text{member } x(y{:}s) = (\text{EQ}_T\, xy) \text{ or } (\text{member } xs)$$

There are of course other representations. For example, we may insist that the lists are to contain no duplicates. In such a case we need to modify the definition of union. Finally, arrays can be implemented as pairs of values: a list and a number that provides the length of the list. We leave the reader to fill in the rest of the details as exercises.

10.4 COMBINING UNIVERSAL AND EXISTENTIAL TYPES

One fruitful application of these notions stems from their combination. One thing to notice about our examples is that we have not parameterized on the base type. For example, in the case of queues we have only captured the abstract notion of a queue on a given type T. However, by employing polymorphism we can capture the more abstract notion.

$$\Pi Y . \Sigma X . \{(s, j, f, r) : s \in X \ \wedge$$

$$j \in X \Rightarrow Y \Rightarrow X \ \wedge$$

$$f \in X \Rightarrow Y \ \wedge$$

$$r \in X \Rightarrow X \ \wedge$$

$$\forall x \in Y[f(jsx) = x] \ \wedge$$

$$\forall q \in X \forall x \in Y \forall y \in Y[f(j(jqx)y) = f(jqx)] \ \wedge$$

$$\forall x \in Y[r(jsx) = s] \ \wedge$$

$$\forall q \in X \forall x \in T \forall y \in T[r(j(jqx)y) = j(r(jqx))y]\}$$

Elements of this type are four-tuples (s, j, f, r) such that, for every type Y, there exists a type X (the type of queues on Y) with respect to which (s, j, f, r) satisfies the signature and laws. Notice that the parameter type Y is universally quantified, indicating that it represents a *generic* type, whereas the parameter X is existentially quantified, indicating that it represents a hidden abstract data type. This has more right to be called the *abstract type of queues*.

Similarly, we can form the polymorphic abstract data type of lists. Once again the base type is universal but the parameter X represents the abstract type of lists on the base type.

$$\Pi Y . \Sigma X . \{(e, h, t, c): e \in X \ \wedge$$

$$h \in X \Rightarrow\!\!\!\gg Y \ \wedge$$

$$t \in X \Rightarrow\!\!\!\gg X \ \wedge$$

$$c \in Y \Rightarrow X \Rightarrow X \ \wedge$$

$$\forall x \in Y \forall y \in X [h(cxy) = x \wedge t(cxy) = y]\}$$

The combination of these two notions thus provides a rather powerful conceptual tool for the programmer. It enables a high level of abstraction to be obtained and protects the programmer from the necessity to get involved in much low-level implementation. More examples of such combinations can be found in the survey article of Cardelli and Wegner (1986).

10.5 SECOND-ORDER COMPREHENSION

There is one further extension we can make to the theory. At present comprehension types are restricted to the first-order fragment of the theory. No universal or existential type quantification is permitted in the defining wff. We now examine the consequences of removing this restriction.

The language of types is extended to include comprehension terms for the full language, including type quantifiers:

$$T ::= X | B | \{x : \phi\} | \Xi[T, S] | (\Pi X . T) | (\Sigma X . T)$$

The axiom is a generalization of that for first-order comprehension.

COMP*. $z \in \{x : \phi\} \leftrightarrow \phi[z/x]$

Unlike its first-order look-alike this is a highly impredicative scheme. The occurrence of type quantifiers in the defining wff means that these types, in their actual definitions, implicitly appeal to themselves. However, with impredicativity comes power—sometimes too much—and the theory becomes inconsistent. Fortunately, in this case we just get more power. We have already seen that first-order comprehension subsumes all the type constructors from Chapters 6 and 7. With second-order comprehension we obtain the rest of the theory.

Theorem 10.1 The scheme of second-order comprehension subsumes PM, ADT and well-founded inductive types.

PROOF For polymorphism and data abstraction the definitions are clear:

$$\Pi X . T = \{ f : \forall X (f \in T) \}$$

$$\Sigma X . T = \{ f : \exists X (f \in T) \}$$

For well-founded inductive types we have to do a little more work. First define:

$$\Xi[T, S] = \{ z : \forall Z [\forall x \in T \{ \forall y ((x, y) \in S \to y \in Z) \to x \in Z \} \to z \in Z] \}$$

We have to show that this type satisfies closure and induction. For the induction axiom we instantiate Z as $\{x : \phi\}$, where ϕ is the induction formula. For closure assume $x \in T$ and $\forall y \{(x, y) \in S \to y \in \Xi[T, S]\}$—$(a)$. We need to show that $x \in \Xi[T, S]$. Assume the following: $\forall u \in T \{ \forall v ((u, v) \in S \to v \in Z) \to u \in Z \}$—$(b)$. Let $(x, y) \in S$. By (a), we obtain $\forall Z [\forall u \in T \{ \forall v ((u, v) \in S \to v \in Z) \to u \in Z \} \to y \in Z]$—$(c)$. By (b) and (c), we obtain $y \in Z$. Therefore $\forall y \{(x, y) \in S \to y \in Z\}$. By (b), $x \in Z$, as required.

Hence a theory based on second-order comprehension would render all the other type constructors redundant. Conversely, first-order comprehension plus PM and ADT yield the second-order scheme.

Theorem 10.2 COMP + ADT + PM subsumes COMP∗.

PROOF By induction on ϕ in $\{x : \phi\}$. The only cases in need of attention are $\{x : \forall X \psi\}$ and $\{x : \exists X \psi\}$ and these follow from PM and ADT. For example, $\{x : \forall X \psi\}$ is subsumed by $\Pi X . \{x : \psi\}$.

In other words, once PM and ADT are included we already have the full second-order scheme.

10.6 ABSTRACT DATA TYPES AS VARIETIES OF ALGEBRA

We have opted for the notion of abstract type which is dual to that of universal polymorphism. However, there is a different approach which arises from the view that an *abstract data type* is *variety of algebras*. According to this notion the elements of the abstract type are *algebras* and therefore consist of a type (the *carrier* of the algebra) and the operations.

10.6.1 Types as Terms

Even at the outset, there is a technical problem with implementing this idea. At the moment only terms can be elements of types. We have not allowed types to occur on the left-hand side of membership assertions. At a purely syntactic level this can be easily remedied. We simply extend the syntax of terms to include types. Our syntax for terms then undergoes the following transformation:

$$t ::= x \,|\, c \,|\, (ts) \,|\, (\lambda x . t) \,|\, T$$

As a consequence of this extension, individual quantification now ranges over types as well as the terms of the lambda calculus. Consequently, we have the following ontological principle:

$$\forall X \exists x (X = x)$$

Under this constraint, types can no longer be considered extensionally. There is a variation where only representatives for types occur as terms and then the types can be considered extensionally even though their term *correlates* must be considered intensionally. Feferman's constructive set theory T_0 (Feferman, 1975, 1979) effectively admits types as terms, but does not allow the polymorphic types of the present theory.

10.6.2 Abstract Types as Algebras

With this extension we can state the axiom for this notion of abstract data type. It reflects the above idea that elements of an abstract data type are pairs consisting of a type and its associated operations.

$$\text{ADT}'. \quad f \in \Sigma X . T \leftrightarrow [f \in \text{PAIR} \wedge \exists Y \{(lf = Y) \wedge rf \in T[Y/X]\}]$$

This notion is actually the *infinite disjoint union* of the family $T[X]$ where the indexing is done through the types themselves. In contrast, the original notion corresponds to ordinary union.

There is, however, a slight problem with this way of proceeding: it is inconsistent. Consider the following instance of the above:

$$R = \Sigma X . \{x : \sim ((x, x) \in X)\}$$

According to the axiom we have the following derivation:

$$(R, R) \in R \leftrightarrow$$

$$(R, R) \in \Sigma X . \{x : \sim ((x, x) \in X)\} \leftrightarrow$$

$$(R, R) \in \text{PAIR} \wedge \exists Y \{(R = Y) \wedge R \in \{x : \sim ((x, x) \in Y)\}\} \leftrightarrow$$

$$R \in \{x : \sim ((x, x) \in R)\} \leftrightarrow$$

$$\sim ((R, R) \in R)$$

We have yet another variation on the Russell set or type. Therefore we cannot add such types to the theory—at least not in the presence of comprehension. The problem stems from the combination *types as terms*, comprehension and this present notion of abstract type.

10.7 A PREDICATIVE THEORY

It appears that the approach of the last section is doomed from the outset. There is, however, a solution (of a kind). We have already alluded to the possibility of introducing a new layer of *types*; polymorphic types and abstract data types would then be admitted into this layer but not into the category of types. If we follow this path then the above derivation is blocked. Moreover, the theory is predicative. In this section we briefly explore this alternative approach.

10.7.1 Kinds

To begin with we introduce a new layer of *types* called *kinds*. The syntax of the theory would then take on the following form:

$$t ::= x \,|\, c \,|\, (ts) \,|\, (\lambda x . t) \,|\, T$$

$$T ::= X \,|\, B \,|\, \{x : \phi'\} \,|\, \Xi[T, T']$$

$$K ::= T \,|\, (\Pi X . K) \,|\, (\Sigma X . K)$$

$$\phi ::= \alpha \,|\, (\phi \wedge \psi) \,|\, (\phi \vee \psi) \,|\, (\phi \to \psi) \,|\, (\forall x \phi) \,|\, (\exists x \phi) \,|\, (\forall X \phi) \,|\, (\exists X \phi)$$

$$\alpha ::= (t \in K) \,|\, (t = s) \,|\, (t \downarrow) \,|\, \Omega$$

Comprehension is now restricted to first-order formulae, i.e. no type quantifiers and membership is restricted to types. The axioms are as before with the modification that the polymorphic and abstract types are kinds.

PM. $\quad f \in \Pi X . K \leftrightarrow \forall X (f \in K)$

ADT'. $\quad f \in \Sigma X . K \leftrightarrow [f \in \text{PAIR} \wedge \exists Y \{ (lf = Y) \wedge rf \in K[Y/X] \}]$

This approach at least avoids the specific problem that caused the inconsistency of the last section. Moreover, the theory is now predicative since the type variables do not range over the polymorphic and abstract types—these are now kinds. However, this theory is not as expressive as the original. Consider again the following functions:

$$\text{Curry} =_{\text{def}} \lambda f x y . f(x, y)$$

$$\text{Uncurry} =_{\text{def}} \lambda f z . f(lz)(rz)$$

Previously, Curry had the type $[\Pi X \cdot (X \otimes X \Rightarrow X)] \Rightarrow [\Pi X \cdot (X \Rightarrow X \Rightarrow X)]$ and Uncurry the type $[\Pi X \cdot (X \Rightarrow X \Rightarrow X)] \Rightarrow [\Pi X \cdot (X \otimes X \Rightarrow X)]$. However, these are neither types nor kinds according to the present theory. They are not types since polymorphic *types* are kinds and they are not kinds since the latter class is not closed under function spaces. However, this is easy enough to rectify by extending the kinds to include second-order comprehension kinds (and for completeness inductive kinds):

$$K ::= T \mid \{x{:}\phi\} \mid \Xi[K, K']$$

The explicit inclusion of the polymorphic and abstract data types is no longer necessary since these are now special instances of the second-order comprehension scheme now added as a kind constructor:

$$\Pi X \cdot K ::= \{f{:}\forall X(f \in K)\}$$

$$\Sigma X \cdot K ::= \{f{:}f \in \text{PAIR} \wedge \exists Y\{(1\!f = Y) \wedge (r\!f \in K[Y/X])\}\}$$

Moreover, the new layer of comprehension kinds permits the formation of function space kinds. This extension therefore enables us to deal with functions whose domains and ranges are polymorphic. Kinds now take much the same shape as types. The only omission concerns kind variables and kind quantification. A similar approach has been recently taken by Feferman (1990) in his theory $\text{QL}_1(\lambda)$, where kinds correspond to his G types (general types) and types to his U types (*user-defined* types).

10.7.2 Higher-Order Polymorphism

For all practical purposes this system is probably expressive enough and there is no need to consider higher-order polymorphism and data abstraction. In most applications only the level of kinds is employed and indeed suffices for the formalization of languages like ML and Miranda™. Conceptually, however, it is rather unsatisfactory. For example, we cannot articulate the idea of a polymorphic function on kinds. Intuitively, the identity function has type $K \Rightarrow K$ for all kinds, not just those that are types. To reflect this intuition we are forced into yet another extension which includes the introduction of kind variables and kind quantification. Indeed, even if this is carried out we will run into the same problem at the next level and so on. To cut a long story short, we generalize the whole theory through a *hierarchy of type levels*:

$$t ::= x \mid c \mid (ts) \mid (\lambda x \cdot t) \mid T_n$$

$$T_0 ::= X_0 \mid B \mid \{x{:}\phi_0\} \mid \Xi[T_0, T_0']$$

$$T_{n+1} ::= T_n \mid X_{n+1} \mid B \mid \{x{:}\phi_{n+1}\} \mid \Xi[T_{n+1}, T_{n+1}']$$

$$\phi ::= \alpha \mid (\phi \wedge \psi) \mid (\phi \vee \psi) \mid (\phi \rightarrow \psi) \mid (\forall x\phi) \mid (\exists x\phi) \mid (\forall X_n\phi) \mid (\exists X_n\phi)$$

$$\alpha ::= (t \in T_n) \mid (t = s) \mid (t{\downarrow}) \mid \Omega$$

In the definition of the comprehension types, the ϕ_0 involve only individual quantification and, generally, $\phi_n(n > 0)$ involve at most quantification with respect to T_{n-1} variables. The rules for the higher-order quantifiers follow the pattern of T_0 quantification.

In essence this is the theory of Henson and Turner (1988). It has some redeeming features and some drawbacks. The most important conceptual point in its favour is its predicativity. However, this has to be weighed against its complexity. Like all hierarchial type systems, the layers of the theory duplicate notions where intuitively we expect there to be just one. Nevertheless, it is an option worthy of further exploration. Indeed, its application to program development can be found in Henson (1989a, 1989b). We shall not investigate it further since our intension is to explore the theory where there is no distinction between kinds and types. We have only included this brief account as an alternative for those readers who are hooked on predicative theories.

10.8 EXPLICIT POLYMORPHISM

The theory we have developed has its roots in the implicit style of polymorphism. The alternative stems from the *second-order lambda calculus*. We finally explore the possibility of adopting this approach—very briefly.

This form of polymorphism arises naturally in a context where the terms themselves contain explicit type information. In the *typed lambda calculus* terms are decorated with types, for example $\lambda x \in X . x$. Polymorphic functions are then introduced by abstracting on the types. In particular, the polymorphic identity function would be expressed as $\lambda X . \lambda x \in X . x$. Such terms can then take types as arguments and the axiom of polymorphic types takes the following form.

PM'. $f \in \Pi X . T \leftrightarrow \forall X (fX \in T)$

According to this notion of polymorphism a function is in the polymorphic type if, for every type, the function applied to the type is a member of the instance determined by the type.

Our terms do not contain explicit type information and do not demand types as arguments. To make sense of this axiom requires a radical reworking of the whole theory including the development of the typed lambda calculus. We only sketch the main ideas. The first revision concerns the syntax of terms, the syntax for types remains intact:

$$t ::= x \mid c \mid (ts) \mid (tT) \mid (\lambda x \in T . t) \mid (\lambda X . t)$$

The axioms that require revision are those of the lambda calculus. For example, the major axioms of the calculus take the following form:

$$\forall y \in X [(\lambda x \in X . t) y = t[y/x]]$$

$$(\lambda X . t) Y = t[Y/X]$$

The second is self-explanatory while the first restricts the application by demanding that the operand be of the correct type.

This appears to be a viable alternative theory, but there is a major technical question that needs to be addressed: is it consistent? The theory extends that of the second-order lambda calculus by including (first-order) comprehension (plus Ξ and Σ types). If we restrict the theory by removing comprehension (and Ξ and Σ types) and adding the types of STT, we have little more than the second-order lambda calculus itself. However, problems may occur because of the presence of comprehension. Theories of this form are currently under investigation (Berretta, 1990).

An alternative might be to adopt this approach together with that of the previous section and admit only the polymorphic types as kinds. This is developed in Feferman (1990) and amounts to his system $QL_1(\Lambda)$.

We shall not explore matters any further here since we have already nailed our flag to the mast. These last two sections have only been included to sketch alternative approaches.

10.9 A PROGRAMMING THEORY

The theory is complete and the time has come to investigate its application to program development. For convenience we spell out the theory in full.

10.9.1 The Theory PT

1. Syntax:

$$t ::= x \,|\, (ts) \,|\, (\lambda x . t)$$
(plus the syntax of Chapter 5)

$$T ::= X \,|\, B \,|\, \{x : \phi\} \,|\, \Xi[T, S] \,|\, SI[\mathbf{T}, \mathbf{C}]$$

$$\phi ::= \alpha \,|\, (\phi \wedge \psi) \,|\, (\phi \vee \psi) \,|\, (\phi \rightarrow \psi) \,|\, (\forall x \phi) \,|\, (\exists x \phi) \,|\, (\forall X \phi) \,|\, (\exists X \phi)$$

$$\alpha ::= (t = s) \,|\, (t \in T) \,|\, (t\downarrow) \,|\, \Omega$$

2. Axioms and axiom scheme:

   (*a*) The axioms of PL*   (Chapter 5)
   (*b*) COMP* + INV   (Sec. 10-5)
   (*c*) Relational and structural induction (Chapters 8 and 9)
        extended to the new language

3. The logic is that of the intuitionistic predicate calculus together with the type quantifier rules of this chapter.

Obviously, COMP* subsumes well-founded and structural induction, but we shall not fuss over this. In any case we shall be most concerned with its negative fragment where COMP is replaced by NCOMP* (i.e. no disjunctions or individual existential quantifications). Call this theory PT_{neg}. In PT_{neg} we need the explicit version of well-founded types since the negative version of comprehension restricts the induction formulae to negative ones.

EXERCISES

10.1 In the theory PT, assign polymorphic types to the following:

$$\lambda xy . x \tag{a}$$

$$\lambda xy . xy \tag{b}$$

$$\lambda xyz . ((xz)(yz)) \tag{c}$$

10.2 Consider the function:

del $pu[\ ] = [\ ]$

del $pu(v{:}x) =$ del pux when puv

del $pu(v{:}x) = v{:}$del pux when not(puv)

Prove, in PT, that it has the type $\Pi X . [(X \Rightarrow X \Rightarrow Bool) \Rightarrow (X \Rightarrow List[X] \Rightarrow List[X])]$.

10.3 Consider the following function:

$$\text{quicksort } p[\ ] = [\ ]$$

$$\text{quicksort } p(x{:}l) = (\text{quicksort } pl') * [x] * (\text{quicksort } pl'')$$
$$\text{where } (l', l'') = (\text{split } pxl)$$

This is a generalization of the function from Theorem 9.1 where the ordering is included as an argument to the function. Assuming that the function split has type $\Pi X . [(X \otimes X \Rightarrow Bool) \Rightarrow X \Rightarrow List[X] \Rightarrow (List[X] \otimes List[X])]$, prove, in PT, that quicksort has type $\Pi X . [(X \otimes X \Rightarrow Bool) \Rightarrow List[X] \Rightarrow List[X]]$.

10.4 Implement the following abstract data types in terms of $List[T]$:

(*a*) Sets on T
(*b*) Arrays on T
(*c*) Queues on T

For each case provide the implementation of the operations of the abstract type as list functions.

REFERENCES AND FURTHER READING

For more details concerning intuitionistic second-order logic the reader should consult Sec. 3.8 of Troelstra and Van Dalen (1988). Hindley and Seldin (1986) is a good starting point from which to embark on a study of the second-order lambda calculus and generalized type systems. The recent collection by Huet (1990a) provides a good summary of recent work on polymorphism. The paper by Cardelli and Wegner (1986) is an excellent survey at a semi-formal level. Feferman (1990) and Henson and Turner (1988) contain more details of the alternative formulations only hinted at in Secs 10.7 and 10.8. Other papers of direct relevance are Burstal and Lampson (1984), Leivant (1983), McQueen and Sethi (1982), Reynolds (1974) and Mitchell and Plotkin (1985).

11

REALIZABILITY

In this chapter and in Chapter 12 we are concerned with the theoretical ideas that support program specification and development. In broad outline the theory of program construction centres upon the precise connections between the following notions:

1. Wff (as program specifications)
2. Proofs
3. Programs
4. Types

In Chapter 2 we outlined a semantics for the predicate calculus in which the meaning of a wff was provided by supplying conditions of verification, the actual means of verification being furnished in terms of algorithms. This *algorithmic interpretation* of the logical connectives forges a link between programs and wff. Indeed, it implicitly links wff and types where the type corresponding to a wff is the type of the programs that verify it. Moreover, given a proof of a wff (specification) a program that meets the specification can be automatically extracted. It is these links and their formal unpacking that form the core of this chapter.

To begin with we supply a more precise account of the semantics and its mathematical foundations. This is not for purely formal reasons. It is the latter that yields the connection between proofs and programs and thus supports the process of program construction. In this chapter we review the traditional ideas on the subject and in the next consider a variation that permits the development of more *natural* programs. In this chapter and the next these ideas will be applied to the actual process of program construction including a brief airing of transformational programming.

11.1 AN ALGORITHMIC INTERPRETATION OF THE PREDICATE CALCULUS

Intuitively, an assertion in intuitionistic logic has to be supported by some means of verification. One way of formally unpacking this semantic conception is based upon the idea that programs supply the means. In Chapter 2 we provided an informal version of this semantics; in this section we provide a precise one. To begin with we restrict ourselves to the first-order part of the language.

11.1.1 The Definition of Realizability

The semantics is furnished by *associating*, with each wff ϕ, a new wff:

$$z\rho\phi$$

to be read as z *realizes* ϕ, where z is a fresh variable not free in ϕ. The association proceeds by way of a recursive translation between wff. We shall motivate matters in much the same way as before but this time, for each connective, provide a precise translation clause.

(a) Conjunction Suppose we are asked to write a program to solve a problem that is specified as the conjunction of two subproblems. Presumably, a program that solves the problem must consist of a pair of programs, one being a program that is a solution to the first subproblem and the other a solution to the second. This leads to the following clause of translation.

R1. $z\rho(\phi \wedge \psi)$ is $[z \in \text{PAIR} \wedge \text{l}z\rho\phi \wedge \text{r}z\rho\psi]$

The fact that we have a precise notion of pairing enables the formulation of a precise version of the original.

(b) Disjunction A problem that is expressed as a disjunction gives us licence to solve either but we must indicate which of the two has been chosen. R2 captures this requirement: a program that is a solution to a disjunction $\phi \vee \psi$ is an injection and, depending upon whether it is a left or right injection, its projection is a solution to ϕ or to ψ.

R2. $z\rho(\phi \vee \psi)$ is $[z \in \text{INJ} \wedge (z \in \text{INL} \rightarrow (\text{proj } z)\rho\phi)$
$\wedge (z \in \text{INR} \rightarrow (\text{proj } z)\rho\psi)]$

Here the nature of the injection (left or right) acts as a flag that indicates which problem has been addressed.

(c) Implication To solve a problem expressed as an implication we must locate a uniform procedure that maps a solution for the antecedent to a solution for the consequent.

R3. $z\rho(\phi \to \psi)$ is $\forall x(x\rho\phi \to zx\rho\psi)$

In this case, the lambda calculus notion of function has been marshalled to formally express the original informal notion of procedure.

(d) Universal quantification A program that verifies or solves $\forall x\phi$ is to be a function that given any element returns a program that solves the corresponding instance of ϕ.

R4. $z\rho(\forall x\phi)$ is $\forall x(zx\rho\phi)$

(e) Existential quantification To solve the problem $\exists x\phi$ we must not only locate an element that satisfies ϕ but also provide evidence that the located element does so. The following reflects this twofold demand.

R5. $z\rho(\exists x\phi)$ is $[z \in \text{PAIR} \wedge \mathrm{l}z\rho\phi[\mathrm{r}z/x]]$

(f) Atomic assertions In order to complete the picture we must say how atomic assertions are to be realized. Such assertions are taken to be realizable just in case they are true.

R6. $z\rho\phi$ is ϕ for atomic ϕ

Given that atomic assertions contain no logical connectives and quantifiers, their assertion is taken to be logically unproblematic. Realizability is a recursive translation procedure where the recursion is unpacked in terms of the structure of wff. It only dictates the form of realizers for compound wff in terms of the realizers of their components. This should dispel any initial shock engendered by R6.

R1 to R6 provide a recursive translation between wff; the clauses recursively associate, with each wff ϕ, a new wff, $z\rho\phi$, whose free variables are those of ϕ plus (except for atomic cases) z itself.

Before we proceed to the more interesting aspects of this notion there is a small technical matter we need to dispense with. There is an apparent ambiguity in the expression $z\rho\phi[s/x]$. The following justifies matters. The proof is by induction on the complexity of the wff and is left for the reader—use the fact that z is a fresh variable.

Theorem 11.1 For each wff ϕ, variable x and term s we have

$$\text{PT} \vdash z\rho(\phi[s/x]) \leftrightarrow (z\rho\phi)[s/x]$$

Despite its simplicity, this interpretation of intutionistic logic is not without its difficulties and does not exactly reflect the *intended* intuitionistic meaning of the logical connectives. We shall explore its strengths and shortcomings shortly and point out, formally, where it parts company with the *intended* interpretation.

11.1.2 The Types of Realizers

In Chapter 7 we employed our type theory to provide a different perspective on the content of R1 to R6 (or rather their informal correlates). If you recall, we provided a version of the following mapping between wff and types:

$$R(\phi) = \{z : \phi\} \quad \text{for } \phi \text{ atomic and } z \text{ not free in } \phi$$

$$R(\phi \wedge \psi) = R(\phi) \otimes R(\psi)$$

$$R(\phi \vee \psi) = R(\phi) \oplus R(\psi)$$

$$R(\phi \rightarrow \psi) = R(\phi) \Rightarrow R(\psi)$$

$$R(\forall x\phi) = \pi x \in \Delta . R(\phi[x])$$

$$R(\exists x\phi) = \sigma x \in \Delta . R(\phi[x])$$

Notice that the last two clauses employ the dependent types and the universal type. For each wff ϕ, $R(\phi)$ is *the type of the realizers for* ϕ. The exact connection between R and realizability is reported in Theorem 11.2.

Theorem 11.2 For any term t, $PT \vdash t\rho\phi$ iff $PT \vdash t \in R(\phi)$.

PROOF By induction on the structure of wff. The atomic case is clear. We illustrate the induction step with universal quantification. Suppose that $t\rho(\forall x\phi)$. By R4, this is equivalent to $\forall x(tx\rho\phi)$. By induction, this is just $\forall x[tx \in R(\phi[x])]$, i.e. $t \in R(\forall x\phi)$.

We have thus made links between three of the listed notions: wff, programs and types. We now bring *proofs* into the picture.

11.2 CHARACTERIZATION OF REALIZABILITY

By itself, realizability does not provide the machinery to obtain programs from proofs; it only lays down the criteria for correctness. To abstract programs we need to systematically link programs with proofs. This involves a mathematical investigation of the notion. The aim of this section is to characterize the notion of realizability and, in particular, to forge a link between provability and realizability.

11.2.1 Negative Formula

We introduced negative formulae in Chapter 7 where we discussed negative comprehension. If you recall, a wff ϕ is negative or ($\exists$, $\vee$ free) iff ϕ does not contain $\vee$ or $\exists$. Indeed, the reader may not be altogether clear as to exactly why they were singled out for special attention. The answer stems from the role they play in realizability. They possess a rather striking property: a negative formula is true iff realizable, and if realizable it is realizable by a canonical term, depending only on the formula.

Theorem 11.3
(a) With each nwff ϕ, there exists a term $t[\phi]$, with free variables at most those of ϕ, such that $STT \vdash (\phi \to t[\phi]\rho\phi)$
(b) For each nwff ϕ, $STT \vdash x\rho\phi \to \phi$
(c) For each wff ϕ, $x\rho\phi$ is nwff

PROOF Parts (a) and (b) are by simultaneous induction on the structure of the wff. If ϕ is atomic then both (a) and (b) are immediate by R6. If ϕ is $\eta \wedge \gamma$, then put $t[\phi] = (t[\eta], t[\gamma])$. By induction, $t[\eta]\rho\eta$ and $t[\gamma]\rho\gamma$. Hence, by R1, $t[\phi]\rho(\eta \wedge \gamma)$. If $x\rho(\eta \wedge \gamma)$ then by R1, $lx\rho\eta$ and $rx\rho\gamma$, by induction we have $\eta \wedge \gamma$. If ϕ is $\eta \to \gamma$, then put $t[\phi] = \lambda x . t[\gamma]$. If $z\rho\phi$, then $\forall x(x\rho\eta \to zx\rho\gamma)$. By induction, using (a) and (b) we have $\eta \to \gamma$. If ϕ is $\forall x\eta$ then put $t[\phi] = \lambda x . t[\eta]$. If $z\rho\phi$ then $\forall x(zx\rho\eta)$. By induction, $\forall x\eta$. Part (c) is immediate by inspection of the definition of R.

Negative formulae are often called *self-realizing* in the sense that they obey (a) of the following theorem.

Theorem 11.4
(a) With each nwff ϕ, $STT \vdash [\exists x(x\rho\phi) \leftrightarrow \phi]$
(b) For each wff ϕ, there is a term t such that $STT \vdash t\rho[\exists x(x\rho\phi) \leftrightarrow \phi]$

PROOF Part (a) follows from the previous theorem. For (b) we have to locate terms for each of the implications. For $\phi \to \exists x(x\rho\phi)$ we need only to observe that $x\rho\phi$ is a nwff and use the canonical realizers given by Theorem 11.3(a): $(t[x\rho\phi], x)\rho\exists x(x\rho\phi)$ and so

$$\lambda x . (t[x\rho\phi], x)\rho(\phi \to \exists x(x\rho\phi))$$

For the converse, note that $z\rho\exists x(x\rho\phi)$ yields, by R5, $lz\rho(rz\rho\phi)$, which by Theorem 11.3(b) yields $rz\rho\phi$. Thus $\lambda z . rz\rho(\exists x(x\rho\phi) \to \phi)$.

The negative formulae behave in an elegant way under realizability. According to Theorem 11.4(a), a negative formula is equivalent to the assertion of its own realizability. However, not all wff are self-realizing. In general, the situation is somewhat more delicate.

11.2.2 Soundness of STT

The soundness theorem insists that what is provable is realizable. To begin with, we restrict our attention to the theory STT—the simple theory of functions and types introduced in Chapters 2 to 6. We shall extend the discussion in the next section.

Theorem 11.5 Let Γ be some set of formulae that are provably realized in STT. If $\Gamma + \text{STT} \vdash \phi$ then there exists a term t such that $\text{STT} \vdash tp\phi$.

PROOF We establish the result by induction on the proofs in $\Gamma + \text{STT}$. We have to consider the proof rules and the axioms. All the axioms of the lazy lambda calculus and its constant extensions (Chapter 5) are negative (verify this claim) and so we need only appeal to Theorem 11.3. Moreover, each of the axioms for the type constructors of STT is a nwff and so we again appeal to Theorem 11.3. For example, the axiom for Cartesian products takes the following form.

CP. $z \in X \otimes Y \;\leftrightarrow\; [z \in \text{PAIR} \wedge \text{l}z \in X \wedge \text{r}z \in Y]$

Since the whole axiom is negative it is canonically realized. For the basic types like Bool and INJ we represent them as structural types. The closure axioms are negative. We leave the induction schemes as an exercise for the reader. In fact, we shall deal with the general case of structural inductive types in the next section. This leaves the proof rules of the logic. For each such rule we shall supply a derived proof rule of realizability which indicates how to compute the realizers of the conclusion from those of the premises.

(a) Conjunction. For each of the connectives and quantifiers we have to consider the introduction and elimination rules. The derived rules for conjunction are given as follows:

$$\frac{tp\phi \qquad sp\psi}{(t,s)p(\phi \wedge \psi)} \qquad \frac{tp(\phi \wedge \psi)}{\text{l}tp\phi} \qquad \frac{sp(\phi \wedge \psi)}{\text{r}sp\psi}$$

To justify the introduction rule we assume, inductively, that for ϕ and ψ provable there are terms that realize them. The conclusion then follows from R1. The soundness of the elimination rules also follows directly from R1.

(b) Disjunction. The derived rules for disjunction take the following form:

$$\frac{tp\phi}{\text{in}_L \, tp(\phi \vee \psi)} \qquad \frac{tp\psi}{\text{in}_R \, tp(\phi \vee \psi)} \qquad \frac{rp(\phi \vee \psi) \quad \overset{[xp\phi]}{\underset{\displaystyle tp\eta}{\vert}} \quad \overset{[yp\psi]}{\underset{\displaystyle sp\eta}{\vert}}}{(\text{case } r \text{ of} [\lambda x.t, \lambda y.s])p\eta}$$

To justify the introduction rule(s) we appeal directly to R2. The elimination rule is more tricky. Assume the premises. By R2, we have two cases to consider. If $r \in$ INL then (proj $r)\rho\phi$ and so, by assumption, $t[(\text{proj } r)/x]\rho\eta$. Moreover, case z of $[\lambda x.t, \lambda y.s] = t[(\text{proj } r)/x]$. The other case is similar.

(c) Implication. In this case the derived rules take the following form:

$$\frac{\begin{array}{c}[x\rho\phi]\\ |\\ t\rho\psi\end{array}}{\lambda x.t\rho(\phi \to \psi)} \qquad \frac{s\rho\phi \qquad t\rho(\phi \to \psi)}{ts\rho\psi}$$

To justify the introduction rule and the elimination rule we appeal directly to R3. For example, from the premise of the introduction rule (and the introduction rules for implication and universal quantification) we obtain $\forall x(x\rho\phi \to t\rho\psi)$. R3 yields $(\lambda x.t)\rho(\phi \to \psi)$.

(d) Universal quantification. These derived rules should be predictable.

$$\frac{t\rho\phi}{\lambda x.t\rho\forall x\phi} \qquad \frac{t\rho\forall x\phi}{tx\rho\phi[x]}$$

We leave the reader the task of justifying them—obviously we appeal to R4.

(e) Existential quantification. These rules are perhaps the most difficult to grasp:

$$\frac{t\rho\phi[x]}{\langle t, x\rangle\rho\exists x\phi} \qquad \frac{t\rho\exists y\phi \qquad \begin{array}{c}[x\rho\phi[y]]\\ |\\ s\rho\eta\end{array}}{(\text{let } (y, x) = (rt, lt) \text{ in } s)\rho\eta}$$

The introduction rule follows from R5 immediately but the elimination rule requires a little work. From R5, $t\rho\exists y\phi$ implies that $(lt)\rho\phi[rt/y]$. By the second premise, $\forall y\forall x(x\rho\phi[y] \to s\rho\eta)$. By R3, $\forall y(\lambda x.s\rho(\phi[y] \to \eta))$. By R4, $\lambda y\lambda x.s\rho\forall y(\phi[y] \to \eta)$. Hence, (let $(y, x) = (rt, lt)$ in $s)\rho\eta$.

(f) Absurdity rule. To justify this we have only to observe that $x\rho\Omega \leftrightarrow \Omega$, since Ω is atomic. We then have the following derived rule:

$$\frac{x\rho\Omega}{x\rho\phi}$$

This completes the proof for the theory STT.

Hence, every theorem of STT is realized by some term. What of the converse? Are there wff that are realizable but are not theorems of STT? There are. In fact, we can be very precise about matters.

11.2.3 Characterization of Realizability: Extended Church's Thesis

Examples of sentences that are realizable but not derivable in intuitionistic logic are given by the following scheme known as *the extended Church's thesis*. In the scheme, ϕ is arbitrary but ψ is restricted to nwff.

$$\text{ECT}_0. \quad \forall x(\psi[x] \to \exists y \phi[x, y]) \to \exists f \forall x(\psi[x] \to \phi[x, fx]) \qquad \psi \text{ nwff}$$

If, given an arbitrary x which satisfies a predicate ψ, we can locate a y such that x and y satisfy ϕ, then, according to ECT_0, we can algorithmically obtain such a y from the x. One can read the assertion

$$\forall x(\psi[x] \to \exists y \phi[x, y])$$

as a program specification where the ψ is the *pre-condition* and ϕ is the *post-condition*. The consequent of ECT_0 then guarantees the existence of a function that meets the specification. In other words, if we can specify a function, then we can find a program for it. This is the interpretation we shall exploit in the last two chapters. However, at this point we are concerned with putting the theory in place. In this regard, ECT_0 is certainly not provable from the axioms of STT (it is in fact independent of them) and it is not generally accepted in intuitionistic mathematics—for the reasons discussed in the introduction. However, it is realizable.

Theorem 11.6 For any instance θ of ECT_0, there exists a term t such that $\text{STT} \vdash t \rho \theta$.

PROOF Let θ be the following instance of ECT_0:

$$\forall x(\psi[x] \to \exists y \phi[x, y]) \to \exists f \forall x(\psi[x] \to \phi[x, fx])$$

Consider the term $\lambda z.(\lambda x w.l(zxt[\psi]), \lambda x.r(zxt[\psi]))$. Claim this is the realizer of the instance in question. To see this suppose that $z \rho \forall x(\psi[x] \to \exists y \phi[x, y])$. Then $zxt[\psi] \rho \exists y \phi[x, y]$. Hence, we have, by R5, $l(zxt[\psi]) \rho \phi[x, r(zxt[\psi])]$. Hence, by clause R3 of realizability, $\lambda w.l(zxt[\psi]) \rho (\psi[x] \to \phi[x, r(zxt[\psi])])$, where w is a fresh variable. Consequently, by clause R4, $\lambda x w.l(zxt[\psi]) \rho \forall x(\psi[x] \to \phi[x, r(zxt[\psi])])$. Thus, by R5, $(\lambda x w.l(zxt[\psi]), \lambda x.r(zxt[\psi])) \rho \exists f \forall x(\psi[x] \to \phi[x, fx])$. By R3 we are finished.

We have located a general scheme whose instances are realizable but which is not intuitionistically provable. In this respect realizability parts company with intuitionism. Indeed, this scheme embodies the exact difference between the two notions.

Theorem 11.7

(a) $STT + ECT_0 \vdash \exists x(x\rho\phi) \leftrightarrow \phi$

(b) $STT + ECT_0 \vdash \phi$ iff $STT \vdash \exists x(x\rho\phi)$

PROOF For part (a) we argue by induction on the complexity of the wff. We illustrate with implication since this employs ECT_0. Inductively, assume that $\exists x(x\rho\phi) \leftrightarrow \phi$ and $\exists x(x\rho\psi) \leftrightarrow \psi$. Assume that $\phi \rightarrow \psi$; we need to establish that $\exists z(z\rho(\phi \rightarrow \psi))$. Suppose that $x\rho\phi$; by induction we may conclude ϕ. Hence, by assumption, we may conclude ψ. By induction again we can conclude $\exists y(y\rho\psi)$. Hence we have $\forall x(x\rho\phi \rightarrow \exists y(y\rho\psi))$. By Theorem 11.3(c), $x\rho\phi$ is nwff. Applying ECT_0, we conclude that $\exists z\forall x(x\rho\phi \rightarrow (zx\rho\psi))$, and we are finished. For the converse suppose that $\exists z(z\rho(\phi \rightarrow \psi))$. Then $\forall x(x\rho\phi \rightarrow zx\rho\psi)$. Assume ϕ. Then by induction, $\exists x(x\rho\phi)$. Hence, if $x\rho\phi$ then $(zx\rho\psi)$ and so $\exists u(u\rho\psi)$. By induction, we obtain ψ. For part (b), the direction from right to left follows from part (a). The other direction follows from Theorem 11.6 and the *soundness* of realizability.

This result offers a precise characterization of realizability: under the government of ECT_0, every assertion is equivalent to the assertion of its own realizability, i.e. self-realizable.

This completes the first stage in our investigation. We have included the above characterization of realizability to provide the reader with some insight into the formal aspects of the notion. However, the actual abstraction of programs from proofs is based on the soundness proof: the derived proof rules of realizability enable the abstraction. Consequently, we must extend the soundness proof to PT_{neg}, the theory we employ in program development. We should point out that we shall not actually employ this notion of realizability in program construction. However, the following is necessary in order to motivate our modified notion of realizability.

11.3 EXTENSIONS OF STT: SOUNDNESS

There are several aspects to the extension. These involve type quantification, inductive types and negative comprehension. Most are easy and not very interesting. The most difficult and the most interesting, at least from the present perspective, concern the induction axioms. We shall get to these shortly.

11.3.1 Type Quantification, Polymorphism and Abstract Data Types

Our first extension involves the rules for type quantification and the axioms for universal and existential types. However, before we prove soundness we must provide a realizability interpretation for the type quantifiers. There are two main options available but we shall adopt the following.

R7. $z\rho\forall X\phi$ is $\forall X(z\rho\phi)$

R8. $z\rho\exists X\phi$ is $\exists X(z\rho\phi)$

According to this notion the realizability *passes through* the type quantifiers. This account of realizability for type quantification is essentially that of Kreisel and Troelstra (1970) and reflects the *implicit* style of polymorphism and data abstraction. Observe that the notion of negative formulae can be extended to include the type quantifiers and that such formulae are self-realizing. We leave the reader to extend the proof of Theorem 11.3.

However, for the second-order lambda calculus version of polymorphism and its dual these clauses would parallel those for the individual quantification.

R7'. $z\rho\forall X\phi$ is $\forall X(zX\rho\phi)$

R8'. $z\rho\exists X\phi$ is $z \in \text{PAIR} \wedge \exists Y[rz = Y \wedge lz\rho\phi[Y/X]]$

Notice that R8 demands that types occur as terms. Since we have not adopted these notions of data abstraction and polymorphism we shall not consider these clauses further. We mention them only to indicate how one might deal with alternative versions of the theory.

With these clauses in place we can return to the main issue, namely the extension of soundness. For this, we must indicate the derived rules of realizability. These are straightforward, given our interpretation.

$$\frac{t\rho\phi[X]}{t\rho\forall X\phi} \qquad \frac{t\rho\forall X\phi}{t\rho\phi[T/X]}$$

$$\frac{t\rho\phi[T/X]}{t\rho\exists X\phi} \qquad \frac{s\rho\exists X\phi \qquad \overset{[x\rho\phi]}{\underset{t\rho\psi}{\mid}}}{t[s/x]\rho\psi}$$

We must also check that the axioms for universal and existential types are realizable. In fact, the axioms are negative and therefore self-realizable. Indeed, they will be subsumed under comprehension. However, for pedagogical reasons we provide the explicit details. The following equivalences follow from the definition of realizability for atomic wff, the axioms of Π and Σ types, realizability for type quantification and the definition of realizability for atomic wff:

$$u\rho(z \in \Pi X . T) \leftrightarrow z \in \Pi X . T \leftrightarrow \forall X(z \in T) \leftrightarrow \forall X(u\rho(z \in T)) \leftrightarrow (u\rho\forall X(z \in T))$$

$$u\rho(z \in \Sigma X . T) \leftrightarrow z \in \Sigma X . T \leftrightarrow \exists X(z \in T) \leftrightarrow \underline{\exists} X(u\rho(z \in T)) \leftrightarrow (u\rho\exists X(z \in T))$$

Hence, $\lambda x . x\rho[z \in \Pi X . T \to \forall X(z \in T)]$ and $\lambda x . x\rho[z \in \Sigma X . T \to \exists X(z \in T)]$. The converse implications are identical.

11.3.2 Structural Inductive Types

From our perspective, the most interesting aspect of realizability concerns the inductive types. For such types the idea is simple enough but the general form rather hides this simplicity, and so we examine a special case. Consider the inductive type, I, given as follows:

Closure

$$\forall x \in T(cx \in I) \wedge$$
$$\forall u \in I \forall v \in I(duv \in I)$$

Induction

$$\frac{\forall x \in T(\phi[cx]) \quad \forall u \in I \forall v \in I((\phi[u] \wedge \phi[v]) \to \phi[duv])}{\forall y \in I(\phi[y])}$$

For convenience, we have expressed the induction axiom as a rule. First observe that the closure axiom is a nwff and so we have nothing to prove. For induction suppose that the premises of the rule are realized by f and g respectively. Then consider the following function:

$$\mathrm{rec}\,(cx)z = fx(t[x \in T])$$

$$\mathrm{rec}\,(duw)z = gu(t[u \in I])w(t[w \in I])((\mathrm{rec}\,uz), (\mathrm{rec}\,wz))$$

We employ I induction to prove that $\forall x \in I((\mathrm{rec}\ xz)\rho\phi[x])$. Set the induction formula to $(\mathrm{rec}\ xz)\rho\phi[x]$. For the base case we have to show that $\forall x \in T(fx(t[x \in T])\rho\phi[cx])$, but this follows from the fact that f realizes the first premise and that $t[x \in T]$ is the canonical realizer for membership in T. For the induction step, assume that $(\mathrm{rec}\ uz)\rho\phi[u]$ and that $(\mathrm{rec}\ wz)\rho\phi[w]$. By the stipulation of g we have that $(\mathrm{rec}\,(duw)z)\rho\phi[duw]$. Hence, by induction, $\forall x \in I((\mathrm{rec}\ xz)\rho\phi[x])$. Hence, by definition of realizability, we obtain the required $\lambda xy.(\mathrm{rec}\ xz)\rho\forall x \in I(\phi[x])$, where y is a fresh variable.

For the special cases of natural numbers and lists we obtain the following recursion schemes:

$$\mathrm{rec}\,0z = f$$
$$\mathrm{rec}\,x'z = gx(t[x \in N])(\mathrm{rec}\ xz)$$

$$\mathrm{rec}\,[\ ]z = f$$
$$\mathrm{rec}\,(u:x)z = gu(t[u \in T])x(t[x \in \mathrm{List}[T]])(\mathrm{rec}\ xz)$$

As an exercise the reader might derive the recursion scheme for sexpressions. These functions look very inelegant and unnatural. In particular, the realizers for the membership assertions need to be passed as arguments. Indeed, this is the main motivation for our major refinement of realizability— the topic of the next chapter.

11.3.3 Well-founded Inductive Types

For these types we proceed in a similar manner. Recall that the axioms take the following form.

CLO. $\forall x \in T\{\forall y[(x, y) \in R \to y \in \Xi[T, R]] \to x \in \Xi[T, R]\}$

IND. $\forall x \in T\{\forall y[(x, y) \in R \to \phi[y]] \to \phi[x]\} \to \forall x \in \Xi[T, R]\{\phi[x]\}$

Once again, the closure axiom is negative so we have only to worry about the induction axiom. Suppose that $f\rho\forall x \in T\{\forall y[(x, y) \in R \to \phi[y]] \to \phi[x]\}$. Then consider the following function:

$$\text{rec } xz = fx(t[x \in T])(\lambda y. \lambda u.(\text{rec } yz))$$

We employ relational induction to prove that $\forall x \in \Xi[T, R]\{(\text{rec } xz)\rho\phi[x]\}$. Assume that $\forall y[(x, y) \in R \to (\text{rec } yz)\rho\phi[y]]$. From the definition of realizability it is easy to see that $\lambda y. \lambda u.(\text{rec } yz)\rho\forall y[(x, y) \in R \to \phi[y]]$, where u is a fresh variable. By assumption, $fx(t[x \in T])(\lambda y. \lambda u.(\text{rec } yz))\rho\phi[x]$. Hence, by induction, $\forall x \in \Xi[T, R]\{(\text{rec } xz)\rho\phi[x]\}$. Thus $\lambda xu.(\text{rec } xz)\rho\forall x \in \Xi[T, R]\{\phi[x]\}$, where u is a fresh variable.

11.3.4 Comprehension Types

Not all forms of comprehension are sound under the stated realizability interpretation. This is not that important since we shall only employ the restricted form in program development and this form is sound. For ϕ a first or second-order nwff we have the following equivalences:

$$u\rho x \in \{x:\phi\} \leftrightarrow x \in \{x:\phi\} \leftrightarrow \phi \leftrightarrow t[\phi]\rho\phi \qquad \phi \text{ nwff}$$

Thus $\lambda u. t[\phi]\rho[x \in \{x:\phi\} \to \phi]$ and $\lambda u. u\rho[\phi \to x \in \{x:\phi\}]$. Notice that the above equivalences fail in the more general case. There is a way out which demands that all types be transformed into *completely presented* ones. However, for program specification and development, the negative comprehension types suffice. The reader should consult Beeson (1986) and Henson (1990) for the full comprehension scheme.

In conclusion, we have extended the soundness proof to include type quantification, universal and existential types, structural and well-founded inductive types and the types given by negative comprehension. We have thus provided a soundness proof for the whole of PT_{neg}.

11.4 EXISTENCE PROPERTIES AND Q REALIZABILITY

The form of realizability we have provided is essentially the original one due to Kleene (1945). However, it differs from Kleene's in several respects. Firstly, we have not made any explicit reference to termination; the Kleene definition does. We shall address this issue shortly. Secondly, the original furnished the interpretation of wff in terms of Turing machines whereas ours employed the extended lambda calculus of Chapter 5. In all other respects the present notion is identical to the original. Indeed, it suffers from a similar short-coming to the original and consequently it will not, as it stands, serve our purposes.

To grasp the problem consider the following rule of inference:

If $\exists x\phi$ then, for some term t, $\phi[t/x]$

This is usually referred to as *the term existence* property. This is an important property since we shall employ proofs of existential statements to derive programs. For this purpose it is essential that the object constructed satisfies its specification. Unfortunately, the present notion of realizability does not guarantee this. This is easy to see if we consider the bare clause R5:

R5. $z\rho(\exists x\phi)$ is $[z \in \text{PAIR} \land \mathrm{l}z\rho\phi[\mathrm{r}z/x]]$

If we can prove $\exists x\phi$ then we can find a term t such that $\mathrm{l}t\rho\phi[\mathrm{r}t/x]$. However, this offers no guarantee that $\phi[\mathrm{r}t/x]$—realizability does not yield truth.

11.4.1 Q Realizability

To rectify this lunacy we need a modified notion of realizability called Q *realizability*. The revisions occur in the clauses for existential quantification, disjunction and implication. For convenience we provide the definition for Q realizability in full.

Q1. $zQ(\phi \land \psi)$ is $[z \in \text{PAIR} \land (\mathrm{l}z)Q\phi \land (\mathrm{r}z)Q\psi]$
Q2. $zQ(\phi \lor \psi)$ is $[z \in \text{INJ} \land \{z \in \text{INL} \to \phi \land (\text{proj } z)Q\phi\} \land$
$\{z \in \text{INR} \to \psi \land (\text{proj } z)Q\psi\}]$
Q3. $zQ(\phi \to \psi)$ is $\forall x((xQ\phi) \land \phi \to zxQ\psi)$
Q4. $zQ(\forall x\phi)$ is $\forall x(zxQ\phi)$
Q5. $zQ(\exists x\phi)$ is $[z \in \text{PAIR} \land \phi[\mathrm{r}z/x] \land (\mathrm{l}z)Q\phi[\mathrm{r}z/x]]$
Q6. $zQ\phi$ is ϕ for ϕ atomic
Q7. $zQ(\forall X\phi)$ is $\forall X(zQ\phi)$
Q8. $zQ(\exists X\phi)$ is $\exists X(zQ\phi)$

Once again realizability commutes with substitution and the self-realizability for negative formula remains intact. We leave the details for the reader.

Theorem 11.8
(*a*) With each nwff ϕ there exists a term $t[\phi]$ with free variables, those of ϕ such that $\text{PT}_{\text{neg}} \vdash \phi \to t[\phi]Q\phi$
(*b*) For each nwff ϕ, $\text{PT}_{\text{neg}} \vdash zQ\phi \to \phi$

The term existence property follows almost directly from the soundness of this notion of realizability.

11.4.2 Soundness for Q Realizability

The proof of soundness is not very different from the original. Most of the steps remain unscathed and so we concentrate on those involving the modifications.

Theorem 11.9 Let Γ be some set of formulae that are provably Q-realized in PT_{neg}. If $\Gamma + PT_{neg} \vdash \phi$, then there exists a term t such that $\Gamma + PT_{neg} \vdash tQ\phi$.

PROOF Once again, we establish the result by induction on the proofs. Notice that the statement differs from the original since the provability of $tQ\phi$ depends upon the underlying assumptions, Γ, and not just their realizability. This fact plays a crucial role in the following cases: implication, disjunction and existential quantification.

(*a*) Implication:

$$\frac{\begin{array}{c}[\phi \wedge xQ\phi]\\|\\tQ\psi\end{array}}{\lambda x . tQ(\phi \to \psi)} \qquad \frac{\phi \wedge sQ\phi \quad tQ(\phi \to \psi)}{tsQ\psi}$$

Notice in the elimination rule that we must use the assumption that ϕ is provable.

(*b*) Disjunction. In the introduction rule we need again to employ the provability of ϕ:

$$\frac{(tQ\phi) \wedge \phi}{(in_L t)Q(\phi \vee \psi)} \qquad \frac{(tQ\psi) \wedge \psi}{(in_R t)Q(\phi \vee \psi)} \qquad \frac{rQ(\phi \vee \psi) \quad \begin{array}{cc}[\phi \wedge xQ\phi] & [\psi \wedge yQ\psi]\\| & |\\tQ\eta & sQ\eta\end{array}}{(\text{case } r \text{ of}[\lambda x . t, \lambda y . s])Q\eta}$$

(*c*) Existential quantification:

$$\frac{\phi \wedge tQ\phi}{(t, x)Q\exists x\phi} \qquad \frac{tQ\exists x\phi \quad \begin{array}{c}[(xQ\phi[y]) \wedge \phi[y]]\\|\\sQ\eta\end{array}}{(\text{let } (y, x) = (rt, lt) \text{ in } s)Q\eta}$$

In the introduction rule we use the assumption that $\phi[x]$ is provable.

Before we deal with the existence property we deal briefly with the following question: what is the connection between these two notions of realizability?

Theorem 11.10 $\text{PT}_{\text{neg}} + \text{ECT}_0 \vdash xQ\phi \leftrightarrow x\rho\phi$

PROOF Employ induction on the structure of wff. The only cases that demand attention are those for disjunction, implication and existential quantification, and these employ the completeness (in the presence of ECT_0) of ρ realizability.

11.4.3 Existence Properties

With the soundness proof in place we can move on to the reason for introducing this modified notion. We need to do just a little work to obtain this result since the modified notion has been designed to guarantee it.

Theorem 11.11 PT_{neg} has the term existence property.

PROOF Suppose that $\text{PT}_{\text{neg}} \vdash \exists x\phi$. By soundness, there is a term t such that $\text{PT}_{\text{neg}} \vdash tQ\exists x\phi$. From the definition of Q realizability, $\phi[\text{r}t/x] \wedge$ $\text{l}tQ\phi[\text{r}t/x]$. The result follows.

In general, we shall be most interested in the existence of terminating objects that satisfy a predicate. The following result captures the abstract idea.

Theorem 11.12 If $\text{PT}_{\text{neg}} \vdash \exists^\circ x\phi$, then $\text{PT}_{\text{neg}} \vdash \phi[t] \wedge t{\downarrow}$, for some term t.

PROOF Assume that $\text{PT}_{\text{neg}} \vdash \exists^\circ x\phi$; then by Q realizability there is a term t such that $\text{PT}_{\text{neg}} \vdash (\text{r}t){\downarrow} \wedge \phi[\text{r}t/x]$, as required.

We also find, as a consequence of soundness, that decidability implies strong decidability; a result promised in Chapter 6.

Theorem 11.13 For PT_{neg} decidability implies strong decidability.

PROOF If $\text{PT}_{\text{neg}} \vdash \forall x(\phi[x] \vee \sim\phi[x])$ then for some term g, we have $\text{PT}_{\text{neg}} \vdash gQ\forall x(\phi[x] \vee \sim\phi[x])$. The witness function f is obtained by putting $fx = w(gx) \longrightarrow \text{t}, \text{f}$, where w is the witness function for the strong decidability of INL relative to IN.

This completes the basic theory of realizability. We have carried out a series of changes and extensions that may have left the reader a little weary. Fortunately, we are nearly at the end of the theoretical development. We consider one more modification to realizability, but this one is motivated by practical as well as certain conceptual considerations.

EXERCISES

11.1 Complete all the details of the soundness of Q realizability. Provide a type theoretic version of Q realizability (i.e. state and prove the Q realizability analogue of Theorem 11.2).

11.2 Modify the original definition of realizability so that the following generalization of Theorem 11.5 holds: for each wff ϕ of STT, if $STT \vdash \phi$, then there exists a term t such that $STT \vdash t \downarrow \wedge t\rho\phi$.

Hint: Modify the clause for conjuction as follows:

$$z\rho(\phi \wedge \psi) \text{ is } [z \in PAIR \wedge (lz)\downarrow \wedge lz\rho\phi \wedge (rz)\downarrow \wedge rz\rho\psi]$$

These changes result from the lazy nature of pairing. Provide a type theoretic version of this notion of realizability.

11.3 Define a notion of realizability as follows. Adopt the clauses R1, R2, R4, R5 and R6 of ordinary realizability but modify R3 as follows:

R3. $z\rho\phi \to \psi$ is $[\forall x(x\rho\phi \to zx\rho\psi) \wedge \phi \to \psi]$

Investigate its properties with respect to soundness and completeness.

REFERENCES AND FURTHER READING

The most accessible account of realizability is Troelstra and Van Dalen (1988, Volume 1). This is also a rich source of exercises. Troelstra (1973) contains a very detailed study of the various options concerning the definition of realizability. Beeson (1985) provides an account under which full comprehension is sound. Dummett (1977) contains some philosophical discussions of realizability. The original source, Kleene (1945), is also worthy of attention, if only for historical reasons. Feferman (1979) provides an account for his constructive set theory T_0 and Beeson (1985) provides a realizability interpretation of Martin-Löf's theories.

12

NEGATIVE REALIZABILITY

In this second chapter on realizability we turn to the more practical aspects of realizability and set the scene for its application to program development. Traditional notions of realizability are fine in principle but next to useless in practice. The soundness proof provides a means of obtaining programs from proofs, but in general we obtain pretty silly programs.

More specifically, realizers often contain *redundant* information. For example, consider the realizer we obtain for the axiom of list induction:

$$\text{rec} \ [\ ]z \ = f$$

$$\text{rec} \ (u{:}x)z = gu(t[u \in T])x(t[x \in \text{List}[T]])(\text{rec} \ xz)$$

The function contains computationally *redundant* information. In particular, the canonical realizers of the membership assertions pass through the recursion without playing any substantial role—they are never invoked. Indeed, it would be preferable if the realizer took the following more natural and elegant form:

$$\text{rec} \ [\ ] \quad = f$$

$$\text{rec} \ (u{:}x) \ \ = gux(\text{rec} \ x)$$

The unfortunate form of the original arises from the need to carry around the information necessary to realize negative formula (in particular, atomic ones), and this information plays no computational role. However, we cannot just erase it; without it the function would not be a sound realizer for the induction scheme. A more radical approach is called for; we need to modify the very definition of realizability. More specifically, we shall remove the redundancy present in the original definition by exploiting the self-realizing properties of negative formulae. To achieve this we introduce a new notion of realizability which is fully cognizant of their self-realizing properties.

12.1 NEGATIVE FORMULAE AND NEGATIVE REALIZABILITY

The fundamental idea arises from the work of Shanin (1958). Shanin regards the meaning of nwff as immediate. This is not reflected in Q realizability since it transforms them into logically more complex formulae. For example, consider the clause for conjunction:

$$zQ(\phi \wedge \psi) \text{ is } [z \in \text{PAIR} \wedge \text{l}zQ\phi \wedge \text{r}zQ\psi]$$

Even when both conjuncts are negative the right-hand side is more complex than the left. While it is true that, for negative formulae, the transformed formulae are provably equivalent to the orginals, this can only be established once the full semantic definition is in place; Q realizability does not distinguish, in its definition, between negative and non-negative formulae. The special properties of the former only emerge after a mathematical investigation. This is the primary reason for the redundant information present in Q realizers. These observations form the beginnings of a solution.

The starting point of the investigation is Shanin's insistence that the meaning of nwff is unproblematic. This is encoded in the following demand:

$$z \text{ realizes } \phi \quad \text{is} \quad \phi \quad \text{where } \phi \text{ nwff}$$

The basic idea is to treat negative formulae along the same lines as the atomic ones: their realizability is taken as totally self-evident. This is justified by their self-realizing nature. In other words, instead of introducing a notion of realizability and then proving that negative formulae are self-realizing, we treat them as such from the very outset. The realizability for the other cases then proceeds by appealing to the structure of non-negative formula and taking advantage of their negative components. Accordingly, each of the clauses for realizability is split according to whether the wff involved are negative or not.

Negative realizability:

q1a. $zh(\phi \wedge \psi)$ is $[\phi \wedge zh\psi]$ only ϕ nwff
q1b. $zh(\phi \wedge \psi)$ is $[zh\phi \wedge \psi]$ only ψ nwff
q1c. $zh(\phi \wedge \psi)$ is $[z \in \text{PAIR} \wedge \text{l}zh\phi \wedge \text{r}zh\psi]$ neither nwff
q2a. $zh(\phi \vee \psi)$ is $[z \in \text{Bool} \wedge (z = \text{t} \to \phi) \wedge (z = \text{f} \to \psi)]$ both nwff
q2b. $zh(\phi \vee \psi)$ is $[z \in \text{INJ} \wedge (z \in \text{INL} \to \phi \wedge (\text{proj } z)h\phi)$ otherwise
         $\wedge (z \in \text{INR} \to \psi \wedge (\text{proj } z)h\psi)]$

q3a. $zh(\phi \to \psi)$ is $(\phi \to zh\psi)$ only ϕ nwff

q3b. $zh(\phi \to \psi)$ is $\forall x((xh\phi) \wedge \phi \to zxh\psi)$ ϕ not nwff

q4. $zh(\forall x\phi)$ is $\forall x(zxh\phi)$

q5a. $zh(\exists x\phi)$ is $\phi[z]$ ϕ nwff

q5b. $zh(\exists x\phi)$ is $[z \in \text{PAIR} \wedge \phi[\text{r}z] \wedge \text{l}zh\phi[\text{r}z]]$ otherwise

q6. $zh\phi$ is ϕ ϕ nwff

q7. $zh(\forall X\phi)$ is $\forall X(zh\phi)$

q8. $zh(\exists X\phi)$ is $\exists X(zh\phi)$

The conjunction case is split into three cases (implicitly four). The first two take advantage of the fact that one component is negative: a realizer has only to realize the non-negative component. When neither are negative then the standard clause is invoked. If both are negative then q6 applies. For disjunction there are two cases. The case where both are negative is catered for by only demanding that the realizer indicates which of the two cases applies. Since they are nwff their truth is sufficient. Otherwise the standard clause takes over. For implication we have two possibilities in the non-negative case. Either the antecedent is negative or it is not. In the second case the normal clause applies. For the other, we take advantage of the negative nature of the antecedent and only insist that the realizer applies to the consequent. For universal quantification there are no further options, since if ϕ is negative so is the quantified formula. Type quantification follows suite. The first-order existential case splits into two: the standard clause and that where ϕ is negative. In the latter case we need only the witness as the realizer since everything realizes the instance. There are further modifications possible (e.g. where only one disjunct of a disjunction is negative) but we leave these as exercises for the reader. They do not appear to be that useful in practice.

Although much more complex than Q realizability, it has the conceptual advantage of reflecting the constructively unproblematic nature of negative formula. Moreover, the new realizers contain much less *information* than the Q variety. This is in accord with our original desire to remove redundant computational information. We have achieved this by taking advantage of the self-realizing nature of negative formula which occur as components of non-negative ones. In these cases only the necessary information is included. As we shall see, this has important implications for program development. However, before we proceed with this aspect we need to investigate this new notion a little and, in particular, indicate its relationship to Q realizability.

12.2 Q AND h REALIZABILITY

The relationship between Q and ρ realizability is quite simple—in the presence of ECT_0, $tQ\phi$ iff $t\rho\phi$. Nothing so obvious characterizes the relationship between Q and h realizers. Indeed, the whole point of this new notion is to obtain realizers that are less *information bound*. Given that they are not equal, the next best thing is to indicate how to mediate between them. Indeed, this is the route we shall explore. We formulate mappings that turn the respective realizers into one another. There appear to be several ways of doing this but the one below captures certain aspects of our informal notion of *information loss*.

12.2.1 From Q Realizers to h Realizers

We first present a mapping that sends Q realizers to h realizers. It is defined recursively on the wff but is more fine grained since it mirrors the recursion of h realizability.

$$\mu(z, \phi) = z \qquad\qquad\qquad\qquad \phi \text{ atomic}$$

$$\mu(z, \phi \wedge \psi) = \mu(rz, \psi) \qquad\qquad\qquad \text{only } \phi \text{ nwff}$$

$$= \mu(lz, \phi) \qquad\qquad\qquad\quad \text{only } \psi \text{ nwff}$$

$$= (\mu(lz, \phi), \mu(rz, \psi)) \qquad\quad \text{otherwise}$$

$$\mu(z, \phi \vee \psi) = \text{case } z \text{ of } [\lambda x . \mathsf{t}, \lambda x . \mathsf{f}] \qquad \text{both nwff}$$

$$= \text{case } z \text{ of } [\lambda x . \text{in}_L(\mu(x, \phi)), \lambda x . \text{in}_R(\mu(x, \psi))] \qquad \text{otherwise}$$

$$\mu(z, \phi \rightarrow \psi) = \mu(zt[\phi], \psi) \qquad\qquad\qquad \text{only } \phi \text{ nwff}$$

$$= \lambda x . \mu(z(\sigma(x, \phi)), \psi) \qquad\qquad \text{otherwise}$$

$$\mu(z, \forall x \phi) = \lambda x . \mu(zx, \phi[x])$$

$$\mu(z, \exists x \phi) = rz \qquad\qquad\qquad\qquad \phi \text{ nwff}$$

$$= (\mu(lz, \phi[rz]), rz) \qquad\qquad \text{otherwise}$$

$$\mu(z, \forall X \phi) = \mu(z, \phi)$$

$$\mu(z, \exists X \phi) = \mu(z, \phi)$$

All the clauses of the recursion arise naturally from the definition of h realizability. Observe that where the whole formula is negative it is included in the general case. This applies to universal quantification, conjunction and implication. This is in keeping with their harmless nature—if true, any realizer will do. Notice also that in the general implication clause the mapping going in the opposite direction is invoked. This is necessary since a Q realizer for the antecedent has to be turned into an h realizer. Thus, to complete the picture, we must supply the details of this converse mapping.

12.2.2 From h Realizers to Q Realizers

Where the first *throws away information*, the second must attempt to recover it. The general strategy is to employ the canonical Q realizers. More precisely, where a non-negative compound formula has negative components, we employ the canonical Q realizers for these components to fill in the holes left by the supplied h realizer.

$$\sigma(z, \phi) = z \qquad\qquad\qquad\qquad\qquad\qquad\qquad \phi \text{ atomic}$$

$$\sigma(z, \phi \wedge \psi) = (t[\phi], \sigma(z, \psi)) \qquad\qquad\qquad\qquad \text{only } \phi \text{ nwff}$$

$$= (\sigma(z, \phi), t[\psi]) \qquad\qquad\qquad\qquad \text{only } \psi \text{ nwff}$$

$$= (\sigma(lz, \phi), \sigma(rz, \psi)) \qquad\qquad\qquad \text{otherwise}$$

$$\sigma(z, \phi \vee \psi) = z \longrightarrow in_L(t[\phi]), in_R(t[\psi]) \qquad\qquad \text{both nwff}$$

$$= \text{case } z \text{ of } [\lambda x . in_L(\sigma(x, \phi)), \lambda x . in_R(\sigma(x, \psi))] \qquad \text{otherwise}$$

$$\sigma(z, \phi \rightarrow \psi) = \lambda x . \sigma(z, \psi), \quad x \text{ fresh variable} \qquad\qquad \text{only } \phi \text{ nwff}$$

$$= \lambda x . \sigma(z(\mu(x, \phi)), \psi) \qquad\qquad\qquad \text{otherwise}$$

$$\sigma(z, \forall x \phi) = \lambda x . \sigma(zx, \phi[x])$$

$$\sigma(z, \exists x \phi) = (t[\phi], z) \qquad\qquad\qquad\qquad\qquad\qquad \phi \text{ nwff}$$

$$= (\sigma(lz, \phi[rz]), rz) \qquad\qquad\qquad\qquad \text{otherwise}$$

$$\sigma(z, \forall X \phi) = \sigma(z, \phi)$$

$$\sigma(z, \exists X \phi) = \sigma(z, \phi)$$

All the clauses are straightforward, but the reader should observe that the implication clause also invokes the mapping in the opposite direction.

12.2.3 Correctness

Finally, we show that these mappings are correct in the sense that they preserve the respective realizers.

Theorem 12.1 For each wff ϕ of PT_{neg},

(a) if $PT_{neg} \vdash zQ\phi$ then $PT_{neg} \vdash \mu(z, \phi)h\phi$.

(b) if $PT_{neg} \vdash zh\phi$ then $PT_{neg} \vdash \sigma(z, \phi)Q\phi$.

PROOF We prove (a) and (b) by simultaneous induction of the wff. The atomic case is trivial since both realizers are identical. We illustrate the others by reference to disjunction, implication and existential quantification. For disjunction we consider the general case. Suppose $zQ(\phi \vee \psi)$. Then if $z \in INL$ then we have $\mu(z, \phi \vee \psi) = in_L(\mu((\text{proj } z), \phi))$. Hence, $\text{proj}(\mu(z, \phi \vee \psi)) = \mu((\text{proj } z), \phi)$ which by induction h-realizes ϕ. The other case is similar. Part (b) is similar. Implication is a little more involved. First suppose that $zQ(\phi \rightarrow \psi)$. By definition we have $\forall x(\phi \wedge xQ\phi \rightarrow zxQ\psi)$. Suppose first that ϕ is not a nwff; then we have to show that $\lambda x. \mu(z\sigma(x, \phi), \psi)h(\phi \to \psi)$. Suppose $xh\phi$ and ϕ. By induction, $\sigma(x, \phi)Q\phi$. Hence, $z\sigma(x, \phi)Q\psi$. Hence, by induction again, $\mu(z\sigma(x, \phi), \psi)h\psi$ and we are finished. In the case where ϕ is nwff we know that $t[\phi]Q\phi$ and so $zt[\phi]Q\psi$; by induction, $\mu(zt[\phi], \psi)h\psi$. Part (b) is similar. For existential quantification the non-negative case is clear. Suppose that ϕ is nwff and that $zQ(\exists x\phi)$. Then we know that $\phi[rz]$. Hence $(rz)h(\exists x\phi)$. For the other mapping assume that $zh(\exists x\phi)$. Then, clearly, $(t[\phi], z)Q\exists x\phi$.

Parts (a) and (b) establish that the mappings are sound relative to the two notions of realizability: any wff realizable with respect to one notion is realizable with respect to the other. In particular, we can conclude that h realizability is sound.

Actually, one can abstract a little more from these mappings. Under a suitable definition of *equivalence* for h realizers one can show that $\mu(\sigma(z, \phi), \phi)$ is *equivalent* to z—under certain obvious assumptions about z; in particular, z must be an h realizer for ϕ. However, the actual notion of equivalence is somewhat combinatorial. Indeed, it must be defined by simultaneous recursion in conjunction with the *types* of realizers. For example, in the general implication case we proceed as follows:

$$T[\phi \to \psi] = \{f : \forall x \in T[\phi](\phi \to fx \in T[\psi]) \wedge \forall x \in T[\phi]\forall y \in T[\phi]$$

$$(x \cong_{\phi} y \to fx \cong_{\psi} fy)\}$$

$$f \cong_{\phi \to \psi} g \leftrightarrow \forall x \in T[\phi]\forall y \in T[\phi](x \cong_{\phi} y \to fx \cong_{\psi} gy)$$

$T[\phi \to \psi]$ is the (*extensional*) type of the $(\phi \to \psi)$ realizers and $\cong_{\phi \to \psi}$ the corresponding notion of equivalence. With the full definition in place, one can show that, for $z \in T[\phi]$, $\mu(\sigma(z, \phi), \phi) \in T[\phi] \wedge \mu(\sigma(z, \phi), \phi) \cong_{\phi} z$. We shall not present the full details here since the result is not required for the actual application of the concept of h realizability to program development. We have, already, sufficiently bored the reader with technical background. We only mention these ideas to indicate the fact that no essential *information* is lost when we pass from h realizers to Q realizers, and back. No such result is forthcoming in the other direction: μ throws away *information*.

12.3 PROGRAM EXTRACTION

In theory, Theorem 12.1 suffices to establish soundness for h realizability. However, to abstract programs from proofs we need to be more explicit about matters: we need to construct a *compiler* from derivations to programs.

Before we present the compiler we need some preliminary notation. Derivations will be represented by $\pi, \pi', \pi'', \pi 1, \pi 2$, etc. When we wish to indicate the conclusion of a derivation we shall write π/ϕ. To indicate that a wff ψ may be discharged when passing to a conclusion we shall write $[\psi]\pi/\phi$.

The actual function (F) is given by a recursion on the structure of proofs. To cater for the fact that a derivation may depend on assumptions, the function will be given relative to an assignment function ρ which maps wff into terms:

$$F: \text{derivations} \rightarrow (\text{assignment functions} \rightarrow \text{terms})$$

As we proceed through the definition of F we shall establish its correctness by induction on the structure of the derivations. More precisely, we show that, if the assignment function provably h-realizes the assumptions of a derivation, then F applied to the derivation provably h-realizes its conclusion.

Theorem 12.2 Let π be a derivation of ϕ from assumptions Γ and ρ any assignment such that for all η in Γ, $\Gamma + \mathrm{PT}_{\mathrm{neg}} \vdash \rho(\eta)h\eta$. Then $\Gamma + \mathrm{PT}_{\mathrm{neg}} \vdash (F\|\pi\|\rho)h\phi$.

The function is defined by recursion on the structure of the derivations where the various cases correspond to the introduction and elimination rules. If the conclusion of a derivation is negative then any realizer will do. This leaves the other cases.

(a) Conjunction: neither nwff We first consider the case of conjunction where neither wff is negative:

$$F\left\|\frac{\pi/\phi \quad \pi'/\psi}{\phi \wedge \psi}\right\|_{\rho} = \left(F\left\|\frac{\pi}{\phi}\right\|_{\rho}, F\left\|\frac{\pi'}{\psi}\right\|_{\rho}\right)$$

$$F\left\|\frac{\pi/\phi \wedge \psi}{\phi}\right\|_{\rho} = \mathrm{l}F\left\|\frac{\pi}{\phi \wedge \psi}\right\|_{\rho}$$

$$F\left\|\frac{\pi/\phi \wedge \psi}{\psi}\right\|_{\rho} = \mathrm{r}F\left\|\frac{\pi}{\phi \wedge \psi}\right\|_{\rho}$$

To see that the function preserves correctness consider the first clause. Suppose, inductively, that the two components of the pair h-realize ϕ and ψ respectively, then clearly the left-hand side h-realizes $\phi \wedge \psi$. The elimination rules are equally obvious.

(b) Conjunction: ϕ nwff Next we consider the case where only the first conjunct is negative:

$$F\left\|\frac{\pi/\phi \quad \pi'/\psi}{\phi \wedge \psi}\right\|_{\rho} = F\left\|\frac{\pi'}{\psi}\right\|_{\rho}$$

$$F\left\|\frac{\pi/\phi \wedge \psi}{\psi}\right\|_{\rho} = F\left\|\frac{\pi}{\phi \wedge \psi}\right\|_{\rho}$$

Once again, if the right-hand sides are h realizers for the conclusions of their derivations then so are the left-hand sides. This follows directly from the definition of h realizability for the case where ϕ is negative. In particular, inductively, F applied to the derivation of ϕ yields a realizer for ϕ. Since ϕ is negative, ϕ follows.

(c) **Conjunction: ψ nwff** In the next alternative only the second conjunct is negative. This is parallel to the previous case.

$$F \left\| \frac{\pi/\phi \quad \pi'/\psi}{\phi \wedge \psi} \right\|_{\rho} = F \left\| \frac{\pi}{\phi} \right\|_{\rho}$$

$$F \left\| \frac{\pi/\phi \wedge \psi}{\phi} \right\|_{\rho} = F \left\| \frac{\pi}{\phi \wedge \psi} \right\|_{\rho}$$

This completes the conjunction cases since if both are negative the whole conjunct is and consequently, if provable, anything is a realizer.

(d) **Disjunction: not both nwff** For disjunction there are two cases. In the first at least one disjunct is not negative.

$$F \left\| \frac{\pi/\phi}{\phi \vee \psi} \right\|_{\rho} = \text{in}_{\text{L}} \, F \left\| \frac{\pi}{\phi} \right\|_{\rho}$$

$$F \left\| \frac{\pi/\psi}{\phi \vee \psi} \right\|_{\rho} = \text{in}_{\text{R}} \, F \left\| \frac{\pi}{\psi} \right\|_{\rho}$$

$$F \left\| \frac{\pi/\phi \vee \psi \quad [\phi]\pi'/\eta \quad [\psi]\pi''/\eta}{\eta} \right\|_{\rho} = \text{case} \, F \left\| \frac{\pi}{\phi \vee \psi} \right\|_{\rho} \text{ of } [f, g]$$

$$\text{where } f = \lambda x . F \left\| \frac{\pi'}{\eta} \right\|_{\rho[\phi/x]}$$

$$\text{and } g = \lambda x . F \left\| \frac{\pi''}{\eta} \right\|_{\rho[\psi/x]}$$

The fact that these clauses preserve correctness may be less obvious. In particular, the elimination rule deserves comment. Assume, inductively, that for $xh\phi$ we have that $fxh\eta$. Inductively, $(F\|\pi/\phi \vee \psi\|_{\rho})h\phi \vee \psi$. If $F\|\pi/\phi \vee \psi\|_{\rho}$ is a left injection then $\text{proj}(F\|\pi/\phi \vee \psi\|_{\rho})h\phi$ and so $f(\text{proj}(F\|\pi/\phi \vee \psi\|_{\rho}))h\eta$. The right injection case is similar.

(*e*) **Disjunction: both nwff** In this case we can take advantage of the unproblematic nature of negative formula.

$$F \left\| \frac{\pi/\phi}{\phi \vee \psi} \right\|_\rho = t$$

$$F \left\| \frac{\pi/\psi}{\phi \vee \psi} \right\|_\rho = f$$

$$F \left\| \frac{\pi/\phi \vee \psi \quad [\phi]\pi'/\eta \quad [\psi]\pi''/\eta}{\eta} \right\|_\rho = F \left\| \frac{\pi}{\phi \vee \psi} \right\|_\rho \longrightarrow F \left\| \frac{\pi'}{\eta} \right\|_\rho, F \left\| \frac{\pi''}{\eta} \right\|_\rho$$

The argument for correctness is similar but this time the realizer for the disjunction is a Boolean and since the disjuncts are negative we have no need to update the assignment function since, if provable, anything will realize them.

(*f*) **Implication: ϕ not nwff** In the introduction case we need to update the assignment function and abstract on the variable assigned to the assumption.

$$F \left\| \frac{[\phi]\pi/\psi}{\phi \to \psi} \right\|_\rho = \lambda x \, . \, F \left\| \frac{\pi}{\psi} \right\|_{\rho[\phi/x]}$$

$$F \left\| \frac{\pi/\phi \to \psi \quad \pi'/\phi}{\psi} \right\|_\rho = F \left\| \frac{\pi}{\phi \to \psi} \right\|_\rho F \left\| \frac{\pi'}{\phi} \right\|_\rho$$

The elimination clause clearly preserves correctness. For the introduction clause we have only to observe that, by induction, if $xh\phi$ then $(F \| \pi/\psi \|_{\rho[\phi/x]})h\psi$.

(*g*) **Implication: ϕ nwff** This time we take advantage of the negative nature of the antecedent.

$$F \left\| \frac{[\phi]\pi/\psi}{\phi \to \psi} \right\|_\rho = F \left\| \frac{\pi}{\psi} \right\|_\rho$$

$$F \left\| \frac{\pi/\phi \to \psi \quad \pi'/\phi}{\psi} \right\|_\rho = F \left\| \frac{\pi}{\phi \to \psi} \right\|_\rho$$

The argument for correctness is unproblematic and follows directly from the induction hypothesis and the definition of negative realizability. Notice, in particular, that in the introduction rule the antecedent is negative and, if provable, any term will realize it. Consequently, there is no need to update the assignment function on the right-hand side.

(**h**) **Universal quantification** This time there is only the general case since if ϕ is negative so is $\forall x \phi$.

$$F \left\| \frac{\pi/\phi[x]}{\forall x \phi} \right\|_\rho = \lambda x . F \left\| \frac{\pi}{\phi[x]} \right\|_\rho$$

$$F \left\| \frac{\pi/\forall x \phi}{\phi[t]} \right\|_\rho = F \left\| \frac{\pi}{\forall x \phi} \right\|_\rho t$$

We leave the reader to ponder on the correctness of these clauses.

(**i**) **Existential quantification: ϕ not nwff** The general case is relatively straightforward, although the correctness for the elimination rule deserves some attention.

$$F \left\| \frac{\pi/\phi[x]}{\exists x \phi} \right\|_\rho = \left(F \left\| \frac{\pi}{\phi[x]} \right\|_\rho , x \right)$$

$$F \left\| \frac{\pi/\exists x \phi \quad [\phi[x]]\pi'/\eta}{\eta} \right\|_\rho = \text{let } (x, y) = (\mathrm{r}f, \mathrm{l}f) \text{ in } F \left\| \frac{\pi'}{\eta} \right\|_{\rho[y/\phi[x]]}$$

$$\text{where } f = F \left\| \frac{\pi}{\exists x \phi} \right\|_\rho$$

The correctness of the introduction clause is evident. For the elimination case, assume, inductively, that $f h \exists x \phi$. Then we know that $\mathrm{l}f h \phi[\mathrm{r}f/x]$. Moreover, under the assumption that $y h \phi[x], (F \| \pi'/\eta \|_{\rho[y/\phi[x]]}) h \eta$. Hence, the right-hand side h-realizes η.

(**j**) **Existential quantification: ϕ nwff** This is a special case of the above which takes note of the negative nature of the wff.

$$F \left\| \frac{\pi/\phi[x]}{\exists x \phi} \right\|_\rho = x$$

$$F \left\| \frac{\pi/\exists x \phi \quad [\phi[x]]\pi'/\eta}{\eta} \right\|_\rho = \text{let } x = f \text{ in } F \left\| \frac{\pi'}{\eta} \right\|_\rho$$

$$\text{where } f = F \left\| \frac{\pi}{\exists x \phi} \right\|_\rho$$

We leave the correctness for the reader. The introduction case follows directly from the definition of h realizability but induction is required for the elimination case.

(*k*) **Universal type quantification** This is quite straightforward since the type quantifiers are unproblematic.

$$F \left\| \frac{\pi/\phi[X]}{\forall X \phi} \right\|_\rho = F \left\| \frac{\pi}{\phi[X]} \right\|_\rho$$

$$F \left\| \frac{\pi/\forall X \phi}{\phi[T]} \right\|_\rho = F \left\| \frac{\pi}{\forall X \phi} \right\|_\rho$$

We leave the reader to establish correctness.

(*l*) **Existential type quantification** Once again the rules present no difficulties and we leave the reader to puzzle over their correctness.

$$F \left\| \frac{\pi/\phi[X]}{\exists X \phi} \right\|_\rho = F \left\| \frac{\pi}{\phi[X]} \right\|_\rho$$

$$F \left\| \frac{\pi/\exists X \phi \quad [\phi[X]]\pi'/\eta}{\eta} \right\|_\rho = \text{let } y = f \text{ in } F \left\| \frac{\pi'}{\eta} \right\|_{\rho[y/\phi[X]]}$$

$$\text{where } f = F \left\| \frac{\pi}{\exists X \phi} \right\|_\rho$$

This completes the definition of the function on the rules of the logic. We must now consider the axioms of the theory. Fortunately, most are negative and the function F can assign an arbitrary realizer. We have only to worry about the induction axioms.

(*m*) **Structural induction** We consider the following case:

$$[\forall x \in T(\phi[cx]) \wedge \forall u \in I \forall v \in I(\phi[u] \wedge \phi[v] \to \phi[duv])] \to \forall y \in I(\phi[y])$$

$$F \| [\forall x \in T(\phi[cx]) \wedge \forall u \in I \forall v \in I(\phi[u] \wedge \phi[v] \to \phi[duv])]$$

$$\to \forall y \in I(\phi[y]) \|_\rho$$

$$= \lambda(f, g) . \text{rec } (f, g)$$

where

$$\text{rec } (f, g)(cx) \quad = fx$$

$$\text{rec } (f, g)(duv) = guv((\text{rec } (f, g)u)(\text{rec } (f, g)v))$$

We can only hope that the reader is impressed by the elegance and naturalness of these recursion equations compared with their Q counterparts. We have still to establish correctness but this is a simple induction using the induction principle of the inductive type itself. We need to establish that, if $fh\forall x \in T(\phi[cx])$ and $gh\forall u \in I \forall v \in I(\phi[u] \wedge \phi[v] \to \phi[duv])$, then

$rec(f, g)h\forall y \in I(\phi[y])$. We set the induction formula to $rec(f, g)yh\phi[y]$. The rest is straightforward.

(n) Well-founded induction For convenience we repeat the axioms of closure and induction.

CLO. $\forall x \in T\{\forall y[(x, y) \in R \to y \in \Xi[T, R]] \to x \in \Xi[T, R]\}$

IND. $\forall x \in T\{\forall y[(x, y) \in R \to \phi[y]] \to \phi[x]\} \to \forall x \in \Xi[T, R](\phi[x])$

The realizer for the induction axiom is computed as follows:

$$F \| \forall x \in T\{\forall y[(x, y) \in R \to \phi[y]] \to \phi[x]\} \to \forall x \in \Xi[T, R](\phi[x]) \|_\rho$$

$$= \lambda f.(rec\ f)$$

where

$$rec\ fx = fx(\lambda y.(rec\ fy))$$

The argument for correctness is by $\Xi[T, R]$ induction, with the induction formula set to $(rec\ fx)h\phi[x]$.

    This completes the definition of the function and its proof of correctness. It may seem rather complicated but this is due to our demand that the realizer contain as little redundant computational information as possible. In any case, the programmer must treat the above as a *compiler for proofs* and should not be concerned with its inner complexity. In the next chapter we shall illustrate its employment in some detail, but this is for purely pedagogical reasons.

    Finally, we should stress that this notion of realizability is not meant to be our final word on the matter. There is no doubt that more *optimized* notions could be developed. Our objective has been only to set the scene.

EXERCISES

12.1 Introduce a notion of h realizability that corresponds to the original definition given in Sec. 11.2. State and prove an analogue of Theorem 12.1.

12.2 Define the analogue of the function F for Q realizability. Examine the relationships between the programs obtainable with this function and F itself. (For example, can we state their relationship in terms of the functions of Theorem 12.1?)

12.3 Complete the definition of the *extensional* types and equivalence for h realizability given at the end of Sec. 12.2. Prove the stated theorem.

12.4 Modify the notion of h realizability to take account of the cases where only one disjunct of a disjunction is negative and where only the consequent of an implication is negative. Generalize the theorems of this chapter with respect to this new notion.

REFERENCES AND FURTHER READING

One major source is Shanin (1958), but the paper is very complex and the technical presentation and objectives are very different to ours. Troelstra and Van Dalen (1988, Volume 1) also make some informal remarks about the content of Shanin's work. For applications to program development see Henson (1989a, 1989b) and the next two chapters. A similar approach has been taken in Hayashi (1987).

13

AN INTRODUCTION TO CONSTRUCTIVE FUNCTIONAL PROGRAMMING

In intuitionistic logic a program specification is an implicit assertion to the effect that a function exists. From a constructive proof of such a specification the required function can be automatically abstracted. This is the central idea that supports *constructive functional programming*. Programming within this paradigm is essentially proof construction in intuitionistic logic. In general, there are three phases to the derivation of a program.

1. Program specification
2. Proof of existence
3. Program extraction

By way of introduction we shall say a brief word about each of these phases.

(a) Program specification Traditionally, the specification of functions is achieved through the statement of two conditions: the so-called *pre-* and *post*-conditions on the function. The latter constitutes a statement of the required relationship between the input and output of the function under the government of the pre-condition placed upon the input. Traditionally, a function specification takes the following form:

$$\forall x(\phi[x] \to \psi[x, fx])$$

The wff ϕ is the pre-condition and ψ the post-condition. Logically, this function specification is a statement of correctness for the required function.

However, as it stands, this is not quite the style of specification we shall employ. In intuitionistic logic, under a realizability interpretation, it is sufficient to specify a function *implicitly*. In other words, we appeal to the antecedent of ECT_0:

$$\forall x(\phi[x] \rightarrow \exists y \psi[x, y])$$

There is one constraint on the general form, namely the pre-condition has to be negative. More generally, for functions of more than one argument, specifications take the following form. For convenience we have separated out the types of the implicit function.

$$\forall x_1 \in T_1 \cdots \forall x_n \in T_n(\phi[x_1, \ldots, x_n] \rightarrow \exists y \in S \psi[x_1, \ldots, x_n, y])$$

For total correctness the total existential quantifier is employed; this guarantees the totality of the implicit function.

$$\forall x_1 \in T_1 \cdots \forall x_n \in T_n(\phi[x_1, \ldots, x_n] \rightarrow \exists^\circ y \in S \psi[x_1, \ldots, x_n, y])$$

Of course, if all elements of S are provably total, this modification is redundant. Indeed, most of our examples will have such a simple format since we shall illustrate the technique with list and numerical programming. We make no apology for this; suffice it to say that our intentions are pedagogical.

(b) Proof of existence In the second phase the specification is viewed as a theorem to be established; a proof of the theorem then amounts to a justification that the specification can be met. This is the creative phase and the one where the majority of work has to be done. Indeed, by hand, the construction of such proofs is a rather tedious activity. Ideally, it needs to be supported by an interactive proof-development system which aids the programmer with proof construction.

In general, the *style* of proof determines the *style* of program that is abstracted during the last phase. Indeed, our examples have been selected in order to illustrate how different proof techniques lead to different *styles* of program.

(c) Program extraction This last phase is not properly part of the programming activity; it is automatic, given the output of the second. The abstraction function of the previous chapter (F) acts as a compiler which, given the proof, yields the required program. Programming is thus reduced to carrying out the existence proof. Moreover, the proof of existence, in conjunction with the correctness proof for F, automatically guarantees that the abstracted program meets the specification.

In this chapter we shall go through several simple examples, illustrating each of the stages and drawing out the theoretical and practical implications of the technique. More specifically, we shall study the development of three sorting algorithms.

1. Insertion sort
2. Mergesort
3. Quicksort

Each will be employed to illustrate a slightly different style of proof. The first involves only a simple structural induction, the second appeals to a complete numerical induction and the last employs a well-founded one.

13.1 INSERTION SORT

Generally, program specifications do not take place in isolation; normally, they are pursued relative to certain predefined functions and relations. Of course, these functions may themselves have been specified and derived but, since we are mainly concerned with the development of the sorting algorithms, we shall assume that certain basic functions are already in place.

In particular, we require two Boolean functions. The first determines whether a list is ordered and the second informs us whether one list is a permutation of another. For simplicity, we shall work with lists of numbers with their standard ordering.

$$\text{ord} [\ ] = t$$

$$\text{ord} [n] = t$$

$$\text{ord}\ m:n:x = \text{ord}\ n:x \qquad \text{when } m \leq n$$

$$\text{ord}\ m:n:x = f \qquad \text{when } n < m$$

$$\text{perm}\ x[\ ] = \text{empty}\ x$$

$$\text{perm}\ x(m:y) = (\text{member}\ mx)\ \text{and}\ (\text{perm}\ (\text{remove}\ mx)y)$$

where

$$\text{remove}\ m[\ ] = [\ ]$$

$$\text{remove}\ m(n:x) = x \qquad \text{when } m = n$$

$$\text{remove}\ m(n:x) = n:(\text{remove}\ mx) \qquad \text{when not}(m = n)$$

In what follows we shall abbreviate $(\text{ord}\ x) = t$ as $O(x)$ and $(\text{perm}\ xy) = t$ as $P(x, y)$. These relations are needed to state the specification of our sorting algorithm. Moreover, in the course of the program development we shall appeal to certain derived properties of these relations. In particular, we shall appeal to the following properties of P:

(a) $\forall x \in \text{List}[N]\{P(x, x)\}$
(b) $\forall x \in \text{List}[N]\forall y \in \text{List}[N]\{P(x, y) \to P(y, x)\}$
(c) $\forall x \in \text{List}[N]\forall y \in \text{List}[N]\forall z \in \text{List}[N]\{P(x, y) \wedge P(y, z) \to P(x, z)\}$
(d) $\forall x \in \text{List}[N]\forall y \in \text{List}[N]\forall u \in \text{List}[N]\forall v \in \text{List}[N]\{P(x, y) \wedge P(u, v) \to$
$$P(x * u, y * v)\}$$

These are not meant to be exhaustive but illustrative. Generally, where appeal is made to any such derived properties we shall indicate this by writing $P \wedge O$. These steps play a background role in the actual development of the sorting algorithms and their proofs and realizers are taken to be already in place. One could proceed in a different manner by supplying an abstract specification of these relations—in which case (a) to (d) would form part of the specification. Since we are primarily concerned with the development of the sorting algorithms it does not matter which route we adopt.

13.1.1 The Specification

The specification of the sorting algorithm will be the same for all three examples:

$$\forall x \in \text{List}[N]\exists y \in \text{List}[N]\{O(y) \wedge P(x, y)\} \qquad (a)$$

i.e. for every list there exists an ordered permutation of it. Notice that since $\text{List}[N]$ is total this specifies a total function.

Obviously, this is only part of the story. In order to prove this assertion we must decide upon a strategy for the proof. The most obvious employs list induction. However, if we attempt this we soon discover that the following lemma is required:

$$\forall n \in N\forall y \in \text{List}[N]\{O(y) \to \exists z \in \text{List}[N](P(n:y, z) \wedge O(z))\} \qquad (b)$$

This asserts that, for every natural number n and ordered list y, there is an ordered list that is a permutation of $n:y$. We shall see exactly where this is required when we prove (a). This completes the specification phase. Of course, it is not independent of the process of proof construction. One cannot determine which auxiliary results will prove necessary until the proof of the main specification is attempted. In this respect our presentation is retrospective.

13.1.2 Existence Proofs

In the constructive paradigm, the main step in program development involves the construction of proofs. We show in principle that such specifications can be met. For the present example we have two proofs to perform corresponding to (a) and (b). We do them in reverse order.

Theorem 13.1 $\forall n \in \mathbb{N} \forall y \in \text{List}[\text{N}]\{O[y] \rightarrow \exists z \in \text{List}[\text{N}](P(n:y, z) \wedge O(z))\}$

PROOF For convenience we shall write $\text{List}[\text{N}]$ as L. The main part of the proof proceeds by list induction with the induction formula: $\phi[y] = \{O[y] \rightarrow \exists z \in \text{List}[\text{N}](P(n:y, z) \wedge O(z))\}$.

$[n \in \text{N}]$	(1)	assumption
Base step		
$[n] \in L \wedge n{:}[\ ] = [n] \wedge P(n{:}[\ ], [n]) \wedge O([n])$	(2)	$P \wedge O$
$\exists z \in L(P(n{:}[\ ], z) \wedge O(z))$	(3)	$\exists$i, (2)
$O([\ ]) \rightarrow \exists z \in L(P(n{:}[\ ], z) \wedge O(z))$	(4)	$\rightarrow$i, (3)
Induction step		
$[m \in N]$	(5)	assumption
$[y \in L]$	(6)	assumption
$[\phi[y]]$	(7)	induction hypothesis
$[O(m{:}y)]$	(8)	assumption
$n \leq m \vee m < n$	(9)	theorem
$[m < n]$	(10)	assumption
$O[y]$	(11)	(8), $P \wedge O$
$\exists z \in L(P(n{:}y, z) \wedge O(z))$	(12)	$\rightarrow$e, (7)
$[z \in L \wedge (P(n{:}y, z) \wedge O(z))]$	(13)	assumption
$(m{:}z) \in L \wedge P(n{:}m{:}y, m{:}z) \wedge O(m{:}z)$	(14)	(13), (10), (8), $P \wedge O$
$\exists z \in L(P(n{:}m{:}y, z) \wedge O(z))$	(15)	$\exists$i, (14)
$\exists z \in L(P(n{:}m{:}y, z) \wedge O(z))$	(16)	$\exists$e, (15), (13), (12)
$[n \leq m]$	(17)	assumption
$O(n{:}m{:}y)$	(18)	$P \wedge O$, (8), (17)
$\exists z \in L(P(n{:}m{:}y, z) \wedge O(z))$	(19)	$\exists$i, (18), $P \wedge O$
$\exists z \in L(P(n{:}m{:}y, z) \wedge O(z))$	(20)	$\vee$e, (19), (16), (9)
$O(m{:}y) \rightarrow \exists z \in L(P(n{:}m{:}y, z) \wedge O(z))$	(21)	$\rightarrow$i, (20), (8)
$\phi[y] \rightarrow \phi[m{:}y]$	(22)	$\rightarrow$i, (21), (7)
$\forall m \in \text{N} \forall y \in L(\phi[y] \rightarrow \phi[m{:}y])$	(23)	$\rightarrow$i, $\forall$i, (22), (5), (6)
This completes the induction step.		
$\forall y \in L\{\phi[y]\}$	(24)	(4), (23), induction
$\forall n \in \text{N} \forall y \in L\{\phi[y]\}$	(25)	$\rightarrow$i, $\forall$i, (1), (24)

This completes the proof of (b). Unfortunately, we have not finished since we still have to deal with the main part of the specification. Fortunately, it is a little easier.

Theorem 13.2 $\forall x \in L \exists z \in L\{P(x, z) \wedge O(z)\}$

PROOF By induction with respect to x. We set the induction formula to $\phi[x] = \exists z \in L\{P(x, z) \wedge O(z)\}$.

Base step

$P([\ ], [\ ]) \wedge O([\ ])$	(1)	$P \wedge O$
$[\ ] \in L \wedge \{P([\ ], [\ ]) \wedge O([\ ])\}$	(2)	$\wedge i$, (1), closure
$\exists z \in L\{P([\ ], z) \wedge O(z)\}$	(3)	$\exists i$, (2)

Induction step

$[m \in N]$	(4)	assumption
$[x \in L]$	(5)	assumption
$\forall n \in N \forall y \in L\{O[y] \to \exists z \in L(P(n:y, z) \wedge O(z))\}$	(6)	Theorem 13.1
$[\phi[x]]$	(7)	induction hypothesis
$[z \in L \wedge P(x, z) \wedge O(z)]$	(8)	assumption
$\exists u \in L(P(m:z, u) \wedge O(u))$	(9)	$\forall e, \to e, \wedge e, (6), (8), (4)$
$[u \in L \wedge P(m:z, u) \wedge O(u)]$	(10)	assumption
$P(m:x, m:z)$	(11)	(8), $\wedge e$, $P \wedge O$
$u \in L \wedge P(m:x, u) \wedge O(u)$	(12)	$P \wedge O$, (10), (11), $\wedge e, \wedge i$
$\exists z \in L\{P(m:x, z) \wedge O(z)\}$	(13)	$\exists i$, (12)
$\exists z \in L\{P(m:x, z) \wedge O(z)\}$	(14)	$\exists e$, (13), (10), (9)
$\exists z \in L\{P(m:x, z) \wedge O(z)\}$	(15)	$\exists e$, (14), (8)
$\phi[x] \to \phi[m:x]$	(16)	$\to i$, (15), (7)
$\forall m \in N \forall x \in L\{\phi[x] \to \phi[m:x]\}$	(17)	$\to i, \forall i$, (4), (5), (16)

This completes the proof.

Notice that we have contracted several steps into one at several places. The finer steps are left to the reader as exercises—including the derived properties of $P \wedge O$. Although quite tedious, we have now done all the essentially creative work in constructing the program. The required program is implicit in the above proof and h realizability provides the means of automatically abstracting it.

13.1.3 Program Extraction

To obtain the sorting program we apply F to the existence proofs. Tables 13.1 and 13.2 contain the details of the computation: Table 13.1 contains the trace of the function F on the proof of (b) and Table 13.2 that for the proof of (a). For convenience, we have represented a proof by its conclusion and its undischarged assumptions. For the first computation (Table 13.1), we assume that the assignment function contains realizers for the basic properties of P and O and a proof for the decidability of the ordering on the natural numbers. For the second proof we employ an assignment function that, in addition, contains a realizer for the first. More precisely, we evaluate the second with respect to an assignment function ρ which satisfies:

$$\rho[\forall n \in N \forall y \in \text{List}[N]\{O[y] \to \exists z \in \text{List}[N](P(n:y, z) \wedge O(z))\}] = \text{insert}$$

Table 13.1

$$\text{F} \left\| \frac{n \in \text{N} \to \forall y \in L\{\phi[y]\}}{\forall n \in \text{N} \forall y \in L\{\phi[y]\}} \right\|_{\rho}$$

$$= \lambda n . \text{F} \left\| \frac{[n \in \text{N}]/\forall y \in L\{\phi[y]\}}{n \in \text{N} \to \forall y \in L\{\phi[y]\}} \right\|_{\rho}$$

$$= \lambda n . \text{F} \left\| \frac{\phi[[\ ]] \quad \forall m \in \text{N} \forall y \in L\{\phi[y] \to \phi[m:y]\}}{\forall y \in L\{\phi[y]\}} \right\|_{\rho}$$

$$= \lambda n . \text{rec} \left(\text{F} \left\| \frac{[O([\ ])/\exists z \in L(P(n:[\ ],z) \wedge O(z))}{\exists z \in L(P(n:[\ ],z) \wedge O(z))} \right\|_{\rho} , \text{F} \left\| \frac{m \in \text{N} \to \forall y \in L\{\phi[y] \to \phi[m:y]\}}{\forall m \in \text{N} \forall y \in L\{\phi[y] \to \phi[m:y]\}} \right\|_{\rho} \right)$$

$$= \lambda n . \text{rec} \left(\text{F} \left\| \frac{[n] \in L \wedge P(n:[\ ],[n]) \wedge O([n])}{\exists z \in L(P(n:[\ ],z) \wedge O(z))} \right\|_{\rho} , \text{F} \left\| \frac{m \in \text{N} \to \forall y \in L\{\phi[y] \to \phi[m:y]\}}{\forall m \in \text{N} \forall y \in L\{\phi[y] \to \phi[m:y]\}} \right\|_{\rho} \right)$$

$$= \lambda n . \text{rec} \left([n], \text{F} \left\| \frac{m \in \text{N} \to \forall y \in L\{\phi[y] \to \phi[m:y]\}}{\forall m \in \text{N} \forall y \in L\{\phi[y] \to \phi[m:y]\}} \right\|_{\rho} \right)$$

$$= \lambda n . \text{rec} \left([n], \lambda m . \text{F} \left\| \frac{[m \in \text{N}]/\forall y \in L\{\phi[y] \to \phi[m:y]\}}{m \in \text{N} \to \forall y \in L\{\phi[y] \to \phi[m:y]\}} \right\|_{\rho} \right)$$

$$= \lambda n . \text{rec} \left([n], \lambda m . \text{F} \left\| \frac{y \in L \to \{\phi[y] \to \phi[m:y]\}}{\forall y \in L\{\phi[y] \to \phi[m:y]\}} \right\|_{\rho} \right)$$

$$= \lambda n . \text{rec} \left([n], \lambda m y . \text{F} \left\| \frac{[y \in L]/\{\phi[y] \to \phi[m:y]\}}{y \in L \to \{\phi[y] \to \phi[m:y]\}} \right\|_{\rho} \right)$$

$$= \lambda n . \text{rec} \left([n], \lambda m y . \text{F} \left\| \frac{[\phi[y]]/\phi[m:y]}{\phi[y] \to \phi[m:y]} \right\|_{\rho} \right)$$

$$= \lambda n . \text{rec} \left([n], \lambda m y i . \text{F} \left\| \frac{[O(m:y)]/\exists z \in L(P(n:m:y,z) \wedge O(z))}{O(m:y) \to \exists z \in L(P(n:m:y,z) \wedge O(z))} \right\|_{\rho[\phi[y]/i]} \right)$$

$$= \lambda n . \text{rec}([n], \lambda m y i . \rho[n \leq m \vee m < n] \longrightarrow f, g)$$

where

$$f = \text{F} \left\| \frac{(P(n:m:y, n:m:y) \wedge O(n:m:y))}{\exists z \in L(P(n:m:y,z) \wedge O(z))} \right\|_{\rho[\phi[y]/i]} = (n:m:y)$$

and

$$g = \text{F} \left\| \frac{\exists z \in L(P(n:y,z) \wedge O(z)) \quad [z \in L \wedge P(n:y,z) \wedge O(z)]/\exists z \in L(P(n:m:y,z) \wedge O(z))}{\exists z \in L(P(n:m:y,z) \wedge O(z))} \right\|_{\rho[\phi[y]/i]}$$

$$= \text{let } z = h \text{ in F} \left\| \frac{(m:z) \in L \wedge P(n:m:y, m:z) \wedge O(m:z)}{\exists z \in L(P(n:m:y, m:z) \wedge O(z))} \right\|_{\rho[\phi[y]/i]} = m:h$$

where

$$h = \text{F} \left\| \frac{\phi[y] \quad O(y)}{\exists z \in L(P(n:y,z) \wedge O(z))} \right\|_{\rho[\phi[y]/i]} = i$$

Inserting these values for f and g we obtain:

$$= \lambda n . \text{rec}([n], \lambda m y i . \rho(n \leq m \vee m < n) \longrightarrow (n:m:y), (m:i))$$

that is

$$\begin{aligned}
&\text{insert } n[\ ] \quad = [n] \\
&\text{insert } n(m:y) = n:m:y \qquad \text{when } n \leq m \\
&\text{insert } n(m:y) = m:(\text{insert } ny) \quad \text{when } m < n
\end{aligned}$$

Table 13.2

$$F \left\| \frac{\phi[[\ ]] \quad \forall m \in \mathbb{N} \forall x \in L\{\phi[x] \to \phi[m:x]\}}{\forall x \in L \exists y \in L\{P(x,y) \land O(y)\}} \right\|_\rho$$

$$= \operatorname{rec}\left([\ ], F \left\| \frac{m \in \mathbb{N} \to \forall x \in L\{O[x] \to \phi[m:x]\}}{\forall m \in \mathbb{N} \forall x \in L\{\phi[x] \to \phi[m:x]\}} \right\|_\rho\right)$$

$$= \operatorname{rec}\left([\ ], \lambda mx. F \left\| \frac{[\phi[x]]/\phi[m:x]}{\phi[x] \to \phi[m:x]} \right\|_\rho\right)$$

$$= \operatorname{rec}\left([\ ], \lambda mxi. F \left\| \frac{\phi[x] \quad [y \in L \land P(x,y) \land O(y)]/\phi[m:x]}{\phi[m:x]} \right\|_{\rho[i/\phi[x]]}\right)$$

Evaluating the second part we obtain:

$$\lambda mxi. \operatorname{let} z = i \operatorname{in} F \left\| \frac{\exists u \in L(P(m:z,u) \land O(u)) \quad [u \in L \land P(m:z,u) \land O(u)]/\phi[m:x]}{\phi[m:x]} \right\|_{\rho[i/\phi[x]]}$$

$$= \lambda mxi. \operatorname{let} z = i \operatorname{in} \left(\operatorname{let} u = f \operatorname{in} F \left\| \frac{u \in L \land P(m:x,u) \land O(u)}{\phi[m:x]} \right\|_{\rho[i/\phi[x]]}\right)$$

$$= \lambda mxi. \operatorname{let} z = i \operatorname{in} f$$

where

$$f = F \left\| \frac{[z \in L \land P(x,z) \land O(z)]}{\exists u \in L(P(m:z,u) \land O(u))} \right\|_{\rho[i/\phi[x]]}$$

$$= \operatorname{insert} mz$$

Putting the parts together again we obtain the following:

$$\operatorname{rec}([\ ], \lambda mxi.(\operatorname{insert} mi))$$

which rewrites as follows:

$$\operatorname{insertsort} [\ ] = [\ ]$$

$$\operatorname{insertsort} (m:x) = \operatorname{insert} m(\operatorname{insertsort} x)$$

where insert is the program obtained from the first computation. In general, the assignment function must contain the realizers for all previously established theorems that are used in the proof; i.e. wherever we write 'theorem' to justify a proof step we are assuming that the realizer is obtained from the underlying assignment function.

Eventually, we obtain the following pair of functions:

$$\operatorname{insert} n[\ ] = [n]$$
$$\operatorname{insert} n(m:y) = n:m:y \qquad \text{when } n \le m$$
$$\operatorname{insert} n(m:y) = m:(\operatorname{insert} ny) \qquad \text{when } m < n$$

$$\operatorname{insertsort} [\ ] = [\ ]$$
$$\operatorname{insertsort} (m:x) = \operatorname{insert} m(\operatorname{insertsort} x)$$

We hope that the reader is impressed with the elegance of these functions; this is the main benefit of negative realizability. Had we employed the Q variety we would have obtained correct but *information-bound* functions.

Finally, notice that we could have been more ambitious in our original specification and not restricted matters to lists of numbers. Somewhat informally, define the type of all total orderings on a type X as follows:

$$\text{TotOrd}(X) = \{f \in \text{List}[X] \otimes \text{List}[X] \Rightarrow \text{Bool}: f \text{ is a total ordering on } X\}$$

With this notion we can extend our original specification:

$$\forall x \in \text{List}[X] \forall f \in \text{TotOrd}(X) \exists y \in \text{List}[X]\{O(y, f) \wedge P(x, y)\}$$

where $O(y, f)$ asserts that y is ordered relative to f. We would then obtain the following function—by an almost identical proof:

$$\text{insertsort}[\ ]f = [\ ]$$

$$\text{insertsort}(m:x)f = \text{insert } mf(\text{insertsort } xf)$$

Moreover, since the proof does not depend upon X, by universal type introduction, insertsort $\in \Pi X . \{\text{List}[X] \Rightarrow \text{TotOrd}(X) \Rightarrow \text{List}[X]\}$. Thus the technique easily extends to facilitate the development of polymorphic functions.

13.2 MERGESORT

We further illustrate the idea of constructive functional programming by reference to a different sorting technique. The reader should by now have grasped the rudiments of the abstraction algorithm and from now on we shall not carry out stage three explicitly (i.e. indicate the trace of the abstraction function on the proof); we only present the results. This is in keeping with the spirit of the present approach. The abstraction function is best viewed as a compiler from proofs to programs and the programmer is only required to carry ou the specifications and the existence proofs.

The top-level specification is the same as before, i.e.

$$\forall x \in \text{List}[N] \exists y \in \text{List}[N]\{O(y) \wedge P(x, y)\} \qquad (a)$$

However, this time we argue by complete numerical induction on the length of lists. For ease of presentation we again adopt a retrospective analysis and first prove any of the auxiliary lemmas.

13.2.1 The Development of Merge

If (a) is attempted by complete numerical induction we require the following lemma:

$$\forall x \in \text{List}[N] \forall y \in \text{List}[N] \exists z \in \text{List}[N]\{O(x) \wedge O(y) \quad \rightarrow \quad P(x * y, z) \wedge O(z)\}$$

$$(b)$$

This is obviously a specification of a merge function which takes two ordered lists u, v and outputs an ordered permutation of $u * v$. The proof involves a nested induction which makes life a little more interesting.

Theorem 13.3 $\forall x \in L \forall y \in L \exists z \in L\{O(x) \wedge O(y) \rightarrow (P(x * y, z) \wedge O(z))\}$

PROOF By list induction: we set the induction formula to
$$\phi[x] = \forall y \in L \exists z \in L\{O(x) \wedge O(y) \quad \rightarrow \quad P(x * y, z) \wedge O(z)\}$$

Base step

$\{O([\ ]) \wedge O(y) \rightarrow (P([\ ] * y, y) \wedge O(y))\}$	(1)	$P \wedge O$, definition (*)
$\exists z \in L\{O([\ ]) \wedge O(y) \rightarrow (P([\ ] * y, z) \wedge O(z))\}$	(2)	$\exists i$, i
$\forall y \in L \exists z \in L\{O([\ ]) \wedge O(y) \rightarrow (P([\ ] * y, z) \wedge O(z))\}$	(3)	$\forall i$, $\rightarrow i$

Induction step

$[m \in N]$	(4)	assumption
$[x \in L]$	(5)	assumption
$[\phi[x]]$	(6)	induction hypothesis

Subinduction: set subinduction formula to:
$$\psi[y] = \exists z \in L\{O(m:x) \wedge O(y) \rightarrow (P((m:x) * y, z) \wedge O(z))\}$$

Base step

$O(m:x) \wedge O([\ ]) \rightarrow (P((m:x) * [\ ], m:x) \wedge O(m:x))$	(7)	$P \wedge O$, definition (*)
$\exists z \in L\{O(m:x) \wedge O([\ ]) \rightarrow (P((m:x) * [\ ], z) \wedge O(z))\}$	(8)	$\exists i$, (7)

Subinduction step

$[y \in L]$	(9)	assumption
$[n \in N]$	(10)	assumption
$[\psi[y]]$	(11)	subinduction hypothesis
$m \leq n \vee n < m$	(12)	theorem
$[m \leq n]$	(13)	assumption
$\exists z \in L\{O(x) \wedge O(n:y) \rightarrow (P(x * (n:y), z) \wedge O(z))\}$	(14)	(6), $\forall e$, $\rightarrow e$
$[z \in L \wedge \{O(x) \wedge O(n:y) \rightarrow (P(x * (n:y), z) \wedge O(z))\}]$	(15)	assumption
$O(m:x) \wedge O(n:y) \rightarrow \{P((m:x) * (n:y), m:z) \wedge O(m:z)\}$	(16)	$P \wedge O$
$\exists z \in L\{O(m:x) \wedge O(n:y) \rightarrow (P((m:x) * (n:y), z) \wedge O(z))\}$	(17)	(16), $\exists i$
$\exists z \in L\{O(m:x) \wedge O(n:y) \rightarrow (P((m:x) * (n:y), z) \wedge O(z))\}$	(18)	$\exists e$, (14), (15)
$[n < m]$	(19)	assumption
$[z \in L \wedge \{O(m:x) \wedge O(y) \rightarrow (P((m:x) * y, z) \wedge O(z))\}]$	(20)	assumption
$O(m:x) \wedge O(n:y) \rightarrow (P((m:x) * (n:y), n:z) \wedge O(n:z))$	(21)	$P \wedge O$
$\exists z \in L\{O(m:x) \wedge O(n:y) \rightarrow (P((m:x) * (n:y), z) \wedge O(z))\}$	(22)	(21), $\exists i$
$\exists z \in L\{O(m:x) \wedge O(n:y) \rightarrow (P((m:x) * (n:y), z) \wedge O(z))\}$	(23)	$\exists e$, (11)
$\exists z \in L\{O(m:x) \wedge O(n:y) \rightarrow (P((m:x) * (n:y), z) \wedge O(z))\}$	(24)	$\vee e$, (12)
$\psi[y] \rightarrow \psi[n:y]$	(25)	$\rightarrow i$, (11), (24)
$\forall y \in L\{\psi[y] \rightarrow \psi[n:y]\}$	(26)	$\forall i$, $\rightarrow i$, (9)
$\forall n \in N \forall y \in L\{\psi[y] \rightarrow \psi[n:y]\}$	(27)	$\forall i$, $\rightarrow i$, (10)
$\forall y \in L\{\psi[y]\}$	(28)	subinduction
$\forall x \in L\{\phi[x] \rightarrow \phi[m:x]\}$	(29)	$\forall i$, $\rightarrow i$, (5)
$\forall m \in N \forall x \in L\{\phi[x] \rightarrow \phi[m:x]\}$	(30)	$\forall i$, $\rightarrow i$, (4)
$\forall x \in L\{\phi[x]\}$	(31)	main induction

This completes the proof

If we apply the abstraction function to the above proof we obtain the following function:

$$\text{merge}\,(m\!:\!x)[\ \ ] \quad = (m\!:\!x)$$

$$\text{merge}\,(m\!:\!x)(n\!:\!y) = m\!:\!\text{merge}\,x\,(n\!:\!y) \qquad \text{when } m \leq n$$

$$\text{merge}\,(m\!:\!x)(n\!:\!y) = n\!:\!(\text{merge}\,(m\!:\!x)y) \qquad \text{when } n < m$$

In this case we assume that the assignment function contains a realizer for the decidability of the ordering on the natural numbers. The function obtained is elegant and natural. Indeed, it is the expected one.

13.2.2 Development of the Sorting Function

This leaves the main theorem to prove. In this case we assume two functions, take and drop, which select initial and final segments of a list. These are given by the following recursion equations:

$$\text{take}\,0x = [\ \ ]$$

$$\text{take}\,n'[\ \ ] = [\ \ ]$$

$$\text{take}\,n'(u\!:\!x) = u\!:\!(\text{take}\,nx)$$

$$\text{drop}\,0x = x$$

$$\text{drop}\,n'[\ \ ] = [\ \ ]$$

$$\text{drop}\,n'(u\!:\!x) = \text{drop}\,nx$$

The length of the segment selected is determined by the first argument. In addition, for convenience, we employ the following abbreviations:

$$\text{int}\,x \quad \text{for} \quad \text{take}\,((\text{len}\,x)/2)x$$

$$\text{end}\,x \quad \text{for} \quad \text{drop}\,((\text{len}\,x)/2)x$$

We shall see the necessity for these as we proceed. We could, of course, take matters further and specify these, but our main objective is to illustrate the use of complete numerical induction.

Theorem 13.4 $\forall x \in \text{List}[\,\text{N}\,]\exists y \in \text{List}[\,\text{N}\,]\{O(y) \wedge P(x, y)\}$

PROOF Let

$$\delta[k] = \forall x \in \text{List}[\,\text{N}\,]((\text{len}\,x) = k \rightarrow \exists y \in \text{List}[\,\text{N}\,]\{O(y) \wedge P(x, y)\}).$$

We establish by complete numerical induction that $\forall n \in N(\delta[n])$. we must prove $\forall n \in N\{\forall k \in N(k < n \to \delta[k]) \to \delta[n]\}$.

$[n \in N]$	(1)	assumption
$[\forall k \in N(k < n \to \delta[k])]$	(2)	assumption
$n < 2 \vee 2 \leq n$	(3)	theorem
$[n < 2]$	(4)	assumption
$[x \in L \wedge (\text{len } x) = n]$	(5)	assumption
$\{O(x) \wedge P(x, x)\}$	(6)	$P \wedge O$
$\exists y \in L\{O(y) \wedge P(x, y)\}$	(7)	$\exists$i, $\to$i from (6)
$(x \in L \wedge (\text{len } x) = n) \to \exists y \in L\{O(y) \wedge P(x, y)\}$	(8)	(7), (5), $\to$i
$\delta[n]$	(9)	$\forall$i, (8)
$[2 \leq n]$	(10)	assumption
$[x \in \text{List}[N] \wedge (\text{len } x) = n]$	(11)	assumption
$\text{len}(\text{init } x) < n$	(12)	definition of init
$\text{len}(\text{end } x) < n$	(13)	definition of end
$\exists y \in \text{List}[N]\{O(y) \wedge P((\text{init } x), y)\}$	(14)	$\forall$e, $\to$e, (2), (12)
$\exists y \in \text{List}[N]\{O(y) \wedge P((\text{end } x), y)\}$	(15)	$\forall$e, $\to$e, (2), (13)
$[O(u) \wedge P((\text{init } x), u)]$	(16)	assumption
$[O(v) \wedge P((\text{end } x), v)]$	(17)	assumption
$O(\text{merge } uv) \wedge P(x, (\text{merge } uv))$	(18)	$P \wedge O$, Theorem 13.3
$\exists y \in \text{List}[N]\{O(y) \wedge P(x, y)\}$	(19)	$\exists$i, (18)
$\exists y \in \text{List}[N]\{O(y) \wedge P(x, y)\}$	(20)	$\exists$e, (19), (17)
$\exists y \in \text{List}[N]\{O(y) \wedge P(x, y)\}$	(21)	$\exists$e, (20), (16)
$(x \in \text{List}[N] \wedge (\text{len } x) = n) \to \exists y \in \text{List}[N]\{O(y) \wedge P(x, y)\}$	(22)	$\to$i, (11), (21)
$\delta[n]$	(23)	$\forall$i, (22)
$\delta[n]$	(24)	$\vee$e, (9), (23)
$\forall k \in N(k < n \to \delta[k]) \to \delta[n]$	(25)	(2), (24), $\to$i
$\forall n \in N\{\forall k \in N(k < n \to \delta[k]) \to \delta[n]\}$	(26)	$\forall$i, $\to$i, (25), (1)

The result now follows by complete numerical induction.

To abstract the program we must assume that the assignment function comes equipped with a realizer (i.e. the merge function) for the first existence proof. We then obtain the following function:

mergesort $x = x$ when $(\text{len } x) < 2$

mergesort $x = \text{merge}(\text{mergesort } u)(\text{mergesort } v)$ otherwise

where $u = \text{take }((\text{len } x)/2)x$

$v = \text{drop }((\text{len } x)/2)x$

Once again we obtain a natural and elegant function. We urge the reader to go through the details of the computation for each of these two derivations. Although this is not strictly part of the programming enterprise the exercise will be instructive. In particular, this example requires the use of the h realizability scheme for complete numerical induction. This is a special case of well-founded induction—which is also employed in our final example.

13.3 QUICKSORT AND WELL-FOUNDED INDUCTION

To complete our introductory exposition we examine one final example of sorting and one that more forcefully illustrates the employment of well-founded induction. Our objective is to derive the quicksort algorithm. To achieve this we employ well-founded induction on the following relation:

$$R = \{(x, y) \in \text{List}[N] \otimes \text{List}[N] : (\text{len } y) < (\text{len } x)\}$$

We know from Chapter 9 that the well-founded type generated by this relation, namely $\Xi[N, R]$, is equivalent to $\text{List}[N]$. We are thus working within this well-founded type even though it is extensionally equivalent to $\text{List}[N]$. If we adopt this proof strategy then we are forced into proving the following auxiliary lemma—where $\text{Mem}(u, v)$ abbreviates $(\text{member } uv) = t$ and $y \ll x$ abbreviates $(x, v) \in R$:

$$\forall n \in N \forall x \in \text{List}[N] \exists y \in \text{List}[N] \otimes \text{List}[N] \{\theta \wedge \gamma \wedge \phi\}$$

where $\theta = ly \ll (n:x) \wedge ry \ll (n:x)$

$$\gamma = \forall x[\text{Mem}(z, ly) \rightarrow z < n] \wedge \forall z[\text{Mem}(z, ry) \rightarrow z \geq n]$$

$$\phi = P((ly) * (ry), (n:x))$$

This specifies a function that, given a number and a list, returns a pair of lists that satisfy three constraints. The first insists that the left and right components are of smaller length than the original (i.e. $n:y$) and the second that every element of the left is less than n and that every element of the right is greater than or equal to n. The final constraint demands that no elements are lost or introduced. More explicitly, we have specified a function:

$$\text{split} \in N \Rightarrow \text{List}[N] \Rightarrow (\text{List}[N] \otimes \text{List}[N])$$

where

$l(\text{split } nx) \ll (n:x) \wedge r(\text{split } nx) \ll (n:x)$

$\forall z[\text{Mem}(z, l(\text{split } nx)) \rightarrow z < n] \wedge \forall z[\text{Mem}(z, r(\text{split } nx)) \rightarrow z \geq n]$

$P((l(\text{split } nx)) * [n] * (r(\text{split } nx)), (n:x))$

However, since our primary aim is to illustrate the employment of well-founded induction, we shall assume that the function split is in place. In this connection, for simplicity, we shall write Lnx for $l(\text{split } nx)$ and Rnx for $r(\text{split } nx)$.

Theorem 13.5 $\forall x \in \text{List}[N] \exists y \in \text{List}[N] \{O(y) \wedge P(x, y)\}$

PROOF By well-founded induction with induction formula set to $\delta[x] =$ $\exists y \in \text{List}[N]\{O(y) \wedge P(x, y)\}$). We have to prove that

$$\forall x \in \text{List}[N]\{\forall z(z \ll x \rightarrow \delta[z]) \rightarrow \delta[x]\}.$$

Again write L for List $[N]$.

$[x \in L]$	(1)	assumption
$x = [\ ] \vee \exists n \in N \exists u \in L(x = n:u)$	(2)	theorem
$[x = [\ ]]$	(3)	assumption
$O([\ ]) \wedge P([\ ], [\ ])$	(4)	$P \wedge O$
$\exists y \in L\{O(y) \wedge P(x, y)\}$	(5)	(4), $\exists$i
$\forall z(z \ll x \rightarrow \delta[z]) \rightarrow \delta[x]$	(6)	$\forall$i, (5), $\rightarrow$i
$[\exists n \in N \exists u \in L(x = n:u)]$	(7)	assumption
$[\forall z(z \ll x \rightarrow \delta[z])]$	(8)	assumption
$[x = n:u]$	(9)	assumption
$Lnu \ll x$	(10)	γ
$Lnu \ll x \rightarrow \delta[Lnu]$	(11)	$\forall$e, (8)
$\delta[Lnu]$	(12)	$\rightarrow$e, (11), (10)
$Rnu \ll x$	(13)	γ
$Rnu \ll x \rightarrow \delta[Rnu]$	(14)	$\forall$e, (8)
$\delta[Rnu]$	(15)	$\rightarrow$e, (13), (14)
$[O[w] \wedge P(Lnu, w)]$	(16)	assumption
$[O[v] \wedge P(Rnu, v)]$	(17)	assumption
$O(w * [n] * v) \wedge P(w * [n] * v, x)$	(18)	$P \wedge O, \theta, \gamma, \phi$
$\delta[x]$	(19)	$\exists$i, (18)
$\delta[x]$	(20)	$\exists$e, (19), (17), (15)
$\delta[x]$	(21)	$\exists$e, (20), (16), (12)
$\delta[x]$	(22)	$\exists$e(twice), (7), (9)
$\forall z(z \ll x \rightarrow \delta[z]) \rightarrow \delta[x]$	(23)	$\rightarrow$i, (8), (22)
$\forall z(z \ll x \rightarrow \delta[z]) \rightarrow \delta[x]$	(24)	$\vee$e, (3), (7), (2)
$x \in L \rightarrow \forall z(z \ll x \rightarrow \delta[z]) \rightarrow \delta[x]$	(25)	$\rightarrow$i, (1), (24)
$\forall x \in L(\forall z(z \ll x \rightarrow \delta[z]) \rightarrow \delta[x])$	(26)	$\forall$i, (25)

By well-founded induction we are finished.
If we apply the abstraction algorithm to this proof we obtain:

$$\text{rec } Fx = Fx(\lambda z.(\text{rec } Fz))$$

where F is the realizer for $\forall x \in L(\forall z(z \ll x \rightarrow \delta[z]) \rightarrow \delta[x])$. Let f be the realizer for the theorem $x = [\ ] \vee \exists n \in N \exists u \in L(x = n:u)$. It is assumed that this is supplied by the assignment function. Then F is given as follows, where we have abbreviated (proj f) as a:

$$\lambda xg.\text{case } f \text{ of } [\lambda z.[\ ], \quad \lambda z.(g(L(ra)(la)) * [ra] * g(R(ra)(la)))]$$

Writing quicksort for rec F and unpacking f we obtain the following:

quicksort $[\ ] = [\ ]$

quicksort $(n:u) = (\text{quicksort } (Lnu)) * [n] * (\text{quicksort } (Rnu))$

that is

$$\text{quicksort} \; [\;] \quad = [\;]$$

$$\text{quicksort} \, (n:u) = (\text{quicksort} \; u') * [n] * \text{quicksort}(u'')$$
$$\text{where} \; (u', u'') = (\text{split} \; nu)$$

Once again negative realizability produces an elegant solution; there is no sign of any redundant computational information.

13.4 SOME MORALS

One might suggest that little has been gained by this approach to program construction since these proofs are extremely tedious. This would be a mistake. If one is concerned with correctness (and this is taken for granted), at some level they cannot be avoided. The advantage of the present approach is that correctness is all that needs to be established; the rest is automatic. Of course, in practice such proof/program development needs to be supported by an interactive proof development system which facilitates the construction of such proofs. Constructive functional programming can only be realistically achieved in such an environment. Such a system is currently under development under SERC support at Essex University. The present system not only automatically abstracts the programs from the proofs but also provides an interactive environment for proof development.

In this chapter we have shown that *natural* programs can be derived via negative realizability. Our examples do not bristle with originality but this is really beside the point. The fact that they are familiar is a pedagogical advantage. However, to demonstrate that the constructive approach is a viable one it needs to be compared with the traditional *specify and derive* paradigm of functional programming, i.e. *transformational programming*.

EXERCISES

13.1 Abstract the programs from the proofs of Theorems 13.3 and 13.4 and 13.5. This is a long and tedious process but the reader should write out at least one derivation in complete detail.

13.2 Carry out the development of each of the sorting algorithms using Q realizability. This can only be done if the abstraction algorithm (set as an exercise in the last chapter) is in place. The reader should pay particular attention to the style of programs obtained.

13.3 Prove and abstract a program for the split function employed in quicksort.

13.4 Derive polymorphic sorting algorithms for each of the sorting techniques studied.

REFERENCES AND FURTHER READING

Henson (1989a, 1989b) contain many more examples carried out using similar realizability techniques. Hayashi and Nakano (1988) contains the details of a system based upon Lisp and Feferman's T_0 with a few example derivations but using a slightly different realizability technique. The work on *the theory of constructions* should also be mentioned. Huet (1990b) provides a fine introduction and Mohring (1986) provides its application to algorithm development.

14

PROGRAM SYNTHESIS

Transformational programming forms one of the central tools in functional program development. One begins with a rather crude version of the required function. This is then subjected to a battery of transformational techniques which result in an *improved* program. In many cases the improvement is motivated by efficiency considerations, but not always. There are many such techniques available in the literature and our goal is not to survey them all. Indeed, the objective of this chapter is not primarily to present any in their traditional format. Instead, we shall study just two from within the paradigm of constructive functional programming.

The two main sections of this chapter are devoted to an exploration of the following transformational techniques:

1. Duplicate computations
2. Accumulating parameters

The account offered is not the standard one but is informed by the ideas of the last three chapters. The traditional technique involves the formulation of an abstract specification of the program (the so-called *eureka* step) and this forms the basis for the transformations. Operations such as *FOLD* and *UNFOLD* then yield the improved program. Within the present paradigm the eureka step is recast as a program specification and then subjected to the constructive treatment. The result is a somewhat better mathematical account of transformational programming where its connection with the corresponding proofs of correctness is made tight and explicit. Indeed, as we shall see, constructive functional programming turns the whole technique of transformational programming on its head.

14.1 AVOIDING DUPLICATE COMPUTATIONS

One technique for improving programs seeks to avoid doing the same computation over and over again. This idea is easily demonstrated by reference to the following function:

$$\text{fib } 0 = 1$$

$$\text{fib } 1 = 1$$

$$\text{fib } (n + 2) = (\text{fib } n) + (\text{fib } n')$$

This is obviously quite inefficient. In fact, it has exponential time complexity since the computation of (fib n) requires at least (fib n) recursive calls of fib. Indeed, it is easy enough to see where the inefficiency resides: each recursive call involves a calculation that has already been carried out at the previous stage. More exactly, the calculations of (fib n) and (fib n') both involve the calculation of fib $(n - 1)$; the heart of the inefficiency stems from the necessity to duplicate computations. To overcome this we need to ensure that each such computation is carried out only once. A simple way of achieving this involves the construction of a function that returns pairs of adjacent values of fib. This leads naturally to the following definition:

$$gn = ((\text{fib } (n + 1)), (\text{fib } n)) \quad (*)$$

Obviously, this is not a solution as it stands. If this is taken as the definition of g it will generate no improvement since we will still have to compute the values of fib twice. It is to be taken not as a definition of a function but rather as a specification. This is the starting point of the transformational approach.

14.1.1 The Transformational Approach

The traditional or transformational approach employs (*) as the basis for the transformation. The original definition of fib is then gradually massaged into a new improved program:

$$g0 = ((\text{fib } 1), (\text{fib } 0)) \qquad \text{instance of } *$$

$$= (1, 1) \qquad \text{UNFOLD fib}$$

$$g(n + 1) = ((\text{fib } (n + 2)), (\text{fib } (n + 1))) \qquad \text{instance of } *$$

$$= ((\text{fib } (n + 1)) + (\text{fib } n), (\text{fib } (n + 1))) \qquad \text{UNFOLD fib}$$

$$= \text{let } (u, v) = ((\text{fib } (n + 1)), (\text{fib } n)) \text{ in } (u + v, u) \qquad \text{definition of let}$$

$$= \text{let } (u, v) = (gn) \text{ in } (u + v, u) \qquad \text{FOLD } g$$

We have thus arrived at a recursive characterization of the function g:

$$g0 = (1, 1)$$

$$g(n + 1) = \text{let } (u, v) = (gn) \text{ in } (u + v, u)$$

Most of the steps are quite obvious but those marked as FOLD and UNFOLD are the significant ones and require comment. Indeed, they form the heart of the transformational approach. The UNFOLD steps correspond to using the definitions of fib in a left-to-right direction. More generally, UNFOLD steps correspond to the replacement, in a term, of instances of the left-hand side of an equation by the right-hand side. FOLD steps do the reverse. Here instances of the right-hand side are replaced by the left. Both procedures appeal to the definitions of functions but employ them in opposite directions. We shall say a little more about the justification for this procedure shortly but first notice that, with g in place, we can define an improved Fibonacci function:

$$\text{fib}' \ 0 \quad = 1$$

$$\text{fib}' \ 1 \quad = 1$$

$$\text{fib}' \ (n + 2) = \text{let } (u, v) = (gn) \text{ in } u + v$$

This is a genuine improvement in that adjacent values of fib' are now computed in tandem by employing the auxillary function g.

All this seems pretty straightforward but there is an important question that needs attention. How do we know that this recursive function meets the original specification? At first sight it seems that we need to offer a proof. The obvious ploy is to employ an induction with the induction hypothesis, $\phi[n]$, set to $gn = ((\text{fib } (n + 1)), (\text{fib } n))$. The proof then proceeds as follows:

Base case

$$
\begin{array}{lll}
g0 = (1, 1) & & \text{definition of } g \\
\ \ = ((\text{fib } 1), (\text{fib } 0)) & & \text{definition of fib}
\end{array}
$$

Induction step

$$
\begin{array}{ll}
g(n + 1) = \text{let } (u, v) = (gn) \text{ in } (u + v, u) & \text{definition of } g \\
\ \ = \text{let } (u, v) = ((\text{fib } (n + 1)), (\text{fib } n)) \text{ in } (u + v, u) & \text{induction} \\
& \text{hypothesis} \\
\ \ = ((\text{fib } (n + 1)) + (\text{fib } n), (\text{fib } (n + 1))) & \text{definition of let} \\
\ \ = ((\text{fib } (n + 2)), (\text{fib } (n + 1))) & \text{definition of fib}
\end{array}
$$

We have thus established that g meets the specification ($*$). However, we seem to have somewhat duplicated matters. The induction proof is nothing more than the original program derivation turned on its head. Could we not, therefore, avoid the proof entirely and just carry out the transformation? We could if we knew that all the steps in the transformation are in some sense *meaning preserving*. At first sight this seems clear since all we have done is to replace equals by equals. Indeed, in our particular example there is no problem. However, in general, matters are more delicate. The issue centres upon the justification of the FOLD step in the original transformation. In general, FOLDING involves the replacement of the right-hand side of an equation by its left. Notice that in the proof this corresponds to the appeal to the induction hypothesis—which is the underlying justification for the move. However, in general, FOLDING *does not preserve total correctness*. A simple example is afforded by the following:

$$fx = 3 \qquad (a)$$

If we fold this expression into itself, i.e. replace 3 on the right by fx, we obtain the following equation:

$$fx = fx \qquad (b)$$

Whereas equation (a) yields f to be total and everywhere equal to 3, any function satisfies (b), in particular $\bot$ does. The upshot is that FOLDING needs to be constrained. Indeed, it is not difficult to see exactly how: it must be restricted so as to be in harmony with the induction hypothesis of the corresponding correctness proof. This is the case with our example. Indeed, if it were not so, we could not have carried out the correctness proof. With this proviso the transformational technique preserves total correctness. More explicitly, providing FOLD steps can be justified by the induction hypothesis, total correctness is preserved. Moreover, we can always check this by carrying out the corresponding induction proof. Nevertheless, this duplicates the amount of work involved in program synthesis. More to the point, it appears to be a rather inverted way of viewing matters. The discipline implicit in the correctness proof is being brought in by the back door. Can we not use the inductive proof itself as a means of transforming the program?

14.1.2 The Constructive Approach

First we must reformulate (∗) as a program specification. Within the constructive framework this pans-out as follows:

$$\forall n \in \mathrm{N} \exists m \in \mathrm{N} \otimes \mathrm{N}[m = ((\mathrm{fib}\,(n + 1)), (\mathrm{fib}\,n))]$$

This demands that for every natural number n (the pre-condition) there exists a pair of numbers, m, that satisfies $m = ((\mathrm{fib}\,(n + 1)), (\mathrm{fib}\,n))$ (the post-condition). This is the required specification of the function g. We must now show that the specification can be met. The following is a slight variation on the above correctness proof—with all the details.

Theorem 14.1 $\forall n \in \mathrm{N} \exists m \in \mathrm{N} \otimes \mathrm{N}[m = ((\mathrm{fib}\,(n + 1)), (\mathrm{fib}\,n))]$

PROOF By induction on the natural numbers. We set the induction formulae to:

$$\phi[x] = \exists m \in \mathrm{N} \otimes \mathrm{N}[m = ((\mathrm{fib}\,x'), (\mathrm{fib}\,x))]$$

Base step

$((\text{fib } 0),(\text{fib } 1)) = (1, 1)$	(1)	definition of fib
$\exists m \in N \otimes N[m = ((\text{fib } 0),(\text{fib } 1))]$	(2)	$\exists$i from (1)

Induction step

$[x \in N]$	(3)	assumption
$\exists m \in N \otimes N[m = ((\text{fib } x'),(\text{fib } x))]$	(4)	induction hypothesis
$[(u, v) \in N \otimes N \wedge (u, v) = ((\text{fib } x'),(\text{fib } x))]$	(5)	assumption
$((\text{fib } (x + 2)),(\text{fib } x')) = ((\text{fib } x') + (\text{fib } x),(\text{fib } x'))$	(6)	definition fib
$(u + v, u) \in N \otimes N \wedge ((\text{fib } (x + 2)),(\text{fib } x')) = (u + v, u)$	(7)	(6), (5),
$\exists m \in N \otimes N[m = ((\text{fib } (x + 2)),(\text{fib } x'))]$	(8)	$\exists$i, (7)
$\exists m \in N \otimes N[m = ((\text{fib } (x + 2)),(\text{fib } x'))]$	(9)	$\exists$e, (4), (8)
$\phi[x] \to \phi[x']$	(10)	$\to$i, (4), (9)
$\forall x \in N(\phi[x] \to \phi[x'])$	(11)	$\forall$i, $\to$i, (3)

The result now follows by numerical induction.

All we have done is to reformulate ($*$) and carry out the implicit form of the original proof of correctness. However, in this form the proof automatically yields the required function. Applying the abstraction function F, we obtain the following:

$$g0 = (1, 1)$$

$$g(n + 1) = (\lambda x . \lambda z .(\text{let } (u, v) = z \text{ in } (u + v, u)))n(gn)$$

This reduces to the following:

$$g0 = (1, 1)$$

$$g(n + 1) = \text{let} (u, v) = (gn) \text{ in } (u + v, u)$$

We have thus arrived at the required function. Moreover, g is guaranteed to meet the original specification. Of course, we have not removed all creativity from the process of program construction. One still has to carry out the original proof and secondly dream up the specification, but the same is true in the transformational approach. The only difference is that the original sequence of transformations is replaced by the existence proof. Consequently, there is no duplication of effort. Both formally and practically the technique is very close to the transformational one, but there is a crucial difference. Of the two basic operations of FOLDING and UNFOLDING only the latter preserves total correctness. In the present setup FOLDING is implicitly carried out but is constrained; it must be justified by appeal to the induction hypothesis. Thus the constructive approach not only provides a mathematical explanation of the legitimate transformations but blocks the ignominious ones.

14.2 ACCUMULATING PARAMETERS

In order to further illustrate the constructive approach to program synthesis we consider one more transformational technique and indicate how it is transformed within the constructive paradigm.

In many cases constructing an improved function involves a generalization of the given function. This is similar to the need to strengthen the
induction hypothesis in proving properties of programs and has been
observed by many authors, e.g. Bird (1977). To illustrate the technique we
turn to yet another well-worn example:

$$\text{reverse } [\ ] = [\ ]$$
$$\text{reverse } a{:}l = (\text{reverse } l) * [a]$$

In this case the observation that is crucial concerns the form of the recursive
call: it involves appending a list to the right of the recursive call. The improved
form of the function is obtained by generalizing the function to capture this
observation. This leads to the following definition:

$$\text{rev } xz = (\text{reverse } x) * z$$

According to our strategy, this is to be viewed as a program specification—in
the constructive style:

$$\forall x \in \text{List}[X] \forall z \in \text{List}[X] \exists y \in \text{List}[X][y = (\text{reverse } x) * z]$$

To obtain the new function all we have to do is prove the specification; the
rest is automatic.

Theorem 14.2 $\forall x \in \text{List}[X] \forall z \in \text{List}[X] \exists y \in \text{List}[X]$
$[y = (\text{reverse } x) * z]$

PROOF Employ induction with the induction formula set to

$$\phi[x] = \forall z \in \text{List}[X] \exists y \in \text{List}[X][y = \text{reverse } x) * z]$$

Base case

$(\text{reverse } [\ ]) * z = [\ ] * z = z$	(1)	definitions of reverse and $*$
$\exists y \in \text{List}[X](y = (\text{reverse } [\ ]) * z)$	(2)	$\exists i, \wedge i, (1)$
$\forall z \in \text{List}[X] \exists y \in \text{List}[X](y = (\text{reverse } [\ ]) * z)$	(3)	$\forall i, \rightarrow i, (2)$

Induction case

$[u \in X]$	(4)	assumption
$[x \in \text{List}[X]]$	(5)	assumption
$\forall z \in \text{List}[X] \exists y \in \text{List}[X](y = (\text{reverse } x) * z)$	(6)	inductive hypothesis
$(\text{reverse } (u{:}x)) * z = ((\text{reverse } x) * [u]) * z$	(7)	definition of reverse
$= (\text{reverse } x) * ([u] * z)$	(8)	$*$ association
$= (\text{reverse } x) * (u{:}([\ ] * z))$	(9)	definition of $*$
$= (\text{reverse } x) * (u{:}z)$	(10)	definition of $*$
$[z \in \text{List}[X]]$	(11)	assumption
$(u{:}z) \in \text{List}[X]$	(12)	(14),(11), list clo.
$\exists y \in \text{List}[X](y = (\text{reverse } x) * (u{:}z))$	(13)	$\forall e, (6)$
$[y \in \text{List}[X] \wedge y = (\text{reverse } x) * (u{:}z)]$	(14)	assumption
$y \in \text{List}[X] \wedge y = (\text{reverse } (u{:}x)) * z$	(15)	(14),(10)
$\exists y \in \text{List}[X](y = (\text{reverse } (u{:}x)) * z)$	(16)	(15), $\exists i$
$\exists y \in \text{List}[X](y = (\text{reverse } (u{:}x)) * z)$	(17)	$\exists e, (13),(14),(16)$
$\exists z \in \text{List}[X] \exists y \in \text{List}[X](y = \text{reverse}(u{:}x) * z)$	(18)	$\rightarrow i, \forall i, (17),(11)$
$\phi[x] \rightarrow \phi[u{:}x]$	(19)	$\rightarrow i, (6),(18)$
$\forall u \in X \forall x \in \text{List}[X]\{\phi[x] \rightarrow \phi[u{:}x]\}$	(20)	$\rightarrow i, (19),(4),(5), \forall i$

The result now follows by induction.

Applying the abstraction function we obtain the following:

$$\text{rev } [\ ] \, z = z$$

$$\text{rev } (u{:}x) \, z = \text{rev } x \, (u{:}z)$$

The new definition of reverse is then a special case where the additional parameter is instantiated with the empty list:

$$\text{reverse}' \, x = \text{rev } x \, [\ ]$$

This is the same program that is obtained from the transformational approach (see, for example, Henson, 1987, Sec. 4.5). However, matters have been turned upside down. The transformations are only implicitly performed within the existence proof.

This completes our brief excursion into transformational programming. We hope that this short chapter has persuaded the reader that the constructive approach has much to offer in providing a more mathematical account of the whole transformational enterprise. At the very least, we should have whetted the reader's appetite for further study. There are many other program transformational techniques (e.g. *generalized parameters* and *continuation*-based program transformations) and we urge the reader to study them within the present framework.

EXERCISES

14.1 Consider the following function which selects the initial segment of a list x of length n:

$$\text{take } 0x = [\ ]$$

$$\text{take } (n + 1)[\ ] = [\ ]$$

$$\text{take } (n + 1)(a{:}x) = a{:}(\text{take } nx)$$

Using the following specification derive a direct program for selecting the initial segment of a list:

$$\forall x \in \text{List}[A] \exists y \in \text{List}[A]\{y = (\text{take } ((\text{len } x) - 1)x)\}$$

14.2 Consider the following functions:

$$\text{fac } 0 \quad = 1$$

$$\text{fac } (n + 1) = (n + 1) * (\text{fac } n)$$

$$\text{fringe } a = [a]$$

$$\text{fringe } (x{:}y) = (\text{fringe } x) * (\text{fringe } y)$$

For each, provide a suitable *eureka* definition to generate an accumulating parameter version and use the constructive approach to obtain the improved function.

14.3 Investigate the *generalized parameter* and *continuation*-based program transformation techniques within the constructive paradigm (see Henson, 1987, for further details).

REFERENCES AND FURTHER READING

The most accessible source for program transformations is the book of Henson (1987). This provides further references. The previously referenced papers of Henson contain further examples and an explanation of the constructive approach. Bird and Wadler (1988) also give a very elementary account of the traditional approach.

15

AFTERTHOUGHTS

It is almost as difficult to end a book as it is to start one. Perhaps it is even harder since one is usually exhausted. The usual way out is to repeat most of the introduction with a sprinkling of hindsight. We shall not adopt this strategy. Nevertheless, there are a couple of points that need to be made. The theory developed here is not meant to be, in any sense, complete. Indeed, there are several holes in the current development. We shall comment upon the two most obvious.

15.1 MODELS OF PT

Firstly, we have not offered the reader any set theoretical interpretations for PT. This is largely because they are rather easy to construct. We only provide a brief guide with pointers to the literature. Our only objective is to convince the reader that their construction is not a problem. The hardest part concerns the models of the lazy lambda calculus. We shall assume a knowledge of *domain theory* and in particular some knowledge of Abramsky (1987).

For the lazy lambda calculus we require a domain that satisfies the equation

$$D \simeq (D \to D)_\perp$$

where $(D \to D)_\perp$ is the *lifted* function space. The terms of the theory are given their denotation in D in the standard way (see Ong, 1988, and Abramsky, 1987, for details). Let $[t]_g$ be the denotation of a lambda term t, in the domain D, with respect to an assignment function g which assigns elements of D to individual variables.

This provides a model for the axioms of the lazy lambda calculus. More precisely, we interpret the wff and types of the theory as follows. Since our objective is only to show that the construction of models is unproblematic, we provide a classical semantics. The assertion $\models_g \phi$ is to be read as ϕ *is true in D with respect to the assignment function g*, where the (extended) assignment function assigns subsets of D to type variables.

$$\models_g s = t \quad \text{iff} \quad [t]_g = [s]_g$$

$$\models_g t\!\downarrow \quad \text{iff} \quad [t]_g \neq \perp$$

$$\models_g t \in T \quad \text{iff} \quad [t]_g \in [T]_g$$

$$\models_g \phi \wedge \psi \quad \text{iff} \quad \models_g \phi \text{ and } \models_g \psi$$

$$_{,}\!\models_g \sim \phi \quad \text{iff} \quad \text{not } \models_g \phi$$

$$\models_g \forall x \phi \quad \text{iff} \quad \text{for all } d \text{ in } D, \models_{g(d/x)} \phi$$

$$\models_g \forall X \phi \quad \text{iff} \quad \text{for all } E \subseteq D, \models_{g(E/X)} \phi$$

The only novel points concern the interpretation of the termination predicate and type membership. Types are interpreted as subsets of the model. This leads to the following semantics for types. Recall, from our previous discussion, that it is sufficient to interpret full second-order comprehension:

$$[\{x:\phi\}]_g = \{d \in D : \models_{g(d/x)} \phi\}$$

We have thus shown how to interpret the language of the theory. The axioms of the lazy lambda calculus are sound (see Ong, 1988, for details) and the axiom of comprehension is immediate.

15.2 LAZY DATA TYPES

This is a much more difficult topic. There are two main approaches in the literature. One is that of Mendler, Panangaden and Constable (1986) and the other that of Martin-Löf (1990). The former employs a construction involving a sequence of types where members of the sequence correspond to the build-up of the infinite data items. The latter employs a variation on the notion of *choice sequence*. Both approaches are formulated within a Martin-Löf style type theory. It is possible to recast both approaches within the present setup, and this is currently under investigation (Hamie, forthcoming Essex PhD thesis).

The theory we have presented is not meant to be our final word. It is to be understood as a first attempt to formulate a constructive theory that reflects the style of argument and the notions of function and type that are implicit in current practice within the functional paradigm. Almost certainly, we have not been totally successful in meeting these objectives. Indeed, they constitute a moving target. Moreover, the present enterprise, if only partially successful, may well move it further.

REFERENCES

Abramsky, S. (1987). 'Domain theory and the logic of observable properties', PhD Thesis, Queen Mary College, London.

Backhouse, R. (1986). 'Notes on Martin-Löf's Theory of Types', Internal Report CSM-80/1, Department of Computer Science, University of Essex.

Barendregt, H. (1984). *The Lambda Calculus: Its Syntax and Semantics*, North Holland Studies in Logic and the Foundations of Mathematics, Vol. 103, North-Holland, Amsterdam.

Barendregt, H. (1990). 'Functional programming and lambda calculus', to appear in *Handbook of Theoretical Computer Science*.

Beeson, M. (1981). 'Formalising constructive mathematics: why and how?' in *Constructive Mathematics: Proceedings, New Mexico, 1980*, Lecture Notes in Mathematics, Vol. 873, pp. 146–190, Springer-Verlag, Berlin.

Beeson, M. (1985). *Foundations of Constructive Mathematics*, Springer-Verlag, Berlin.

Beeson, M. (1986). 'Proving programs and programming proofs', in *Logic, Methodology and Philosophy of Science*, Vol. VII, pp. 51–82, Elsevier, Amsterdam.

Beeson, M. (1989). 'Towards a computation system based on set theory', Internal Memo, Stanford University.

Berretta, R. (1990). 'Program Development in a typed constructive type theory', Internal Memo, Department of Computer Science, University of Essex, forthcoming PhD Thesis.

Bird, R. (1977). 'Improving programs by the introduction of recursion', *Commun. ACM*, **20**, 856–863.

Bird, R. and Wadler, P. (1988). *Introduction to Functional Programming*, Prentice-Hall, Englewood Cliffs, N.J.

Bishop, E. (1967). *Foundations of Constructive Analysis*, McGraw-Hill, New York.

Bishop, E. and Bridges, D. (1985). *Constructive Analysis*, Springer-Verlag, Berlin.

Burstall, R. and Lampson, B. (1984). 'A kernel language for abstract data types and modules', in *Symposium on Semantics of Data Types*, Lecture Notes in Computer Science, Vol. 173, pp. 1–50, Springer-Verlag, Berlin.

Cardelli, L. and Wegner, P. (1986). 'On understanding types, data abstraction and polymorphism', *ACM Computing Surveys*, **17** (4).

Church, A. (1941). *The Calculi of Lambda Conversion*, Princeton University Press, Princeton, N.J.

Constable, R. L. (1986). *Implementing Mathematics*, Prentice-Hall, London.

Curry, H. B. and Feys, R. (1958). *Combinatory Logic*, Vol. 1, North-Holland Studies in Logic, North-Holland, Amsterdam.

Curry, H. B., Hindley, R. and Seldin, J. (1972). *Combinatory Logic*, Vol. 2, North-Holland Studies on Logic, North Holland, Amsterdam.

de Bruijn, N. G. (1970). *The Mathematical Language AUTOMATH, Its Usage, and Some of Its Extensions*, Lecture Notes in Mathematics, Springer-Verlag, Berlin.

Dummett, M. (1977). *Elements of Intuitionism*, Oxford University Press.

Feferman, S. (1975). 'A language and axioms for explicit mathematics', in *Algebra and Logic*, Lecture Notes in Mathematics, Vol. 450, pp. 87–139, North-Holland, Amsterdam.

Feferman, S. (1979). 'Constructive Theories of Functions and Classes', in N. Boffa, D. Van Dalen and K. McAloon (eds), *Logic Colloquium 78*, North-Holland Studies in Logic and the Foundations of Mathematics, pp. 159–224, North-Holland, Amsterdam.

Feferman, S. (1990). 'Logics for termination and correctness of functional programs', Internal Report, Department of Mathematics, Stanford University.

Field, A. J. and Harrison, P. G. (1988). *Functional Programming*, Addison-Wesley, Wokingham.

Hamilton, A. G. (1989). *Logic for Mathematicians*, Cambridge University Press.

Hayashi, S. (1987). 'The PX systems—a computational logic', Technical report, University of Tokyo.

Hayashi, S. and Nakano, M. (1988). *PX: A Computational Logic*, MIT Press, Cambridge, Mass.

Henson, M. C. (1987). *Elements of Functional Languages*, Blackwells, Oxford.

Henson, M. C. (1989a). 'Program development in the constructive set theory TK', *Formal Aspects of Computing*, **1**, 173–192.

Henson, M. C. (1989b). 'Realizability models for program construction', in *Proceedings of Conference on Mathematics of Program Construction*, Gröningen, LNCS 375, pp. 256–272, Springer-Verlag, Berlin.

Henson, M. C. (1990). 'Information loss in the programming logic TK', in *Proceedings of IFIP TC2 Working Conference on Programming Concepts and Methods*, pp. 509–545, Elsevier, Amsterdam.

Henson, M. C. and Turner, R. (1988). 'A constructive set theory for program development', in *Proceedings of 8th Conference on FST & TCs*, Bangalore, LNCS 338, pp. 329–347, Springer-Verlag, Berlin.

Heyting, A. (1934). 'Mathematische Grundlagenforschung Intuitionismus, Beweistheorie', Springer-Verlag, Berlin.

Heyting, A. (1958). 'Intuitionism in mathematics', In R. Klibarsky (Ed.), *Philosophy in the Mid-Century: A Survey*, pp. 101–115, La Nuova Italia Editrice, Firenze.

Hindley, J. R. (1969). 'The principal type-scheme of an object in combinatory logics', *Trans. Am. Math. Soc.*, **146**, 29–60.

Hindley, J. R. and Seldin, J. P. (1986). *Introduction to Combinators and Lambda Calculus'*, London Mathematical Society Students Texts, Vol. 1, Cambridge University Press.

Huet, G. (1990a). *Logical Foundations of Functional Programming*, Addison-Wesley, Wokingham.

Huet, G. (1990b). 'A uniform approach to type theory', in *Logical Foundations of Functional Programming*, Addison-Wesley, Wokingham.

Jones, C. (1986). *Systematic Software Development Using VDM*, Prentice-Hall, Englewood Cliffs, N.J.

Kleene, S. (1945). 'On the interpretation of intuitionistic number theory', *J. Symb. Logic*, **10**, 109–124.

Kreisel, G. and Troelstra, A. (1970). 'Formal systems for some branches of intuitionistic analysis', *Ann. Math. Logic*, **1**, 229–387.

Landin, P. A. (1966). 'A lambda calculus approach', in *Advances in Programming and Non-numerical Programming*, pp. 97–141, Pergamon Press, New York.

Leivant, D. (1983). 'Polymorphic type inference', in *Proceedings of 10th ACM Symposium on Principles of Programming Languages*, ACM, New York.

McQueen, D. and Sethi, R. (1982). 'A semantic model of types for applicative languages', in *Proceedings of ACM Conference on LISP and Functional Programming*, pp. 243–52, ACM, New York.

Manna, Z. and Waldinger, R. (1984). *The Logical Basis of Computer Programming*, Vol. 1, Addison-Wesley, Reading, Mass.

Martin-Löf, P. (1975). 'An intuitionistic theory of types: predicative part', in *Logic Colloquim 73*, North Holland, Amsterdam.

Martin-Löf, P. (1979). Preprint of Martin-Lof (1982), Report 11, University of Stockholm.

Martin-Löf, P. (1982). 'Constructive mathematics and computer programming', in *Logic, Methodology and Philosophy of Science*, Vol. VI, pp. 153–179, North Holland, Amsterdam.

Martin-Löf, P. (1990). *Mathematics of Infinity*, COLOG-88, Springer-Verlag.

Mendler, N. P., Panangaden, P. and Constable, R. L. (1986). 'Infinite objects in type theory', Proceedings of Symposium on Logic in Computer Science, pp. 249–58, Cambridge, Mass.

Mitchell, J. and Plotkin, G. (1985). 'Abstract types have existential type', in *Proceedings of 12th ACM Conference on Principles of Programming Languages*, pp. 37–51, ACM, New York.

Mitschke, G. (1976). 'λ-Kalkül, δ-Konversion und Axiomatishe Rekursion theorie' Report No 274, Technische Hochschule, Dormstadt, Fachbeveil-Mathematik.

Mohring, C. (1986). 'Algorithm development in the calculus of constructions', in *Proceedings of IEEE Symposium on Logic in Computer Science*, IEEE, New York.

Moschovakis, Y. N. (1974). *Elementary Induction on Abstract Structures*, North Holland Studies in Logic, Vol. 77, North Holland, Amsterdam.

Ong, C. H. Luke (1988). 'The lazy lambda calculus: an investigation into the foundations of functional programming', PhD Thesis, Imperial College, London.

Paulson, L. C. (1986). 'Constructing recursion operators in intuitionistic type theory', *J. Symbolic Computation*, **2**, 325–355.

Peyton-Jones, S. (1986). *The Implementation of Functional Programming Languages*, Prentice-Hall.

Plotkin, G. (1985). 'Lectures on predomains and partial functions', Notes for course at CSLI, Stanford.

Reade, C. (1989). *Elements of Functional Programming*, Addison-Wesley, Wokingham.

Reynolds, J. C. (1974). 'Towards a theory of type structures', in *Proceedings of Programming Symposium*, Lecture Notes in Computer Science, Vol. 19, Springer-Verlag, Berlin.

Scott, D. S. (1970). 'Constructive Validity', Lecture Notes in Mathematics, Vol. 125, 237–75, Springer-Verlag, Berlin.

Scott, D. S. (1979). 'Identity and existence in intuitionistic logic', in *Applications of Sheaves, Proceedings London Mathematical Society, Durham Symposium*, Lecture Notes in Mathematics, 753, Springer-Verlag, Berlin.

Shanin, N. A. (1958). 'On the constructive interpretation of mathematical judgements', *Am. Math. Soc. Transl.*, **II**, Ser. 23, 109–189.

Smith, J. M., Peterssön, K. and Nordström, B. (1990). *Programming in Martin-Löf's Type Theory: An Introduction*, International Series of Monographs on Computer Science No. 7, Oxford University Press.

Stenlund, S. (1972). *Combinators, Lambda Terms and Proof Theory*, Reidel, Amsterdam.

Tennant, N. W. (1978). *Natural Logic*, Edinburgh University Press.

Thomson, S. (1989). 'A logic for Miranda™', Internal Report, Computing Laboratory, University of Kent at Canterbury.

Troelstra, A. S. (1973). *Metamathematical Investigations of Intuitionistic, Arithmetic and Analysis*, Springer-Verlag, Berlin.

Troelstra, A. S. and Van Dalen, D. (1988). *Constructivism in Mathematics*, Vol. 1, North-Holland Studies in Logic and the Foundations of Mathematics, North-Holland, Amsterdam.

Wadsworth, C. P. (1971). *Semantics and Pragmatics of the Lambda Calculus*. DPhil Thesis, Oxford.

AUTHOR INDEX

SUBJECT INDEX

INDEX OF SYMBOLS